THE POETICS OF
Motoori Norinaga
A Hermeneutical Journey

Translated and Edited by
MICHAEL F. MARRA

University of Hawai'i Press
Honolulu

© 2007 University of Hawai'i Press
All rights reserved
Printed in the United States of America
12 11 10 09 08 07   6 5 4 3 2 1

Library of Congress Cataloging-in-Publication Data

Motoori, Norinaga, 1730–1801.
[Selections. English & Japanese. 2007.]
The poetics of Motoori Norinaga : a hermeneutical journey / translated and edited by Michael F. Marra.
p. cm.
English and romanized Japanese.
Includes English translation of Sugagasa no nikki.
Includes bibliographical references and index.
ISBN-13: 978-0-8248-3078-6 (hardcover : alk. paper)
1. Japanese poetry—Philosophy—Early works to 1800. 2. Poetics—Early works to 1800. 3. Kinki Region (Japan)—Description and travel—Early works to 1800. I. Marra, Michael F. II. Motoori, Norinaga, 1730–1801. Sugagasa no nikki. English.
III. Title.
PL727.A2M68213 2007
895.6'134—dc22
2006032801

University of Hawai'i Press books are printed on acid-free paper and meet the guidelines for permanence and durability of the Council on Library Resources.

Designed by University of Hawai'i Press production staff
Printed by The Maple-Vail Book Manufacturing Group

To a world that is no more—
In memory of Michele Marra and his children:
Mario, Riccardo, Gemma, and Aldo

Contents

Preface ix
Acknowledgments xi

Translator's Introduction
Motoori Norinaga's Poetics 3

Translations

Diary and Poetry
The Sedge Hat Diary *(Sugagasa no Nikki)* 33
Songs on *"Aware"* (Pathos): Selection from *Suzunoya Shū* 96

Essays
The Province of Ise 105
The Tomb of Emperor Jinmu 106
The Mikumari Shrine in Yoshino 107
The Asuka Shrine 109
The Fire Deity 109
Poems on Deities 110
The Imose Mountains 112
Again on the Imose Mountains 115
The Tatsuta River 116
Again on the Tatsuta River 118
The Tatsuta-Ogura Peak 119
The Minase River 120
The Floating Bridge of Dreams 121
The Meaning of the Poem "Is This Not the Same Moon?"
  by Lord Narihira 123
The Last Words of Lord Narihira 124
A Debate on Flowers 125

Focusing on Fragrance in Poems on Plum Blossoms	126
The Cherry and Orange Trees at the Stairway of the Shishinden	127
On Calling the Cherry Blossoms "Flowers"	128
The Way of Poetry and the Cherry Blossoms	128
The Logic of Priest Kenkō	129
The Habit of Creating Appearances	130
On Paintings	131
Again on Paintings, 1	131
Again on Paintings, 2	131
Again on Paintings, 3	132
Again on Paintings, 4	132
The Beginning of Poetry	136
On Songs *(Uta)*	138
Again on Songs	146
On Yamato	149
On *Mono no Aware*	172
On Love Poems	194
Notes	201
Glossary	275
Bibliography	279
Index of First Lines	285
Index	289

Preface

This book is a study of the poetics of one of Japan's most renowned thinkers, Motoori Norinaga (1730-1801). It follows an earlier publication on the poetry and poetics of the philosopher Kuki Shūzō (1888-1941).[1] Norinaga and Kuki shared a deep interest in the composition of poetry: both provided readers with a full-fledged poetics with which to make sense of their poems. Neither of them made poetry his main activity, and both of them are known today for their original thoughts on aesthetics. Norinaga is recognized for his notion of *"mono no aware,"* a detailed description of the workings of emotions as the precondition for the poetic act. Kuki became famous for his idea of *"iki,"* a mixture of refinement, renunciation, and pride, making up the portrait of his ideal woman. Both thinkers shared a strong commitment to the construction of a metaphysical system. Norinaga believed in the power of the poetic word to recapture the spontaneity and immediacy of the voice of the gods *(kami)*. Kuki thought that poetry could voice the Being of a reality that, otherwise, could hardly be captured in its ontological state. Both were distrustful of the logic of proposition, the logic of statements, on which law and science were based, although they both had scientific interests: Norinaga in medicine, Kuki in the natural sciences. Both proposed powerful thoughts on the ideas of space and time, working towards hermeneutical theories that would allow them to capture the past in the present. A man of modernity, well traveled all over the world and conversant in several languages, Kuki made time the focus of his philosophy, dedicating his energies to define the contingencies of reality and the qualitative nature of time. On the other hand, Norinaga, a man well versed in the classical Chinese language who never left his native land, privileged space in his account of the local poetic production and belief system, showing that space did not necessarily need to be reduced to quantitative time, as Kuki believed.

Norinaga's interest in developing a poetics of space should become apparent to the reader of this book, who will find a translation of a diary that Norinaga wrote on a journey to the heartland of Japanese culture: the Yamato province (from which the name Yamato derived as a general term that was applied to the whole Japanese country), and the Yoshino area. The diary, known as *Sugagasa no Nikki* (The Sedge Hat Diary, 1772) from the name of the traveler's straw hat, is written in the classical style of Heian prose, interspersed with fifty-five poems, in the classical tradition, which Norinaga wrote during the journey. The diary offers an insight into Norinaga the poet, the scholar of ancient texts, the devout believer in Shintō deities, and the archeologist searching for traces of ancient capitals, palaces, shrines, and imperial tombs of the pre-Nara period. In his poetic journey, Norinaga followed in the footsteps of earlier traveler poets, whose destinations were dictated by poetic tradition. Manuals of "poetic pillows" *(uta-makura)* were readily available to poets, listing locations made famous by poetic geniuses such as Saigyō (1118–1190), Fujiwara no Teika (1162–1241), and Matsuo Bashō (1644–1694). Yoshino was one of those places—a revered locale whose mountains, rivers, and the vestiges of an imperial palace had been materials for poetic compositions since the age of the *Kaifūsō* (Fond Recollections of Poetry, 751) and the *Man'yōshū* (Ten Thousand Leaves, 759). In 1799, two years before his death, Norinaga made another trip to the Yamato province, during which he composed an additional "One Hundred Songs on Yoshino" *(Yoshino Hyakushu)*. Norinaga presents Yoshino as a "common poetic space" that readers must inhabit in order to develop the "common sense" that makes them live ethically in the poet's ideal society. This society is deeply imbued with the knowledge of poetry and the understanding of emotions, as one can see from the translation of Norinaga's twenty-six songs on *"aware"* (pathos) from his poetic collection.

The introductory essay on Norinaga's poetics should serve as guide through the dense arguments that he developed both practically in his poems and theoretically in his numerous essays, some of which I translated for this volume. The selection of essays deals with the history of places that Norinaga visited during his trip to Yoshino, as well as with the main topic of his scholarly interests: the sound of the songs *(uta)* from his beloved land of Yamato.

Acknowledgments

I want to thank Professor Suzuki Jun of the National Institute of Japanese Literature (Kokubungaku Kenkyū Shiryōkan) for accepting my invitation to teach a course on the *Sugagasa no Nikki* at UCLA in the winter quarter of 2000. It would have been impossible to have a better teacher of Norinaga's work in the classroom than the editor of the *Diary*'s most recent edition in the prestigious *Shin Nihon Koten Bungaku Taikei* series of the Iwanami publisher. During his stay on campus Professor Suzuki completed his edition of Norinaga's *Ashiwake Obune* for the new *Nihon Koten Bungaku Zenshū* series of the Shōgakukan publisher. Winter 2000 was definitely the Norinaga year at UCLA. The UCLA Institute of International Studies and the UCLA Center for Japanese Studies sponsored Professor Suzuki's visit. The Japan Foundation has made several additional meetings with Professor Suzuki in Tokyo possible, thanks to a research fellowship I received in fall 2004.

I would also like to express my gratitude to Toshie Marra, librarian of Japanese studies at UCLA, who brought to my attention the CD-ROM version of the *Shinpen Kokka Taikan*, which includes over 450,000 poems from 1,162 poetic collections. This tool enabled me to work on the sources of Norinaga's poems on Yoshino.

Catharine McGraw has been trying for a number of years to make English my first language, but I am afraid it still remains my fifth, despite her prodigious knowledge of English and her superb skills as a teacher.

Patricia Crosby, executive editor, and Cheri Dunn, managing editor, for Hawai'i University Press have made possible the publication of yet another book. To them and to my copy editor, Barbara Folsom, go my deepest thanks.

All this generous assistance does not guarantee that readers will find no mistakes in the translations; it simply means that, without it, they would find many more mistakes.

One additional note on the format of this book: sentences that appear in square brackets are translations of Norinaga's original text, which makes use of square brackets in lieu of footnotes.

THE POETICS OF
Motoori Norinaga

Translator's Introduction

Motoori Norinaga's Poetics

A medical doctor by training and profession, Motoori Norinaga (1730-1801) has left a profound imprint on the world of Japanese letters thanks to his pioneering efforts as a philologist who spent thirty years of his life deciphering one of Japan's earliest mythological records, the *Kojiki* (Records of Ancient Matters, 712).[1] Norinaga's antiquarian interests in literary records led him to in-depth studies of what are considered today the major classics of Japan's literary canon—classics written in the vernacular Yamato language that poets used in their composition of non-Chinese poems *(waka)*. Poetry continued to be at the center of Norinaga's humanistic interests during his whole life, as we can see from his continued efforts to talk about it in theoretical works such as *Ashiwake Obune* (A Small Boat amidst the Reeds, 1757), which he wrote as a young man during his training in Kyoto; *Shibun Yōryō* (The Essentials of the *Tale of Genji*, 1763); *Isonokami no Sasamegoto* (Personal Views on Poetry, 1763); *Genji Monogatari Tama no Ogushi* (The Jeweled Comb of the *Tale of Genji*, 1799); and the collection of essays *Tamakatsuma* (The Jeweled Comb Basket, 1793-1801). Like most members of the Japanese intelligentsia up to modern times, Norinaga enjoyed composing poems, mainly thirty-one-syllable poems, although he tried his hand at a variety of styles, including the ancient long-poem meter *(chōka)*. His best-known poems are collected in his private collection, which is known under the title *Suzunoya Shū* (The Collection of the House of Bells, 1798-1800), taken from the name of his private school. Norinaga is credited with the composition of over ten thousand verses.[2]

Norinaga's discovery of poetry coincided with the time he spent in Kyoto studying medicine. In 1752 he joined the school of Morikawa Akitada, a student of the revered Reizei Tamemura (1712-1774). Norinaga also became a disciple of Aruga Chōsen (1712-1774) and attended his poetry gatherings. Norinaga indicates in his diary that he was impressed by the *Hyakunin Isshu Kaikanshō* (Revised Views on One Poem by a Hundred Poets), Keichū's (1640-1701) commentary on Fujiwara Teika's renowned selection of one hundred poems.³ Keichū was quite critical of the traditional Nijō School that had introduced Norinaga to the world of poetic composition. The Nijō School was the inheritor of a tradition known as *Kokindenju*, or "Secret Teachings of Ancient and Modern Poems," an institution that had kept the confines of poetry restricted to the diction of the first three imperial collections: *Kokinshū* (Collection of Ancient and Modern Poems, 905), *Gosenshū* (Later Collection, 951), and *Shūishū* (Collection of Gleanings, 1005–1007). Despite the impact that the revolutionary work of Keichū had on Norinaga's poetics, Norinaga seems to have been unwilling to break free from the powerful Nijō School, as we can see from the indebtedness to *Kokinshū, Gosenshū,* and *Shūishū* shown in the following poem on the Yoshino Mountains:

Miwataseba	When I look far away
Tada shirakumo zo	Only white clouds
Niounaru	Shine in their splendors—
Sakura wa izura	Where are the cherry trees,
Miyoshino no yama	Mountains of fair Yoshino?⁴

In the first three imperial collections Mount Yoshino was sung for its white snow, which was often compared to the whiteness of the cherry blossoms, for which the mountain came to be known only after the compilation of the *Shinkokinshū* (New Collection of Ancient and Modern Poems, 1205). Norinaga relies on a set of images that were well known to poets of the Nijō School—a combination of topoi developed in the first three imperial collections (the whiteness of snow and clouds capping Mount Yoshino) with further images (the beauty of the cherry blossoms and the act of looking far in the distance), which appear in an anthology that Norinaga revered: the eighth imperial collection *Shinkokinshū*.

Miyoshino no	Flowering cherries
Yamabe ni sakeru	Blossoming in the mountains
Sakurabana	Of fair Yoshino—
Yuki ka to nomi zo	Betrayed by unwary eyes,
Ayamatarekeru	We mistake them for snowflakes.⁵

Miyoshino no	Flowering cherries
Yoshino no yama no	On the Yoshino mountains
Sakurabana	The fair, good field,

Shirakumo to nomi	I have taken them to be
Miemagaitsutsu	Nothing but white clouds.⁶

Yoshinoyama	The Yoshino mountains
Kiesenu yuki to	Have been seen as a place
Mietsuru wa	Where the snow does not melt!
Mine tsuzuki sae	The cherry trees have bloomed
Sakura narikeri	On the ranges of its peaks.⁷

Whereas in poetic composition Norinaga became a strong supporter of the traditionalism of the Nijō School, in the study of poetic texts he did not hesitate to confront interpretations that were based exclusively on authority rather than on philology. When it came to scholarship, Norinaga clearly sided with Keichū against the repetition of hollow theories promoted by the secrecy of the *Kokindenju* tradition. A thorough study of the ancient language allowed Norinaga to formulate a sophisticated poetics in which he attempted to recover the voices of the past—a realm of sounds that he associated with primordial voices heard in the most ancient texts. This explains the great attention he paid to the most ancient collection of Japanese verse, the *Man'yōshū*, despite his admiration for the aristocratic texts of the Nijō School. One might have reservations about the quality of Norinaga's poetic production due to his tendency to follow the rules and regulations of poetic precedent religiously. However, it would be disingenuous to dismiss the complexity of his poetics in which he dealt with linguistic, aesthetic, and ethical issues. The following is a summary of Norinaga's technical description of the poetic voice, the poetic sign, and the role played by poetry in the formation of interpretative communities.

Voice

In his discussion of poetry Norinaga emphasizes four key concepts: *"koe"* (voice), *"aya"* (pattern), *"sama/sugata"* (form), and *"mono no aware"* (the pathos of things). Simply stated, the sound of words *(koe)* takes on a poetic form *(sama* or *sugata)* by being externalized into written signs *(aya)*, a process informed by the poet's ability to be moved by the external surroundings *(mono no aware)*. This basic idea had been the working hypothesis for any Japanese poet or scholar working in the field of classical poetics since the time it was formulated at the very beginning of a document that is considered to be the first theoretical statement on *waka*, Ki no Tsurayuki's (868?-945?)

vernacular preface *(Kana-jo)* to the first imperial anthology of Japanese poetry, the *Kokin Waka Shū* (Collection of Ancient and Modern Poems, 905): "Japanese poetry *(Yamato-uta)* has the human heart *(kokoro)* as seed and myriads of words as leaves *(koto no ha)*. It comes into being when men use the seen and the heard to give voice to feelings aroused by the innumerable events in their lives."[8]

Tsurayuki's metaphor privileges the human heart (or mind) as the repository of feelings (or ideas) that, like a seed, sprout into words *(kotoba)* (or leaves, *koto no ha*) under the pressure of the surrounding reality (the perception of what is seen and heard), thus making a poem come into being. Literally, a "word" *(kotoba)* is "the leaf of *koto*" *(koto no ha)*. The question is, what does the word *koto* mean? The linguist Ōno Susumu argues that prior to the eighth century *koto* meant both "words" (*koto* 言) and "things" (*koto* 事). He states that a differentiation between an object and its naming came to be made only during the Nara period, a time when "words" eventually came into being as the "expressions of things" *(kotoba or koto no ha)*.[9] Ōno's debatable theory is rooted in a belief shared by thinkers such as Motoori Norinaga, who were later classified as members of the "School of National Learning," or "Nativism" *(Kokugaku)*.[10] In mythological times prior to history, no separation existed between things and the perceptions of them. Things were the way they appeared to be and the way they were named. This theory, known as *kotodama* (the spirit of words/things), provided Nativist scholars with powerful arguments in favor of an allegedly sacred origin of the voice, "a divine sign expressed in words," as Keichū (1640–1701), the alleged father of *Kokugaku*, argued in *Waji Shōranshō* (Rectification of Japanese Names, 1695). Keichū based this belief on the observation that in the *Man'yōshū* (Collection of Ten Thousand Leaves, 759), one of Japan's most ancient poetic collections, the Chinese characters for "word" and "thing" were interchangeable in the writing of the word *kotodama* (言霊/事霊).[11] This observation led to the formulation of a coextension between expression and event, a belief that is still at work in Ōno's modern explanation of the word *koto*. The spirit of language *(kotodama)* had the power to create reality, inasmuch as naming (*koto* 言) had a direct bearing on the construction of things (*koto* 事). The *Man'yōshū* provided Norinaga with evidence of the ancient liturgical practice of "lifting up words" *(kotoage)*—the practice of correct naming that was the prerogative of deities. To use a biblical example, God said "light," and light came into being. Wishing to praise the strength of a warrior who could translate his plans of victory into reality, Takahashi Mushimaro (fl. ca. 720–737) sang the brave soldier as someone who could achieve the result of the *kotoage* liturgy with his own actions, without having to rely on any linguistic ritual:

Chiyorozu no	Though you faced a foe
Ikusa naritomo	A thousand myriads in strength,
Kotoage sezu	You are such a man
Torite kinubeki	As without lifting up words
Onokoi to so omou	Could bring them captive back.[12]

The recovery of correct naming, therefore, was paramount to the recovery of the original, divine voice. Norinaga thus committed himself to the ambitious task of uncovering "the true voice of the spirit of language" *(kotodama no shingon)* that could be found in ancient poetry.[13] Nativist hermeneuticians achieved this task by using the homophonies of the Yamato language and by entrusting "ancient words" *(furukoto* 古言*)* with the voicing of "ancient facts/history" *(furukoto* 古事*)*. In *Isonokami no Sasamegoto* (Personal Views on Poetry), Norinaga emphasizes the futility of applying the hermeneutical enterprise to scriptive traces—the imported mass of Chinese signs—before understanding the meaning of the voice to which, Norinaga argues, Chinese characters have been improperly attached. He takes issue with the graphically oriented struggle of philologists who "read foreign characters in Yamato language" *(wakun)*. In Norinaga's opinion, such an act privileged the sign *(moji)*—the character for poetry, *uta* 歌, for example—rather than focusing attention on the native sound that Norinaga recorded in *man'yōgana* as 干多, and that he argues "was expressed in words since the age of the gods." Norinaga believed that words *(kotoba* 詞*)* are the root of signification, whereas signs *(moji)* are the tree's twigs. While the sound was "the master" *(shu)*, its written representation was nothing but "a servant" *(bokujū)*, "a borrowed temporary device" *(kari no mono)* that could easily be replaced by a different Chinese character, thus making writing an unreliable object of study.[14]

The fracture of meaning following the improper association of a foreign script with the native language was already a major concern for the philosopher Ogyū Sorai (1666–1728), whose theories Norinaga knew from his teacher Hori Keizan (1688–1757). It was Keizan who in *Fujingen* (Things That Cannot be Fully Expressed in Words, 1742) had noticed the awkwardness of translating Japanese language into Chinese characters, thus providing alien shapes for native meaning.[15] Norinaga took up his teacher's lesson in an earlier poetic treatise, *Ashiwake Obune* (A Small Boat amidst the Reeds), in which he attacked the practice of earlier commentators who analyzed the Chinese character for *uta* rather than its sound, not realizing that "*kanji* are harmful to the language of our country."[16]

Norinaga's privileging of speech/action over representation/object is rooted in his attempt to distinguish native speech from the "alien" continental script inherited from China. Paradoxically, he based his defense of the lyric nature of native poetry (*uta* 干多), to be distinguished from Chinese poetic language *(shi)*, on the canonical Chinese definition of poetry that appears in the *Shu jing* (Book of Documents): "The poem *(shi)* articulates what is on the mind intently *(zhi)*; song makes language *(yan)* last long" 詩言志歌永言.[17] The *Shu jing* explains poetry as the articulation of the poet's intentionality by a special language whose musical pattern makes the word last a long time through the chanting of "elongated" words. Norinaga, however, forced this text by disjoining the sentence as if the author were dealing with two different kinds of activities, one more prosaic resulting from an act of will, and the other more spontaneous following the singing impulse of a lyrical heart. It goes without saying that Norinaga read the first clause—"poetry expresses intent *(kokorozashi)*"—as the definition of Chinese poetry, while using the second —"the act of singing *(utau wa)* makes language last long"—to characterize the native voice.[18]

The "sustained elongation of the voice" (=song; *nagamu)*[19] becomes for Norinaga a distinctive mark of the native *uta* that keeps it apart from the intellectualistic bent of Chinese poetry aiming at "expressing intentionality" *(kokorozashi o iu)*. As Keichū already noted in his annotation of the *Kokinshū*, the *Kokin Yozai Shō* (Excess Material of the *Kokinshū*, 1692), *shi* stops at the level of intentionality *(kokorozashi no koto*, or, literally, "the words of the will"), while *uta* implies the presence of the language of music. However, Keichū denied that there was any difference between the two forms of lyric, arguing that "in the *Shoku Nihongi* [Chronicles of Japan, Continued, 797] and in the *Man'yōshū*, songs *(uta)* are called poems *(shi).*"[20]

Norinaga makes it a priority to recover the native voice. His philological agenda outlines the rift between "the voice of writing" *(moji no koe, ji no koe)* forming "scriptive meaning" *(jigi, moji no giri)*, and the native voice or "voice of speech" permeating "local meaning" *(kotoba no kokoro, konata no kotoba no gi)*. This defense of song as the voice of speech is based on the realization of the musical origin of poetry as a performative act.[21] In order to prove the primacy of the voice in the process of signification, Norinaga used the discrepancy between signifiers and signified to attack the philological methodology that explained local terms according to the etymology of Chinese characters.[22] He addressed his criticism to scholars such as Hosokawa Yūsai (1534–1610) and Keichū, whose interpretation of the word "song" *(uta)* followed the explanation that Liu Xi gave of the Chinese character *ge* (to sing) in *Shi ming* (Explanation of Terms, ca. 200 C.E.): Liu Xi found the etymon of *ka* (歌) in the character *ke* (柯), which means "branches," since "the upward and downward modulation [=pitch] of the singing voice was like the movement of leaves on a branch [when the wind blows]."[23] Norinaga faulted Japanese scholars for corrupting the meaning of native expression—in this instance the phoneme *uta*—with a scriptive trace that could well be explained in light of Liu Xi's theory, but that, basically, fractured the local voice with an alien sign. The freezing of speech in writing implied a series of contextual translations that distanced the native signifier—graphically represented in *man'yōgana* (于多 for *uta*)—from its scriptive representation (歌). This explains Motoori's skepticism towards the etymological enterprise that was alleged to recapture a universal meaning from an alien root of signification.

Addressing the question of the etymology of "song" *(uta)*, Norinaga relied on a work by the Ise Shintō scholar Tanigawa Kotosuga (1709–1776), the *Nihon Shoki Tsūshō* (A Compendium Treatise on the *Nihon Shoki*, 1762), a commentary of the *Nihon Shoki* (Chronicles of Japan, 720). Kotosuga quoted a senior colleague, Tamaki Masahide, arguing that "the act of singing, reciting a poem aloud" *(utau)*, was related to "the act of appealing to someone" *(uttau)*. Hori Keizan had further explained the same etymology as "an expression of grievances piling up in one's heart, which needed to be relieved in order to dispel the heart's gloom."[24] Poetry, thus, was seen as the explosion of an excess of feeling that the heart could hardly contain; it acted as a safety valve that would guarantee the person's physical and mental well-being. Norinaga refused to either corroborate or reject his teacher's theory, dismissing the matter with a curt statement, "now there is nothing more we can say about it."

In a later work addressed to beginning scholars, the *Uiyamabumi* (First Steps into the Mountain, 1798) Norinaga openly voiced his distrust of the etymological method, stating that "etymologies are not that essential . . . and they do not deserve too much scholarly attention."[25] Norinaga was clearly skeptical of a method that would attempt to recapture meaning from the root of a scriptive trace from which meaning had originally been separated. Therefore, he encouraged a more historical approach to the study of language that would analyze temporal changes in the usage of words and in the meanings attributed to them. As he states in *Uiyamabumi,* "more than being concerned with the original meaning *(moto no kokoro)* of such and such a word, we should think to which uses such words were put by the ancients, and we should clarify what meaning such and such a word had at that time."²⁶ If the etymological enterprise could find a justification, this was limited to the uncovering of the roots of speech, the study of native words whose transcription into an alien script was purely phonetic *(man'yōgana)*.

As an example of the etymologist of the native voice at work, Motoori's philological explanation of the notion of "making a poem" *(uta o yomu)* is particularly eloquent. He focuses on the several Chinese characters—読/誦/作—that were associated with the sound *yomu* (与牟 in *man'yōgana*) indicating, in Norinaga's words, "the act of reading/making a poem by having the voice imitate words/concepts already in use . . . as in the case of counting numbers . . . without any melody attached to it or any particular intonation."²⁷ On the other hand, the presence of melody or intonation explains the expression "to sing a poem" *(uta o utau)*, with particular regard to an ancient composition that is not a creative act on the reciter's part. Norinaga reminds his readers that the sound *utau* 干多布 ("to sing") was also conveyed by the character *ei* 詠, whose other reading, *nagamuru* ("to sing/to sigh"), becomes Norinaga's ground for an act of philological bravery. He explains the poetic act *(nagamuru)* as "a long reverberation of the voice" *(koe o nagaku hiku)* expressing the "lamenting heart lost in deep thoughts" *(monoomoi shite nageku koto)*. Norinaga relates the act of singing *(nagamuru)* to the act of sighing *(nageku)*, which, according to what Tanigawa Kotosuga and Kamo no Mabuchi had previously argued, derived from the expression "a long breath" *(nagaiki)*.²⁸ As Norinaga himself points out in the *Kojiki-den*, "a lament *(nageki)* is the shortening of a long breath *(nagaiki)*." It was also the shortening of "a long life" *(nagaiki)*, a widespread popular etymology lent credit by Kaibara Ekiken (1630–1714) when he wrote in his *Nihon Shakumyō* (Japanese Etymologies, 1699), "the living *(iki-taru)* human being has breath *(iki)*; with death there is no breath."²⁹ "To sustain the breath" *(iki o nagaku suru)* in poetry meant to reproduce semantically the process of life at the time when "the shortening of breath" deriving from human emotions threatened the body's organic functions.

The complex web of signification surrounding the meaning of *uta* included a pneumatological theory of existence that made breath the major component of poetry, as well as of life, translating sighs of regret and relief into the articulations of poetry. Poetic language restores life to a body deeply threatened by overwhelming passions. Poetry then, is defined as "the spontaneous sigh of relief following the deep movement of the heart, the clearing of a gloomy disposition."[30] Several organs and senses are engaged in the poetic process. In particular, Norinaga singles out the role played by the voice *(koe)* that transforms the deep breath *(nagaiki)* into exclamatory particles—*ana, aya, aa, aware*—which, as I will mention later, are at the center of Norinaga's theory of *mono no aware*. The eye also, Norinaga continues, came to play a fundamental role in the process of poetic signification, starting from the time of the *Senzaishū* (Collection of a Thousand Years, 1187) and *Shinkokinshū* (New Collection of Ancient and Modern Times, 1205), when *nagamuru* came to include the meaning, "staring at an object." The fixed gaze of the observer contributed further to the depressed state of the man "sunk in deep thoughts" to which the word *nagamuru* also refers.[31] By combining all the different meanings that make up the Japanese word for poetry, the poetic act could then be defined, in somewhat Heideggerian fashion, as "the voicing of the deep breath of the long life of a still, pensive Being" *(nagaiku/nageku/nagamuru)*.[32]

The same distrust for the written word that sets Norinaga apart from several generations of philologists can be seen in Norinaga's reconstruction of the etymology of the word "Yamato." First conceived as the name of the geographical area where the capital was located (the Yamato province), it eventually became a general term that included in its meaning the entire land of Japan *(ame no shita no sōmyō)*. Norinaga challenges the explanation given to this name in the *Nihongi Shiki* (Private Notes on the Chronicles of Japan), a record of commentaries of the *Nihon Shoki* compiled during the Heian period. According to this work, after the separation of heaven and earth, people were forced to live in the mountains because the ground had not yet solidified and still remained in a muddy state. This would explain the large number of "footprints left in the mountains" (*yamaato* 山跡), from which the name Yamato 山跡 allegedly derived. Moreover—the document continues—since in ancient times "to live, to dwell" was indicated by the character *"to"* 止 (to stop), Yamato 山止 also means "to dwell in the mountains."[33] Norinaga contends that, according to eighth-century mythological records, the early history of a not yet solidified land preceded the birth of the two ancestral gods, and therefore the Japanese land (Ōyashimaguni) could not have been created. He argues that, as there was no textual proof of people living in the mountains during the first stage of human history, the argument advanced in the *Nihongi Shiki* must be rejected. Keichū, Norinaga admits, was already very critical of an interpretation that would single out only one land, the Yamato province, as the place where the ground had not yet solidified. However, by still accepting the theory that the name Yamato derived "from the many traces left by people in the mountains because the Yamato province was surrounded on four sides by mountains,"[34] Keichū ignored the fact that his explanation was based on an interpretation of Chinese characters—Yamato 山跡—that were meant to be taken phonetically rather than literally. Norinaga also points out that this incorrect interpretation caused the malpractice of incorrect intonation during poetry meetings in which the singer would linger on the word "Yamato" as if it were made of two words, *yama* and *ato*.[35]

Norinaga also criticizes as "modern philosophizing" *(nochi no yo no gakumonzata)* and "self-affectation" *(sakashidachitaru setsu)* the theory that explains Yamato as a contraction of "Ya(shi)ma(mo)to" or "the original land among the myriad islands." Norinaga defends his rejection of this theory on the basis that, unlike the *Nihon Shoki*, the *Kojiki* states that the first island created by the ancestral deities of what is known today as the Japanese archipelago was Awaji, while Yamato—the island of Honshū—was the last. Norinaga continues, saying that too much reliance on a work marred by concerns for rhetorical embellishments *(kazari)* such as the *Nihon Shoki*, at the expense of the natural simplicity *(sunao)* of expression found in the *Kojiki*, has led to the loss of the signifying codes in use during the age of the gods—codes that the philologist has the duty of making readable once again.[36] Norinaga further took issue with the interpretation that explained Yamato as an auspicious name *(kagō)* attached to a sound that was destined to become the signifying mark of the entire land. Such an interpretation wrongly privileged debates centered on the need to find a proper character for Yamato *(moji no sata)* rather than explaining what for Norinaga counted the most, the meaning behind the voice of the word *(kotoba* 言*)*.[37]

Where, then, should one look for the correct etymology of the sound "Yamato"? Given the foundational status Norinaga accorded to the mythological accounts of the *Record of Ancient Matters*, the answer could only be found in the oldest native songs, such as in the following, which the *Kojiki* attributes to the legendary Yamato Takeru no Mikoto:

Yamato wa	Yamato is
Kuni no mahoroba	The highest part of the land;
Tatanazuku	The mountains are green partitions
Aokaki	Lying layer upon layer.
Yamagomoreru	Nestled among the mountains,
Yamato shi uruwashi	How beautiful is Yamato![38]

Being a land surrounded by mountains—"the green fences" that, according to another poem quoted by Norinaga, "shield" the land, protecting it from the outside[39]—Yamato 山処 simply means "mountainous place." North, behind this land, lies the Yamashiro province—today's Kyoto prefecture—whose name literally means "behind the mountains."[40] Norinaga found a legitimate etymology in the voice of poetry, a voice that for centuries had been silenced by the alien traces of Chinese characters.

Signs

Norinaga never denied the fact that the voice of poetry is inscribed in scriptive signs. He never took issue with the fact that words were recorded in the phonetical system *(man'yōgana)* used in the earliest records of the Yamato language, the *Kojiki* and the *Man'yōshū*. Phonetic signs were part of the poetic voice that stood in opposition to daily expressions used for the practical reason *(jitsuyō)* of communication. For Norinaga, the difference between poetic language and common language could be compared to the difference between appreciating a cherry tree for the beauty of its blossoms and valuing the same tree as firewood. Poetic language was made of what he called "pattern words" *(aya)*, the unmediated expression of a pristine voice transmitting "the heart of things" *(koto no kokoro/mono no kokoro)*. On the other hand, daily language was conveyed by "common words" *(tada no kotoba)*, simplified signs communicating the "reason" *(kotowari)* and "meaning" *(i)* of objects. It was certainly not unusual for poets to define the language of their trade with a vocabulary that distinguished the refinement of the poetic voice from the crudeness of daily expression. The eleventh-century poet Fujiwara Michitoshi (1047–1099), for example, stressed "the needlework like" *(nuimono)* nature of poetic words, "brocade patterns" *(nishiki nuimono)* that he singled out as one of poetry's distinctive marks, together with "heart" *(kokoro)* and "voice" *(koe)*. Fujiwara no Shunzei (1114–1204) quoted Michitoshi in one of the most influential poetic treatises of the middle ages, the *Korai Fūteishō* (Poetic Styles Past and Present, 1197).[41]

For Norinaga "patterns" *(aya)* were graphic visualizations of poetic speech, the translation of sound into "spontaneous expressions" *(onozukara kotoba)*, which were grounded in the wondrous nature of "the principle of spontaneity" *(jinen no myō)*—the principle that let things "be what they are" *(ari no mama)*. The articulation of spontaneity relies more on the language of exclamations than on logic of the proposition. Norinaga argues that, whereas the common word for expressing sadness would be a simple repetition of the adjective "sad" *(kanashi kanashi)*, only the sigh of sadness that arises spontaneously—"Oh, how sad, oh, oh!" *(ara kanashi ya, nō nō)*—can free the heart from gloom and convey the depth of human sensitivity *(fukaki aware)*.[42] Such a spontaneous sigh can be conveyed only by poetry. Norinaga's reduction of the notion of "pattern" to the idea of spontaneity exonerated him from any further explanation. The etymology of the character *"aya"*—a method of which Norinaga would not have approved—actually provides some further clarification.

An etymological analysis of *aya* (Ch. *wen*; J. *fumi, bun*), which Norinaga used to indicate the word "pattern" and its most distinguished extensions—"letters" and "literature"—indicates that this character "consists of intersecting strokes, representing a crisscross pattern." We find this definition in the *Shuo Wen Jie Zi* (Explanations of Simple and Compound Graphs, ca. 100 C.E.), China's most ancient etymological dictionary by Xu Shen. In it, we read that Can Jie, a scribe in the service of the Yellow Emperor, devised the system of Chinese writing by observing the prints of birds and other animals on the ground, thus representing graphically the configuration of things by a process of analogy.[43] The *Zhouyi* (Book of Changes) explains *"aya"* as "an image in writing of the shape of the things written about." According to this work, after noticing the marks *(wen/bun)* on the bodies of birds and other animals, Pao Xi traced the first scriptural marks—the eight trigrammes of the *Book of Changes*—in order to communicate the power of the universe *(shenming)*.[44] These two definitions include both the symbolic and the syntactic/semantic aspects of "literary patterns"[45] and emphasize the fictional nature of the sign that subsumes under its representational power the "natural qualities" or "inner substances" *(zhi)* of the objects of representation. The privileging of the "likely" over the closure of mimetic reproduction keeps the process of signification open to the possibility of production, the divine source of infinite creation. Thus, the poet becomes an extension of the god by using words (*koto* 言 = voice and written sign) to enable the representation of things (*koto* 事) "just as they are," open as they are to the realm of possibilities.

In order for words to be transparent and immediate vehicles for the articulation of things, the sign cannot interfere with the purity of the word's voice, but must convey it in its total immediacy. Norinaga had to address the question of how scriptive signs relate to the voice, the source of signification—a question that is at the core of all metaphysical systems. Relying on grammatical studies by Kamo no Mabuchi, Norinaga found in the fifty letters of the Japanese syllabary *(gojū onzu)* repositories of sacred speech, the utterances of the gods. He accepted the argument developed by Mabuchi in *Goi Kō* (Reflections on the Meaning of Words, 1769), according to which "the voice of the unseen" *(itsura no koe)*, whose secret source only the gods knew *(itsura* means "somewhere, although no one knows where"), was "the voice of the fifty linkages" *(itsura no koe)*, "the sacred voice that is subjected to no transformation," "the voice of heaven and earth" *(ametsuchi no koe)*.[46] Mabuchi's ideas led Norinaga to categorize five kinds of "divine expressions" *(kami no kotoba)*, which he listed in the eleventh book of the *Kojiki-den*, arguing that they actually existed.[47]

Known as "the theory of sound/meaning" *(ongi setsu)*, this interpretative model was rooted in commentaries of Buddhist scriptures, such as the *Hannyakyō Ongi* (Sound and Meaning in the Heart Sutra), and the *Hokekyō Ongi* (Sound and Meaning in the Lotus Sutra). By applying this theory to the reading of Japan's ancient records—*Kojiki, Nihongi*, and *Man'yōshū*—Nativist scholars believed that they could recover divine speech either in the sound of each syllable *(ichion ichigi ha)* or in each line *(ichigyō ichigi ha)* of the *kana* system. In this regard we see a common pattern developing among late Nativist scholars who shared the view that "nothing is outside language" (Suzuki Shigetane, 1812–1863), and that, as the breath of heaven and earth "*kotodama* was god *(kami)* dwelling in the spoken word" (Kawagita Tanrei). The productive power of the fifty sounds was also underlined by Tachibana Moribe (1741–1849), who argued that "the first sound of the syllabary, 'a,' was the origin of the world" *(aji hongen setsu)*. His debt to Buddhist philosophy is apparent when we consider that Moribe was resurrecting an ancient Buddhist doctrine developed in the Shingon school, according to which, the sound "a" was the alpha and omega of the world, the principle of the imperishable truth of emptiness *(aji honfushō)*. Other Nativists followed suit by finding the principle of truth in different letters of the syllabary. Fujitani Mitsue (1768–1823), for example, believed that the key to the explanation of the world was in the letter "u" *(uji hongen setsu)*.[48]

It goes without saying that Norinaga was quite indebted to what James J.Y. Liu has called a "metaphysical concept of literature"[49] as it was developed by Chinese thinkers. Although it might appear paradoxical to search for interpretative keys in what Norinaga rejected as a misleading root of signification, the relevance that Chinese discourses on literature had for him can hardly be underestimated. His notion of "pattern" *(aya)* and the importance that he gave to the rhetorical dimension of poetic language would hardly exist without the analogy developed by Chinese thinkers between the *wen* of men and the *wen* of the Sky *(tianwen-renwen)*.⁵⁰ The locus classicus of this analogical patterning is a passage from the *Yi jing* (The Book of Changes) that exhorts readers to "contemplate the patterns *(wen)* of heaven in order to observe the changes of season, as well as to contemplate the patterns *(wen)* of men in order to accomplish the cultural transformation of the world."⁵¹ The French sinologist François Jullien has called the relationship between the Dao and the immanence of *wen* "co-naturality" that the Sage must reestablish in order to understand the configurations of the cosmos.⁵² For Norinaga, the poet fulfills the task of the Sage whenever the poet reenacts the language of the gods with his words.

The theory of "patterns analogy" penetrated Chinese poetry as well. Bo Juyi (772–846), a Chinese poet well known in Japan since the Heian period, had developed the concept of the three patterns—celestial, terrestrial, and human. He and his followers gave analogical readings of the *wen* of the Sky (sun, moon, and the stars), the *wen* of Earth (mountains, rivers, and trees), and the *wen* of Man (the content of his conscience as shaped by education). The reciprocity of Being, beings, and representation implied the notion of an omnipervasive Dao as the origin *(yuan)* of a creative process whose mechanisms poets reproduced in their acts of literary production. Liu Xie (465?–520?) opened his famous *Wenxin Diaolong* (The Literary Mind and Carving of Dragons, 5th c. C.E.) with a quotation from *The Book of Changes* indicating "the power of Words to initiate the movement of the World." This resulted from the fact that "words are the pattern *(wen)* of Dao."⁵³

Within such an analogical typology, linkage becomes of the utmost importance in relating divine/cosmic utterances to human language. Since nature *(tiandao* or *daoti)* was considered the root and the poet's emotions the branches, the analogical pattern of poetry articulates itself through rhetorical devices playing on the coextension of what the West has hierarchized as *natura naturans* and *natura naturata*. The use of several types of linkages in Chinese and Japanese rhetoric can be seen from a variety of poetic techniques such as, for example, "analogical rapprochement" *(lian lei)* and "metaphorical projections" *(tuo wu, jie wu yi yin huai)*—rhetorical devices that Norinaga felt were essential to the composition of a successful poem.⁵⁴ How the reciprocity between god and man, divine and poetic languages, works in Norinaga's poetics is the subject of his theory of communication *(mono no aware)*. Once he had established the perfect correspondence between sound and sign, he could then proceed to explain how the divine prelinguistic model allowed people to communicate in this world.

Mono no Aware

Norinaga's name has been most vividly associated with the notion of *"mono no aware,"* a person's ability to realize the moving power of external reality and, as a result, to understand and, thus, communicate with others.[55] I know of no better introduction to this theory than the following words from Jean-Jacques Rousseau's *On the Origin of Languages,* which Rousseau wrote in 1763, the same year that Norinaga developed his theory of *mono no aware* in *Shibun Yōryō* (The Essentials of the Tale of Genji) and *Isonokami no Sasamegoto* (Personal Views on Poetry):

> How are we moved to pity? By getting outside ourselves and identifying with a being who suffers. We suffer only as much as we believe him to suffer. It is not in ourselves, but in him that we suffer. It is clear that such transport supposes a great deal of acquired knowledge. How am I to imagine ills of which I have no idea? How would I suffer in seeing another suffer, if I know not why he is suffering, if I am ignorant of what he and I have in common. He who has never been reflective is incapable of being merciful or just or pitying. He is just as incapable of being malicious and vindictive. He who imagines nothing is aware only of himself; he is isolated in the midst of mankind.[56]

Although for Rousseau knowledge preceded rather than followed (as Norinaga argued) the encounter with others, they both agreed on the idea that it is impossible to understand others unless one shares with others a "common sense" that allows one to communicate with them. Norinaga interpreted what he called "the moving power of things" *(mono no aware)* as the restoration of godly nature to those who understand how to be moved by the awesomeness of external reality. The potential for intersubjectivity—the very possibility of communication—was contained in the power of things (=words) to elicit the same emotions from different perceivers. The subjugation of difference by a universal principle of sameness—"sacred speech" inscribed in "pattern signs"—made communication possible through recording. Norinaga did not reduce the idea of *mono no aware* to suffering alone; for him, communication was a pathic experience originating from the sum of human feelings. He did not shy away from speculative etymologies when it came to an explanation of the word *aware*.

In *Shibun Yōryō* he interpreted it as the combination of two emotive particles—*"aa"* + *"hare"* = *"aware"*—indicating the initial surprise that the subject experiences before "the heart is moved" by the surrounding reality. He considered *aware* the Japanese translation of the Chinese exclamation "Ah!" (Ch. *Wu hu;* J. *Aa*)—an expression of grief kept hidden *(tansoku)* but in need of linguistic articulation.⁵⁷ This etymology replaced an earlier etymological explanation of *aware* that Norinaga first defended in *Aware Ben* (A Discussion of *Aware*, 1758), and then rejected in *Isonokami no Sasamegoto*. This earlier explanation was based on a passage from the *Kogo Shūi* (Gleanings from Ancient Stories, 807), recording the happiness and awe that followed the sun's reappearance in the sky after the Sun Goddess Amaterasu was taken out of her cave, a famous episode that originally appeared in the *Kojiki*. According to this etymological theory, the "amazement" *(aware)* of the gods at the view of the Sun Goddess was the result of "the clearing of the sky" *(amehare)* after a long period of total darkness. This was a commonly accepted interpretation during the Edo period; Kaibara Ekiken included it in his *Nihon Shakumyō* (Japanese Etymologies).⁵⁸ Eventually, Norinaga rejected this explanation on the ground that *aware* did not simply refer to sighs of relief; rather, it conveyed the entire range of human feelings and perceptions.⁵⁹

Norinaga found the first expression of *aware* in a passage from the *Kojiki*—a passage that he also considered the "origin" *(hajime)* of poetry in the Yamato language: the vocal exchange between the deities Izanami and Izanagi prior to their copulation and the production of the land. This passage is quoted in *Isonokami no Sasamegoto* as follows: "Then Izanagi no Mikoto said first: 'Ah, what a cute girl!' *(ana ni yashi, e otome o)*. Afterwards, his spouse, little sister Izanami no Mikoto said: 'Ah, what a handsome lad!' *(ana ni yashi, e otoko o)*."⁶⁰ Norinaga explains *"ana"* as an exclamatory particle like *"aya"* and *"aa,"* indicating the reciprocal surprise that the "young man" *(otoko)*⁶¹ and the "young woman" *(otome)* felt at the discovery of sexual difference. The choral nature of the exchange—vocal expression *(tonau)* followed by a reply *(kotau)*—underscores the need for a dialogic structure in all acts of communication. An uttered trace of the heart's outburst, *aware* requires the presence of likeminded witnesses who share in the emotional experience and help the experiencing subject to get free from the oppressive power of feelings by becoming new transmitting agents in a chain of communications.⁶²

Norinaga made *mono no aware* the key concept for the understanding of classical stories *(monogatari)*, a genre whose distinction was marked by its commitment to "recording human feelings just as they are" *(ninjō no ari no mama o kakishirushite)*. In *Shibun Yōryō* he argues that *monogatari* offer a glimpse into a concealed world of feelings and perceptions. This allows the reader to recognize himself in the story's characters, thus reducing his own psychological burden, of which he thought originally he was the only victim. This ability to relate to the feelings of others also functions as a yardstick to measure the degree of one's sensitivity and to make sure of one's ability "to rejoice at a person's joy and to be sad in the presence of sadness."[63] The insensitive person—"the person who does not know *mono no aware*" *(mono no aware o shiranu hito)*—is the one who does not cry when someone is in tears, and is deaf to the "ah-invoking nature" of things. Norinaga was, again, indebted to Chinese poetics, especially the poetics of "inter emotivity," which were central to the composition and interpretation of Chinese poetry since the first commentaries on the *Book of Odes*, eventually culminating in the theories of Bo Juyi. According to such poetics, human nature *(xing)* is moved *(dong)* by external reality *(wu)* thanks to its sensitivity to emotions *(gan)*. The *Wenxin Diaolong* describes this process as follows: "Man is endowed by nature with seven kinds of sentiments that are the results of an incitation *(xing)* produced by the external World. Moved by this external World, man sings what he feels in his interiority: nothing is there that is not natural." This natural incitation puts in motion a relational process in which exteriority/objectivity and interiority/subjectivity move back and forth as a net of unending correspondences.[64]

Norinaga's "rediscovery" of the Japanese classics *(monogatari* and *waka)* was directly related to his belief that their aesthetic appeal—an appeal directed to one's "senses" *(aisthesis* in its etymological meaning)—would create an ethical community whose members could eventually communicate without relying on the distortions of language. In other words, membership in Norinaga's community came with the benefits of transparent communication, which was guaranteed by the fact that each member, after mastering the language of the classics, would be able to speak the language of the gods. To use the words of the contemporary philosopher Sakabe Megumi, Norinaga's theory of *mono no aware* becomes the basis of "an aesthetics *(bigaku)* and of an hyper-ethics *(chō-rinri)* that transcends the level of the intramundane *(naisekaisei)* properly known as human."[65] The language of *mono no aware* provided Norinaga with an allegedly universal pattern of signification beyond the articulation of language into words and sentences. He believed that poetry and *monogatari* had the power to trigger a silent communication that brought expression back to its original locus—the gods.[66]

Norinaga's contribution to the field of aesthetics is particularly striking when seen within the context of a science that in the West was witnessing its birth as the "science of sensible knowledge" *(scientia cognitionis sensitivae)*,

Alexander Gottlieb Baumgarten's (1714–1762) well-known definition of aesthetics, with which he opened his *Aesthetica* of 1750.[67] Unlike the reductive conceptualizations of logic that limit the possibility of communication to the stiffness of formal linguistic categories, thus distorting the truth of all messages, the realm of feelings (aesthetics) recaptures the ontological truth of messages by going beyond mere verbal communication. Norinaga argued that the purpose of poetry had been "to sing human feelings" in order to awaken others to the depths of human nature since the time when the "Great Preface" *(Daxu)* to *The Books of Odes* was compiled in China in the first century C.E. He believed that later exegetical traditions misunderstood the language of poetry and took pride in misreading the "truth of emotions" *(hito no makoto no nasake)* as the common language of craft, cunning, and action. On this issue Norinaga followed an argument that Ogyū Sorai developed in *Bendō* (Distinguishing the Way, 1717):

> The bad practices of Tsu Ssu, Mêng Tzu, and those after them consist in that, when they explained [the Way], they made it in the minutest detail [wishing thereby] to make the listeners easily comprehend [the truth]. This is the way of the disputants; they are those who want to sell their theories quickly. . . . When we arrive at Mêng Tzu, we find that he proclaimed his clamorous message by means of casuistry and quibble; and he wished thereby to make people submit themselves. Now, a person who [attempts] to make people submit by words is certainly a person who is not [yet] able to make people submit themselves. For a teacher ministers to people who trust him.[68]

For Norinaga, poetry cannot be reduced to a rhetorical world of self-interest. His stand against neo-Confucian interpretations of literary texts was firm: the idea that poetry could be taken as a yardstick for measuring good and evil was nothing but an act of self-affectation *(sakashigenaru koto)* on the part of scholars who were insensitive to the truth of *mono no aware*. Only the spontaneity of perception, which is best represented in the "language of women and children" *(onna warabe no kotomeki)*, could avoid wearing the "deceptive mask" *(itsuwareru uwabe)* of gratuitous "rhetorical flourishes" *(tsukuroikazari;* lit., embellishing makeup).[69] This tension between logic and aesthetics came to assume strong political undertones. In Norinaga's opinion, the Chinese logic of dynastic succession encouraged new dynasties to devise words of legitimization, thus forging a language whose false virtue led to disloyalty and immorality. On the other hand, the language of the native soil sprang from the immediacy of nature, whose order the deities maintained by delegating power to their imperial epiphanies.[70]

Norinaga argues that the recovery of perfect language takes place in the realm of native poetry, in which the particularity of history is bracketed, and the universality of mythical times—"the age of the gods" *(kami no yo)*—is preserved in poetic form *(kokoro kotoba)*. This was made possible by the alleged power of poetry to short-circuit any mediation between expression *(kotoba)* and intention *(kokoro)*, and to find in the language of the gods the immediacy and directness *(nahoku)* of words and things. According to Norinaga, the spontaneity and immediacy of the senses must be translated into poetic language in order to avoid the analytical mediation of reason in the formation of knowledge. The "movement of the heart" or "emotions" *(nasake)* are, then, recognized as a privileged topos of the native poetic voice, not to be confused with "the passion of desire and craving" *(yoku)*, which is still rooted in the intentionality of self-interest, and as such cannot reach the depth of true feelings *(mono no aware)*.[71]

Norinaga interpreted the immediacy of feelings as "an original presence" *(moto no aru yō)*, "the essence of things" *(moto no tai)*, which he classified grammatically as "nouns" *(tai)*—the noninflected parts of a discourse. At the same time, the articulation of *mono no aware* produced effects in the realm of praxis to be appropriated for hermeneutical purposes. Norinaga called this effect, "the virtuous merit" *(kudoku)* of poetry, the "pragmatics of inflection" *(yō)*, that worked in the real world in the same way that a verb *(yō)*, or any other inflected parts of a discourse, functioned in a sentence.[72] As an example of the latter, Norinaga quotes Ki no Tsurayuki's remarks in his preface to the *Kokinshū* that poetry is believed to have the power of moving heaven and earth, influencing the realm of the unseen, and appeasing domestic relations. Norinaga explained the inflection of *mono no aware* in the world of the seen hermeneutically as the potential embedded in the poetic word to achieve concrete results that were otherwise inexplicable, such as, for example, the sudden fall of rain, or the resuscitation of the dead—what is known as "the theory of poetic merit" *(kadoku setsuwa)*.[73]

However, the concept of inflection is a major crux of Norinaga's philosophy, since immediacy cannot be retained if it needs the mediation of articulation in order to be communicated. How could a fracturing sign convey the truth of immediacy? The straightforwardness of immediacy, Norinaga argued, requires a communicational vessel capable of expressing the reality of the senses in the same way that those essences were perceived when they came into being during the age of the gods. Because of the changes undergone by the senses and by expression since that age, the recovery of meaning must be conducted by getting as close as possible to the language of the Sun Goddess. Here is where rhetoric comes into play, since it is the art of words that allows the poet to escape the distortions of contemporary language and to reconstruct the expressions of an otherwise irrecoverable past. Rhetoric, however, is a problematic concept, as Norinaga himself pointed out when he attacked Chinese texts on the ground of their alleged embellishments with rhetorical flourishes. Norinaga was confronted with the paradox of entrusting the recovery of the "truth of emotions" *(makoto no kokoro)* to the working of a "linguistic deception" *(itsuwari)*.[74] He tried to resolve it by stating that the spontaneity of the present moment is far from being equivalent to spontaneity itself. In other words, poetic truth *(makoto)* is not the expression of the poet's "immediate inner thoughts crossing his mind now" at the time of poetic creation *(ima omou koto o arinomama ni yomu)*. Instead, it is the result of the poet's exposure to and mastery of "the correct, refined heart of the past" *(uruwashiku miyabiyakanaru inishie no kokoro)*. Norinaga explained this deferral of immediacy by arguing that what at first might look like a forced attempt at appropriating the past, eventually develops into a natural habit that enables the poet to present rather than re-present the perfect language of self-presence.[75]

Since this immediacy was recovered within poetic form, the exclusion of the present in terms of both language and experience from the act of poetic composition did not limit the validity of poetry as a heuristic act. Norinaga shows that a poet cannot allow himself to "be inspired" by his own contemporary world and follow his "natural talents" on the ground that immediacy was created using rhetorical "skills" *(takumi)* even (in opposition to the claims of other Nativists) in the most ancient native songs.[76] For Norinaga, immediacy meant the complication of expression—the inscription of the unseen into the pattern of the seen text. Far from conveying the immediacy of presence, an uncomplicated, clear expression was a recipe for the composition of a second-rate poem *(ni no machi no koto)*.[77]

The bypassing of the historical present in the recuperation of immediacy had, for Norinaga, noteworthy consequences on the political level, inasmuch as the consumers of poetry dwelt in a shared space (the space of immediacy) and lived in the ahistorical time of what the philosopher Nishida Kitarō (1870–1945) has called "the eternal present" (the age of the gods). While the mastery over perfect language allowed an emperor to sympathize with his subjects and assume the persona of a farmer in his compositions,[78] the lower classes were made to experience the world above the clouds by bracketing the reality of the present in the immediacy of the imperial presence.[79] This bracketing of human time in Norinaga's poetics was not an innocent act of retrieval from the historical world. On the contrary, the inclusion in the circuit of courtly values of the knowledge of *mono no aware* points at the loyalty that Norinaga felt toward the aristocracy in power. Whether his allegiance was to the court's aristocracy (the emperor), or to the military aristocracy (the shogun) at a time of profound political changes, is for historians to establish.[80]

Hermeneutics

The *Sugagasa no Nikki* (The Sedge Hat Diary, 1772), Norinaga's account of a trip he made to the Yoshino area, is a translation in poetic language of the theories examined above. Norinaga left his native Matsusaka in the Ise province and headed west towards the Yamato province—the source of the process of signification that makes his journey so compelling. This was a real journey to Yoshino, witnessed by his adopted son, Ōhira (1756–1833), and other travel companions,[81] as well as a hermeneutical journey through texts and other historical traces—ancient capitals, imperial villas, shrines, and imperial tombs. The complexity of the diary that follows in translation is lost unless the reader is aware of Norinaga's formidable knowledge of poetry and history—a knowledge that becomes apparent when one reads his poetry in light of a thousand years of poetic sources and the essays Norinaga wrote about the places visited during his trip.[82] The diary is an excellent example of the philologist at work—a scholar committed to uncovering the allegedly original meaning of things. Norinaga was deeply concerned that interpretations through the centuries had inevitably distorted the meaning of the original texts. He wanted to witness in person the places that had generated the most remarkable poems in his country, and see which interpretations could be accepted and which should be discarded. His hermeneutical method aimed at recovering the root of signification, as one can see, for example, in the painstaking arguments that he developed in order to explain the origin of the word "song" *(uta)*.

Norinaga pointed out that the expression "Yamato song" *(Yamato uta)*—song in the native Yamato language—came from using the Japanese pronunciation in reading the Chinese characters used to record the word *waka* 倭歌. This word, Norinaga continues, was either modeled on the Chinese practice of defining types of poetry according to the geographical area where the poem was produced, or, more generally speaking, it indicated a kind of poetry not to be confused with the poetry of China *(Morokoshi no kashi)*. Norinaga seems to prefer the latter explanation because of the need to distinguish the local poetic production (Yamato) from the alien one (Kara, or China). By focusing on the rare passages where the word *waka* appears in the *Man'yōshū*, Norinaga warns his readers not to confuse the expression *waka* 倭歌, indicating "Japanese song," with the homophonous word currently employed in Japan to indicate native poetry (*waka* 和歌). He explains that the latter expression originally referred to a poem written in response to another poem *(kotauru uta)*—what came to be known in later poetic collections as "envoy" *(kaeshi)*. Far from meaning "a song from the country of harmony," as it was generally believed, this latter use of the word *waka* derived from the Chinese practice of replying to a poem *(shi)* by using the same rhyming pattern employed in the original poem. This was known in China as *heyun* (J. *wain*), or "fitting rhyme."[83]

Therefore, according to Norinaga, the association of "song" *(uta)* and "the Yamato land" (Yamato) in the expression *Yamato uta* with which Ki no Tsurayuki opened his preface to the *Kokinshū*—"Japanese poetry has the human heart as seed" *(Yamatouta wa hito no kokoro o tane to shite)*—was then a misreading of a word that simply meant "song" (*waka* 倭歌) and nothing more. Norinaga took issue with traditional medieval interpretations of the word "song" that read into it the history and mythology of the land. He leveled his criticism against works such as Sōgi's (1421–1502) commentary on the *Kokinshū*, the *Kokin Waka Shū Ryōdo Kikigaki* (The Verbatim Notes of Both Scholars Tsuneyori and Sōgi, 1472), in which *Yamato uta* is interpreted as "the poem that softens the heart of the Yamato people," with reference to the harmonizing role played by the ancestral deities Izanagi and Izanami as symbolized in the union of sun and moon.[84] Norinaga was also rejecting a theory introduced by the Shintō scholar Asai Shigetō, according to whom *Yamato uta* indicated a form of poetry enriched by the capital's courtly refinement, as opposed to the vulgar verses made in the countryside *(hinaburi)*.[85]

Norinaga was extremely critical of other Japanese scholars who based their interpretations on what he considered to be alien theories that could hardly be applied to his native land. In his critique, he did not spare even master Keichū, since Keichū had resorted to *yin yang* philosophy in his interpretation of the 5/7/5/7/7 pattern of *waka*. Giving credence to the *yin yang* doctrine, according to which odd numbers were considered symbols of the sun *(yang)* while even ones represented the moon *(yin)*, Keichū argued in the *Kokin Yozai Shō* that the three upper verses of a song *(kami no ku)* and their seventeen syllables were related to the sun. On the other hand, the two lower verses *(shimo no ku)* and their fourteen syllables were to be read as symbols of the moon. For Keichū, the relation of the *kami no ku* to the sky explained the length and the power of the first three verses in comparison to the shorter and less important final verses that were closer to earth.[86]

Keichū also advocated the practice of relating each of the five verses to the Five Elements *(wuxing)* of metal, wood, water, fire, and earth, as well as to the Five Constant Virtues *(wuchang)* of humanity, righteousness, propriety, wisdom, and faithfulness. This latter theory found many supporters in the mid-Edo period thanks to the efforts of neo-Confucian scholars, such as Yamazaki Ansai (1618-1682), to interpret the native Shintō creed in the light of Confucian and other Chinese philosophies. Models of symbolic interpretations reached the public through very popular publications on poetry, such as *Waka Yaegaki* (The Manifold Fence of *Waka,* 1700) by Aruga Chōhaku (1661-1737).[87] Norinaga based his rejection of the Chinese symbolism of heaven on what he believed to be the "truth" of local mythology. Far from being a powerful male figure, the sun in the *Kojiki* was represented by a female deity, Amaterasu, while the moon was no other than the brave male deity Tsukiyomi no Mikoto.[88] Once again, theology came to the rescue of an interpreter who resisted the idea of relying on interpretations of the "local" poetic voice that derived from "alien" epistemological systems. Norinaga warned his readers against the temptation to inject gratuitous meaning into the process of interpretation. He addressed his criticism to ancient and modern critics alike, with a particular animosity toward those who practiced a contextual reading of poetry. According to him, the contextualization of the poetic act that characterized the development of native literature from its inception by forging compositional "occasions" of poems and by freezing them in historical time had robbed poetry of its "eternal" and ontological dimension.[89] For Norinaga, poetic language was the carrier of a privileged signification uncontaminated by any mark of contingency.

An excellent example of Norinaga's hermeneutics is his interpretation of a famous song, allegedly composed by the deity Susanoo after he descended to earth, subjugated the dragon, and married Kushihinadahime, the daughter of an earthly deity. Both *Kojiki* and *Nihon Shoki* present the poem in the context of Susanoo's settling down with his new bride in the newly constructed palace at Suga, in the province of Izumo. Standard translations of this poem all refer to the contextualized meaning of the mythical accounts. A well-known English translation gives the following version of the poem:

Yakumo tatsu   The many-fenced palace of Izumo
Izumo iyaegaki   Of the many clouds rising—
Tsumagomi ni   To dwell there with my spouse
Yaegaki tsukuru   Do I build a many-fenced palace:
Ssono yaegaki o   Ah, that many-fenced palace![90]

Although this translation is indebted to his critical work, Norinaga would have undoubtedly quibbled with it. He would probably have accepted the rendering of the first word *yakumo* as "many clouds." Following Keichū's explanation in the *Kokin Yozai Shō*, Norinaga noticed that this expression, which literally means "eight clouds," does not refer to a precise numerical layer of clouds—it is not "eightfold" *(yae)*—but, more generally, that it describes a multiple number of layers, as in the expressions "double cherry blossoms" *(yaezakura)* and "double-petal Japanese yellow rose" *(yaeyamabuki)*.[91] Keichū challenged an earlier allegorical reading of the poem by the critic Kitamura Kigin (1624–1705) who, in *Hachidaishū Shō* (A Commentary on the Eight Imperial Collections, 1682), had related what he interpreted as "clouds of eight different colors" *(yairo)* to the place where the eight-tailed dragon *(yamata no orochi)*, slain by Susanoo, lived. The place was now the residence of the victorious god, who was reminded of his achievements by the constant presence of these symbolic clouds.[92] Keichū was also disproving a medieval interpretation presented in *Kokin-jo Chū* (Notes on the Preface to the *Kokinshū*, ca. 1320), according to which the expression *yakumo* was a contraction of *yakigumo*, or "burning clouds," from the smoke rising from the dragon slain and burnt by Susanoo.[93]

In order to lend further credence to Keichū's theory, Norinaga reminds his readers of the etymological meaning of the word "eight" *(yatsu)*. For this purpose he relied on Tanigawa Kotosuga's *Nihon Shoki Tsūshō*, in which we read that *yatsu* derives from *iya*, meaning "many, numberless," and *tsu*, meaning "ports."[94] The indeterminacy of the etymological root transforms the precise representation of a contingent reality into the veiled expression of Norinaga's poetic truth. Then, Susanoo's dwelling becomes the metaphorical reading of metaphor itself that displaces everything without ever allowing the reader to enjoy the safety of a temporal, geographical, "historical" interpretation. Many are the clouds that rise in a multilayered structure over the house of poetry. How, then, can poetry be made banal by reading the name of a geographical area such as the "Izumo province" 出雲 in these "rising clouds" *(izumo* 出雲*)*—literally, "the clouds that are coming out"? It is on this issue that Norinaga would have disagreed with the poem's standard translations.

Keichū had already criticized the contextualized reading of the poem that the compilers of the *Kojiki* and *Nihon Shoki* made in the eighth century. He had pointed out that "since the name Izumo was given to the province after the time of its composition, we cannot read the verse 'many clouds rising' *(yakumo tatsu)* as a 'pillow word' *(makurakotoba)*—the rhetorical technique that has concrete names preceded by epithets—of 'Izumo.'" Keichū argued that *izumo* was the contraction of *izuru kumo* ("clouds that are coming out"), the attributive form of the *shimo nidan* verb *izu* (to come out) modifying the name *kumo* (clouds). Therefore, rather than being in the presence of a riddle, the reader was faced with a simple repetition—"many clouds" *(yakumo)*, "clouds coming out" *(izumo)*.[95]

By fully supporting Keichū's theory, Norinaga lays the ground for rejecting the making of the "numerous fences" *(iyaegaki)* into the historical walls of Susanoo's palace. The "fences" are simply "the many layers of rising clouds" *(izumo iyaegaki)* hiding the locus of signification, poetry, from view. In the present case poetry is female because, as Norinaga says in his explanation, "the clouds build numerous fences by piling one upon the other in order to hide my woman from view" *(tsumagomi ni yaegaki tsukuru)*.[96] The novelty of Norinaga's interpretation lies in seeing the "fences" as barriers made by clouds, which he compares to "mist" *(kiri)* in their power "to obstruct from view something from which the viewer departs." These barriers are metaphorical walls that block the object of the viewer's admiration from sight. They are not, as both Kitamura Kigin and Keichū had argued,[97] real dwellings within which the viewer lives together with his beloved. Given this, Norinaga might have been less critical of the following translation that fits well with his definition of the poem as a repetitive variation around the theme of clouds:

Yakumo tatsu	Many clouds rising,
Izumo yaegaki	Many layered clouds raising a manifold-fence
Tsumagomi ni	Hiding my bride from sight,
Yaegaki tsukuru	Clouds are forming a manifold fence,
Sono yaegaki o	Oh, that manifold fence!

The clouds have been veiling the truth of this poem for centuries—a truth that Norinaga felt it was his responsibility to uncover. This meant peeling off centuries of interpretations and the encroachments of a history of details. Despite the presence of a scientific drive pushing him towards the goal of objectivity in the reconstruction of truth, Norinaga's working hypothesis was firmly grounded in his belief in a theological truth—the truth of the gods. Despite his tour of hermeneutical force that allows us today to see in this ancient poem the simplicity of an archaic rhetorical structure, Norinaga never questioned the "truth" that the poem was written by a god—the divine voice of Susanoo. For Norinaga, it would have been anathema to recognize the fact that the voice of the god—and the source of Yamato songs—was nothing other than the composition of a Buddhist monk assuming the persona of the Sun Goddess' evil brother. In this sense, Norinaga belongs to the history of philology and aesthetics, disciplines that have translated theology into the secular idiom of science. The gods may have changed their names, but they have never left the stage: they have come to be called literature, history, the work of art, and so on. Behind the clouds is Norinaga's truth—the beautiful cherry trees blooming in Yoshino that only poetry can capture "the way they are." He might have been pleased by words that a later aesthetician, who was unaware of his notion of *mono no aware,* used to define poetry: "A veil of sadness seems to wrap Beauty, but it is not a veil, it is the face itself of Beauty."[98]

Translations

Diary and Poetry

The Sedge Hat Diary
(Sugagasa no Nikki)[1]

Book One

This is the ninth year of the Myōwa era (1772). I wonder what good year this might turn out to be. I finally made up my mind to go see the cherry blossoms at Yoshino—the good field—about which the following verse was left, "Good men took a good look at this good place!" [The verse comes from the *Man'yōshū*:

Yoki hito no	Good men from the past
Yoshi to yoku mite	Took a good look saying what a good place it was.
Yoshi to iishi	Take a good look at Yoshino, the good field
Yoshino yoku miyo	About which they said, "It was good!"
Yoki hito yoku mitsu	The good men of nowadays should take a good look.][2]

It has already been about twenty years since I had planned to wear the garment of the traveler, but every spring something always came up and my plans had come to nothing. However, thinking that this should not be the case, I mustered the determination and finally set up to do it. I felt quite restless, although there was no particular hurry, since this was not a journey that would take a long time to accomplish. Because I could not find any time to occupy myself with the proper offering to the deities early in the morning on the day before my departure, I jotted down a poem and attached it to my pouch:

(1)
Ukeyo nao	Please, do accept
Hana no nishiki ni	This offering
Aku kami mo	To which I put my heart this spring—
Kokoro kudakishi	The gods have gotten tired
Haru no tamuke wa	Of the brocades of flowers.[3]

We left at dawn, still hidden by the night, at the beginning of the Third Month, on the Fifth Day. By the time we reached Ichiba-no-Shō, it was completely clear. The road turned left from the edge of the bridge crossing over Miwatari River; we went up a little way alongside the river, and then crossed a wooden bridge. Up to this point the place was familiar to me since occasionally I took care of some business in this area. However, from here the road, known as the Aho crossing, went through Iga province, leading to Hatsuse. In the past I had gone on this road once or twice, but since so much time had gone by, I had completely forgotten. Everything looked new to me as if this were my first time on this road. Since the night before, the sky had been clouded and rain fell occasionally. There was no clear weather in sight. It is interesting to see a face suddenly become reproachful at the sight of the wet sleeves on a traveler's garment. We passed through a hamlet by the name of Tsuyajō and, after going all the way through faraway fields, we reached the village of Ogawa.

(2)   *Ame fureba*   Since the rain has been falling
       Kyō wa Ogawa no   Today this place befits its name—
       Na ni shi oite   Small River,
       Shimizu nagaruru   The road in the middle of a village
       Sato no nakamichi   Where clear waters flow.[4]

After leaving this village, we crossed a narrow wooden bridge on a river called the Miyako River—Capital River—leading to the village of Miyako (Ancient Court). There is a spring of water by the name of Well of Forgetfulness (Wasurei) that an attendant of the Ise Priestess sang in a poem. [The poem appears in the travel section of the *Senzaishū*:

       Wakareyuku   The water of the Well of Forgetfulness!
       Miyako no kata no   Let me scoop it with my hands
       Koishiki ni   Yearning
       Iza musubimimu   For the capital
       Wasurei no mizu   Whence we went our separate ways.][5]

Although other places have markers and monuments shaped like a well claiming to be the site of this well, these claims are false. Recently someone who comes from the same province as mine, after visiting this place, confirmed that this village is the site of the well—and this is the truth.[6] When I look at the poem, I see that the *Senzaishū* indicates that it was composed "at the time of the procession" to Ise. However, when I consulted ancient documents, I noticed that when the priestess returned to the capital, her attendants separated and took two different roads for Kyoto from the temporary palace at Ichishi that was located in this area. This explains the verse "yearning for the capital/from which we went our separate ways" that was inspired by the name of the village, Miyako (=capital). I always thought that this was the case, and for many years I had wanted to see this place with my own eyes. As I was thinking that I wanted to see it, since today would have been a good time to do so, I decided to go, and there it was—the ancient well! What a wonderful spring of water—a well that refused to dry up despite the many terrible droughts that had taken place in the past. However, the villagers were saying that there were not many old legends about this well; as a matter of fact, it did not look as one would expect the famous Well of Forgetfulness to look. I was quite skeptical. I wanted to ask more details about it but we were in a hurry to get to our destination, and we kept going. I had heard that in the mountains in this area there were the ruins of the Tengeji fortress, and also the ruins of the temple. I wonder whether the Ogawa Shrine still stands—the one that is mentioned in the *Jinmyōchō* (Register of Deities), where we read that the god of Ogawa village is enshrined in this village.[7]

In a place about six miles from Miwatari there was a post town called Hata.[8] A wooden bridge crossed the Hata River. The rain kept pouring without ever stopping. On the way I kept talking with my travel companions, wondering "what might happen to the cherry blossoms in Yoshino given the present weather," and I composed the following poem:

(3)   *Harusame ni*   On this trip
    Hosanu sode yori   I think with more pain of the cherry blossoms' color
    Kono tabi wa   Fading away
    Shioremu hana no   Than of my sleeves
    Iro o koso omoe   That do not dry under the spring rains.

From the village of Tajiri we gradually proceeded through a mountain road and passed by the villages of Tanido, Ōnoki, and so on. Up to this point we could see cherry trees in bloom here and there. We rested and then went our way, looking at the blossoms.

(4)   *Shibashi to te*   Even if I stop
    Tachitomarite mo   Watching them for a brief moment,
    Tomarinishi   Here I am beneath the flowers

Tomo koi shinobu Yearning with love for the friends
Hana no ko no moto Who stayed at home.[9]

The Ōnoki River is very big. People say that it constitutes the headwaters of the Kumozu River. On the other side of the river a group of houses stood in a row; the village has the same name as the river. The scenery as we were going up the riverside was quite beautiful. There were many massive boulders in the mountains, along the way, and even in the river. The view of the pools surrounded by rocks was quite frightening. Master Agatai was right when he said that this was the area where we could find "the boulders lying on the long mountain flanks of Hata," about which Fukinotoji sang in a poem from the *Man'yōshū*:[10]

[*Kawanoe no* A girl I want to be for ever,
Yutsu iwamura ni Eternally
Kusa musazu As the sacred group of boulders,
Tsune ni mogamo na On the riverbank,
Tokootome nite From which no grass is ever born.][11]

It was originally a mistake to think that traces of this place could be found in Suzuka.

As we were going through this area, it stopped raining. We ate something at an inn called "The Two Trees of Small Yamato" (Oyamato-no-Nihongi) and rested there for a while. The distance from Hata to this place is about six miles. Three and a half miles beyond this place there is an inn by the name of "Inside the Fence" (Kaito). We were about to cross the mountain path of Aho after leaving this inn when it started raining again—how sad! At that time I heard the song of a bush warbler:

(5) *Tabigoromo* As the rain goes through the sleeves
Tamoto tōrite Of the traveler's garb
Ukuizu to That sadly do not dry,
Ware koso nakame Here I am crying—the crying bush warbler:
Harusame no sora The sky of spring rains.

[This poem was inspired by the following poem on the bush warbler from the *Kokinshū*'s book on "the name of things" *(mono-no-na)*:

Kokoro kara	From his heart
Hana no shizuku ni	The idea came to get wet
Sobochitsutsu	Under the drops from the flowers—
Ukuhizu to nomi	Why should the bush warbler cry:
Tori no nakuramu	Sadly my plumage does not dry?]¹²

We kept going and we reached Tamuke. Up to this point we were in the district of Ichishi. From here on we were entering the Iga district of the Iga province. The mountain path from Kaito that we had passed continued for about seven miles until the place known as Iseji. We kept going without ever coming to an end, while the amount of rain kept increasing. The day was drawing to a close, and we forced ourselves through an unknown mountain path in the midst of total darkness. We were wondering why we should have come to such a place, although we did not have to—how wretched! With great difficulty we reached the post town of Iseji. There is no way I can tell you how happy we were. We stayed at the house of someone by the name of Matsumoto something.

THE SIXTH DAY OF THE THIRD MONTH

This morning we left our lodgings at dawn. We went about two-thirds of a mile;¹³ on the lefthand side of the road there is a mountain called Nakayama whose boulders are quite impressive.

(6)	*Kawazura no*	When I look
	Iga no Nakayama	At the Nakayama mountains of Iga
	Nakanakani	Alongside the river,
	Mireba sugiuki	A village of boulders on the shore
	Kishi no iwamura	Makes the passage hard.

This was the area around the Aho River that runs from the Aho Mountains, which we crossed yesterday. In the morning we crossed the river and went along the river bank. We passed the villages of Okada, Beffu, and others. Close by on the lefthand side a deity by the name of Ōmori Myōjin is enshrined. Wasn't this name the result of the wrong reading of the "Ōmura Shrine"? We kept going along the river until we crossed it at the entrance of the post town of Aho. Because of the heavy rains of the day before, the bridge had been washed away; we lifted up our clothes and walked through the waters. The water was very cold. From Iseji to this post town was about two and a half miles. At a place called Hane we forded the same river again through a wooden bridge. Here the river is called Hane River. After going a while, we climbed up a slope for approximately four or five hundred yards. The villagers told us that this place was known as the Seven Views Pass (Nanami-tōge) because from the slope you could see the seven villages of Aho. However, today, because of the deep clouds and fog, we could not see very well. Although today, again, the sky was not clear, we felt relieved that it did not rain. About two and a half miles away from Aho, past Namiki-no-Matsubara, there is a place called Shinden. At the end of this village was a temporary hut. In front of the hut there was a garden with a pond in it. I noticed a place where a drooping cherry tree was blooming in an interesting way.

(7) *Itozakura*   Standing
   Kurushiki tabi mo   In the shade of the flowers,
     Wasurekeri   Watching the drooping cherry tree,
Tachiyorite miru   I forgot
Hana no kokage ni   This distressful journey.

In this province the cherry trees were not yet in bloom. Only early bloomers such as the drooping cherry tree and the equinoctial cherry tree could be seen here and there.

From here we followed a peaceful mountain road covered with pine trees; the scenery was beautiful. Beginning with this area, we entered the Ibari district. In the past, during an imperial visit to the Ise province, the wife of someone in the emperor's service stayed back in the capital of Yamato. Being truly worried about her husband's journey, she composed the lines, "Will he be crossing today/the Nabari Mountains?" [In the *Man'yōshū* we read:

   Wa ga seko wa   Where will he be going
Izuku yukuramu   My dear husband?
    Okitsumo no   Will he be crossing today
Nabari no yama o   The Nabari Mountains—
Kyō ka koyuramu   Algae of the offshore sea?][14]

She must have been referring to this mountain road. Finally the sky cleared and I could reflect on the Nunobiki (Cloth Stretched Out to Dry) Mountain that we had left far behind.

(8)   *Konogoro no*   Washed
       Ame ni araite   By the recent rains
          Mezurashiku   How strange today,
      Kyō wa hoshitaru   Cloth Stretched Out to Dry Mountain
      Nunobiki no yama   Is drying.

I can see this mountain from my hometown every day. Its shape is exactly the same when I look at it from here—truly a cloth that has been stretched out. We went down the slope for a while, and when we asked the name of the place at the foot of the mountain, we were told it was Kuramochi. From here we left the mountain and followed an even road for one mile that took us to Nabari. It was about seven miles from Aho. In the town was the house of Lord Tōdo something who administered this area; we passed in front of the gate of his mansion. At the edge of the town's houses we crossed two wooden bridges where two rivers—the Nabari and the Yanase rivers—meet and become one river. The reference in the past to the "Nabari Yokogawa River" seems to have been to this river.[15] We kept going until we found a mountain stream. There were many unusual rocky formations along the way in the mountain and in the river. From Nabari it had started raining again, and by the time we reached this area the rain had started pouring so violently that it would seep through our raincoats. At Kataka I composed the following poem:

(9)   *Kinō kyō*   Yesterday, today
      Furimi furazumi   It rained off and on—
        Kumo haruru   How difficult
  Koko to wa Kataka no   For the clouds to clear:
    Haru no ame kana   Spring rains in Kataka.[16]

We were going along a massive boulder that jutted from the mountain out to the middle of the river when, from the mountains on our righthand side, a fall came streaming down close to us—a truly interesting scene difficult to capture in words. A rock towered about three yards[17] above the road, all by itself, from the forefront of a range of boulders that appeared to rise all the way up to the sky. As I was passing under the boulder, I felt as if I was in great danger—as if the boulder would fall on my head. What a frightful sight when I looked back more carefully, after I had proceeded a little farther! People around this area call it "the boulder of the lion dance." Indeed, it truly reminds one of a lion holding out his head.

Well, we climbed the mountain for a while and, as we were going to descend, I noticed a stony statue of Jizō. This was the border between the Iga and Yamato provinces. It was about three and a half miles from Nabari, five miles to the post town of Sanbonmatsu. Two or three hundred yards from the street, on the left, I spotted another strange boulder in the area of the temple called Ōnodera. Since this was a famous place and the destination of many pilgrims, I had to see it. Indeed, someone had gone to the trouble of making a sculpture on the front of the boulder—an image of Miroku Bosatsu that could be faintly seen. Although the Buddha was sixteen yards high, there was still plenty of room left at the top of the boulder. The back of the sculpture was the mountain from which we saw the banks of a mountain stream. I faintly remember that I read somewhere that the emperor visited this place when he abdicated. I wonder which emperor it might have been; I cannot remember right now.[18] We went up a little along this river and, as we were looking for a narrow path among the mountains, we surfaced again on the big main street. Meanwhile we found the road going to Murō[19] but, since there is no stone marker on the way, this must be a place where one is bound to become lost. Although today we had planned to go until Hase, it was raining, the road was bad, our feet were hurting, and we were tired. Therefore, we decided not to go, and stop instead at a place called Haibara. When I noticed that the name of this village was written with the characters "field of bush clover," I felt somehow homesick, and I kept thinking that if only the time had been autumn, I could have applied the scent of the bush clover to the sleeves of the traveler:

(10)	*Utsushite mo*	I only wish
	Yukamashi mono o	I could transfer their fragrance, but . . .
	Saku hana no	Village of bush clovers—
	Oritagaetaru	You have mistaken the time
	Hakihara no sato	Of the flowers' bloom.[20]

Tonight the rain was heavy and the wind strong, so that I could not think of my hometown's sky. All my thoughts were directed to the mountains in Yoshino as I wondered most of all about the tops of the cherry trees, without finding any peace the whole night. As I was unable to sleep at all, someone who I believe was the inn's owner got up in the middle of the night and said, from outside: "Oh, what a terrible wind and rain. Tomorrow it will clear up for sure!" As I lay there listening to him, I prayed that this might be the case.

THE SEVENTH DAY

Since dawn it had stopped raining. When I got up and looked outside, the clouds had gradually thinned out and the sky looked as if it was going to clear up. I was extremely happy to see that the forecast of the master of the house had been correct. During the past few days of rain the road had been very bad. Hearing that there was going to be a mountain path again, this morning everybody left after getting on a palanquin. It was a shabby means of transportation, quite painful to ride, so narrow that one could not move inside. My buttocks were hurting and, on top of that, unfortunately a chilly wind from the valley began to blow. Although it was quite distressful, the heart of the traveler who is bound to suffer on the way endured the experience quite well. How strange it was to think that this was a much better way of traveling than by foot. From the beginning, our party was made up of six people, including the monk Kaigon[21] from the Kakushōin, Koizumi something,[22] Inagake Munetaka[23] and his son Shigeo, and Nakazato Tsuneo.[24] We all climbed together in the same palanquin. We made conversation by talking to and calling the person behind or in front of us, and so we proceeded, sometimes late, sometimes in advance of schedule. We passed the mountain villages of Nishitōge, Tsunogara, and so on, and we arrived at Yonabari. Since I had found several ancient records on this place, I went there paying great attention to what I was seeing. A reference to the Ikai Hills is found in a poem from the *Man'yōshū* ["the Ikai Hills of Yonabari"];[25] a reference to the imperial tomb is found in the *Codes*[26] ["the imperial tomb of Yonabari—the mother of Emperor Kōnin"]. I asked the men shouldering the palanquin about these places, but they did not know anything. I also asked the villagers, but they knew nothing about it—what a sad state of affairs! Moreover, I cannot understand why in the *Man'yōshū* this place is read "Funabari." The character is difficult to read, and the present-day villagers simply say "Yonabari." Although it might be a little annoying to make such a point in a travel diary, I wanted to mention it, entrusting the matter to my brush.

We kept going on a steep mountain road. When we approached Hatsuse, we began seeing Mounts Katsuragi and Unebi emerging far in the distance, through the folds of hills across from us. Although this was a foreign province, we were so used to these famous places that were mentioned in our daily readings and that were sung in poetry, that we felt we were meeting with people of our own hometown; all of a sudden, we felt very close to them. We descended for a while along a steep slope known as Kehaisaka. From this slope, the Hatsuse Temple and the village seemed very close to us. The vivid sight around us defies description. In general, the road up to this point was in the heart of mountains; nothing particularly outstanding had caught our eyes. To see all of a sudden so many solemn monasteries and halls standing together gave us the impression that we were in a different world. We came down until we reached the front of a shrine called Yoki-no-Tenjin. Here the river flowing beneath the wooden bridge was the Hatsuse River, the river by the early rapids. In other words, on the other side of the river stood the village of Hatsuse. We stopped at a local inn, had something to eat, and took a rest. Since the back of the house was set against the riverbank, the waves resounded beneath the floor.

(11)   *Hatsusegawa*   River by the early rapids,
        Hayaku no yo yori   You came flowing from early times—
        Nagare kite   The waves on the rocks
        Na ni tachiwataru   Make the rapids
        Seze no iwanami   That gave you a name.

We left with the intention of visiting the Main Hall. First we entered the main gate; we were about to climb the stairs when someone, I do not know who, pointed out the mausoleum of Dōmyō Shōnin, which we saw on our righthand side. We went up a little and, in a place that was winding like a broken elbow, we found Tsurayuki's plum of the eaves.[27] Moreover, the Hall of Zaō, the Shrine of the God of Creation, and so on, stood next to each other. Up from here the place is known as Kumoizaka, the Slope of Clouds.[28] When we arrived at the Main Hall they had just raised the curtains, so that we could see the neat figure of an extremely large Buddha image. Since people were worshipping, I also prostrated myself to pray. As we were going around seeing things here and there, I noticed that, although we had already passed the heyday of bloom on this mountain, there were still many places where the cherry trees were blooming here and there. At the hour of the snake (10 a.m.) someone blew the conch shells and hit the bell. A long time ago Sei Shōnagon wrote about her surprise at the sudden sound of the conch shell during her pilgrimage; I remembered this episode, and I felt as if I were witnessing the scene as it unfolded in the past.[29] The sound of the bell soon spread to the area around the Main Hall, reaching up to the tower above the stair I had just climbed.

(12)   *Na mo takaku*   Now I am finally listening
        Hatsuse no tera no   To the well-known
        Kanete yori   Sound of the bell

Kikikoshi oto o	Of Hatsuse temple
Ima zo kikikeru	Which I heard in the past.[30]

Many old poems were sung about this bell in the past; I felt a sense of nostalgia at the thought that it might have been the same bell.[31] The fact that places like this draw us into everything we happen to see or to hear, even when there is nothing special to experience, is the result of the heart's habit of yearning after the past. As I was walking and standing for a while in the area, I heard the sound of an elegant piece, not the popular tunes of nowadays. I asked our guide what was the reason for such a performance, and he replied: "It is the anniversary of the death of the founder of this temple;[32] at this time a thousand sutras are chanted. This is the sound of court music *(gagaku)* which introduces the ceremony everyday." I hurried, as I truly wanted to hear that music but, by the time I reached the place, the sound had already stopped—unbearably painful!

On my way back I went through the Main Hall again and, when I descended a little way past Tsurayuki's plum, I noticed a small cedar that is said to be what is left of the twin-trunked cedar around the dwellings of the monks of great virtue who dedicated their life to scholarship.[33] Down a little farther there were five stones piled up on each other, which are known as the pagoda of the Middle Counselor Teika.[34] Since it looked like a recent construction, I could not accept the association at all. There is also a place called Yashio-no-Oka. We descended a little farther and came out on the riverbank; we crossed the bridge, and on the opposite bank was a small house that is said to be the place of Lady Tamakazura.[35] Although people say that we can also find her tomb here, the nun in charge of the place had gone somewhere else that day and, since she was not present, the gate was locked. There are so many claims about ancient ruins at Hatsuse. Among the many whose validity is debatable, the claim related to Tamakazura is the most preposterous. This place was probably built by someone who ignored the fact that *The Tale of Genji* is totally fiction, and that its characters are not real persons. When you go a little farther inside, you see a pile of thirteen stones known as the pagoda of Ietaka of the Second Rank.[36] This looks old somehow. Here stood two old cedars. There was also a shrine dedicated to the Heavenly King Gozu; next to it, one could see the water flowing beneath the moss.[37] Up to this point everything was located on the side of the mountain, near the river.

From here we went to the Yoki-no-Tenjin Shrine. The shrine was located on the flat land of the mountainside. This must be why this place is also known as "The Shrine at the Start of the Ascent of Mount Hatsuse" (Hatsuse-no-Yamaguchi-ni-Masu-no-Jinja). Since nowadays no one knows anything about this matter, I did not bother asking any question about the name. In other words, all the shrines that were probably well known in the past nowadays have become the Hachiman Shrine or the Gozu Shrine. This area was covered with dense vegetation, and there were many cedars; and yet I could not see the field of cypresses for which this place was famous.[38] Our guide told us that there were many cypresses upstream. By the time we had completed our tour of the mountain and were coming back to the village, it started raining again. That day the sky had begun to clear up in the morning, eventually becoming all blue, so that I had put away my raincoat, thinking that it had become unnecessary. How troublesome it was to take it out again all of a sudden, and have to put it on.

(13)   *Nugitsuredo*   Although I had taken it off
       Mata mo furikite   It is coming down again—
       Amagoromo   Again and again
       Kaesugaesu mo   The sleeves of my raincoat
       Sode nurasu kana   Are wet.

However, after a while, as we were leaving the village, it stopped raining completely. A large red torii gate stood at the entrance, on the opposite side.[39]

We left from there and got far away, passing through the villages of Izumo, Kurozaki, and so on. Since I had come hearing of the ruins of Asakura-no-Miya and Namiki-no-Miya [Asakura-no-Miya of Hase was the capital of Emperor Yūryaku; Hase-no-Namiki-no-Miya, the capital of Emperor Buretsu], I wanted to visit them. In Kurozaki every house was making and selling *manjū*—cakes.[40] As I wanted to ask about these ancient capitals, I found a house that appeared to belong to an old man, and I stopped there to eat a *manjū*. While I was eating I asked about the capitals, and he said, "I have heard about the ruins of the ancient capitals, but actually there is no evidence of their existence." When I asked him where Mount Takamato was, he answered that it was behind the house. When I looked following his indication, I faintly saw the top of a moderately high mountain south of this village. He told me that the mountain was now called Tokama. Since the real Mount Takamato is located in the area of Kasuga, I wonder whether this mountain was named so because Tokama sounded like Takamato, or whether the villagers had simply forced the name of Takamato onto their mountain. Which of these two hypotheses might be true? We proceeded to the villages of Wakimoto, Jionji, and so on. From here we could see Mount Tokama very close. At the end of this village the road bifurcated—a crossing with two streets, one leading to Miwa and the other to Sakurai. We turned on the first left, crossed a bridge, and took a narrow path going to Tamu-no-mine.[41] The bridge crossed over the Hatsuse River.

Actually, the correct way to Tamu-no-mine was from Sakurai. Since the famous village of Tobi was on that way, I wanted to visit it. However, everybody was too weary to go the long way, so we decided to take the present route. When we asked which mountain on the Eastern side was so high, we were told it was Mount Otowa. The village of Otowa is located at the foot of this mountain. The village of Osaka stood in the folds of the mountains on the lefthand side of the road; soon we were going to pass by this village, which is mentioned in an ancient poem.[42] Although there was a shrine there, we were in a hurry to proceed so we could not visit it.

We kept following the steep mountain road until we reached the village of Kurahashi. From here we took the road that came from Sakurai. We were about five miles away from Hatsuse, and about two and a half miles away from Tamu-no-mine. At the house where we stopped a moment to rest I asked the whereabouts of that capital. [Kurahashi-no-Shibagaki-no-Miya was the capital of Emperor Sushun.] The owner answered: "You will find the remains of the capital at a temple called Kinfukuji in the middle of the village. It is in the direction you were coming from." He called a boy twelve or thirteen years of age, who might have been his son, and assigned him as our guide. We followed the boy and went back two or three hundred yards. There was no gate in front of the temple, which looked like a truly temporary hut. Well, I wanted to know more about this place; I called for the priest in charge of the temple, but no one was there. In front there was a small hall with a thatched roof called Goma-dō (Hall for Cedar-Stick Burning). When I peeked inside, I noticed a statue of Fudō surrounded by Shōtoku Taishi and Emperor Sushun, with a sign indicating their names. However, these statues looked absolutely new; there was no hint that would make one think of the past. The Kurahashi River ran behind this dwelling. Everything here—mountain and river—were quite well-known places.[43]

We went back to the man's house, and I asked him the location of the imperial tomb [the Kurahashi-no-Oka Mound, tomb of Emperor Sushun]. He replied: "About six hundred yards south-east of a village called Osaka there is a place called Misasagi-yama (Mount Imperial Mound); in the middle of a luxuriant forest you will find three caves one hundred or one hundred and twenty yards deep.[44] Although from here it is quite faraway, the whole area up to that place is called Kurahashi." I was disappointed to hear that we had passed Osaka without knowing that we missed the road to Emperor Sushun's tomb—how regrettable! Since the man told us that it was about well over a mile from here, I gave up the idea of visiting that place. We could see the mountain known as Otowa standing tall, east of us. From reading ancient poetry I knew that Mount Kurahashi was a high peak, and now I could verify it with my own eyes.[45]

We left the village, went on for about six hundred yards, crossed an earthen bridge, and found a place called Orii on our righthand side. The owner of that house had told us that the hilly forest up the mountain was the tomb of Emperor Yōmei, but I felt that this was wrong. However, I thought it was worth visiting, so we climbed up to that place and found in the middle of the forest a small shrine called the Kasuga Shrine. A little way down the road there was a mountain temple. We approached it, and I asked the priest in charge of the temple about this place. He answered that this was not an imperial tomb, and that the tomb of Emperor Yōmei was located in a village by the name of Nagato. Now I was finally convinced that the indication I had gotten earlier from that man was incorrect. Yet this forest looked as if it were worth seeing. According to ancient documents *[Montoku Jitsuroku*, 9, and also *Jinmyōchō]*, the god of Kurahashi Orii was worshipped in this village. After crossing the earthen bridge we had the Kurahashi River on our lefthand side; we went along the river and kept climbing while following its current. This river comes out of Tamu-no-mine and flows northward, going through the village of Kurahashi. On this road from Sakurai until Tamu-no-mine a stone stands every one hundred yards with the fifty-two rankings of the bodhisattva according to *The Sutra on a Bodhisattva's Original Action*.[46] We could rely on these markings to calculate how far we had gone and how much farther we needed to go. As we were gradually going up along the bank of the same river, we found ourselves in the shade of a ravine dense with trees and reached a spot where the left and right branches of the mountain stream joined. The sight of the rapid current caught my eye. After we had crossed a bridge over there, a teahouse immediately appeared. We were told that this was the entrance to Tamu-no-mine.

The houses stood in a row for about two or three hundred yards. We crossed a beautiful bridge again, proceeded for a while, and entered a main gate—the eastern gate. The dwellings of the monks were lined up on the right and the left sides. The area in front of the mausoleum was wide open; the mausoleum faced south in the mountainside.[47] It is a solemn building; the sight of this radiant and polished construction makes one's eyes dazzle. The thirteen-story pagoda and the shrine are located in the west side. It goes without saying that everything around the shrine was truly gorgeous; but even the area beside the monks' dwelling—even every nook and cranny of the pathways —was swept spotless. Not a single fallen leaf could be found in this mountain—I don't think any other place matches this one. The cherry blossoms were at their peak. Treetops as white as mulberry trees were in full bloom— no words can describe the appeal of this place. I wonder if all these trees were moved from somewhere else and planted here. None was the same; they were all of different types. I had never heard that there were so many cherry trees in this mountain.

(14)   *Tani fukaku*   Oh, the mountain cherries
        Wakeiru Tamu no   Of Tamu-no-mine
            Yamazakura   Where I entered deep into the gorge—
        Kai aru hana no   How worthy it is
        Iro o miru kana   To see the color of their flowers![48]

We turned west and passed in front of a torii gate; there stood another main entrance—the western gate. From there we went straight down and found a road of nearly four miles going to Asuka-no-Oka. When I heard that halfway down this road there was a village by the name of Hosokawa, I wondered whether this was the place where the poem "Mount Hosokawa in Minabuchi" was composed.[49] I also wondered whether the river originating from the mountains of Tamu-no-mine flowed there. [We read in the *Man'yōshū*,

        Uchi taori   Is it because the mist on Mount Tamu
        Tamu no yamagiri   Of the breaking flowers
            Shigemi ka mo   Is so thick
        Hosokawa no se ni   That the waves are so noisy
        Nami no sawakeru   In the rapids of the Hosokawa River?][50]

I wanted to ask all these questions, but we could not go there. From this gate we had to make a sharp left turn in order to go to Yoshino. We went far up the mountain path; on the summit we found a teahouse from which we could view the entire Yamato Plain. We proceeded on the same mountain path until we reached another peak. From here we could see Yoshino Mountain in the distance among the clouds.[51] How happy I was to have finally seen, albeit faintly, the cherry blossoms as white as clouds on which my mind had been set day and night.[52] The view of the shade in the ravine where we were descending, and of the mountain stream flowing on the rocks, far from the world, was refreshingly pure. Four miles from Tamu-no-mine there was a mountain village called Taki-no-hata—the Field of Rapids. Indeed this area was run through by a furious stream. In the shady gorge that we found after crossing another mountain, we encountered the road that went from the hill to Kamiichi. Although we had planned to arrive in Yoshino today, while we had been doing this and that, the spring sun had set. Therefore, we stopped at a village in the heart of the mountains called Chimata, the Crossroad. That night I composed the following poem:

(15)   *Furusato ni*   I wish to follow
        Kayou yumeji ya   The path of dreams
            Tadoramashi   Taking me to my hometown,
        Chimata no sato ni   Since I will certainly spend the night
        Tabine shitsureba   In Chimata, the village of Crossroads.

When I asked some guidance at the inn about Ryūmon-no-taki, the Waterfall of the Dragon's Gate,[53] the owner said, "If you go directly to Kamiichi from here, it is about two and a half miles, but if you go through Ryūmon-no-taki, it is about five miles—two and a half miles from this village to that place and, then, another two and a half miles to Kamiichi." Since I had wanted to see this waterfall for a long time, I thought that I would go there that day from the Tamu peak. However, our guide had discouraged us, saying that it was very far away and that the path was steep—so I did not go. To hear now that from here the place was not so far made me feel pangs of regret. And yet, at the news that the cherry blossoms at Yoshino had already passed their peak, no one expressed a desire to visit the waterfall on the following day. The place known as Ryūmon was on the way that led from Ise to both Yoshino and the Ki province through Mount Takami. People say that the waterfall is located in a concave space about two-thirds of a mile from the road. They also say that this is a sacred fall. When people pray for rain in days of great drought, a sign always appears: when the eels climb the fall, the rain falls shortly.

(16)	*Tachiyorade*	I have passed by
	Yoso ni kikitsutsu	While hearing from others
	Suguru kana	Without a chance to get close to it—
	Kokoro ni kakeshi	The white thread of the waterfall
	Taki no shiraito	Hanging from my heart.[54]

THE EIGHTH DAY

It had not rained since we left Hatsuse yesterday, the light creeping over the hills;[55] by the time we had reached the Tamu-no-mine area the sky had completely cleared. Today, again, was a fair day. As we were approaching Yoshino, the fair field, we all felt lightness in our legs. It might have been because we were so cheerful on the way that we reached Kamiichi in no time. We were told that the distance was about two and a half miles, but I felt that it was much closer, less than one mile. A boat had reached the bank of the Yoshino River on our side, jostling through the rafts floating all over without leaving any gap. Since it was not getting late, the ferryman did not invite us to hurry up, and yet everybody got into the boat quickly. [In the *Tales of Ise* we read, "The ferryman said, 'Come aboard quickly; it's getting late.'"][56] When I asked where I could find the Imose Mountains, I learned that the river splits in its upper course; the mountains that I could see near to me were Mount Imo on the eastern side and Mount Se on the western side. However, there was no doubt that the mountains carrying this name were in the Ki province. And yet, the fact that someone set this place as the location of the mountains indicates that this was the act of a man of taste, totally dedicated to the arts, who was inspired by the famous verse, "the Yoshino River, whose course falls between...."[57] In this vein I composed my poem:

(17)	*Imoseyama*	This is what a name is about:
	Naki na mo yoshi ya	Even if your name is not Imose Mountains
	Yoshinogawa	The currents of the Yoshino River
	Yo ni nagarete wa	Flowing through generations
	Sore to koso mime	See them as such.

On the opposite shore was the village of Igai. We went west for a while along the river and approached the entrance to the mountain from a place called Tanji. As we went deeper and deeper into the mountain, we found Shidekake-no-Myōjin enshrined in the middle of a cedar forest; I wonder whether this was the Yoshino-no-Yamanoguchi Shrine.[58] However, it did not look as gorgeous as I had expected. All around these woods, above and beneath, there were many cherry trees in the midst of which we kept climbing. At the end of our climb there was a teahouse in a place where our road met with the road from Mutsuda. We stopped here to rest awhile. This house was located at a very high spot, so that we had a wonderful view from there after coming up from the steep road. As I was looking far in the distance, I noticed a place called Hitomesenbon (A Thousand Trees in one View) that is generally known in Yoshino as the place with the most cherry trees. As a matter of fact, that is exactly how the place looks, but I find the name unpleasant; I wonder what fool came up with such a vulgar name. Basically, full bloom had already passed, and now I could spot here and there treetops that looked like patches of melted snow. People say that every year the cherry trees on this mountain bloom sixty-five days after the spring equinox.[59] Moreover, someone from my province had asked those who had come to Yoshino when was a good time to see the cherry blossom there. Several people had answered that, looking at the bloom in our area, this must be a perfect time over there. We had waited for the right time to come, and we had left accordingly. Many people whom we had asked on the way had told us that the time was perfect for the bloom, and someone even told us that it was early. The thought that we could be late never even crossed our minds. Now, when I asked more details here on the spot, I was told that this year the bloom had come earlier, probably because of the heat they had during the latter part of the Second Month. What could be called full bloom had taken place three or four days earlier. Because of the heavy rains and the blowing winds, the flowers had scattered without actually having time for a full bloom. Listening to this news I realized that not even local people can predict with any certainty the time of the blossoms, which could be either late or early depending on the heat or cold of that particular year.

On the northeastern side Mount Mifune came into view. [In the *Man'yōshū* we find the poem, "Along the crest of Mifune,/over the waterfall."][60] However, since the poem says that this mountain is "over the waterfall," I don't think Mount Mifune is in this area. This must be another baseless name. Here was the entrance to the village of Yoshino; from here a row of merchant houses began to unfold. We continued for two or three hundred yards, and, after climbing a few stone steps, I noticed an extremely large copper-colored torii gate. A plaque was inscribed with the name "Gate of Faith" (Hosshin-mon); people say that the inscription was by the hand of Kōbō Daishi. About two hundred yards farther, on top of the stone steps, stood the

Gate of the Two Kings.[61] In this area there were cherry trees, many of which were in bloom. Across from here the mountain they called Mifune looked quite close. Since we were concerned with finding lodgings, we kept going without visiting the Zaō Hall.[62] Because the hall faced in the opposite direction, the gate stood in the back of the hall. We searched for a clean place to stay in the area; after we decided on the inn, we rested for a while, had some food, and discussed what we wanted to see today and tomorrow. We hired a guide, and we left with the idea of beginning our visit with the places closest to us.

Since next to the room we had rented from a man by the name of Hakoya something was the Yoshimizu-in, we began by paying our respects to that place.[63] This temple was located on a hill removed from the village—we had to go down for a while on the left off the road, and then climb a little. The surrounding area was like a ravine. People say that Emperor Go-Daigo lived here for a while. When we entered this place in which things had stayed the way they were in the past, the building indeed exuded an ancient atmosphere; it did not look like an ordinary place. With great trepidation and respect I put forward the following words:

(18) *Inishie no*　　　　　　Imagining
　　Kokoro o kumite　　　The suffering heart of the past,
　　　　Yoshimizu no　　My sleeves are drenched
　Fukaki aware ni　　　　By the deep sadness
　Sode wa nurekeri　　　Brought about by these good waters.[64]

People say that Emperor Go-Murakami[65] sculpted with his own hands a statue of Emperor Go-Daigo, to which I addressed a poem as my worship:

(19)　　*Aware kimi*　　　　How sad, the Lord,
　　Kono yoshimizu ni　　Uprooted, to these good waters
　　　　Utsuri kite　　　He came—
　Nokoru mikage o　　　With trepidation I see
　Miru mo kashikoshi　　The august image left behind.[66]

There were other ancient treasures of that age; there were so many that, although I saw them, I cannot remember them all. Inside the compound of this temple a small building was wide open, allowing an unobstructed view of the wonderful scenery. I entered it and gazed while smoking. I could see the mountain of the Komori Shrine standing tall in front of me. Cherry trees were all over, on the mountain as well as in the adjacent ravine, with no gaps between them. I have no words to express my regret at the view now of their green leaves. And yet I could see, deeper inside those leaves, many flowers still blooming:

(20)   *Miyoshino no*   There is no limit
         Hana wa hikazu mo   To the number of days
              Kagiri nashi   In which the flowers bloom in fair Yoshino—
         Aoba no oku mo   Deep into the green leaves
         Nao sakari ni te   Is the bloom.[67]

Someone told me that over there was the place called Takizakura—The Waterfall Cherry.

(21)   *Sakiniou*   Oh, the white thread of the waterfall!
         Hana no yosome wa   Seen from afar
              Tachiyorite   The flowers blooming fragrantly
         Miru ni mo masaru   Excel those
         Taki no shiraito   Seen from nearby.

One could keep looking until the sun has set and no tiredness would dawn on him. Moreover, there was also a place called Kumoizakura—"Cherries above the Clouds." I thought of the poem that Emperor Go-Daigo wrote when he saw these trees in bloom:

              Koko nite mo   When I think
         Kumoi no sakura   Of my temporary dwelling,
              Sakinikeri   The cherry flowers above the clouds
         Tada karisome no   Bloom
         Yado to omou ni   Here as well.[68]

I added my own poem:

(22)   *Yoyo o hete*   The remains of the palace above the clouds
         Mukai no yama no   Have aged—
              Hana no na ni   They survive through the ages
         Nokoru kumoi no   In the name of the cherry blossoms
         Ato wa furiniki   On the mountain opposite.

Then, we visited the Zaō Hall. I asked to have the curtain rolled up, and when I looked I saw an extremely huge statue of a truly frightening deity standing with an angry face and one leg lifted in midair—Zaō Gongen. Actually, there were three statues that looked exactly the same, so that I could not tell them apart. The hall faced south and was over thirty-three yards long and wide. The building looked very ancient. In front of the hall there was a place where someone had planted cherry trees in the four corners—it is called Shihonzakura, the Four Cherries. An extremely big piece of iron shaped like a pot was lying broken on one side. When I asked what it was, someone replied that this was what was left of the nine rings at the top of an old pagoda that had burned and crumbled to the ground. The diameter of the foundation appeared to be two yards—a fact that made me guess the huge size of the pagoda. We went west from the side of the hall, and after going down a few stone stairs, there it was—the Jitsujōji temple![69] On the left of the main statue stood the mortuary tablet of Emperor Go-Daigo; on the right stood Go-Murakami's. Only the front of this temple continued into the Zaō Hall: its left, right, and back sides all descended into a ravine. And yet it was slightly larger than the Yoshimizu-in. I wonder if it is true what they say that this place was the residence, albeit temporary, of three emperors [Emperor Go-Daigo, Emperor Go-Murakami, and Emperor Go-Kameyama] over fifty years.[70] Although things seem to have been different, this must have been the imperial dwelling from time to time. Nowadays, the hall and everything else have been rebuilt, so that we cannot find vestiges of that age; and yet, it is a fascinating, appealing place—something that one cannot find elsewhere. We left this temple, went back to our original road, and saw a place called Sakuramoto-bō—the Monastery at the Bottom of the Cherry Trees. Since the Katte Shrine has burned in recent years,[71] today one can see only a small temporary building; I prayed there and went beyond. Near this shrine there was also a small forest on a hill by the name of Sodefuruyama, Mount Waving Sleeve,[72] but it burned down at the same time as the shrine. Mount Mikage is a continuation of this hill—a forest dense with trees.

In front of the hall of the Chikurin-in—the Temple of the Bamboo Forest—there was a curious bamboo: at every joint a branch came out in all directions. Behind it was an unusually remarkable garden.[73] From there we climbed to a slightly higher location and saw a most spectacular view of all the mountains round about. First of all, in the northern direction I saw the Zaō Hall—a continuation of the peddlers' houses at their end—which drew my attention because of its height towering over all other buildings. Far in the distance I could see Mount Tamu, Mount Takatori, and, northeast along the same line, Ryūmon-no-Dake, the Peak of the Dragon's Gate. On the other side of the gorge, a range of mountains unfolded on the east side and west side: the mountain of the Komori Shrine topped all other mountains in the south, while in the northwest Mount Katsuraki raised itself over the mist, far away. My words cannot do justice to this place—it was an eye-catching view.

(23)   *Hana to nomi*   Oh, Yoshino Mountain,
    Omoiirinuru   I went deep into you
        Yoshinoyama   Thinking only of the cherry blossoms!
    Yomo no nagame mo   Is there a match for the vistas
    Tagui ya wa aru   You produce in all directions?

I stayed there admiring the view for a long time. I was alerted that there were still many places ahead of us we should be seeing, and that the sun would be setting soon, but I could not bring myself to listen. While humming to myself, "If the sun sets/I will take shelter . . . "—[a verse from the *Kokinshū* poem:

    Iza kyō wa   Oh, today
    Haru no yamabe ni   I will make my way
        Majiri namu   Into the mountains of spring!
    Kurenaba nage no   If the sun sets I will take shelter
    Hana no kage ka wa   In the shadow of the transient flowers.][74]—

I composed the following poem:

(24)   *Akanaku ni*   As I cannot see enough,
    Hitoyo wa nenan   One night I will sleep
        Miyoshino no   At the base of a flowering tree
    Take no hayashi no   In the bamboo forest
    Hana no ko no moto   Of fair Yoshino.[75]

Despite my words, since I was drawn by the many places still lying ahead, I tied this poem to the branch of a cherry tree that was standing there, and I left. Around the road I noticed many mistletoes[76] of the cherry trees, and wondering what people did with them, I composed the poem,

(25)   *Urayamashi*   How envious I am!
    Ware mo koishiki   What promise did you make

Hana no eda o	When you began dwelling
Ika ni chigirite	In the branches of the flowers
Yadori somekemu	That are so dear to me?

We kept going until we reached a place called the Kannon Exorcizing Dreams.[77] There was also a place called Nunobiki-no-Sakura (The Cherry Blossom of the Cloth Stretched Out to Dry) but, as the place had changed its garment and was now in the shade of green leaves, those wearing the robe of the traveler would have been unable to see the bloom, even were they to stop. In this area there were also cherry trees shaped like waterfalls and cherry trees shaped like clouds that I had seen from the Yoshimizu-in. The Sesonji was an outworn temple with a big, ancient bell. We climbed again for a while, and we reached a place two miles from the Zaō Hall where Komori-no-Kami, the God Protecting Children, is enshrined.[78] In this shrine I prayed quietly, with more devotion than in any other of the many places I had visited before. The reason is that many years ago my father, deeply grieving over the fact that he did not have any child, came to this distant place to pray to this god. The prayer was effective since, after a short while, my mother became pregnant. My father was ecstatic at the thought that all his prayers had come true. He immersed himself in even deeper prayers, asking the god to grant him, if possible, a son. Eventually, I was born. At every possible occasion my mother kept telling me, in tears: "Father repeated to me several times his intention to pay his respects to the god by visiting him together with you, my son, as soon as you turned thirteen. Now, it is unbearable for me to think that father died when you were only eleven years old." When I became thirteen, my mother firmly made me go and make a pilgrimage to the shrine in order to fulfill my father's wishes. When I think now that even my mother has died, it all seems like a dream.

(26)	*Omoiizuru*	My tears fall more densely
	Sono kamigaki ni	Than the dense offerings
	Tamuke shite	Presented
	Nusa yori shigeku	To this shrine
	Chiru namida ka na	That has brought back so many memories.

There was no way I could squeeze my sleeves to make them dry. At that time I was very young and I did not know very much. Little by little I became an adult and, as I became able to understand the meaning of things, listening to this old story, I realized that the blessings of the god were not such a common thing. Keeping this in mind, every morning I worshipped facing this shrine. Although I kept thinking about my desire to make a pilgrimage to the shrine, the pressure of many things took all my time. Thirty years went by; the fact that this year I made the pilgrimage at the age of forty-three is the proof of a deep karma. I feel extremely happy to know that my hope of many years has finally been realized; and yet, I could not help crying.[79] The viewing of the cherry blossoms might make my faith look a little shallow, but I believe that the god will forgive all the diverse reasons for my journey, and I totally rely on his understanding for accepting my plea.[80]

Because of this deep connection I felt that everything related to this deity was not someone else's concern. I put all my efforts into the study of it by looking at documents for a number of years. Earlier on I thought that the "Yoshino Mikumari Shrine" was related to this deity. However, the *Shoku Nihongi* (The Chronicles of Japan, Continued) mentions the "god of Mikumari Peak,"[81] and I wondered whether such a place existed. I wanted to check the shape of the place myself, and this had been a source of anxiety for several years. Now that I was able to see it with my own eyes, I had no doubt. This place was on a peak towering over all the neighboring mountains, the highest place in the area. This was definitely the place described in *The Chronicles of Japan, Continued*. The place sung in an ancient poem as "Mount Mikumari" refers to this place;[82] however, the characters used to indicate the mountain were erroneously read "Mizuwake"—a name that was also used to indicate another mountain in a different place, which is not unusual. Moreover, in middle antiquity people mispronounced "Mikumari," calling it instead "Mikomori-no-Kami," "the God Protecting Children." Nowadays, they simply say, "Komori"—the deity invoked for the prosperity of one's offspring. As a matter of fact, my father also addressed his prayers to this god in this place.

In front of the shrine's gate there were many cherry trees at the peak of their bloom. As I was resting after stopping at a teahouse beneath the trees, I noticed a gentleman who said he was from the Owari province, and who had also come to see the cherry blossoms. He liked poetry in Chinese, and his name sounded like a Chinese name—I have forgotten it. His wife composed poetry in the Yamato language; they had come together. Although she had passed the prime of her life, she was attractive. The day before yesterday I had seen them as I was resting in Nabari of Iga province. Yesterday we were fellow pilgrims at Tamu-no-mine, and today we met again at the Chikurin-in. That man had been speaking with Koizumi[83] and exchanging poems in Chinese with him; I heard that he was asking many things in detail about us. Without knowing all this, today we met again here. As we were having a conversation, talking about this and that, the long day of spring came to a close, and the sound of the bell tolling at sunset made me hurry.[84] As I was making my departure from them beneath a tree, I recited:

(27)   *Ima wa mata*   Let me see next time
    Kimi ga kotoba no   The flowers
        Hana mo min   Of your words—
    Yoshino no yama wa   Yoshino Mountain that we visited today
    Wakekurashikeri   Has become dark.[85]

Saying that we would entrust to tomorrow what was left to see, from here today we returned to the inn. That night, two poems were sent to me from the inn where the man from Owari was staying. They must have been written by that lady who had passed her prime. Since the poems were on how beautiful the cherry blossoms were that day, I replied with the following poem:

(28)   *Yoshinoyama*   Adding further glow
    Hiru mishi hana no   To the image of the flowers
        Omokage mo   That I saw today
    Nioi o soete   On Mount Yoshino—
    Kasumu tsukikage   Misty moonlight.

I wrote this poem because the name of the lady who had written those two poems was Kagetsu, Misty Moon. Since she had sent her poems along with some fruits, I also wrote the following poem:

(29)   *Miyoshino no*   Oh, the deep kindness
    Yama yori fukaki   Coming from the mountain of Yoshino!
        Nasake o ya   It will be my souvenir
    Hana no kaesa no   On my return
    Iezuto ni sen   From viewing the flowers.

As I happened to have a container, I sent her some tea from the Kawakami village of the Ise province, adding the following poem to the wrapping paper:

(30)   *Chigiri are ya*   It must have been our destiny!
    Yamaji wakekite   To have come to this mountain road,

Sugigate no	And to have met for a while
Ko *no shitakage ni*	In the shade of the trees
Shibashi aishi mo	So difficult to pass by.

I wonder whether she understood the message I hid in the poem, "a little tea."[86] Several other people added their poems, which we sent to the couple. As the man had sent word that they were rushing to get to the capital Kyoto, and that they would be getting up early the next morning, I wrote the following lines:

(31)	*Tabigoromo*	The sleeves of the traveler's robe
	Sode koso nureru	Are drenched with tears.
	Yoshinogawa	Your early parting
	Hana yori hayaki	Is faster than the flowers
	Hito no wakare ni	Scattered in the Yoshino river.

THE NINTH DAY

I got up early, went out onto the porch, and saw that the sky was not covered by the tiniest particle of clouds; it was clear all over. The morning sun came out radiantly beautiful. This morning the buds on the trees and the view deep into the mountains in spring were not covered by any haze—one could see clearly far into the distance. The Yoshimizu-in was at a crawling distance; signs of people coming and going appeared very close to one's eyes. Generally speaking, this village was on top of a narrow mountain—a continuation downwards from Mikumari peak. Seen from the front, people's houses looked normal, like everywhere else; however, the backs of the houses were built on top of a gorge. Since these were three-story houses, every single house came with an incredible view. In other words, the top floor was reserved for paying guests or for selling something, and one had access to this floor directly from the street. The middle floor was reserved for the family; being beneath the top floor, one had to use a stair to come down from the entrance. If one goes one story farther down, he will not find any floor. Everything lies on the dirt—a truly messy sight. Since the bathtub and the latrines are there, for the legs of the traveler who is exhausted by a day-long journey, to go up and down the stairs in order to get to these places is like crossing many mountain ridges—extremely hard! However, the atmosphere is so interesting that these minor things never become a problem. Forgetting that "people will wait for me/once the flowers have scattered," [In the *Shinkokinshū* Saigyō says,

Yoshinoyama	This body of mine knows
Yagate ideji to	That it will never come out
Omou mi o	From Mount Yoshino.
Hana chirinaba to	Will people wait for me
Hito ya matsuramu	Once the flowers have scattered?]87

I wished I could stop and live there.

Today we left with the idea of seeing the waterfall. We asked our guide to be our leader, and to carry the food and the rice wine. In the area of the Chikurin-in there was a continuous line of mercantile houses, mixed with a few solemn monasteries. As we proceeded away from it, the houses became more and more scattered, until they totally disappeared after we entered into the recess of the mountain from the Komori Shrine. We proceeded, clearing our path through an area completely covered by cypresses. When we finally reached an open space, I saw on my left side a place called Haruka-no-tani, The Far-away-Ravine. There one could see many cherry trees in full bloom.

(32)	Takane yori	The flowers
	Hodo mo Haruka no	White as white clouds
	Tani kakete	Span
	Tachitsuzukitaru	The far away ravine
	Hana no shirakumo	That faraway I see from this high peak.

We kept going until we met a big red torii gate that is called Ni-no-torii (The Second Gate), or also, Shugyō-mon (The Gate of Spiritual Training). Nowadays the Kane-no-mitake Shrine is called Konshō Daimyōjin, which is the name of the deity ruling over this mountain. From the front of this shrine we turned left and descended a little; I saw an ancient-looking pagoda called Kenuke-no-tō. People say that in the past, as he was pursued by the enemy, Minamoto no Yoshitsune hid himself in this pagoda.88 When they found him, he kicked open the roof and fled. I took a look, but since I was not interested in this event, I did not see anything, even though I kept my eyes on the place. We went deeper into the mountain and reached a teahouse. From there we went down for a while on the righthand side until [we reached] the Anzen-ji Temple. The Zaō Hall was built by the Ōsaka Minister of the Right.89 On the east side there was a mountain covered with trees, called Aoge-ga-mine, the Peak of Green Roots, which from the front of the hall appeared to be quite close.90 Two or three hundred yards deep into the mountain a hall with a bombastic name appeared. From the back of this hall we continued two hundred yards downwards through a shady path and came to a place called Kokeshimizu, The Mossy Spring Water, where water was trickling down from the crevices between rocks. Our guide recited a poem that he said was by Saigyō. As soon as I heard it, I felt that the poem was not in the style of that famous poet; it was a vulgar fake. We proceeded one hundred yards farther and found, on slightly flat ground, the remains of the place where Saigyō had lived—a temporary hut about three yards long, still standing today. I could see cherry trees here and there.

(33) *Hana mitsutsu*   When I visited the remains of a past
     Sumishi mukashi no   In which he lived
         Ato toeba   Admiring the flowers,
     Koke no shimizu ni   The image floated
     Ukabu omokage   On the mossy spring water.

Recently a recluse spent three years shut in this place.

People here say simply *maki*[91] (the good tree) for what in the capital is called *koya-maki* (good tree from the high field). When I think about it, I realize that in the past when people said *maki*, they meant this tree—another name for *hinoki* (cypress). This is certainly not the place I should be making this point. However, someone asked this question after seeing that in this area the mountains were covered by these trees. When I heard the answer, these thoughts came to my mind immediately, and I entrusted them to my brush. We took the main road and returned to the teahouse in front of Anzen-ji. Then, we took the road leading to the peak.[92] When we thought we had come over four hundred yards, we turned left at a stony sign indicating that from here women were not allowed to climb to the peak. In other words, this mountain was Aoge-ga-mine, which we had seen earlier. We went a little farther, and far at the bottom of the gorge on the eastern side was the village of Natsumi.[93] We kept going and, when we asked the name of the village down in the east valley, we were told that it was "Kuzu"—The Country's Nest. The distance along the ridge of this mountain, which was open to a great view, was quite extensive. The steepness of the path as we were descending was unmatched—and yet, it was not as hard as when we were going up. At the end of the descent was the village of Nijikō. Although we were told that the distance from Anzen-ji to this place was about two and a half miles, I felt it was much farther away. Surrounded by mountains, this village had no spot from which one could look into the distance; at every house people were manufacturing paper, and there was plenty drying in front of the gates. Since I had never seen this process, I wanted to take a look; my legs would not rest and took me inside, where I witnessed the procedure of making and lifting the paper sheet by sheet and superimposing it one on top of the other. It was so unusual that I forgot I had to go.

After leaving the village, we went on about four hundred yards on the righthand side, left behind a wooden bridge crossing the mountain stream, and climbed a while towards the left. After going across a fold of hills, suddenly we were in the village of Ōtaki, The Great Fall—no more than six hundred yards in length. What was called "fall" was outside the village, in the vicinity of the Yoshino River. It was nothing but the rapids that one could see from the front of the house facing the river; it was not a real waterfall falling straight from above. I had learned from Master Kaibara that "since, seen from far away, this fall is no different from any other waterfall, one should look at it up close."[94] Therefore, we managed to climb on top of the rocks and, once we got there and looked up close, I saw the water of this large river flowing and falling through the many boulders piled on top of each other. The view of the white waves rising after touching and breaking against the rocks was at the same time beautiful and frightful—expressions that only estrange one from the actual experience. I had also learned that "in the past, rafts passed through these rapids but, because the current was so violent, every time they went through, they risked being swept away; therefore people opened a path where the boulders were a little more smooth. Nowadays every raft passes through that place." When I looked in that direction I saw a separate path for the water that actually looked a little calmer than the rapids on this side. As I was saying, "Oh, if only a raft would descend the current right now! I would like to see it going through these rapids," we were eating and drinking rice wine when something that looked like a raft coming down faraway from the upper stream drew closer and closer. When the raft reached this fall, people on board jumped left and right onto the top of the boulder; meanwhile, the ferryman was holding the raft with a rope. While everybody was running along the current, the raft took off down the current like an arrow. Then, on the last boulder, everybody jumped back onto the raft. To see those people jumping effortlessly onto the logs that bobbed up and down, shaken by waves furiously rising, in a place where the strength of the water was particularly impressive, was to witness something extremely dangerous. And yet, it was strangely beautiful—an unparalleled experience. We were all taken by the view of the raft, and we stopped asking whose turn it was to drink from the *sake* cup.[95] Then, the raft got away from the fall and went down a smoother rapid. When I had a chance to look at it more carefully, I noticed that the raft was made of sixteen bundles of logs tied together, each bundle being three or four logs almost four meters long. The full length of the raft was quite big. There were four people riding on it. From this fall the rapids break towards the other side and flow between the mountains across. The sight of the rafts passing at the bottom of a rocky shore so steep that one could hit everything left and right, was something out of a painting. In such a place my mouth was shut and no poem came out of it. Since to pick my brain and keep thinking would have been awkward, I gave up the idea of composing a poem.

The place where in the past the Yoshino Palace was located—a place often visited by the empress—which Kakinomoto no Hitomaro called "the palace by the surging rapids" in one of his poems while he was in attendance on the empress, must be related to this Ōtaki.[96] When I think about several poems, matching them to the locations they describe, I have no doubt that the places sung as "the plain of Akizu"[97] and "along the crest of Mifune over the waterfall"[98] are definitely in this area. Thinking that this must be the mountain in question, I looked around with great attention. I turned left from the river and, when I looked back, saw a mountain that could be said to be Mount Mifune, Boat Mountain. If we want to compare it to a boat, we could say that the front and back of the mountain are flat and long, while only the central part is elevated; this mountain looks like a roofed boat.[99] Although I think that this should be it, I am not really sure. There seems to be a discrepancy between the actual location of this mountain below the waterfall and the poem's indication, "above the waterfall." However, is there a reason why we should not call these mountains "above the waterfall"? If anyone yearning after the past comes to this place, he should definitely ponder over this matter. This is the mountain immediately above the village.

We passed again through the village and returned to Nijikō. This time we crossed the wooden bridge that I mentioned earlier, climbed the stone steps for about one hundred yards, and made our way through the shade of an overgrown ravine until we saw what is called Seimei-ga-taki, The Clear Waterfall. The shape of this fall was different from the one we saw at Ōtaki. This one fell about thirty meters straight down from the boulder of a mountain completely covered with trees. Since our observation point was a cliff protruding a little from the side located close to the middle part of the waterfall, we kept looking up and down. The top part of the fall was narrow; then it gradually expanded to over three meters, and fell down. Its end was mantled by the dense foliage of the mountain here and there; that was the bottom of the dark ravine. The water landed violently in a place that looked like a peeping hole, creating a roar in the mountain—a truly frightening view that gave one the chills. On one side there was a small hall; from there we took hold of the vines and ivy growing over the boulder and climbed a little. When I looked towards the top of the waterfall, I saw the water coming down from above and falling into a pool surrounded by rocks. The diameter of this pool was about six meters; although it was narrow, it looked quite deep. The waterfall came down, suddenly overfilling the pool with its water. Sometime in the past I had heard that the villagers of this place performed an act known as "Iwatobi," Jumping from the Boulder, and at that time they actually were jumping from the boulder. Earlier on at Nijikō I had asked the guide whether someone would be performing the jump, and he answered that recently there was too much water because of what was left of the long rains; it was too dangerous and no one would do it. He said that for a fee people would jump from the top of the rock adjacent to the waterfall into the bottom of the pool, and then they would float out of it. However, when the water was too stormy, there was the danger of being swept away when coming up to the surface, and of getting trapped at Chōshi-no-guchi, The Neck of the *Sake* Bottle—then, it would have been all over. Chōshi-no-guchi indicates the spot where the water falls from the edge of the pool downwards.

Someone argues that the name of the waterfall, Seimei-ga-taki, derives from the place-name Kagerō-no-ono, The Field of Mayflies, since the insect known as mayfly *(kagerō)* is also called *seimei*. I don't believe this is true. It might have been true at the beginning, as local people also refer to it as "Semi-no-taki," The Cicada's Waterfall. However, later on they played it smart and came up with the name "The Clear *(seimei)* Waterfall." Now that I see the fall, I notice that the top part is narrow; then it becomes broader and broader as it comes down. It definitely looks like the shape of a cicada. Moreover, the roar produced by the fall reminds one of the cicada's shrill. It was only natural that it would be given the name Cicada's Waterfall. Someone argues that Semi-no-taki is not here, but refers to a different waterfall—a thesis that local people deny, insisting that this is Cicada's Waterfall. Be that as it may, the reference to the mayfly must be wrong. Kagerō-no-ono is a mistaken reading of Akizuno, Fields of Akizu. Not only does a place called The Field of Mayflies not exist, but Fields of Akizu is not located in this area. From this fall comes the Otonashi-gawa, Soundless River. The strangest thing about this river is that during the first half of each month its upper course is dry; during the second half, the lower course becomes dry. One wonders where the waters coming from the upper stream go. It actually penetrates the cracks in the rocks, gradually impregnating the sand below. While disappearing, it keeps going farther and farther down, until it resurfaces again. Although this is what happens, the constant alternating appearance of the upper and the lower courses without fail is truly a wondrous thing. However, today the fact that this river looks like any other river is due to the recent large amount of water. In other words, the river crossed by the wooden bridge that I mentioned earlier is this river; the lower stream flows through the village of Nijikō.

We returned to the village of Nijikō and took again the road from which we had descended this morning. I had not felt that it was so bad this morning, but now that we were going up it I felt that the path was indescribably hard, as if we had taken a different road. When the ascent came to a stop, we took the path going to the right—a truly steep slope going up a mountain by the name of Hotoke-ga-mine, Buddha's Peak. Although the descending path was smooth, I still found it stressful, perhaps because my legs were tired. I rested for a while at a teahouse, where I asked about the Kashiono Shrine. I was told that nowadays the deity is called Ōkura Myōjin—the god of the three villages of Kashio, Nijikō, and Ōtaki, who is enshrined in the mountain between Nijikō and Kashio. Since I heard that the shrine was quite faraway from the road, I did not visit it. As we were going down the slope, I looked down on the righthand side, and from the bottom of the mountain I saw the Yoshino River flowing. Kuzu, Natsumi, and other villages were located along the river; from here they looked quite close. The village at the end of our descent was called Higuchi; the village at the foot of the mountain opposite was Miyataki, the Palace's Waterfall. The Yoshino River flowed between these two villages. It must have been a little over one hundred yards from Nijikō to here. Kuzu and Natsumi were located by the river's upper course, while the lower course was closer to Kamiichi. A long time ago, a temporary palace was built in this area, which became the destination of several imperial visits and the scene of many imperial strolls. I wonder whether this village, Palace's Waterfall, was named after the building. In this area the boulders along the river were again frightening and strange. While the rocks in the area of Ōtaki were all smooth, without edges, here they were sharp, filled with edges—a continuous bank of rocks. Basically, the entire riverbank is made of boulders. There are many absurd old stories about Yoshitsune and these boulders, but since it would be annoying to relate them, I will refrain from doing so. The river in this area is constricted between these boulders; although the water is quite deep, the river flows quietly, without any rapids. The bridge going from rock to rock must have been about nine meters long. It is called Miyataki-no-shibabashi, the Brushwood Bridge of the Palace's Waterfall: it was plaited with brushwood. The bridge rocked as we were crossing it, and I could not get used to this feeling of danger.

Here as well there was a person jumping from the rocks—we asked him, and made him jump. The place where he jumped was straight beneath this bridge. The riverbanks were rock everywhere; they looked like standing screens, seven and a half meters above the water. We looked from this side of the river at the man jumping from the top of a rock on the other side. He took off his clothes and became nude. He pulled down his arms and kept them tight to his sides. It was a rare sight to see him standing up properly, with his eyes closed, jumping into the water—a frightening view that made those who were watching feel faint as if they were losing consciousness. At this spot the water was high—about eight yards. He resurfaced after a while quite a way downstream; he grabbed a rock of the riverbank and climbed onto it, without showing any sign of distress. Although he asked, "Should I jump some more?" we were too frightened and made him stop. Nevertheless, he jumped three times, in the same position as his earlier jump, as well as jumping backwards and headfirst. The man told us that it took many years to learn these jumping techniques, and that, since it was not an easy thing to do, there were only one or two people in the village who could do it.

Although there were less than two and a half miles on our way back, as the sun was getting close to the mountain's ridge, we decided that it was time to return to the inn. We left the riverbank, entered the shady ravine on the left, went four or five hundred yards, and found along the road a place called Sakuragi-no-miya, the Shrine of the Cherry Trees. We paid our respects to this place after crossing a bridge on a mountain stream that was flowing in front of the shrine. Then, we went up along the river, passed the village of Kisatani, and took a mountain path. After climbing a while, we reached a waterfall called Takataki, High Fall. A good-sized fall, this was not a continuous waterfall, but it had bumps here and there from which the water was falling—again, a truly eye-catching view! The famous "brook of Kisa"[100] is the flow of this waterfall; it runs in front of Sakuragi-no-miya, which we had just passed, flowing into the big river—the Yoshino River. The famous "Kisa Mountains" are also located in this area.[101] Here there are many cherry trees. Among the many green leaves one could still see in places some flowers that had not yet scattered. Generally speaking, I noticed that the places in Yoshino where the cherry trees are especially numerous are the place with the vulgar name[102] and this area. While looking at the waterfall on our righthand side, we kept climbing the slope; the path going down on the other side was smooth. In this area as well there were many cherry trees. However, I believe that now they have become much fewer than in the past. As a rule, the cutting of trees on these mountains is severely prohibited because the trees are just too dear to the gods. However, nowadays people plant cedars everywhere, to the point that, when these trees grow thicker and thicker, the cherry trees are naturally forced into the shade. Many of them die and, even if they do not die, they decay, while their branches rot and fall—I wonder what the gods think about all this! I personally believe that to plant cedars is harder on the cherry trees than actually cutting them down. Meanwhile it became dark, and we returned to the inn. Actually, on the way back and with great effort, I was finally able to come up with a poem on Ōtaki, The Great Fall:

(34)   *Nagarete no*   The capital of the falls
         Yo ni wa taekeru   In fair Yoshino
             Miyoshino no   Has endured
         Taki no miyako ni   Through flowing generations—
         Nokoru takitsuse   Lasting rapids of the waterfall.[103]

I also composed a poem on Miyataki, The Palace's Waterfall:

(35)   *Inishie no*   At the Palace's Waterfall
         Ato wa furinishi   Where the vestiges of the past
             Miyataki ni   Have aged,
         Sato no na shinobu   The name of the village brings them back to my memory—
         Sode zo nurekeru   My sleeves are drenched with tears.

Book Two

THE TENTH DAY

Today we left Yoshino. Yesterday we were planning to visit the Nyoirinji temple on our way back but, since it was late, we decided to pay our respects this morning. This temple is located across the mountain from the Katte Shrine, down into the ravine. We crossed a mountain stream and, once we were deep into the mountain, our road was surrounded by cherry trees. The temple is an old building in the middle of the mountain. Next to the hall was the treasure storehouse with the statue of Zaō Gongen in it.[104] On the back of the shrine's door there was a painting attributed to Kose no Kanaoka[105]—a truly ancient-looking painting worth seeing. A Chinese poem composed by Emperor Go-Daigo, who caught the flavor of the painting, was pasted on it. On one side there was also a statue of the emperor that people say Go-Daigo sculpted with his own hands. We were also shown other items written by the emperor, as well the inkstone with which he had practiced calligraphy. This storehouse also preserves the poem that Kusunoki no Masatsura[106] inscribed with the tip of his arrow on the door of the pagoda when he left for battle:

Kaeraji to	Oh, bow of the catalpa tree!—
Kanete omoeba	Already thinking
Azusayumi	That I will not come back,
Naki kazu ni iru	I fix here my name
Na o zo todomuru	Adding it to the many who no longer are.

Because he was so loyal to the emperor, I was deeply moved by this person, unlike the story of Yoshitsune that I had heard earlier. From the back of this hall we climbed the mountain for a while to a place called the Tōnō Mound; this is the emperor's tomb, deep in the shade of trees. We visited it, and I saw a somehow elevated hill covered with trees. The fence of stones surrounding the area was a little warped and was missing some parts—a really sad view that moved me deeply. I remembered the poem that Shin-Taikenmon-in composed long ago when she visited this tomb:

Kokonoe no	Is this a dream—
Tama no utena mo	The jeweled dais
Yume nare ya	Of the imperial palace,
Koke no shita ni shi	When I think of my Lord
Kimi o omoeba	Beneath the moss?[107]

I was inspired by this poem when I composed mine, with great trepidation:

(36) *Koke no tsuyu* Even under
Kakaru miyama no The deep mountain
Shita ni te mo Splashed with dew on the moss
Tama no utena wa The jeweled dais
Wasureshi mo seji Will not forget.[108]

68   Translation

We returned to our inn and rested for a while. Then we left, this time planning to go down to Mutsuda. We left the village, proceeded along the ridge of the mountain, went down the slope, and there it was—the village of Mutsuda. Apparently, nowadays the villagers call it "Muda." This place by the Yoshino River was often sung in the past for its many willow trees.[109] Wondering whether they were still there, I looked around and composed the following poem:

(37)   *Ari to shi mo*   One cannot see
    Mienu Mutsuda no   The willows by the river
        Kawayanagi   That everyone says are there:
    Haru no kasumi ya   I wonder whether the spring mist
    Hedate hatsuran   Has removed them from sight.

We crossed the river by boat, and descended for a while along the river. A place by the name of Tsuchida was a post town at the intersection of the road going to the Ki province from Kamiichi and the one going to Yoshino from the north. Although people say that it is about two and a half miles from Mutsuda, I felt it was quite close. Here I had some buckwheat *(soba)*. Although the house and the plates were shabby and dirty, I found some consolation in the thought that my present situation was better than piling food "on an oak leaf"; I ate. [In the *Man'yōshū* there is the following poem:

    Ie ni areba   When I am at home
    Ke ni moru ii o   My rice piles in a lunch box;
        Kusamakura   When I am journeying
    Tabi ni shi areba   On a pillow of grass,
    Shii no ha ni moru   Is piled on an oak leaf.][110]

From here we were planning to visit the Kannon of Tsubo Slope.[111] We kept going on a flat road, turned right, took a mountainous path, passed the village of Hataya, and reached a place where we could look back at the village of Yoshino and the mountains from the mountainous path that we had just climbed.

(38)   *Kaerimiru*   Now it is the last time
    Yosome mo ima o   For me
        Kagiri ni te   To look back somehow—

| Mata mo wakaruru | Village of fair Yoshino |
| Miyoshino no sato | From which again I depart. |

This was the last peak of the Yoshino Prefecture. As we were going down the slope, the entire province of Yamato unfolded in front of our eyes. Although we were told that from here we could see Mount Hie, Mount Atago, and other mountains, today the mist was so thick that we could not see so far away. As we descended a little farther, suddenly the temple Tsubosakadera appeared. This temple is located in a shady ravine south of Mount Takatori, about six thousand yards from Tsuchida, according to the road that we were following. There was the Gate of the Benevolent Kings (Ninnōmon), with a plaque inscribed with the characters, "Fumonkan"—Kannon of the Universal Gate.[112] On the hall where Kannon was worshipped the plaque said "Minami Hokkeji"—Southern Temple of the Lotus Blossom of the Fine Dharma. A three-story pagoda stood across the hall. The sanctum sanctorum was deep inside the compound; there, many statues of the Buddha stood in a row.[113] There was a strange-looking rock that everybody worshipped, but I was not feeling well, and I did not go there. As I was waiting and trying to recover at a teahouse in front of the temple, everybody came back and told me about this rock—a truly awesome boulder! From here we turned right, down the path of the ravine for about a thousand yards until we reached the village of Shimizu-dani—The Clear-Water Ravine. This village is on the road that enters Yoshino through the Ashihara Pass from this province. About one hundred yards from here there was a line of peddlers' houses in a place called Tosa. This village was located at the foot of Mount Takatori. On top of the mountain there is a castle that looked very close from this village. Since the castle was located on the peak of a tall mountain, the view from there all over the area was splendid.

Since I had heard before that Hinokuma was in this area, I went to visit the place. We left the village of Tosa, took a narrow road going about three hundred yards to the right, and there we found the village. As I usually did, I asked an old man about the history of the place, but he did not know for certain. He had heard about the remains of the capital. He also said that the imperial tombs were located in the villages of Hirata, Noguchi, and others, and that in the past all this area was called Hinokuma. He also pointed out the shrine of the village's god—an area inside the forest where an ancient pagoda made with thirteen stones piled on each other stood about six and a half yards tall. When I looked around, I noticed an extremely large foundation stone that appeared to be the remains of a pagoda, or something like it. Recently, wishing to put this stone in his garden, someone had entrusted a laborer with the digging. However, the stone was so big that it became impossible to excavate, and they had to stop. Shortly thereafter this person became sick and died. People said that this was the result of the god's rage. In front of this stone was a temporary hut. When I asked the head priest about the pagoda, he told me the following: "This temple was built on the ruins of the capital of Emperor Senka.[114][Hinokuma-no-Iorino-no-Miya was the name of this capital.] This was a truly beautiful religious complex, but it burned down, and this is what is left. In this area you can still find many fragments of tiles from that time." As a matter of fact, when I looked around, I noticed everywhere, in front of this hut and along the road, pieces of ancient tiles mixed with the soil. I picked up one or two, and judging by their patterns that resembled the texture of cloth, they looked quite ancient. Since this hut was part of the ruins of the ancient temple, I enquired about the name, and he replied, "Dōkōji." I asked him what characters were used to indicate this name. The priest shook his head, saying that he could not write and did not know the characters of this name. My desire to ask and curiosity cooled, so I refrained from asking any other questions. In this world there is a priest who does not know how to write the name of the temple where he lives! Even if someone has absolutely no knowledge of writing, he could at least ask someone to teach him how to write a name. It was funny to think that, despite his indifference, he would vaguely hear about ancient events and tell us about them. Later on I asked another villager about the name. He replied that the name means "light on the path"—I do not know whether this is true or not.

Since I have been literally recording in this diary the words of ignorant villagers who do not understand the meaning of things, mistakes are unavoidable. Moreover, there are also passages recording things that I heard incorrectly, so that errors are mixed with truth. I decided to keep the diary the way it is, as it would be troublesome and distressful to revise. I hope that people who read this diary in the future will not look at it with suspicion and consider it pure humbug. Again, this is something I should not be mentioning here, but I simply follow my recollections. Since the Hinokuma River was not coming into view, I wrote:

(39)   *Kikiwataru*   Even if the Hinokuma River
         Hinokumagawa wa   Of which I have heard so much
            Taenu tomo   Ceases to flow,

Shibashi tazune yo	Let's search for a while:
Ato o dani min	You will see at least the ruins.

I was inspired by the following poem from the *Kokinshū*:

Sasanokuma	Stop the horse
Hinokumagawa ni	By the Hinokuma River,
Koma tomete	The nook of cypresses,
Shibashi mizu kae	And let him drink the water for a while!
Kage o dani mimu	Won't I see your reflection at least?[115]

We walked here and there, asking about this river. Although we saw one or two small streams, not even the villagers knew for sure which one was the Hinokuma River.

We reached the village of Hirata following the way that we were told. As we were enquiring about the imperial tomb, we found on a hilly surface in a field a mound that had collapsed on one side, surrounded by three or four pine tress. We were told that this was the tomb of Emperor Monmu.[116] We went beyond this point and, as we were asking questions after arriving at the village of Noguchi, we followed a path through the rice paddies and reached a place where there was an imperial tomb. Here, on top of a somewhat high hill there was a place built with gigantic boulders. When I looked inside, facing south, from an opening twenty centimeters in width and height, I saw something like a grotto, narrow inside. The lower part was buried in the ground; it was barely possible to crawl inside. The upper part was made of a flat, big boulder, over three yards long and wide, that was covering the place like a lid. As a continuation in the back of this tomb there was a flat place, hollow in the middle, about four yards deep. We were told that these were the remains of a quarry from which people in recent times had excavated big boulders in order to build the castle of Takatori. While saying that this was the action of ignorant and greedy samurai in this confused world, I felt deeply depressed at the thought of someone excavating a truly august imperial tomb. When I saw the traces of straw fires lying around, I thought that this must have been the dwelling of some vulgar beggar. I was right! Many people like these were gathering at the foot of this mountain.

We were told that this was the tomb of Emperor Buretsu,[117] but as I believed that his tomb was somewhere else, I asked several people about it. Everybody insisted that this was indeed Buretsu's tomb, but I am still unconvinced.

The *Engishiki* records all the imperial tombs of Hinokuma. According to this document, the Hinokuma no-Sakai mound is the tomb of the emperor who ruled over the land at Shikishima-no-Miya;[118] the Ōuchi mound is the tomb of the emperor who ruled from Asuka-no-Kiyomibara-no-Miya, as well as of the sovereign ruling from Fujiwara-no-Miya;[119] the Ako-no-Oka mound is the tomb of Emperor Monmu, who governed the land from the same capital. I could not tell which mound belonged to which emperor; now I was unable to distinguish them with any certainty. People say that this is the tomb of Buretsu, but it is a mistake. We cannot even entirely trust the accounts of the villagers. Some time ago Nabika something wrote a work titled *Gokinai Shi* (An Account of the Five Provinces in the Kinai Region).[120] After obtaining permission for a survey from the authorities, he walked everywhere in each province, enquiring with extreme diligence about even these kinds of things. Even among the villagers of this area old people remember him well and talk about that time. He writes with great confidence about which ruins can be found in this village, and where, and what the imperial tombs in this village are called today. I wonder on what proof he bases all this information. Is it that, even though this is a remarkably recent work, the villagers at the time he interviewed them were very knowledgeable? Or, is it simply the result of his speculations? I have many doubts about this work. To see so much clarity and detail—now that I am going here and there with my little enquiries, realizing how many things are uncertain—made me understand how unusual the achievements of that man actually were.

We proceeded a while from this tomb, and before long we came out onto a broad road. This was the road going straight from Tosa to Oka. We kept going a little until we saw the village of Kawara on our lefthand side. At the eastern end of this village there was a small temple by the name of Gufukuji. In the past it was called Kawaradera.[121] The foundation stones of this temple are still lying there nowadays in the area of the hall. Moreover, there are a few other stones scattered here and there in the rice field in front of the temple. Among them was a completely white, transparent stone known as agate that had come from China. It was half hidden beneath the walls of a house standing on the side of the hall—a truly curious stone that travelers should see! It is located in a place that villagers call Kannondō, Kannon's Hall, quite close to the street. Next, we visited the Tachibana Temple.[122] I saw it across the Kawaradera, about one hundred yards from it. Even today this temple is quite vast, with wide halls, and the foundation stones are still there from the past. The village of Tachibana is located next to the temple. It was getting late, so we stopped at the village of Oka, which is quite close to the Tachibana temple. Between them was a river crossed by an earthen bridge. This was the Asuka River.[123] Is not the place which is now called Oka the same as the one mentioned in the *Nihongi* as "Asuka-no-Oka, the Hill of Asuka"?[124] If this is the case, since the Palace of Okamoto [the capital of three sovereigns: Emperor Jomei, Empress Kōgyoku, and Empress Saimei] was in this area, I believe it is not too far. Moreover, since the Kiyomibara Palace is south of this place, its ruins should be close as well.

THE ELEVENTH DAY

We left the inn early in the morning and visited the Oka temple.[125] From the village we climbed the eastern mountain for about three hundred yards and found the Ninnōmon, the Gate of the Benevolent Kings; the plaque said "Ryūgaiji." Going left on the road in front of this gate one can find a shrine called Hachiman. The pilgrims, who had come to visit the several temples in whose main hall Kannon was worshipped, were wearing rough clothing known as the satchel-rubbing kimono.[126] So many of them had come to worship—men, women, old and young people—that it was impossible to count them all. They sat down next to each other, leaving no gap between them, straining their voices while singing loudly the pilgrims' songs. They rocked the hall with their songs. It was so noisy that I could vaguely catch the words, "the moss in the garden of the Temple of the Dewy Hill,"[127] in the midst of many tunes that I could not understand.

We returned to the village of Oka and proceeded three or four hundred yards north. We went to a higher spot on our righthand side and, after climbing about one hundred yards, we saw a large, strange-looking boulder in a field. It was about four yards high and a little over two yards wide at is largest spot. It was very flat, as if someone had placed an inkstone on the field. Inside there was a round, long spot that had been carved, six or seven inches deep,[128] whose bottom was flat as well. Moreover, in the section that could be thought of as the boulder's head, there were three small, round carved spots that looked like the big hollow section. The central one was the biggest, while the two on the sides were equally small. From the hollow part in the middle of the boulder's head three narrow channels had been carved going down the boulder. The central channel continued straight to the big hollow place, going to the edge beneath the boulder. The two lateral hollow spaces descended obliquely, going to the right and left edges of the boulder. On each edge of the channels there was a branch going to a tiny place that had been carved on the left and on the right. The overall appearance of the boulder was round, without corners; the shape of the head was large at the top and became increasingly narrow at the bottom. I had truly a hard time figuring out when this boulder had been shaped the way it was, and for what reason. The villagers called it Mukashi-no-Chōja-no-Sakabune, the Brewing Boat of the Old Millionaire. The name of the field in this area was also Sakabune, the Brewing Boat. Apparently this rock had been much bigger in the past, but people took a big chunk out of it during the construction of the Takatori castle.

We kept going a while, until we reached the village of Asuka. Only a few remains of the Asuka temple were left at the edge of the village.[129] There was no gate, and a large Buddha by the name of the Great Buddha stood in a tiny temporary hall. In other words, this was the main image of the ancient temple, a five-yard-tall Shakyamuni Buddha. It looked truly ancient and noble. Next to it there was the statue of Shōtoku Taishi, but it looked quite modern. Moreover, I looked for tiles of the ancient halls, and I found a few that were quite old, about three or four centimeters thick. On a ridge between fields around the temple there were five stones piled one on top of the other—a pagoda known as Iruka's Mound, half buried in the ground.[130] However, it did not look so ancient. The Asuka Shrine stood on top of a high hill, east of the village. In front of the gate at the bottom of the hill were the ruins of Asukai, Asuka's well; only the shape was left, as the water had dried up. This, also, did not look like the real well. I climbed the stone steps, and I noticed that the four deities were now enshrined in the same temporary building. Originally, this shrine had been located in a place called Kaminabi Mountain. However, according to the *Nihon Kōki* (Japan's Later Chronicles), following a divine omen, it was moved to Torikata Mountain during the reign of Emperor Junna, in the sixth year of Tenchō (829).[131] As a result, when in the past people mentioned "Kaminamiyama—the Sacred Mountain—in Asuka,"[132] and "Kamioka," the Kami Hill,[133] they were not referring to this place. They referred to a place known today as the village of Ikazuchi, fourteen or fifteen miles from here. Therefore, nowadays the shrine is located on Mount Torikatayama, the Mountain Shaped Like a Bird. This is why the Asuka temple is also called Chōgyōzan, after the Chinese pronunciation for Torikatayama. Since even today the temple is no more than one hundred yards away from the mountain, in the past, when the temple was larger, it must have been quite close to the mountain, extending up to its edge. This explains why the temple was named after the mountain.

We went about two hundred yards south of this shrine, and we reached a place that was surrounded by a large rock inside a forest, along the road. A little hollow inside, the boulder was over three yards thick and over two yards wide. I wonder whether these were not the ruins of the real Well of Asuka. People say that this is the place where the minister Kamatari was born, but I cannot accept this idea.[134] Near to this place there was the Ōharadera, the Temple of the Big Field, also known as Tōgenji,[135] the Temple of the Wisterias' Field. Despite its small size, it was such a beautiful and polished construction that it caught my eye, and I decided to enter. There were no halls; only a splendid shrine called Ōhara Myōjin, the God of the Big Field. In this shrine people worship the mother of Minister Kamatari.[136] Moreover, a priest here told us that this temple was the remains of Fujiwara-no-Miya of Empress Jitō, and that we could see the village of Ōhara very close along the southern mountain.[137] He also told us that the place called Fujiwara was this Ōhara, and this was certainly reasonable. However, what is known as Fujiwara-no-Miya of Empress Jitō is not here. We know from a *Man'yōshū* poem that the Fujiwara capital was in the area of Mount Kagu.[138] Previously I had thought that the village of Ōhara was located near Mount Kagu, and that Fujiwara-no-Miya was also in that area. Now that I have seen it with my own eyes, unlike what I had thought, Mount Kagu is quite far away from here. Although I am quite confused, I can speculate that the village of Fujiwara is actually this Ōhara, while the Fujiwara capital is a different place, near Mount Kagu. From here we found the village of Kamiyatori on the road leading to Abe. Since Kamiyatori is written with the characters "eight hooks," this is certainly the place of Emperor's Kenzō's capital, Chikatsu-Asuka-no-Yatsuri-no-Miya, the Palace of the Eight Hooks Nearby Asuka.[139] The narrow mountain stream flowing in front of this village is called "Yatsuri River."[140] We went ahead for a while, until we came out on a broad road. This was the road that connected Asuka directly to Abe. We reached the village of Yamada. People say that in the mountains of this area the oak trees produce chestnuts. We passed the village of Oida, and reached Abe[141]—about two and a half miles from Oka.

The bodhisattva Mañjuśri worshipped in this village is a Buddha well known all over the land.[142] Within the temple there was a tumulus (the Western Tumulus), whose height and width inside was about two yards, and whose depth was almost four yards. What is known as the sanctum sanctorum (the Eastern Tumulus) was also shaped like a tumulus, about six yards deep, with a spring of water flowing inside. We left this temple and proceeded for another four or five hundred yards; another tumulus stood on a high plain.[143] Since this place was not very much visited by people and there was no clear sign, we kept going, asking the farmers of the area. This was a tumulus with approximately the same large size as the previous one. One could walk about four yards inside; the interior's height and length were quite big. Something stood inside which was built in the shape of a house, whose height and width was about two yards, and whose depth was three yards. It also had a roof from which the light penetrated, allowing a dim view of the surroundings. Although I went to the rear, it was too dark to be able to see anything. There was nothing that looked like an entrance, neither in the front nor in the back. There was an opening of about thirty centimeters in the back. I put my hand inside, but I could not feel anything. The inside was completely hollow. A villager told me that in the past Abe no Seimei had put many treasures here, but in later ages thieves had entered the place, destroyed a corner, and taken everything out.[144]

However, this was again an unreliable story. In truth, the two tumuli of the Mañjuśrī Temple and this tumulus were all tombs where noble people were buried a very long time ago. This explains why the tumulus looked like an imperial tomb, and why the stony chamber inside made one think of a sarcophagus. The construction was comprised of a large stony square, carved inside, where a coffin was laid, and a stone that looked like a roof to cover the tomb. There must have been many clay images *(haniwa)* standing around but, after such a long time, they had been scattered and disappeared. Moreover, thieves broke into the sarcophagus, stealing everything that was inside. The two tumuli of that temple and this sarcophagus as well were all missing parts of their original structure; only the external rocks were left. As we were visiting these tumuli, our guide said, "Five or six hundred yards southeast of Oka, in a place called Shima-no-shō, there is a tumulus on top of a hill that people say is the tomb of Empress Suiko.[145] The inside is the size of an eight-tatami straw mat. Moreover, one hundred yards from Oka in the same direction, in the village of Sakata, there is a place called Miyakozuka, the Capital's Mound, where Emperor Yōmei is buried.[146] On top of this mound you can see somehow the corners of a big boulder." I wonder what these imperial tombs looked like. Since both Sakata[147] and Shima[148] were ancient places, I was curious about them.

We returned to our original road up to the Mañjuśrī temple, and we passed the village of Abe. Although we were told that in the rice fields were the Mound of Abe no Nakamaro and the ruins of his house, this was again difficult to accept.[149] Generally speaking, I believe that all the things related to Nakamaro and Seimei in this area are legends derived from local names. There was a place with some stagnant water here and there that was called the Seven Wells of the Empress Picking up Parsley. I wonder whether this name derives from the verse "Does the ancient proverb/'to pick up parsley. . . .'"[150] This is something that I do not understand. From there we went to Kaijū. Here there was a large road going from Yagi to Sakurai. We passed a village by the name of Yokōchi, and saw on our righthand side the village of Daifuku. We kept going for a while and, at a crossroad, there was a Jizō Hall.[151] If one goes straight, one reaches Yagi; if, instead, one takes the northern route, one follows the road going to Miwa; if one goes south, then, one reaches the village of Kibi on the road for Mount Kagu. Now we took this road and entered Kibi. On the side of the road within the village there is a mound with a five-stone pagoda standing on top of it; people say that this is the tomb of the Kibi Minister.[152] The stones did not look so ancient. Moreover, I marveled at the sight of a torii gate standing at a place where corpses were cremated. When I asked for an explanation, I was told that this was the case all over this province. We left the village and went south for a while; then we turned west and passed the village of Ikejiri. In an area south of the village of Kashiwade there was a forest. We enquired about it, and found out that it was the Kōjin Shrine, the Shrine of the Fierce God. The shrine faced north, although in the past it used to face south. Since this god was particularly fierce, every time someone would pass in front of this shrine on a horse, he would necessarily fall from the saddle. The situation became so troublesome that people decided to change the shrine's direction, making it facing north.

This shrine was located a little north on the road that we were now following, in an area in the northern foot of Mount Kagu. Although this is a small, low mountain, its name is so well known since ancient times that everybody under the sky recognizes it. One can imagine how someone like me, who yearns after the past, turns his thoughts to this place every time he encounters it in a book. Since this was a place I had always wanted to visit, I was truly impatient to climb the mountain as soon as possible. I was very happy:

(40)   *Itsushika to*   When, when will I ever see it,
    Omoikakeshi mo   I kept thinking for such long time—
    Hisakata no   Today I finally opened my way
    Ame no Kaguyama   Through heavenly
    Kyō zo wakeiru   Mount Kagu.[153]

Everybody shared my feelings; we all rushed to climb the mountain. As we approached the slope, we saw on our lefthand side a pond about one hundred yards long. The ancient Haniyasu pond immediately came to my mind;[154] however, there was no sign indicating that this was the case. Since it was not very tall, we were at the top of the mountain in a dash. On the peak there was a place that was slightly flat; here five or six people, who looked as if they were from this area, sat in a circle on the grass, drinking *sake* and other drinks. There was still someone who would climb this mountain and enjoy the view! We also saw two or three women from the village, young and old, walking and searching for brackens to pick. This mountain was a field all covered with young groves, where one could rarely see an old tree. The view from the peak was excellent; nothing stood in the way, so that one could see in every direction. In the east, a long meander of mountain ridges continued, all covered with groves. Unlike the views in the other directions, this one was somehow hampered. We rested for a while beneath what was left of a gigantic, withered pine tree standing in front of a small shrine called the Shrine of the Dragon Kings.[155] As we were having some food, the view of all the mountains and villages in all directions was so outstanding that it is impossible to put it into words. I felt as if with their beautiful voices young people were chanting ancient verses such as, "When I climb it/and look out across the land,/over the land-plain." [We read in the first volume of the *Man'yōshū* the following long poem: "But our rampart/is Heavenly Mt. Kagu:/when I climb it/and look out across the land,/over the land-plain/smoke rises and rises;/over the sea-plain. . . .][156] Now here I was, longing even more for the past. I was in the mood of adding something to the image of a world that I could not see with my eyes:

(41)   *Momoshiki no*   When I look at Mount Kagu
         Ōmiyabito o   Where the inhabitants of the court
         Asobikemu   Of the one hundred stones
         Kaguyama mireba   Disported themselves,
         Inishie omōyu   The past comes to my mind as if I were there.[157]

The villagers who were drinking *sake* approached us and asked us where we came from. They told us old stories about this mountain. I was absorbed by what they were saying, paying full attention to each word. When I realized that they were only talking about unreasonable events that took place in the age of the gods, and that there was nothing believable in what they said, I stopped paying attention. However, when I asked about the places that I was seeing all around, they were quite knowledgeable. First of all, Mount Unebi stood by itself in the west, away from and without connection to any other mountain, looking quite close to us. Although we were told that it was about two and a half miles from here, I thought it was not so far. In the same western direction one could see Mount Kongō, very tall in the distance.[158] In line with it in the north there was another mountain, almost equally tall; slightly lower than Mount Kongō, this is now called Mount Katsuraki. In the past, however, both mountains were called Mount Katsuraki. The name Kongō must have been given to the mountain after the temple was built.[159]

In later generations a practice began of naming mountains and everything else with Chinese-sounding names, so that the ancient names became extinct. It is truly regrettable that people became ignorant of those original names. And yet it is wonderful that many ancient names survived in the names of temples. Again in the northern direction, slightly separated from Mount Katsuraki, one could see Mount Futagami, the Twin Peaks, standing next to each other.[160] Nowadays this mountain is called Nijō Peak, following the hateful habit of using the sound of Chinese characters. While in the northwest we could vaguely see Mount Ikoma, which was not hidden by clouds ["Yesterday and today/clouds rose/hiding the mountain from view—/it was painful to show the forest of flowers"],[161] only Mount Yoshino could not be seen from here, as its view was obstructed by the nearby mountains. Moreover, we could see all the mountains of this province without any exception, east and south. Furthermore, the land inside the province was flat, as if someone had spread and lined up straw mats; this village, that forest, everything came into view like clusters of discrete formations. We were able to see far away, particularly in a northern direction, to the point that the eyes could not catch the end shrouded in clouds. Although I could not see the edge of the mountains, only Mount Miminashi stood by itself in a northern, rather than a northwestern corner, as if someone had put something in that place. Now, this mountain looked a little bit closer to us than Mount Unebi. The view of the mountains was wide open everywhere, in all directions.

(42) *Toriyorou*   The well-shaped
      Ame no Kaguyama   Heavenly Mount Kagu,
        Yorozuyo ni   Will I ever get tired of looking at it
      Mitomo akame ya   Even ten thousand years?
      Ame no Kaguyama   Oh, Heavenly Mount Kagu![162]

Since someone blamed me, asking me why today I came up with such an old-fashioned poem, I recited the following poem, and the blame stopped:

(43) *Inishie no*   If you do not search
      Fukaki kokoro o   For the deep heart
        Tazunezu wa   Of the past,

>   *Miru kai araji* It becomes meaningless to look at it,
>   *Ame no Kaguyama* Heavenly Mount Kagu.

As we were planning to leave this place, I recited one more poem, as a consolation for this forced departure:

> (44) *Wakarutomo* Although I must depart,
>   *Ame no Kaguyama* Heavenly Mount Kagu,
>   *Fumi mitsutsu* As I look at written records,
>   *Kokoro wa tsune ni* My heart
>   *Omoiokosen* Will always call up your image.[163]

This time, we descended the mountain in a southern direction.

Halfway down the slope there was a small shrine called Kami-no-Miya, the Upper Shrine. At the foot of the mountain were the village of Minamiura, the Southern Bay, and also the Nikkō temple. In front of the temple there was a large, withered pine tree. In this area was also the Shimo-no-Miya, the Lower Shrine. Generally, on this mountain there are many ancient famous shrines here and there. Since nowadays no one knew which shrine corresponded to which, the shrines that I was seeing might well have been the remnants of ancient ones; this is why they draw my attention. At the eastern edge of this village was Mikagami-no-ike, the Pond of the Mirror. Although someone argued that this was actually the Haniyasu pond, I have a hard time believing it. On the edge of this pond a temple called the Mañjuśri of Mount Kagu was located. The village of Kaguyama was located east of the temple. About three hundred yards south of Minamiura thirty-six foundation stones were left from what someone said were the ruins of the Golden Hall and the Lecture Hall. I wonder which temple this might have been. It would have been possible to ascertain the identity of places like this by matching them later on to places described in ancient documents. However, since it would be annoying to do a thing like this in a travel diary, I won't say more on this issue, as I have been doing in similar situations. Moreover, in the bamboo grove of this village there is a rock that tells the ancient events of the age of the gods.[164] About two yards of this area were enclosed within a fence. I was told that there was something miraculous with regard to the bamboo growing inside, and I thought that I would be writing about this later, but I forgot all about it. We left the village and went westward. In the rice fields along the road, a cluster of thin bamboos grew in a place about three yards long, known as the Yuzasa Grove.

We continued west; in the village of Bessho there was a shrine by the name of Ōmiya. When we heard that this was the Takechi Shrine,[165] we asked for directions and paid a visit. It was located slightly west of Mount Kagu. Here, the god was enshrined that today is worshipped in the northern village of Takadono. West of this shrine there was a pond; Fujiwara-no-Miya, the capital of Empress Jitō, seems to have been in this area. I wonder whether this is the origin of the present name of Takadono—the High Palace. I heard that the Haniyasu pond was definitely in this area; I wondered whether the many low hills, which ran here and there discontinuously, were the remains of its crumbled banks. These were famous banks, which are also mentioned in ancient poems.[166] Moreover, west of this place was Mount Hizatsuki, Small Knee Mat; on one side was a low and long hill covered with pine trees. Again, we were told that this place was related to events that occurred in the age of the gods; but, as always, this story was groundless. Once we climbed the hill and looked around, the Asuka River appeared in the south, quite long, flowing in a northwestern direction. South of the hill was the village of Kamiida, written with the characters *"kami no hiza"*—god's knees. We proceeded a little farther from there and then crossed the Asuka River that we had just seen from the hill. In this area the river was quite wide. The road that went south along the river connected Oka to Yagi. We followed this road for about one hundred yards upstream, passing through the village of Tanaka, and reached the village of Toyora. The only thing left of the Toyora Temple was the Yakushi Hall.[167] Nowadays it is called Kōgenji, the Temple Across the Field. [In the *Nihon Shoki* we find the name "Mukuhara."][168] Several ancient foundation stones were still there. Although I asked the location of the Enoha well, the Well of the Hackberry Leaf, no one knew it.[169] There was also a small pond that we were told was the Canal of Naniwa, but I had a hard time believing it. The place where the famous Buddhist statue was thrown was the Canal of Naniwa in the province of Tsu.[170]

Now, this village was located on the western side of the Asuka River; across the river was Ikazuchi-mura, the Village of Thunder. In the past this was the place where stood the Asuka Shrine; it was called both "Kaminami-yama" (the Sacred Mountain) and "Kamioka" (God's Hill). Now that I had come here and I was seeing the place with my own eyes, the mountain was standing there, befitting the verse that says, "The Asuka River/surrounded by the sacred mountain."[171] The river was flowing along the bottom of the mountain. It goes without saying that in the past all the area up to this point was called Asuka; even now, this place is only fifteen or eighteen yards from the village of Asuka. Moreover, since Hitomaro said in a poem, "above the thunder," the name of the village where I was now traveling was definitely old.[172] The forest of Iwase must certainly have been in this area.[173] We passed again through Toyora, went west, and reached the village of Wada. From there we climbed for a while, crossed west between mountains, and saw Tsurugi-no-ike, Sword Pond, on the lefthand side of the road.[174] There were low mountains on the southwestern and northern sides; the length and width of the pond was about two hundred yards. Inside there was a small hill—an imperial tomb. We went south, west, and north inside the pond; only in the east was the pond connected with the rear of the hill. Beneath the western banks of the pond was the village of Ishikawa. Although there was no doubt about the resident of this tomb, I thought of asking somebody in order to make sure. I approached an old person in the village, as I usually did, and asked him about it. He answered, "This is the tomb of the eighteenth emperor, what was his name?" As he was tilting his head over and over, I said, "No, it is not the eighteenth emperor; it is the eighth, Emperor Kōgen."[175] He nodded, saying, "That's right, that's right!" It was funny that I was the one providing the answer to the person whom I was asking. We left this village, and in no time the village of Ōkaru was in front of us. This was the capital of that emperor (Kōgen). Karunoichi—the Karu market— must have been here.[176]

We left Karu, proceeding west, until we reached a slightly elevated place. A tall and round hill appeared south of the road. We were told that on the hill's southern edge there was a cave called Tsukaana, the Mound's Hole.[177] We followed a narrow path and, once we reached it, I saw an extremely small opening. I looked inside and it appeared to be quite large and deep; however, since it was dark, I could not be sure of what I was seeing. Water was gathering beneath; I could hear it flowing inside. I asked what mound could this be, but our guide did not know. I wonder whether this might have been the "Musa-no-tsuki Sakanoe Misagi" (the Imperial Tomb above the Slope at Musa) of Emperor Senka. The reason is that beneath the hill there is a village called Mise, where I heard the Musanimasu Shrine now stands.[178] I believe that Musa should be in this area; moreover, the word "Sakanoe" (above the slope) fits a description of these environs perfectly. Now that I think again about this issue, I wonder whether even the name Mise might have been written with the characters for Musa and read Mise. Or, even if this is not the case, the pronunciation of the name might have changed naturally from Musa to Mise under the influence of the local accent. We kept going down for a while westbound, until we arrived at the village of Mise. Here there was a highway going from Yagi to Tosa. It was already dusk, and although in this village, which was quite large, many decent houses were standing next to each other, we were told that there was no place that would accommodate travelers. We wondered whether to continue on to Yagi or to go back to Oka. Everyone was worried about the fact that, unless we moved fast, it would become dark. What should we do? We should stay in this village. As someone was saying, "No matter how uncomfortable, let's inquire if there is a house where we can spend one night," a person of our group walked through the village, asking for a place to stay, and eventually, and with great difficulty, found a dwelling.

(45)	*Omoudochi*	While waving their sleeves,
	Sode furihaete	The fellow travelers
	Tabigoromo	Wear the traveler's garments—
	Harubi kurenuru	They set foot on the mountains today,
	Kyō no yamabumi	A long day of spring that has come to an end.

Although today our journey was not particularly long, we had visited many places and kept walking the whole day, so that we were really extremely tired and in a daze. However, we wanted to know more about this area, and we began by calling the owner of the house. He looked about fifty years of age, had a thick beard, and an unattractive face. It was quite funny to listen to him saying, "Well, the famous places and historic spots of this area . . ." with such a serious expression and tone of voice. The young people could not contain their smiles. I asked him what kind of ruin the Mound's Hole was that we saw on the mountain east of us. He replied, "It was built by Kōbō Daishi at the time of Shōtoku Taishi."[179] Everyone had a hard time putting up with this answer, but because we were all interested in what else he had to say, we stood it and asked, "It is truly an interesting place; how deep do you think it is?" He said, "The inside is endless; it reaches the Samusa pond in Nara."[180] I asked where we could find that pond, and he said: "It is a very famous pond in front of the gate of Kōfukuji temple. I guess someone still does not know about it."[181] Everyone understood that he meant the Sarusawa Pond and burst out laughing with their mouths wide open. As he was talking about Mount Unebi, he referred to the events of Empress Jingū.[182] It was even funnier to listen to him mispronouncing the empress' name—"Jinnikun." From then on we all referred to this man as Jinnikun; he became the object of our ridicule. Although we had many questions on the shrines of this area, how could we inquire of a man like this?—A truly regretful situation!

THE TWELFTH DAY

We left Mise and went north for a while. We turned left and continued for about three hundred yards, until we reached the Kume temple in the village of Kume. Even today it is still a nice temple. However, a priest told us that in the past the temple was located west of the present site, and that here the ruins were left of the ancient pagoda. We could see Mount Unebi to the north, very close to us. I was reminded of ancient words:

(46) *Tamadasuki*   Mount Unebi,
      Unebi no yama wa   The jewel-sash mount,
      Mizuyama to   The lush mountain,
      Ima mo Yamato ni   Even now rises perfectly
      Yamasabiimasu   In Yamato.

[We read in the first volume of the *Man'yōshū* the following long poem: "Unebi/that lush mountain,/at the set-of-sun/great western palace gate,/a lush mountain,/rises mountain-perfect. . . .]¹⁸³

We guessed the way leading to this mountain and, after turning west for a while, we reached the village of Unebi. In other words, we were at the southeastern foot of the mountain. As we were about to enter the village, fifty yards on our right there was a small forest with a shrine standing inside. Although we were told that this was the tomb of Emperor Itoku,¹⁸⁴ the location did not fit the description that the south of this mountain is "above the ravine of Manago." Moreover, it did not look like an imperial tomb, and there were just too many doubts about it. We asked an old villager for details, who answered, "Actually the matter is quite doubtful; however, since we do not know with any certainty about Emperor Itoku's real tomb, nowadays we take the forest to be his resting place." Thinking that Kashibara-no-Miya [Kashibara-no-Miya, southeast of Mount Unebi, was the capital of Emperor Jinmu]¹⁸⁵ should be in this area, I recited the following poem:

(47) *Unebiyama*   When I look at Mount Unebi
      Mireba kashikoshi   It is awe-inspiring—
      Kashibara no   The place of the capital
      Hijiri no miyo no   During the reign of the Master of the Sun
      Ōmiyadokoro   At Kashibara.¹⁸⁶

I asked whether the name Kashibara still existed today, and I was told that the village with this name was located over two and a half miles southwest of here. No place with such a name could be found in this area. Nowadays this mountain is called Mount Jimyōji; however, this does not mean that it is not called Mount Unebi. In this case, the final syllable of the name is pronounced without sonant—Unehi. Moreover, villagers of this area also call it Omineyama, Mount Peak, probably because of the fact that on the peak of the mountain there is a shrine where Empress Jingū is worshipped. This is what Jinnikun had mentioned to us the other night. There was a path going up the mountain from Unebi village. When I heard that it was about five hundred yards long, I encouraged everybody to climb it, but everyone had already grown too fatigued over mountain paths during the past several days, and said, "There does not seem to be anything special to see up there; it would be useless to make our legs tired." Since they were reluctant, I could not force them to go. Then, we passed through the village going west, crossed the southern range of the mountains, and descended, until we reached the village of Yoshida. On the lefthand side on our way, I noticed that the names of Mount Manago and Masago Pond were still there; the pond being dry, only its shape was left. The imperial tomb of Emperor Itoku must have been in this area—how regretful it was not to know where!

In Yoshida I searched for the usual old man. When I asked him about the Mihotoinoue imperial tomb,[187] this old man, who knew about many things, was particularly knowledgeable about this tomb and spoke about it in great detail. In recent years, surveys of imperial tombs have been ordered from Edo;[188] generally, once every twenty years many people from the capital would come upon governmental command and stay in this village. While doing a thorough investigation, they would set up nameplates, surrounding the whole area with a fence. The graciousness of caring about the disappearance of ancient sites and the carrying out of such surveys were indeed welcome regulations. However, low-ranking officials did not share these lofty ideals. They only privileged wealthy families; compared to places with no historical sites, their behavior caused lots of trouble to villages where imperial tombs were located. As no gain whatsoever came from these surveys but only hardship, there were also people who concealed the truth, arguing that in this village such a place did not exist. As a result, the truth became even more deeply buried—a truly sad destiny for the imperial tombs. Did not these surveys actually defeat their original purpose? If the authorities had made these villages different from others, even slightly, showing some favor towards them, people would have rejoiced, and they would have increasingly protected these tombs as venerable places. The old man also mentioned the survey made by Nabika.[189]

Along the road inside the village one can still find the Mihoto Well. Shaped like a well, it had some water in it; it was a typical, small well. The imperial tomb was over one hundred yards northwest from the well; in other words, it was located on a high hill on the western foot of Mount Unebi, with a few pine trees here and there. Albeit with great trepidation, I climbed the hill. The place where I think the imperial body was buried was a huge, round hill; moreover, the part that I thought to be the front of the tomb was a very long structure, which descended a little, becoming narrower. The old man, who had guided us up to here, said: "All ancient imperial tombs are built like this one, everywhere. They all have a stone chamber; the earth crumbles from the top, exposing the inside of the tomb." I thought that this fit perfectly with my recollection of the stone chamber inside the Abe Mound. In front of the path leading from the entrance to the inner chamber there was a long structure. The old man said: "All tombs in the past were surrounded by a dry moat. Until about seventy years ago, there was one here as well." Nowadays the area was surrounded by fields and bamboo groves; there was no trace of a moat. The old man said that the bamboo grove was a remnant of it. This tomb looked perfectly intact, exactly the way it had been in the past. Someone may blame me for getting lost in so many questions with regard to this imperial tomb, as if I had lost my sanity, and for writing about it in such detail. However, nothing has been preserved from ancient times up to the end of history as well as these tombs. The imperial tomb on Mount Unebi is especially ancient among tumuli, and historically reliable. For many years my heart had been set on it; I kept on thinking longingly about going and seeing it in all its details. If it were not someone like me who cherishes the past, a man prejudiced towards whatever is ancient, no one would make the point of coming and seeing a tomb that, no matter where you go, is the same as any other tomb—nothing special worthy of particular attention. People might think that this is a peculiar enterprise, and I completely agree with them.

We left Yoshida, turned north, passed the village of Ōtani and, as we were about to enter the village of Jimyōji, saw a temple at the foot of the mountain on our righthand side.[190] The place that looked like a big mound on top of the hill in front of us was the tomb of Emperor Suizei, which the villagers call the Suizei Mound.[191] It was built on the northwestern foot of Mount Unebi; this tomb also was a high hill. We climbed it, as we had done before, and noticed that its shape was exactly the same as the one in Yoshida.[192] On the eastern foot of the mountain was the village of Yamamoto. The village of Jimyōji was reached by continuing north on this hill. After leaving the village for a while, again in the same northern direction, there was the village of Shijō. One hundred yards east of Shijō, one pine tree and one cherry tree were growing in a field five or six hundred yards northeast of Mount Unebi. There was a small mound, only three or four feet in height, that is said to be the tomb of Emperor Jinmu.[193] However, this did not look like a tumulus. Moreover, the *Kojiki* (Account of Ancient Matters) states that Jinmu's tomb was "atop the oak ridge."[194] Not only did this place not match this description, being faraway from the mountains; it was not plausible that, whereas the tumuli of Suizei and Annei were tall and large, only this one would be so modest. After putting everything together, this is a difficult matter to understand. Once we think it through, the tomb of Emperor Suizei should be the one belonging to Jinmu. Since there are examples in the past of confusion between the tumuli of Emperor Seimu and Empress Jingū,[195] this could well be a mistake. Since ancient times, people might have kept saying that this was the tomb of Emperor Suizei. The reason why I believe this is that, first of all, many imperial tombs in this area are always described as "such and such a tumulus on Mount Unebi." If the tomb of Emperor Suizei was indeed in the actual place, it should be described in this way too. However, the fact that all documents only mention "atop the hill of Tsukida" indicates that the mountain in question is not in this area. Could the tomb be located in the area where the *Jinmyōchō* states that the Tsukida shrine stands? Then, the place would be the prefecture of Shimokatsuragi. This might look like a mistake when we think of documents indicating that the tomb of Suizei is in the prefecture of Takechi. However, this is not really a problem if we think that the prefectures of Shimokatsuragi and Takechi are next to each other. In the ancient documents there are many examples in which the names of prefectures of places on the border are mixed up. This matter should be settled only after a thorough enquiry into the place called Tsukida. Moreover, both *Nihongi* and *Engishiki* indicate that Jinmu's tomb is "northeast of the mountain."[196] It is true that there is room for suspicion when we think that the tomb of Suizei was northwest of the mountain. However, the *Kojiki* states that Jinmu's tomb was "north of Mount Unebi." Moreover, although the Mihotoinoue tomb is west of the mountain, the *Nihongi* presents a different account and says that it was "south." We should not stick too much to the indication "northeast." This is something for later people to study and to settle.

After going two or three hundred yards from Shijō we arrived at a big village called Imai. We went through the town and, after leaving it behind us, we reached Yagi, where we rested for awhile and had something to eat. These past few days the sky had been totally clear, and we did not need to worry about any clouds in the sky. Since last night it had become cloudy, and this morning it looked as if it were going to rain. Therefore, we had left the inn with our eyes turned only to the sky; however, the sky cleared gradually and, by the time we were going around Mount Unebi, the weather was good again, so that everybody was in very high spirits. Since this was the way for Taima, Tatsuta, Nara, and so on, I consulted with my companions whether they would like to go there; many expressed their desire to visit these places, saying that it was a good occasion to do so. However, we were pulled back by someone who said: "We will have other chances to visit those places. Since, this time, I have some business that cannot wait, I need to go back as soon as possible." Therefore, it became impossible for anybody to go. These kinds of things happen all the time when traveling; everybody hurries back to his hometown. And yet it was truly regretful!

We left Yagi proceeding east and, after four or five hundred yards we saw the mountain of Miminashi, about two hundred yards north off the road. Mount Unebi, Mount Kagu, and this mountain stand by themselves in the middle of the land, facing each other. None of them continues into a different chain of mountains. Whereas the other two mountains look quite close to the neighboring heights, this one is particularly removed from anything else. Not one single spot is contiguous with other mountains. Among these equally not-very-high mountains, Miminashi is moderately high. Mount Kagu is the lowest, while Unebi is the highest. Moreover, when I compare their distance, from this mountain Mount Unebi is the closest, followed by Mount Kagu. The distance between Mount Unebi and Mount Kagu is the longest. In the past, these three mountains competed over their mate: since Mount Unebi and Mount Miminashi were male mountains, while Mount Kagu was a female mountain, the first two mountains fought in their courtship over the third one.[197] This is an old legend; and yet, when one looks at the mountains nowadays, one sees that indeed the first two mountains look manly, while Mount Kagu looks more feminine. Mount Miminashi is also called Tenjin-yama, Mount Heavenly God, because of the presence of a shrine on its peak.

(48) *Samo koso wa*　　　It must be because of its name
　　　Negikoto kikanu　　　That the god

	Kami narame	Does not listen to my prayers:
	Miminashiyama ni	Having put a shrine
	Yashiro sadamete	On Miminashi, the Mountain without Ears.[198]

I wondered whether the Miminashi Pond, into which Kazurako threw herself, was in this area.[199] Even now there is a pond on the side of the road.

(49)	*Inishie no*	Although I ask
	Sore ka aranu ka	The Miminashi Pond
	Miminashi no	Whether in the past
	Ike wa tou tomo	Such a thing happened or not,
	Shiraji to zo omou	I don't think the Pond without Ears would know.

Since we were thinking of paying a visit to the Miwa Shrine,[200] we kept going a while, and turned north at the crossroad with the Jizō Hall that we had left yesterday. Thinking of Nara, I was looking in that direction, and I saw in a village a branch of a cherry tree in bloom mixed with other treetops.

(50)	*Omoiyaru*	Many layers of mist
	Sora wa kasumi no	Rise in the sky
	Yaezakura	To which go my thoughts—
	Nara no miyako mo	Double cherry trees must be blooming
	Ima ya sakuran	Now, in the capital.[201]

As we kept going, I saw the Hatsuse River flowing behind the village of Miwa. We crossed the bridge, and went right in front of the torii gate of that shrine. Here there was an incessant flow of travelers. It looked so lively compared to the past few days spent on the road. From this gate we followed a road shadowed by lines of pine trees and entered about three hundred yards into the foot of the mountain. On our lefthand side I saw a temple whose name was written with the characters "Ōmiwadera," the Temple of the Big Wheel, but was read "Daigorinji." The Gate of the Benevolent Kings and a three-story pagoda were there. An Eleven-Face Kannon was enshrined in the hall; next to her on the left, in the same hall, stood a god by the name of Miwa-no-Wakamiya, the Young God of Miwa.[202] We continued to go an additional one hundred yards on our original road and climbed a few stone steps until we reached the shrine's gate. In this area several very large and venerably aged cedars stood here and there;[203] they drew the attention of viewers more than anything else around. Remembering an earlier visit to this shrine, I composed the following poem:

(51)   *Sugi no kado*   Gate of cedars,
     Mata sugigate ni   It would be difficult to pass by without stopping!
         Tazune kite   Now that I have come again to visit,
     Kawaranu iro o   Its appearance is unchanged:
     Miwa no yamamoto   The foot of Mount Miwa.

[In the *Kokinshū* we read:

         Waga yado wa   My dwelling
     Miwa no yamamoto   Is at the foot of Mount Miwa—
         Koishiku wa   If you pine for me,
     Toburai kimase   Come and visit!
     Sugi tateru kado   The gate where the cedar stands.][204]

There was no shrine; I worshipped deep inside the mountain, which was covered with trees. The worship hall at the entrance was truly venerable and auspicious. People who looked like priests and shrine maids sat down in a line. The sound of the swinging bells made the occasion even more sacred.

We did not go back to our original road; there was a narrow path going straight to Hatsuse. We followed a steep mountain road and reached a place called Kanaya. Here was the highway going from Nara to Hatsuse. Then, we went along the banks of the Hatsuse River. I heard that the ruins of Shikishima-no-Miya were in this area.[205] From this road there was nothing hiding Mount Tokama from sight; it looked tall in the direction we were going. We were told that Oiwake was in the intersection between this road and the one coming from Sakurai. Earlier on we had branched off from this place, going towards Tamu-no-mine. We went through the village of Hatsuse again, and as we were to cross the bridge I recited:

(52)   *Futamoto no*   I returned
     Sugitsuru michi ni   To the road
         Kaeri kite   Where the twin-trunked cedar has aged—
     Furu kawanobe o   Again I have seen
     Mata mo aimitsu   The banks of the ancient river.

[In the *Kokinshū* we read:

Hatsusegawa	A twin-trunked cedar stands
Furukawa no he ni	Beside the ancient river
Futamoto aru sugi	Of Hatsuse River—
Toshi o hete	I want to see it again
Mata mo aimimu	After many years have passed,
Futamoto aru sugi	The twin-trunked cedar.][206]

Tonight we stopped at the same inn in the village of Haibara where we stayed on our way to Yoshino. We discussed the possibility of taking a different road from here on our way back home, and to go towards Akabanegoe. When the route was explained to our guide, he shook his head and said: "Oh, this sounds frightening! The road that you mention goes again and again through steep mountains; there would be so many dreadful slopes to cross, such as Kaisaka and Hitsusaka.[207] Since it looks like tomorrow it is going to rain, the road will become even worse. How can you cross all these places safely? It is absolutely impossible." Listening to these words, everybody became fainthearted and hesitated, wondering what to do. The venerable Kaigon[208] said: "No, no! If it were such a frightening road, no one would use it. However, since it looks as if everybody goes there, there is nothing to worry about. As long as we have legs, we should be able to cross." At these words of encouragement the fear disappeared, and everybody calmed down, saying, "That is exactly so."

THE THIRTEENTH DAY

We left for that dreadful road in the midst of a drizzle, still deep in the night. This road branched off on the righthand side from the middle of the village. This morning I was not feeling very well; feeling truly helpless, I worried about what we could expect on this mountain road. Although we heard that we were not too far from Murō, we decided not to visit the mountain, as the rain was getting worse and the road was truly bad. There were about eight and a half miles from Haibara to the post town of Taguchi. First of all, we crossed a place called Ishiwarizaka—a very long distance. From Taguchi we again crossed many mountains—five miles until Momo-no-mata. We crossed another mountain and proceeded for another five miles until the village of Sugano. From here to the village of Tage it was ten miles. In between was the border between the Yamato and Ise provinces. Today we were scheduled to travel until Tage. However, the rain was heavy and the wind strong. As we were going to the top of the mountain, our sedge hats were blown away. The wind made us lose our footing; if we had not been careful enough, we would have fallen to the bottom of the gorge. Moreover, Kaisaka, which was well known for its steepness, was still lying ahead. Thinking that, under these circumstances, we would not be able to cross it, we stopped at a place called Ishinahara. We had spent the whole day in the middle of mountains that looked all the same from Haibara to here; there was nothing particularly worth seeing. However, many cherry trees still in bloom could be seen here and there. And yet the weather was bad, and I continued to feel very sick; as a result, I kept going without any particular thoughts. I ended up not recording any poem.

THE FOURTEENTH DAY

Although the rain had stopped, since I was still feeling sick, I got on the shabby palanquin that I have already described and climbed Kaisaka. It was indeed a steep mountain path. However, as I was not on foot, I did not have to experience that steepness. I felt deep pain looking at everybody climbing, though, as they kept resting every short while, completely out of breath. Our guide climbed little by little, far behind us, perhaps because of the luggage he was carrying. Yet I could see immediately beneath me the whole area where the road came up in a winding fashion, as if it were very close. We rested for a while at the pass' teahouse. When I looked down the slope, I saw the village of Tage. This was the place where the Kitabatake lords, whom my ancestors had served for many generations, lived for centuries.[209] Therefore, I felt as if this were my hometown; a sense of nostalgia took hold of me, for no apparent reason. This time, too, we had chosen this road with the specific intention of visiting ruins. This place, which was surrounded by mountains, was not especially broad; yet, compared to the villages that we had seen yesterday, it looked like an open, wide, long valley. What was left of the Kitabatake castle was only a small temple called Shinzen-in at the foot of the northern mountain, about four or five hundred yards away from the village. Apparently, to this very day the villagers keep referring to this place as Kokushi, "the Provincial Governor."[210] Here there was the Kitabatake's Hachimangū—a shrine where people worshipped the spirit of the chief councilor of state Tomonori. [The religious name of this governor was Jakkōin Fuchi.][211] I prostrated myself in prayer with all my heart, thinking about my ancestors. Since, at that time, it was raining a little, I recited the following poem:

(53)　　Shitagusa no　　　　　Even the last leaves
　　　Sueba mo nurete　　　　Of the grasses beneath the trees are wet—
　　　　Harusame ni　　　　　I think of the blessings
　　　Karenishi kimi no　　　　This lord bestowed long time ago,
　　　Megumi o zo omou　　　Now dry under the spring rains.[212]

As I was looking at the pond in the garden and the stones set in the pond, standing in front of the hall as they did in the past, I could only think of the wonderful reputation he had left behind; I felt sad thinking of his prosperity in the past.

(54)　　Kimi masade　　　　　Without its lord
　　　Furinuru ike no　　　　　The ancient pond
　　　　Kokoro ni mo　　　　　Is unable to express,
　　　Ii koso idene　　　　　　Not even in its bosom,
　　　Mukashi kouran　　　　How much it longs for the past.

The mountain on top is called Kiri-ga-mine, Fog's Peak; apparently, the ruins of the castle are still up there. However, since the mountain was high, we did not try to climb it.

I went to visit the priest of this temple in order to ask him whether he had some records of ancient events, but the abbot was not there, having had some business to attend to elsewhere. Apparently, the person who indicated to me the place where the records of this village were kept was the temple's keeper. In order to see these records I had to return to the village. I looked for the house where the records were kept. When I explained the reason for my visit, I was shown an old illustration of this place. Everything was reproduced in detail, starting with the dwellings of the nobility, the houses of the servants, the temples in the various gorges, and all the private houses. There was also a volume in which were gathered all the names of those who had served the Kitabatake family. When I opened the scroll and looked at the names, I also found among names that I had heard before, and among the ancestors of families that still survive to this day here and there, the name of my ancestor [Motoori Sōsuke].[213] Although I checked with great care whether his house appeared in the illustration, I was unable to find it.

Then, we asked at this house to have some food prepared. The road going to Ise from here went south, passing through the infamous Hitsusaka slope. Since it would have been a long way to go by that road, we were thinking of going back through the Horisaka slope. However, we were told that this road was not for travelers, and that we would not find any food; that's why we arranged for our food here. Again we passed in front of that temple (the Shinzen-in), went to Shimotage, crossed the mountain, passed the mountain villages of Ogawa, Yunohara, and so on, and arrived at the Ibuta Temple.[214] This was not a road that people would take, because it turned into the shadow of the northern mountains. It was an imitation of the sacred peak,[215] where the local people would come for their spiritual training. I had heard of this place earlier on, and I actually came here. Seizing this good chance, we made the detour and visited the area. Although this mountain did not go very deep inside, there were huge boulders, and the water in the gorge was pure—a place removed from the world. Then we came out onto the village of Yohara, entered the temple, rested a while, and then climbed the Horisaka slope. This was a very high mountain. Now we climbed half the slope, following a road that was taking us across to the other side while looking up at the pass that was still lying far away south. From the pass we could see up to the southern islands, as well as to the mountains of Owari and Mikawa. For many days we had been used to seeing only mountains. Now that I was faced with the unusual view of the sea all around, I felt as if I were waking up. When I realized that I was so close to the treetops of the place where I lived that I could touch them with my hand, I felt as if I wanted to cry out.

The way down the slope was very long; by the time we passed the Ise Temple it was already evening. Since, when we took the detour at the Ibuta Temple I had the guide go back home first, everyone from the houses of the people who had joined me on the trip came to welcome us back. It was already quite dark when we went back home together. I was truly happy that the journey had gone smoothly. At the same time, realizing that it was over, I was reluctant to cast off the traveler's clothes I had worn for the past few days—a reluctance that was truly out of the ordinary!

(55) *Nugu mo oshi*   How much I regret to take it off,
      Yoshino no hana no   The small sedge hat
         Shita kaze ni   Blown away
      Fukare kinikeru   By the wind
      Suge no ogasa wa   Beneath the flowers in Yoshino!

Thinking that even if my cap could not retain the fragrance of those flowers, I would preserve at least its name as a memento to cherish at future times, I decided to preserve everything in words, and I called this work "The Sedge Hat Diary."

Motoori Norinaga

Songs on *"Aware"* (Pathos)
Selection from *Suzunoya Shū*

(1) AN OLD WILLOW TREE BY THE WATER:
    Kage miru mo   How many springs now
Ima iku haru to   Has it lasted through,
    Kuchinokoru   Watching its reflection?
Aware mo fukaki   The deeply moving
Kawa yanagi ka na   Willow tree by the river.[1]

(2) INSECTS IN FRONT OF THE MOON:
    Mushi no ne ka   Is it because of the sound of insects?
Izure ni otsuru   Where are these tears
    Aware to mo   From a deeply moved heart falling—
Namida wakarenu   Tears that never leave
Aki no yo no tsuki   The moon on an autumn night?[2]

THE MOON:
(3)   *Kokoro aru*   How will it be for a person
Hito ika naramu   With sensitivity,
    Aki no tsuki   The sky at night
Shiranu aware mo   Whose feelings are deep—
Fukaki yo no sora   A night that does not know the autumn moon?[3]

(4)   *Hitori ite*   When, alone,
Irigata chikaki   I gaze upon the moon
    Tsuki mireba   Close to setting,
Yoi no aware wa   The moving power of early night
Kazu naranu ka na   Is beyond words.[4]

(5) THE MOON REFLECTED IN THE DEW ON THE GRASS:
    Murasaki no   Wondering what kind of relationship
Tsuki wa nani zo no   The purple

Yukari to te	Moon has,
Kusaba mo awaremu	The leaves of grass must be moved to tears!
Musashino no tsuyu	Dew on the Musashi plain.⁵

(6) THE MOON'S COURSE IN THE FIELDS:

Nobe no tsuyu	It must not know
Wakezu wa shiraji	How not to distinguish the dew on the fields!
Kokoro naki	Oh, the moving power of the moon,
Sode ni mo kakaru	Whose rays fall on my sleeves
Tsuki no aware o	That have no sensitivity.⁶

(7) THE MOON AT THE BARRIER:

Yoso ni ninu	How fierce
Aware mo soite	Is the moonlight
Fuwa-no-seki	On The Impenetrable Barrier,
Areshi zo tsuki no	Adding a moving power,
Hikari narikeru	Which is unlike anything that can be experienced anywhere else!⁷

FEELINGS IN FRONT OF THE MOON:

(8) *Towaba ya na*	How much I would like to ask
Mono no aware o	The person who knows
Shiru hito ni	The moving power of things
Tsuki miru aki no	The feelings he feels during an autumn night,
Yowa no kokoro o	As he gazes upon the moon!⁸

(9) *Aki o hete*	The moving power of the moon
Tsuki no aware wa	Passing through autumn
Masukagami	Is like a clear mirror
Waga yo fukeyuku	In which I see my reflection
Kage o miru ni mo	As I get older, and as the night deepens.⁹

(10) QUAILS IN THE MIST:

Aware naru	Increasingly sad
Uzura no koe mo	Is the mist rising in the evening,
Tachisoite	As the cry of the moving quails
Itodo sabishiki	By the moving power rise,
Nobe no yūgiri	Adding sadness to sadness.¹⁰

(11) Mist:

Are hateshi	Oh how dense
Nobe no aware wa	Is the moving power of the fields!
Tachikomete	Nothing more than the evening mist
Tada yūgiri no	Lying around
Fukakusa no sato	Fukakusa village, the village of "Deep Grass."[11]

(12) Geese in front of the moon:

Akugareshi	Is this the autumn
Kari no tokoyo no	Of everlasting darkness,
Aki ya ika ni	When the geese fly away in the sky?
Miyako no tsuki mo	And yet, this moonlit night in the capital
Aware naru yo o	Is so moving![12]

(13) Clouds in late autumn:

Kaze kiou	The sky in the dusk,
Kumo no yukue mo	Looking upon the moving power
Yuku aki no	Of autumn,
Aware o misuru	In which even the going of the clouds
Yūgure no sora	Hustling in the wind goes.[13]

(14) Snow in the capital:

Shirayuki no	Even the moving power
Aware mo fukashi	Of the white snow is deep:
Furukoto no	The capital, where even the traces
Ato sae yoyo ni	Of ancient things
Tsumoru miyako wa	Pile up generation after generation.[14]

(15) Praying for love:

Aware to mo	If you have some compassion,
Omowaba kami mo	Dear gods,
Shirube seyo	Show a sign
Isamenu michi ni	To this self who is lost
Mayou kono mi o	On a path which is not forbidden.[15]

(16) Entrusting love to the image of the miscanthus reed:

| *Aware to mo* | The heart that does not say, |
| *Iwanu kokoro no* | "Ah!" |

Diary and Poetry: Songs on *"Aware"* 99

  Asa wa no ni   Has no cord to bind
Midaruru kaya no   The disordered miscanthus reeds
Tsukaneo mo nashi   In the morning fields.[16]

(17) ENTRUSTING LOVE TO THE IMAGE OF THE PILLOW:
  Aware to mo   Will only my pillow
Makura bakari wa   Know
  Shirinuramu   How pitiable I am?
Uku bakari naru   Waking up in the middle of the night,
Yowa no nezame o   I am unable to find any repose.[17]

(18) ENTRUSTING LOVE TO THE IMAGE OF A FLUTE:
  Aware to mo   If you had heard
Kikaba hitoyo wa   How deeply I feel,
  Fuetake no   I wish you would come and visit
Ne ni naku yado o   The dwelling where the bamboo flute
Kite mo towanamu   Cries the whole night.[18]

(19) ENTRUSTING LOVE TO THE IMAGE OF A BOAT:
  Aware chō   A man
Hito mo nagisa ni   Known for his deep feelings
  Tadayoite   Drifts on the beach:
Nado sutebune no   Why is the discarded boat
Kuchinokoruramu   Left to lie?[19]

(20) GAZING UPON THE MOON ON THE TWENTIETH DAY OF THE EIGHTH
  MONTH, ON THE YEAR I TURNED FIFTY:
  Aware to wa   The pathos of things,
Mizu ya isoji no   Will I not see it?—
  Aki no tsuki   The depth of the dew
Yadokasu sode no   On my sleeves where
Tsuyu no fukasa o   My fiftieth birthday dwells?[20]

(21) A JAPANESE HARP:
  Nezame shite   A jeweled koto in the middle of the night,
Aware naru ne ni   In which the person wakes up,
  Kiku hito mo   And, listening

Namida kakiyaru	To the moving sound,
Yowa no tamagoto	Writes a letter in tears.[21]

(22) As I was leaving the capital Kyoto on the Tenth of the Fourth Month, I looked back at the Eikandō. Since everybody went to worship the main statue, I also joined them, and looking at the Buddha, I composed the following song:

Kaerimiru	How moving is the Buddha
Hotoke mo aware	That I turned back to see,
Asu wa mata	Since, as I will be reflecting on it tomorrow again,
Ware mo miyako o	I never thought
Kaku ya to omoeba	The capital would be like this![22]

(23) The inn on a journey:

Aware naru	Oh, to rest on my journey
Utsu no yamabe no	Beside
Tabine ka na	The moving Mount Utsu!
Makura ni kakaru	Dew dripping from the ivy
Tsuta no shitatsuyu	Onto my pillow.[23]

(24) Thinking nostalgically of old things in the snow at the wake of Ozu Masahira:

Atotoite	Paying my respects,
Aramashikaba to	As I was thinking,
Omou ni wa	If he were only here,
Aware mo fukaki	White snow on his dwelling,
Yado no shirayuki	Deep with moving power.[24]

(25) A song composed for a painting in which the poems known as the "Three Dusks" were scribbled together:

Atsumete wa	To put them together
Itodo aware mo	Exceeds all measures
Masarikeri	Of *aware*:
Ura yama sawa no	Autumn dusk
Aki no yūgure	On the bay, the mountain, and the marsh.[25]

(26) At the Tsukiyomi Shrine:

Te o orite	Bending my fingers I count the months:
Ima wa uzuki to	It is now the Fourth Month, "Sunflower Moon"—
Tsukiyomi no	How moving the name
Yashiro no na aware	Of the Tsukiyomi Shrine, "Moon Counting"—
Tabi no kenagami	Since I have spent many days on my journey.[26]

Essays

The Province of Ise[1]

An ancient document calls the province of Ise "a secluded and pleasant land."[2] From the northern to the southern tips, chains of mountains range on the western side, truly making a fence of green. On the eastern side there is a bay known as the Ise Sea. A flat plain spreads out everywhere between mountains and sea. From Kuwana in the north to Yamada in the south a plain continues uninterrupted for over fifty miles, without a single mountain needing to be crossed. In between, among the many spacious villages, we find the particularly large and lively towns of Yamada, Anotsu, Matsusaka, Kuwana, and others. Generally speaking, while going through the seven or eight provinces separating the capital from Edo, we cannot find towns as big as these, with the exception of Otsu in the Ōmi province and Suruga-no-fu.[3] Keeping in mind the size of towns of other provinces, I should point out, after the ones mentioned above, the beautiful villages of Yokkaichi, Shiroko, and others. This province is not all about sea, mountains, and fields. Compared to other provinces, the weather, both hot and cold, is not severe, although it becomes increasingly cold as one goes north, since the wind often blows in this province. It is a very lively place because of the many travelers who constantly visit the Ise Shrine. The place is particularly busy in spring and summer. Basically, this province has no match in the entire world. Its soil is fertile and the quality of its rice excellent; its grains and produce are equally good.

Matsusaka, in particular, is a lovely town. Although in size it is second to Yamada, Matsusaka has many wealthy houses that have their stores in Edo, where business is entrusted to many clerks. The owners stay in the province and have a good time. One would not be able to tell from the outward appearances, but inside their houses they truly live a life of wealth and luxury. The alleys in this town are crooked, never straight. The way the houses are lined up is bad. They protrude three or four meters from each other, so that the surface is uneven—truly a town without planning! The houses do not look very solemn; however, inside they are truly lovely. The quality of water is uneven, since there are good and bad places for water. There is little water from rivers and, since the tide does not come in, boats cannot reach town. Matsusaka is located a little over two and a half miles from the mountains, and a little over one mile from the sea. Communication with the other provinces is good, especially with the capital, Edo, and Osaka. Since this is a place where people come from all over the land, it is easy to go anywhere. People's disposition is not very good: they tend to be proud, and not very truthful. The inhabitants of the town, both men and women, do not look rustic at all; their appearance is quite good. The women's appearance and deportment are good and appropriate to a prosperous and busy town. This town is not inferior to the capital in any aspect. People living in the provinces east of Owari tend to have a strong accent. However, generally speaking, people from Ise do not have any accent. And yet, somehow, in the provinces of Yamashiro and Yamato the intonation and the words are often coarse. In other words, when it comes to clothes and fancy goods, people in Matsusaka use excellent quality. Places such as the port of Yamada get the best possible goods. Therefore, merchants here are more powerful than in the capital. Especially in Matsusaka, everything is of the highest quality. Merchants from Kyoto regularly visit this town. There is no lack of fashionable items. Since all kinds of arts and technologies converge on this town, some objects are bound to be bad. Workmanship is truly excellent and the city is busy with commerce. Theaters, shows, shrines, and Buddhist temples are packed. Since this is a province with many travelers from other provinces, there are also many things of dubious quality, and many thieves. Matsusaka has an abundance of fishes and vegetables. However, among the fishes there are few carps, and among the vegetables, arrowhead bulbs and lotus roots are scarce. The weak points of Matsusaka are the crooked alleys, which do not follow any plan, and the fact that boats cannot get to town.

The Tomb of Emperor Jinmu[4]

Some time ago, in a diary on my journey to Yoshino,[5] I wrote that the place of Emperor Jinmu's tomb was not where people currently said it was, and that I believed that what people thought to be the tomb of Emperor Suizei was actually the resting place of Emperor Jinmu. However, during the past four or five years, a man from the Yamato province by the name of Takeguchi Eisai has been arguing that the tomb of Emperor Suizei is indeed Suizei's, and that Emperor Jinmu's tomb is actually the place that I visited—a place that matches the direction indicated in the *Nihongi* well: the northeastern foot of Mount Unebi, a mountain where a shrine is found called "the Imperial Shrine."

Takeguchi argues that here one can find a place called Kashi, which appears in the *Kojiki*. This must be the place to which the *Kojiki* refers by the name of "*kashi no ue*" (atop the oak ridge). This place is located in the area of a village called Horamura, east of the mountain where Kamuyaimimi-no-Mikoto[6] is buried in the village of Yamamoto, south of the village of Kosedō and west of the village of Ōkubo. Takeguchi says that in the nearby zone of Tadokoro one can find places called Jibutei and Misanzai. In his book he also adds a truly detailed map of the area, which includes all the imperial tombs of Mount Unebi. Takeguchi also reports that, since he comes from the same province that he describes, and since he is particularly close to all these places, he had visited them often, so he could be sure of his ideas. When I look at his publications, I realize that my earlier hypothesis was incorrect, and I definitely believe that the truth ultimately rests with this man. I thought he was quite sharp to point out that, if indeed the tomb of Emperor Suizei was not his, contrary to what was commonly believed, then it did not belong to any emperor. Now this Eisai has studied the subject of imperial tombs quite broadly, beginning with the tombs of all sovereigns, and going as far as to inquire about the resting places of empresses, princes, and princesses. I was extremely happy to see that all his work on a topic to which I had given so much thought had finally come out in a publication titled *A Record of Imperial Tombs*.[7] I cannot recommend it enough, and definitely suggest taking a look at this book.

The Mikumari Shrine in Yoshino[8]

With regard to the Mikumari Shrine, we read in the *Jinmyōchō* (A List of Gods' Names) that "the Mikumari Shrine is located in the prefecture of Yoshino, in the Yamato province" (*Tsukinami* [Annual Festival], *Niiname* [Festival of the Consumption of the New Grains]). We read in the first volume of the *Shoku Nihongi* (Chronicles of Japan, Continued), Fourth Month, Second Year of the reign of Emperor Monmu (698), that "he offered a horse to the god of the Mikumari Peak in Yoshino, asking the deity for rain." We read in the ninth volume of the *Shoku Kōki* (The Later Chronicles, Continued), Tenth Month, winter, Seventh Year of the Shōwa era (840), that "the god of Mikumari was bestowed the junior fifth rank." The second book of the *Sandai Jitsuroku* (The True Records of Three Reigns), New Year's Day, First Year of the Jōgan era (859), reports that "in the area of the capital and of the five provinces new ranks were conferred upon all the gods all over the land; a total of 267 shrines received the junior, lower fifth rank; the god of Mikumari received the senior, lower fifth rank." The entry for the Ninth Month of the same year indicates that "a messenger was sent with offerings to the god of Mikumari of Yoshino, in the land of Yamato, with a prayer for rain." All these documents speak of the god of Mikumari. The *Kojiki* (A Record of Ancient Matters) states that "after Izanagi-no-Mikoto and Izanami-no-Mikoto finished bearing the land, they went on to bear deities . . . ; next they bore the deity of the sea-straits, whose name was Hayaakitsuhiko-no-Kami; next, his spouse Hayaakitsu-hime-no-Kami. These two deities Hayaakitsuhiko-no-Kami and Hayaakitsu-hime-no-Kami rule, respectively, the rivers and the seas. . . . next they bore the heavenly Mikumari-no-Kami (written with the character for '*kubaru*' [to distribute], but read '*kumari*')."[9] "*Kumari*" means "to distribute" *(kubaru)*—a reference to the god who bestows water, distributing it to the paddies. This is why even at the Prayer Festival and the Annual Festival this deity is singled out and prayers *(norito)* are addressed to him. The *Jinmyōchō* states that "this deity is enshrined in the Mikumari Shrine of Yoshino, in the land of Yamato; in the Mikumari Shrine of Uda, in the Uda prefecture (Annual Festival, Festival of the Consumption of the New Grains); in the Mikumari Shrine of Tsuke, in the Yamanobe prefecture (Annual Festival, Festival of the Consumption of the New Grains); and in the Mikumari Shrine of Katsuragi, in the Upper Katsuragi prefecture (major deity, Annual Festival, Festival of the Consumption of the New Grains). There are other Mikumari shrines here and there in various provinces. Prayers are presented to the deity of Mizukumari at the Prayer Festival and the Annual Festival; the names of Yoshino, Uda, Tsuke, and Katsuragi are all spelled out." Since middle antiquity the word "Mikumari" came to be mispronounced as "Mikomari," and "Mikomori," because of local dialects. Even the Mikumari of Yoshino came to be sung in a poem of the *Kokin Rokujō*[10] and in the *Makura no Sōshi* (Pillow Book)[11] as "Mikomori-no-Kami," the God Protecting Children. Even today, the god called Komori Daimyōjin is this deity. The poem in book seven of the *Man'yōshū*, "How sad I am when I look/at Mount Mikumari/of fair Yoshino/standing on the bluff/of divine boulders,"[12] refers to the mountain of this shrine. However, the reading of the mountain as "Mizuwake-yama" is a mistaken reading of this deity's name.[13] Furthermore, to call Mikumari the shrine in the village of Tanjimura, near Yoshino, is an enormous mistake. The Mikumari Shrine is located on the peak of Mount Mikumari, as the *Shoku Nihongi* indicates, pointing at the God of the Peak; there is no doubt that the shrine is what is called today Komori Myōjin. However, when it comes to the shrine at Tanjimura, people called it Mikomori (Hidden Water), thinking that the place of the shrine should be close to the river. The location of this shrine fits their speculation well; their deity is not a deity of the mountain. This interpretation of the deity as being connected with water does not match the content of the poems from the *Man'yōshū*. When one looks nowadays at the whole area of the Yoshino Mountain, Zaō Gongen is worshipped as the lord of this mountain.[14] The god of Mikumari and all the other excellent gods are all enshrined in the Zaō Hall as subdeities. As a matter of fact, since antiquity the deity known as Zaō was not an orthodox deity; his name did not enter the ancient lists of gods. We do not see him in the orthodox books of the past, and he was not worshipped at the court. He was a Buddhist deity established by the Buddhist priests. Since middle antiquity, thanks to the work of Buddhist priests, all famous places everywhere became places for the worship of the Buddha. The transformation of gods, who had been enshrined as lords from the beginning of time, into servants of the Buddha was an unmentionably sad operation. Because of a personal relation with this Mikumari Shrine,[15] I wanted to let everybody know about the correct sequence of things in the past. This is why I wrote this essay.

The Asuka Shrine[16]

The Asuka Shrine in the Takaichi prefecture of the Yamato province is especially excellent among the religious institutions known as larger shrines *(taisha)*. I visited the shrine for the first time long ago, when I was young, when I went to admire the cherry blossoms in Yoshino.[17] I heard that recently it burned down to the ground—proof of the extreme fragility of temporary shrines. I visited the shrine again as I passed in front of it, during my trip to the Ki province in the spring of the eleventh year of the Kansei era (1799). The shrine was totally different from the first time I saw it. As was common practice with shrines, someone had built the sacred hall and fence, as well as the annexed sub-shrines. When I asked whether the shrine had been rebuilt by the court, I was told that no, that was not the case. It had been built by a local lord who ruled over the area. I felt that this was a rare and noble action. I wrote this down since I was surprised by the fact that they had not got rid of it.

The Fire Deity[18]

The two pillar gods Izanagi and Izanami gave birth to our land and all the deities. Until they produced Fire God, there were only good things and no evil.[19]

As a result of giving birth to the Fire God, Izanami passed away,[20] and evil began in the world. Therefore, because the Fire God stands at the border between the end of good and the beginning of evil, he is the deity joining good and evil. Since nothing is like fire in, on the one hand, the power of softening and setting up everything in the world and, on the other, in burning and destroying all things, it stands at the boundary between good and evil. The joining of good and evil is brought about by the spirit *(mitama)* of this deity. Someone asked me the following question: "We should say that the beginning of evil in the world coincides with the birth of a bad child, the island of Awa, the leech-child. This came as a result of Izanami, the female deity, having spoken first during intercourse. How can you say that evil began with the death of Izanami?"[21] I answered: "Although for a female deity to speak first was improper, her expression of delight[22] was actually a good thing. Moreover, since the birth of the bad child was rare indeed, it would be difficult to consider this event an evil thing. We should say that in a world in which troublesome things are bound to happen, the episode of the leech-child was a natural occurrence."

Poems on Deities[23]

In the section on deities of the *Fūgashū* (Collection of Elegance, 1349) we read the following poem:

Moto yori mo	Since the deity
Chiri ni majiwaru	Is originally mixed
Kami nareba	With dust,
Tsuki no sawari mo	What is painful about
Nani ka kurushiki	The menses?[24]

This poem was an oracle that came to Izumi Shikibu in a dream as she was sleeping at night,[25] after having composed the following poem:

Hare yaranu	How sad
Mi no ukigumo no	The menses each moon
Tanabikite	In front of which the drifting cloud of my impure body
Tsuki no sawari to	Trails,
Naru zo kanashiki	Without ever clearing.

Izumi Shikibu composed this poem during a pilgrimage to Kumano, when she was having her period and her prayers would not be answered. This attitude does not stand up to the true way; it is an expression of Buddhist sentiments. By middle antiquity this had become the practice all over the land. Even people like Izumi Shikibu had already become used to listening to only the words of Buddhist priests. It was because her heart was impregnated with Buddhist sentiments that she had that dream! How could a god's heart be impure? The expression, "to be mixed with dust" appears in the *Lao Tzu*, a Chinese document.[26] The extrapolation from this scripture of the expression, "soften the light and identify with the dust" *(wakō dōjin)* was pure humbug;[27] this is not something that should be applied to gods. We should never be led astray by this kind of mistake and soil the gods with impurities. In the same section of the *Fūgashū* we find the following poem by Watarai no Tomomune:

Katasogi no	Although the rafter ends on the gables
Chigi wa naigai ni	Are split in different ways
Kawaredomo	At the inner and the outer shrines,
Chikai wa onaji	The goddess' vow remains the same—
Ise no kamikaze	The divine wind of Ise.[28]

Not only this poem, but all poems mentioning the words "vow" and "manifest trace"[29] are mistaken. From middle antiquity up to the present time, poets have been singing the events of the gods with profoundly Buddhist sentiments. They strayed in the theory of "Original Ground and Manifest Trace," developing the habit of speaking as if all the original grounds, even of gods, were buddhas. Even priests who serve the gods at the Ise Shrine fell prey to this mistake. How can things such as vows, which belong to buddhas and bodhisattvas, and the notion of "manifest trace," be applied to all gods?

Moreover, today we find poems that are attributed to such and such a god, or that were composed at such and such a shrine. Most of them have been fraudulently made by Buddhist priests in order to convert people to their religion. As a result, these poems do not satisfy the feelings of the way of the gods; they are all expressions of Buddhist sentiments. Generally speaking, since a long time ago priests have not hesitated to fabricate lies in order to draw people to their faith. They must have learned from the skillful means of the man known as Śakyamuni.[30]

The Imose Mountains[31]

Mount Se is mentioned in the book on Emperor Kōtoku in the *Nihon Shoki*, in the edict on the regulation of the borders of the home provinces: "The home provinces shall include the region from Mount Se in the Kii province on the south."[32] A note indicates that the character used to name this mountain, which literally means "elder brother," should be read "Se." The mountains appear for the first time in the *Man'yōshū* in the first volume, during the reign of Empress Jitō.[33] Many references to this mountain can be found in the prefaces and the poems of this collection. Mount Imo appears in two poems of book seven in the same collection,[34] and in one poem in book thirteen.[35] The two mountains together, the Imose Mountains, are sung in volumes four and seven.[36] The *Shūchūshō* (Notes in the Sleeve) by Kenshō[37] mentions the fact that the Imose Mountains are two mountains known as Mount Imo and Mount Se, located in the Ki province, and separated by the Yoshino River. Keichū argues in his *Shōchi Tokai Hen* (An Exposition of Places of Scenic Beauty)[38] that the Imose Mountains are separated by the Ki River—the Husband Mountain in the north and the Wife Mountain in the south. A document on the Ki province states that Mount Se is located in the Kaseta area of the Ito prefecture, northwest of the village of Senoyama; Mount Imo is about two hundred yards south of this village, in an area south of the Ki River. After giving a good deal of thought to this matter, I believe that there is no doubt about the location of Mount Se, which is mentioned in early times in Kōtoku's chronicles, and is sung in the poems of the *Man'yōshū*. However, I don't believe that Mount Imo, the Wife Mountain, existed in reality; the name simply derived from Mount Se, the Husband Mountain. For example, in the poem from the third book of the *Man'yōshū*, "I want to say her name badly," the poet tries to see what would happen if the name of Mount Se, Husband Mountain, was exchanged with the name of his beloved wife.[39] Moreover, the poem that says, "He will never call 'beloved wife'/this mountain of Se," plays with the idea of a possible substitution of names.[40] The poem is devised by creating the expression Mount Imo, Wife Mountain. Therefore, although we find poems on Mount Se, we do not find poems pointing exclusively to Mount Imo. We only find expressions such as crossing the Imo and Se Mountains, or the Imose Mountains, or Mount Imo, Mount Se. It sounds as if Wife Mountain has been added to the pattern of words developing from Husband Mountain. There is no example of a poem on Wife Mountain that is not accompanied by the presence of Husband Mountain. Even the example in book seven—"People say that Mount Imo, the Mount of the Beloved Wife,/is along the path toward the land of Ki"[41]—in which the name appears alone, indicates that the poem is not built on this name alone. Again, even in the poem in book seven that says, "Has Mount Imo/forgiven/Mount Se/that stands straight in front of her?/A bridge I cross between the two,"[42] the poet sees a makeshift bridge by which to cross the mountain stream while going over Husband Mountain. He sees another mountain in the area standing in line with Mount Se and gives it the temporary name of Mount Imo, Wife Mountain. The end of the poem in the record on the roads of the Ki province I mentioned earlier, "Two-Peak Mountain as well/has its Wife Mountain," means that, although in reality on Mount Futagami there is no such a thing as Mount Imo, Wife Mountain, this name was devised because Mount Futagami has two peaks. Being located in the same Ki province as Mount Se, Husband Mountain, the association became immediate.

I have been thinking that no mountain by the name of Mount Imo ever existed in reality, based on the fact that, whereas up to now there has been evidence of the existence of Husband Mountain and of the presence of the village of Senoyamamura, Wife Mountain has been an ambiguous and ungrounded matter. This is why, generally speaking, it is difficult to take as proof of the existence of Mount Imo the reference to the *Kokinshū* poem quoted in the *Shūchūshō* that I mentioned above.[43] While Keichū is not very specific on this subject, the record on the Ki province is quite detailed. And yet, when it says that Mount Imo is located in the area south of the Ki River, it is not very clear to which mountain it refers. In my opinion, it must be referring to a rocky mountain in the middle of the Ki River. However, when I went down the river by boat, I saw that, although the mountain was in the middle of the river, it was in an area close to its northern bank. Since the water was flowing along the southern foot of the mountain, this mountain cannot be located south of the river. Although I think that this could be the result of the rapids' movements—something that would fit the *Kokinshū* poem—I am puzzled by the record's reference to the southern area. Kaibara no Atsunobu was also puzzled when he talked about his "journey to the famous Mount Se, Mount Rapids."[44] Kaibara argues that, if the Imose Mountains were in this place, Mount Imo should be found across from Mount Se, but there is no mountain by the name of Mount Imo. He also says that, since this mountain is in the middle of the river's rapids, this is Mount Se, Mount Rapids, and not the Imose Mountains. That's why, according to him, the villagers at that time called the mountain in the middle of this river Senoyama. However, the mountain inside the river should not be sought within the borders of the Kinai region. Moreover, we know from the poems sung in the *Man'yōshū* that Husband Mountain is the mountain northwest of Senoyamamura. Therefore, Kaibara is wrong on this matter. And yet, if the mountain in the middle of the river was Mount Imo, it goes without saying that Kaibara would not state that there is no mountain that should be called Mount Imo. Moreover, the fact that he did not say that this mountain was Mount Imo, although he should have said it, indicates that he thought that it was not Mount Imo. Things get even more confusing when we see that the record on the Ki province states that this actually is Mount Imo. The reason why things get so confused is that from the beginning Mount Imo did not exist. Moreover, in recent years a man from the Ki province pointed out that the *Kokinshū* poem "This is what/the world of love/ is about" appears in the *Kokin Rokujō* with the variation "the Yoshino waterfall/whose course falls between."[45] He also points out the following poem by Emperor Daigo from the *Shokukokinshū* (Collection of Ancient and Modern Times Continued, 1265):

Sue taenu	Oh, the upper stream
Yoshino no kawa no	Of the Yoshino River
Minakami ya	That does not know an end!—
Imose no yama no	It must be going through
Naka o yukuran	The Imose Mountains.

And, he mentions the poem by Ono no Takamura from the *Gyokuyōshū* (Collection of Jeweled Leaves, 1313), "I wish the Yoshino River/which flows in between,"[46] as well as the reply from his beloved, "I see not even the shadow/ of the Imose Mountains."[47] This man says that, according to these poems, we should reach the conclusion that the mountain was located, not in the Ki province, but in Yoshino. He also says that, although in the *Man'yōshū* the Ki province is mentioned, this is a mistake, due to the fact that this mountain is erroneously taken for Mount Se, Mount Rapids, located in the middle of the famous river, and that master Kaibara also points to the Yoshino region. This theory is a mistake that does not take account of the *Man'yōshū*, relying only on later poetry. The content of the *Man'yōshū* leaves no doubt of the fact that the mountain in question is located in the Ki province.

Even today, when people say the Imose Mountains are in Yoshino, they are actually following the poem from the *Kokinshū*—a poem from a later time when this name was given to other suitable mountains. As a matter of fact, the

Kokinshū poem, "This is what/the world of love/ is about," derives from the poems in volume seven of the *Man'yōshū*, "Has Mount Imo/forgiven/Mount Se/ ... A bridge I cross between the two"[48] and "Mount Imo Younger Sister and Mount Se Elder brother/nearby the Ki River."[49] The *Kokinshū* poem says that the river falls between Mount Imo and Mount Se. The addition of the expression *"yoshi ya to"* (well, with a sense of approval) indicates that, since the poet is talking about rivers, the Yoshino River can well substitute for the Ki River. Moreover, this poem mentions the Yoshino River, and because it says that the river "falls," the *Kokin Rokujō* had to change the word "river" to "waterfall." Although they were composed in later ages, all the poems singing famous places and things that were observed after the poet had reached such scenic spots, are based on more ancient poems. Since, when it comes to love poems, even ancient ones, many are rhetorical embellishments of old poems, generally speaking, they can hardly be taken as evidence for any study of these famous places. It was not a very good thing for people to be thinking—since ancient times—of these Imose Mountains solely in relation to this poem from the *Kokinshū*. Moreover, the poem that is attributed to Emperor Daigo in the *Shokukokinshū*, and the one attributed to Lord Takamura in the *Gyokuyōshū*, are products of much later ages. They are not stylistically compatible with the age of their alleged authors. Their diction is definitely indebted to the *Kokinshū*. Even if they were the work of the people to whom these poems are attributed, there is no doubt that, as they sound ancient, they were influenced by the *Kokinshū*. Then how can they be taken as proof of the location of the Imose Mountains?

Again on the Imose Mountains[50]

In the spring of the eleventh year of the Kansei era (1779) I visited the Ki province again.[51] I wanted to inquire as much as possible about the matter of the Imose Mountains. On my way to that place I went down the Ki River by boat. However, after a while I landed and crossed this mountain. I crossed the mountain again on my way back, paying further attention to this place. About ten miles west of the station of Hashimoto in the prefecture of Ito of the Ki province there is a place called Senoyamamura. In other words, the mountain of this village is Mount Se. It is not a particularly high mountain. It is located in an area north of the Ki River. The tip of its southern end narrows until it reaches the riverbank. The village is located in the eastern belly of the mountain. The highway crosses the village in the northern part along a slightly raised point of the tip of the riverbank. Along the road there are several houses that belong to the people of Senoyamamura. Up to this mountain we are in the Ito prefecture; west of it we find the Kaga prefecture, close to a famous station. As I mentioned earlier in the "Snow Flowers" roll,[52] Mount Imo is nowhere to be found. In the midst of the river at the southern foot of Mount Se there is a long and narrow island. Although I think that Mount Imo refers to this place, in this island there are only trees growing on boulders that are lying around. I could not find any elevation that could possibly be called a mountain. Moreover, it would be a mistake to call this island Mount Se. To call it Mount Rapids because of the river's rapids is a misconception. Although some think that the name of Senoyamamura comes from this island, this is not the case. Since we find in the *Man'yōshū* the sentence "crossing Mount Se,"[53] it is clear that it refers to the mountain of this village. How would it be possible to cross the island in the river? Furthermore, south of the river there is also a mountain that comes down to the riverbank. Although we should say that this is Mount Imo since it stands across from Mount Se, this mountain is slightly higher than Senoyama. Its shape also looks manlier than Senoyama's. It should not be called Mount Imo, Woman Mountain. Moreover, it is on the other side of the river, and not on the highway. Since this mountain cannot be crossed, it does not fit the description of the poet who says, "I crossed Mount Imo and Mount Se."[54] In any case, the expression "Mount Imo" (Wife Mountain) is nothing but a rhetorical device attached to the word "Mount Se" (Husband Mountain). In other words, it is a rhetorical technique like prefaces and pillow words.

The Tatsuta River[55]

In the *Kokinshū*'s second volume on autumn poems we read the following poem on the maple leaves flowing downstream, composed while fording the Tatsuta River after crossing the sacred Mount Tatsuta:

Kamunabi no	Since autumn is the traveler
Yama o sugiyuku	Crossing
Aki nareba	Mount Kannabi the sacred mountain,
Tatsutagawa ni zo	Autumn makes its offerings
Nusa wa tamukuru	To the Tatsuta River.[56]

Mount Kannabi is located in the Otokuni district of the Yamashiro province. This is the same place mentioned in another section of the same poetic collection, in which we read, "Composed when several people, who had gone from Yamazaki to the sacred Forest of Tatsuta...."[57] The *Minamoto no Shigeyuki Shū* (Collection of Minamoto no Shigeyuki, ca. 1000) says that the Yamazaki River is called the Tatsuta River. In this collection we find the following poem, composed while saying that he was going to Kyūshū:

Shiranami no	After leaving
Tatsuta no kawa o	The Tatsuta River
Ideshi yori	By the white waves,
Ato kuyashiki wa	The voyage
Funaji narikeri	Has become filled with regrets.

According to this, the Tatsuta River is also located across from Yamazaki, in the Shimagami district of the Tsu province, close to Mount Kannabi, on the way to Kyūshū. The Tatsuta River of the Yamato Province is a different river. However, since Mount Kannabi and Tatsuta are very well known places in Yamato, people since ancient times, including the author of the *Kokinshū* poem mentioned above, believed that they could only be found in the Yamato province. Realizing this problem, Keichū skeptically pointed out that, "Since Mount Kannabi is located in the district of Takaichi, while Tatsuta is far away in the district of Heguri, it would be illogical to think that the maple leaves of that mountain flow in the Tatsuta River."[58] And yet, since the headnote says that the poet himself crossed this mountain and forded this river, it is hard to believe that it is a mistake. To argue, as my teacher does, that this poem is basically wrong, and that the headnote was made up by the compiler, is going too far.[59] Even if the poet went astray while composing these verses, I don't believe that the headnote is apocryphal. Although in the *Man'yōshū* there are fourteen or fifteen poems on Tatsuta in Yamato, they are all about the mountain; not a single poem mentions the river. Other ancient records as well only refer to the mountain when they mention the name "Tatsuta," never to the river. Only from the time when Kyoto became the capital did poets begin singing the Tatsuta River, saying that it was located across Yamazaki, as I mentioned earlier. If the poem "Maple leaves float/in random patterns"[60] was indeed composed by the Nara emperor, then the author should be Emperor Heizei.[61] The version of the poem "Maple leaves float/in the Tatsuta River"[62] with the first verse "Asuka River" instead of "Tatsuta" is the correct one—a definite reference to Yamato. Although references were made to Mount Kannabi across Yamazaki, this should not be considered to be Mount Mimuro.[63]

Yet, we find the following poem in the section on "the name of things" in the *Shūishū* (Collection of Gleanings, 1005-1007):

Kamunabi no	The cliff of Mount Kannabi,
Mimuro no kishi ya	The sacred Mount Mimuro,
Kuzururan	Must have crumbled:
Tatsuta no kawa no	The waters of the Tatsuta River
Mizu no nigoreru	Are muddy.[64]

This is an early example of the influence of the *Kokinshū* poem that led to this strange combination, confusing the river with the one in the Yamato province. Poems of later ages followed suit.

Again on the Tatsuta River[65]

As I mentioned in the previous book (*Tamakatsuma* 1:3), the Tatsuta River is actually the Yamazaki River. However, we do not know to which river the Yamazaki River corresponds today. I have been discussing this issue for a number of years. This year, in the Third Month of the fifth year of the Kansei era (1793), on my way back on a trip from Kyoto to Osaka, I had the boat approach the land at Yamazaki, and I took a good look at the area. As I was inquiring about this river, I was told generally that from Yamazaki up to the other side there is not a single river aside from the Minase River. After giving the matter a good deal of thought, I realized that the name Minase was given to this river at a later time; originally, it must have been the ancient Tatsuta River. This river is located on the boundary between Yamazaki and Minase. The border between the provinces of Yamashiro and Tsu is slightly on this side of the river, so that the river is located in the Shimagami district of the Tsu province. Although nowadays the river is shallow, here and there the banks are high. When I think about the good amount of water flowing in it, I guess that in the past this river must have been quite broad. When high banks were built at a later time, the river became narrower, as we see it today. Mount Kannabi, the sacred mountain, and the Kannabi Shrine are the ones mentioned in the *Jinmyōchō*: "In the Otokuni district of the Yamashiro province we find the Sakatoke Shrine that people come to worship from Tamate (principal deity, major, *Tsukinami* and *Niiname* festivals)."[66] Since this shrine is called Yamazaki-no-kami (the god of Yamazaki) in the *Shoku Kōki* and the *Rinji Saishiki* (Special Festivals),[67] the name Kannabi (lit., "sacred") came from this shrine. In other words, Mount Kannabi must be Mount Yamazaki. This shrine is the one that nowadays is also called Yamazaki Tennō, the Heavenly King of Yamazaki. I passed the village of Minase and I saw, faraway across from it, a village called Kōnai-mura, Inside the Shrine. In this area there was a small forest. Although people call it Kannabi-no-mori (The Sacred Forest), this place does not match the description of ancient poems; there is no river next to it. People must have moved the Yamazaki Shrine to this area at a later time, maintaining the ancient name. The shape of the forest must also be the product of a later age. The headnote to the *Kokinshū* poem says, "From Yamazaki to the sacred forest."[68] This sounds as if the poet was leaving Yamazaki and going away from it. While all this was taking place within the area of Yamazaki, the poet must have moved from the village to the forest.

The Tatsuta-Ogura Peak[69]

According to one theory, Mount Tatsuta, which in the past one had to cross every time one went from Yamato to Naniwa, corresponds to today's Kuragari Pass.[70] The name Mount Tatsuta appears in book nine of the *Man'yōshū*, in which the poet is on his way to the Ogura Peak.[71] Moreover, this name is also the name of the road, which is today the only main road crossing the mountain. This theory finds further support in the fact that in this area there is a village by the name of Oguradera-mura. Not understanding why, if this were true, the Tatsuta Shrine would be so far away from this mountain, someone has argued that the Tatsutayama-Ogura Peak is not the Kuragari Pass, but what is known today as the Tatsuno Pass. Recently this theory has been supported by someone whose name is Ueda Akinari, who has added his own commentary to my master's *Ancient Meaning of the Tales of Ise*.[72] Ueda has argued cogently his reasons for this theory, and I fully agree with him. However, it would be a mistake to argue that the river nearby is the Tatsuta River. This is an issue to which everyone should pay attention. Although, since ancient times, people came to believe that the Tatsuta River was the river near Mount Tatsuta, the name Tatsuta River does not appear in any poem or any document until the age of the *Man'yōshū*. It began to appear often in poems composed after Kyoto became the capital. As a result, we can argue that the Tatsuta River was located in a different place from Mount Tatsuta. As I already explained in detail in the first book of this work, it was not located in the Yamato province.[73]

The Minase River[74]

In the past, the expression "Minase-gawa" did not refer to any specific river. It simply meant a river without water, or a river whose water flowed beneath the sand, thus not showing any water in its bed. This is the meaning that this expression has in the following poems from the *Man'yōshū*:

Book four:

Koi ni mo so	People die
Hito wa shi ni suru	Even of love—
Minasegawa	I become emaciated,
Shita yu are yasu	Unknown to others like the hidden current,
Tsuki ni hi ni ke ni	Day after day, month after month.[75]

Book eleven:

Kochitaku wa	If people start talking about it,
Naka wa yodomase	Rest for a while in the middle!
Minashigawa	Do not cease to be present,
Tayu to iu koto o	And do not hide from sight,
Arikosu na yume	Like the hidden current.[76]

Uraburete	Despondent,
Mono wa omowaji	I will not be lost in thoughts:
Minasegawa	Even if hidden from sight,
Arite mo mizu wa	The current of water
Yuku to iu mono o	Keeps flowing.[77]

The expression *"minasegawa"* appears with the same meaning in the following poems from the *Kokinshū*:

Fifth book on love:

Aimineba	Since I do not meet with you,
Koi koso masare	My love only increases—
Minasegawa	Why should I be thinking
Nani ni fukamete	So deeply
Omoisomekemu	Of that person hidden from sight like the hidden current?[78]

Minasegawa	If there were no water
Arite yuku mizu	In the hidden current
Naku wa koso	That actually is and flows,
Tsui ni waga mi o	I think that eventually
Taenu to omowame	I would cease to be.[79]

The following poem from the tenth book of the *Man'yōshū* refers to the Milky Way. The meaning of *minasegawa* in this poem is definitely "without water":

Hisakata no	I resent
Ama no shirushi to	The age of the gods
Minashigawa	Who put a waterless river
Hedatete okishi	As mark
Kamiyo shi urameshi	Of the everlasting heavens.[80]

Therefore, it would be a mistake to interpret the word *minasegawa* in all the poems quoted as the Minase River located on the other side of Yamazaki. As I mentioned earlier, in the past the river across from Yamazaki was called the Yamazaki River or the Tatsuta River. The name Minase River came later, after the time of the compilation of the *Kokinshū*. The *Ruijū Kokushi* (Classified Histories of the Land)[81] reports several entries according to which the emperor went hunting in Minashino, the Field Producing Water, during the Enryaku (782–805) and Kōnin (810–823) eras. The name Minashimura also appears. In other words, this is what is called Minase today. Therefore, the name of the Minase River was created at a later time, based on the name of this place. The name is written with the characters for "water" and "to become," and it is read "Minashi." In the *Man'yōshū*, the three characters for "water," "not," and "river" should be read in the same way. I wonder why the character *nashi* became difficult to read. In any event, since ancient times, both the name of the place and the name of the river were "Minashi" and "Minase." Apparently people were able to understand both pronunciations.

The Floating Bridge of Dreams[82]

The name "floating bridge of dreams" (*yume-no-ukihashi*) comes from the following ancient poem:

Yo no naka wa	Are the affairs of the world
Ime no watari no	Like the floating bridge
Ukihashi ka	Across Ime-no-Wada, the Bay of Dreams?
Uchiwatashitsutsu	Absorbed I am in painful thoughts
Mono o koso omoe	As I look far into the distance.[83]

When we look at the following poem from the third book of the *Man'yōshū*,

Aga yuki wa	Not much is left
Hisa ni wa araji	Of my journey:
Ime-no-Wada	I pray that Ime-no-Wada, the Bay of Dreams,
Se to wa narazute	Will not become rapids,
Fuchi nite are mo	Only a deep pool.[84]

and, also, at the following poem from the seventh book of the *Man'yōshū*,

Ime-no-Wada	Ime-no-Wada, the Bay of Dreams,
Koto ni shi arikeri	Exists only in words:
Utsutsu ni mo	I keep on thinking
Mite koshi mono o	That you might come to me
Omoishi omoeba	In reality as well.[85]

the expression "the floating bridge across Ime-no-Wada, the Bay of Dreams" is actually a reference to a real bridge across a famous site known as Ime-no-Wada, which is found in the Yoshino River. We find the name Ime-no-Wada in a poem from the *Kaifūsō* by Yoshida Yoroshi on "a visit to the Yoshino Palace by palanquin"—another reference to this place.[86]

Although we do not know in which anthology the poem "Are the affairs of the world" was originally collected, it is quoted in the *Kakai Shō* (Treatise on Rivers and Seas).[87] The poem's meaning is that, although the poet tries to cross that floating bridge, he is having difficulties doing so, since this is a truly dangerous bridge, and he becomes prey to anxieties. He is simply absorbed in thoughts as he looks far into the distance. However, gazing in rapture and being absorbed in painful thoughts—are these good examples to describe the unreliable affairs of the world? The expression "as I look far into the distance" indicates the act of looking across. This is a reinforcement of the act of gazing in pain. Moreover, the second and third verses should be interpreted as other ways of saying simply, "as I look far into the distance." Aside from these thoughts, and letting things be as they may, Ime-no-Wada is a famous place in Yoshino. In *The Tale of Genji* a chapter is titled after the notion of dreams.[88] Genji's lament, "Is it a floating bridge of dreams?" in the "Wisps of Clouds" chapter of the same story, simply means, "Is this simply a dream?" Therefore, I wonder whether Murasaki Shikibu, ignoring that Ime-no-Wada was a famous place, erroneously took the poem to refer to "dreams." After this became the title of a chapter in *The Tale of Genji* with the meaning of "dreams," everyone began to use the expression "the floating bridge over Ime" to mean "the floating bridge of dreams," including Sagoromo's poem:

Hakanashi ya	Ah, what a vain desire!
Yume no watari no	There is no end
Ukihashi o	To this heart that relies on
Tanomu kokoro no	The floating bridge
Tae mo hatenu yo	Of dreams.[89]

The Meaning of the Poem "Is This Not the Same Moon?" by Lord Narihira[90]

Tsuki ya aranu	Is this not the same moon?
Haru ya Mukashi no	Is this not
Haru naranu	The spring of old?
Waga mi hitotsu wa	Only this body of mine
Moto no mi ni shite	Is the original body.[91]

This poem has been interpreted in different ways,[92] and yet all these interpretations are somehow troublesome. They do not convey the flavor of the poem. As a result, let me try to articulate its flavor based on my present understanding. First of all, the two particles *"ya"* introduce a rhetorical question, thus indicating that both moon and spring have not changed since last year. Then, the poem would mean the following: The moon, which is not the same moon I saw in the past, appears to me in the same way as it did in the past; the spring, which is not the same as the spring I experienced in the past, has come this year as it did in the past. However, this body of mine, which is the same body as in the past, does not feel in the same way as it did in the past.

The past is the time when the poet met with the woman he loved. The expression *moto no mi* (original body) indicates the body at that time. The expression *mi ni shite* means "while remaining myself"; it includes the meaning, "I am certainly not as I was in the past, now that I feel that I am at the end of my life." I feel an added meaning in the power of the word *shite,* which highlights the idea in the upper verse that both moon and spring are the same as in the past. This is what the author of the preface of the *Kokinshū* must have had in mind when he said that the poetry of this man "had a surplus of meaning and not enough words."[93] The sentence in the *Ise Monogatari,* "He stood up and looked, he looked sitting down; although he kept looking, it did not look like the previous year,"[94] shows this additional meaning. The expression "did not look like the previous year" does not mean that moon and spring were not the same as in the previous year; it means that the feelings of the poet who is looking are not the same as last year's. We can hear this interpretation in the following poem by Kiyohara no Fukayabu from the upper miscellanea section of the *Shin Kokinshū*—a poem that looks like a commentary on the verses by Lord Narihira:

Mukashi mishi	While the spring
Haru wa mukashi no	Which I saw in the past
Haru nagara	Is the same as the spring of old,
Waga mi hitotsu no	Only this body of mine
Arazu mo aru kana	Is not the same.[95]

The Last Words of Lord Narihira[96]

We find in the *Kokinshū* the following poem by Lord Narihira, which he wrote "when he became weak, due to an illness:"

Tsui ni yuku	Although I had heard earlier on
Michi to wa kanete	That this is the path
Kikishikado	Which we must take in the end,
Kinō kyō to wa	I never thought
Omowazarishi o	That it would be yesterday or today.[97]

Keichū has made the following comment:[98] "This poem shows the true feelings of man. This is also a useful poem for didactic purposes. When they were on verge of death, people of later ages composed pompous verses, or poems on how to follow the path to enlightenment. These are awful poems, devoid of any truth. I understand the poets' desire to embellish their poems with fictive utterances[99] at normal times in their life; however, when the end comes, I wish they would return to expressing their true, sincere feelings. Lord Narihira expressed the truth of his whole life in this poem. People in later ages have died showing the falsity of their whole life." This does not sound like the words of a priest; they are truly precious. This is what a man who possesses the spirit of the land of Yamato says, even while being a man of the Buddhist faith. How could a Shinto believer or a scholar of poetics who possesses the spirit of China express himself the way Keichū did? Priest Keichū has taught the truth to the world. Shinto believers and scholars of poetics teach only falsehoods.

A Debate on Flowers[100]

When I think of flowers, I think of the cherry blossoms *(sakura)*; when I think of cherry blossoms, I think of the mountain cherries *(yamazakura)*.[101] Among them are those which bloom thick with flowers, with red shining leaves, slender, mixed with sparser bloom. Moreover, there are those whose beauty goes unmatched, which people think cannot be of this uncertain world, with green leaves and sparse flowers, blooming splendidly later than all other cherry trees. Basically speaking, there are many different types of mountain cherries. When one looks at them carefully, one notices slight differences in every tree; no two are the same. The many-layered cherry blossoms *(yaehitoe)*[102] are of a special beauty, truly appealing. When one looks up to the sky on a clouded day, they are particularly beautiful, blooming remarkably green at a time when the colors of all other flowers, including the pine trees, are not bright at all; their color is even further reinforced, and they look different from everything else. Their fragrance is remarkably different when one looks at them from the direction of the incoming sunshine on a clear day, when the sky is translucent. One would not even think that they are the same flowers! It goes without saying how beautiful they are in the morning sun.

In the light of the setting sun, among the plum blossoms *(ume)*, the red ones *(kōbai)* are truly fascinating when they burst open into bloom. However, it is truly regretful that, as they bloom, they become gradually white, losing all their appeal. They do not know how to scatter by the time the cherries have bloomed, and they do not have any fragrance; they age and shrink. When I look at them surviving, every spring, I am reminded of the pain of lingering in the world—a pain that is associated with everything.[103] The white plum blossoms are all fragrant but less appealing to the eye. Basically, plum blossoms are more remarkable when they are cut as twigs and put into a vase, so as to be looked at from close by, rather than being admired as treetops.

The peach blossoms *(momo no hana)*, which are quite superior from their treetops down, keep on blooming in great numbers. It is nice to look at them from a distance. However, if one observes them from close by, they look quite rustic. Japanese roses *(yamabuki)*, irises *(kakitsubata)*, pinks *(nadeshiko)*, bush clovers *(hagi)*, eulalias *(susuki)*, maiden flowers *(ominaeshi)*, and others, are appealing in their own ways. As for chrysanthemums *(kiku)*, they are good enough to be bred into new types. However, if they are arranged too beautifully and solemnly, they end up looking vulgar and unappealing. Azaleas *(tsutsuji)* bloom in great numbers in the wild and make one wake up filled with surprise. The flower called "aronia" *(kaidō)* looks Chinese; it is a beautiful, fine flower. Basically, this is what I think about flowers. Other people might feel differently, but this is not a matter that should be settled in the same way. There are many flowers in the world of which contemporary people are fond. And yet, the reason I did not mention them—and I did it intentionally—is that they are not sung in poems. The fact that they go unmentioned even in ancient documents make them unappealing to me—am I too cold-hearted? Again, this might simply be the result of a devious mind!

Focusing on Fragrance in Poems on Plum Blossoms[104]

Although poems on plum blossoms *(ume no hana)* usually focus on their fragrance, in the *Man'yōshū* there is only one poem which does so in book twenty, despite the many poems we find in the collection on this flower:

Ume no hana	Since superb is the fragrance
Ka o kaguwashimi	Of the plum blossoms,
Tōkedomo	No matter how far you are,
Kokoro mo shinuni	I will think of you
Kimi o shi zo omou.	Until my heart fades away.[105]

With this exception, we cannot find any other poem on this topic. On the whole, in the past people did not praise the fragrance of flowers. Although in the *Man'yōshū* we find many poems on the orange tree *(tachibana)*, only two sing its fragrance, one in book seventeen and one in eighteen.[106] Besides these poems, we only find one more poem on mushrooms in book ten, that says,

| *Takamato no* | Like an umbrella standing |
| *Kono mine mo se ni* | On this narrow peak |

Kasa tatete	Of Takamato,
Michisakaritaru	It fills autumn
Aki no ka no yosa	With a good fragrance.[107]

With these exceptions we do not find any other poem praising the fragrance of anything. The many poems on *nioi* (smell) are actually poems on the beauty of colors; they are not poems on the fragrance that can be smelled by the nose. Now, going back to the poem from book ten that I mentioned above, the poem sings about the mushroom known as *matsutake*.[108] A title precedes the poem that states, "a poem on fragrance" *(ka o yomu)*. The character for "fragrance" *(ka)* is a copyist's mistake for the character "mushroom" *(take)*.[109]

The Cherry and Orange Trees at the Stairway of the Shishinden[110]

The *Rekitai Hennen Shūsei* (The Collection of Chronicles of Various Generations)[111] states: "Originally, the cherry tree of the Shishinden was a plum tree. This tree was planted when Emperor Kammu[112] moved the capital to Heian. However, during the Shōwa era (834–847), the plum tree withered and died. Consequently, Emperor Ninmyō[113] planted a new tree. The tree was destroyed when the palace burned down. When the imperial palace was rebuilt, a cherry tree was moved from the house of Prince Rihō (Prince Shigeaki)[114] and planted here. The tree was originally a cherry tree from Mount Yoshino." It also says that, "However, in a head-note to a poem from the Shūishū by Lord Kintada[115] we read that 'during the Engi era (901–922) I saw the flowers of the Shishinden.' Therefore, does this mean that also prior to the Tentoku era (957–960) there was a cherry tree? This should be taken as the time when the switch between the plum tree and the cherry tree took place. Originally, this was the place where an orange tree grew. Prior to the transfer of the capital, this was the site of the house of Lord Tachibana." The *Bankiroku* (Record of a Watchman)[116] states that "during the reign of Emperor Murakami,[117] on the Seventh Day of the Twelfth Month of the Third Year of the Tentoku era (959), a new orange tree was moved and planted southwest of the Shishinden (it was three and a half yards high). This tree came from the house of the Prince Inspector of Eastern Sanjō, who gave it to the court following an imperial order. It was planted by the Captain of the Guards of the Right." Another document indicates that "At the time of the transfer of the capital the place where that tree was located was called Tachibana-tayu; it was the inner garden of the house of the person with the same name. In this garden there was an orange tree. This was the place that became the front of the Shishinden—something worthy of admiration! Later on, after a fire, the tree of the person from Eastern Sanjō was planted." *The Record of the Minister of the Left Small First Ward (Shōichijō Sadaijin Ki)* states that "the original owner of the orange tree was Hata no Yasukuni. The next fire took place on the Third Year of the Tentoku era (959)." The *Taikai Hishō*[118] indicates that "The orange tree of the Shishinden predates the construction of the imperial palace in this capital. Although it belonged to the person whose house was located here, being a tree, it was not cut down. The courtiers ate the oranges on the floor of the Shishinden, taking them directly from the tree's branches." I wonder whether this was true. Was that tree indeed the old one?[119]

On Calling the Cherry Blossoms "Flowers"[120]

Until the age of the *Kokinshū* the custom of calling the cherry blossoms simply "flowers" was unheard of. As he has argued in detail in *Yozai Shō*,[121] priest Keichū points out a passage on plum blossoms from the "Spring Shoots I" chapter[122] of the *Genji Monogatari* (The Tale of Genji), which says, "Why don't we line up the plum blossoms with the blossoms of the flowers, and take a look at them?" Clearly, in this passage the cherry blossoms are singled out, and they are referred to as "the flowers."

The Way of Poetry and the Cherry Blossoms[123]

The expressions "the way of Shikishima" *(Shikishima no michi)*,[124] and "the way of poetry" *(uta no michi)* became usual terms in later ages. However, when we look at the preface of the *Kokinshū*, we read the statement, "It may have happened because His Majesty was especially skilled in understanding the meaning of poetry *(uta no kokoro)*."[125] We also find the statements, "Since then, some people have understood the meaning of poetry *(uta no kokoro)*"[126] and "Although Hitomaro is dead, the practice of poetry *(uta no koto)* remains with us."[127] If these were all statements from a later age, then we would necessarily encounter the expression "the way of poetry" *(uta no michi)*. Instead, we find the expressions "the meaning of poetry" and "the practice of poetry"; the preface does not use the word "way" *(michi)*. In the Chinese preface[128] to the *Kokinshū* we find the expressions "this way" *(kono michi)*[129] and "our way" *(waga michi)*.[130] However, in the *kana* preface the word "way" is never associated with poetry.

Moreover, the expression *sakurabana* for "cherry blossoms" is also the product of a later age. In all the headnotes to the poems from the *Kokinshū*, only the expression *sakura no hana* appears. The word *sakurabana* appears only in poetry; not one single instance can be found in prose. Basically, this difference is associated with the difference between ancient language and more modern expressions in the composition of poetry and prose; or, the difference between classical Chinese and the language of our country; or, the mixing of poetic language and the language of prose. We should pay attention to all these issues, even if only slightly, and understand these differences. We should be alert to these things as we read and understand the *Kokinshū*.

The Logic of Priest Kenkō[131]

What should we think of Kenkō's question "Are we to look at cherry blossoms only in full bloom, the moon only when it is cloudless?"[132] When we look at ancient poems, we see that there are more poems on lamenting the wind under the blooming cherry trees and on despising the clouds on a moonlit night, or on waiting for the flowers to bloom and for the moon to come out, or on regretting the scattering of the cherry blossoms and the disappearance of the moon, than poems on seeing the cherries in full bloom, or the cloudless moon. These more numerous poems are also the most deeply inspired. The reason why these types of poems are more numerous is that everyone wants to see the cherry blossoms in full bloom and the moon with no clouds in front of it. They grieve over the fact that this is simply impossible. In which poem do you find someone who is waiting for the wind to scatter the blossoms, or who is praying for the clouds to trail over the moon? What this priest says is simply a violation of man's innermost feelings, the result of pretended smartness on the part of people living in later ages. This is a fake refinement; it is not the result of a truly refined heart. Kenkō made many statements like this, all of the same type. The creation of an aesthetic by opposing the feelings of most people lends itself to the formation of many artificial statements. The fact that, when it comes to love, love poems expressing joy at meeting one's beloved are not deeply inspired, whereas those lamenting the impossibility of the meeting are more numerous and more deeply felt, indicates the hope on the part of the poet to actually meet with his or her beloved. Since people are not as deeply moved by joy as they are by something that wounds their heart, all poems expressing joy are not deeply moving, whereas many of those expressing the sadness and distress of an unfulfilled heart are of profound inspiration. If this is the case, is the true sentiment of people to hope for being lonesome and sad, since these are refined feelings?

Moreover, the same priest argues that "To die, at the latest, before one reaches forty, is the least unattractive."[133] Since the Middle Ages everybody has been putting this line into poetry—a line that is on everybody's lips in their daily conversations. They argue that to hope for a long life is the sign of an impure heart, and that an early death is attractive. To say that to hate this world is an act of purity is flirting with the Buddhist way—a basic fallacy. They say it with their lips, but who would actually believe such a thing in his heart? Even if, in a rare case, someone were to truly believe this, such a belief would not come from his true and natural heart; it would be the result of having got lost in Buddhist teachings. No matter how lonesome one may be, the true nature of man does not make him willing to die an early death. There is no one who does not cherish life. Until the age of the *Man'yōshū*, poetry only prayed for a long life. Poems from the Middle Ages up to this day have reversed this desire. We should know that the violation of this general human desire and the idealization of what is different from reality have been carried over from foreign customs—an artificial concealment of the human heart.

The Habit of Creating Appearances[134]

The desire to eat good food, to wear good clothes, to live in a good house, to have money, to be respected by others, and to live a long life is part of everybody's true feelings. And yet everybody says that these are not good things, and that not to possess these desires is quite admirable. The fact that there are so many people in the world who pretend to be free from these desires and not to be asking for them is simply an annoying lie. Moreover, intellectuals whom the world looks upon as teachers,[135] or priests who are worshipped as saints,[136] whenever they see the moon and the flowers, pretend to praise them, saying how moving they are. And yet, when they see a beautiful woman, they pass by, feigning that they did not see her. Was that really true? If they were truly moved by the sight of the moon and the flowers, shouldn't they turn their eyes even more to a beautiful woman? To argue that moon and flowers are moving but the glow of a woman does not draw one's attention is not the product of a human heart. It is nothing but a terrible lie. This being the case, since to fabricate and to embellish appearances has become a habit everywhere, shouldn't we blame this habit and denounce it as a deceit?

On Paintings[137]

The drawing of a person's picture requires on the part of the painter the creation of a resemblance of the person drawn to the best of the painter's ability. He must strive to reproduce not only the person's face and outward looks with a perfect resemblance—something that goes without saying. He must also re-create a good resemblance of the person's attitude and of his garments. As a result, the picture of a person must be drawn with great attention to fine detail. However, in today's world,[138] painters simply strive to show the strength of their brush and give a graceful appearance to their paintings. They are not concerned at all with faithfully reproducing the true shapes of their models, and they do not even think that it is necessary to do so. Since they only aim at showing the strength of their brush and producing a graceful painting, they tend to simplify, without paying any attention to detail. As a result of their glib drawings, not only do the faces they paint not look like the originals, but they appear to be the vulgar faces of shabby mountain folks; these are not the virtuous faces of superior men. I truly detest these paintings!

Again on Paintings, 1[139]

In drawing people from the past, painters should strive to match the status and the knowledge of that person, since we do not know what those people looked like. The portrait of a nobleman should be elegant and should look like the portrait of a really noble person. A knowledgeable person should be portrayed exactly as a man of knowledge. However, artists of later ages did not share my belief. They only tried to show the power of their brush, drawing noblemen and men of learning as if they were vulgar peasants and ignorant fools.

Again on Paintings, 2[140]

Even when they paint an attractive woman with a beautiful face, these painters end up by drawing an ugly face as a result of their obsession with the power of the brush. Apparently, they say that by making the face too graceful, the painting becomes vulgar. However, I believe this happens with bad paintings. One should draw a beautiful face and make a nice painting. There is no reason to depict a beautiful face unattractively for fear of creating a bad painting. One should do his best to make the face of an attractive woman beautiful. It is very unpleasant to see an ugly face. And yet, in today's world, we cannot say that Edo paintings[141] are bad because they force themselves to present beautiful faces. In these paintings the faces look quite ugly; many of them are truly bad paintings.

Again on Paintings, 3[142]

There is a genre of painting called "warrior paintings" that depict scenes of fierce warriors fighting each other. Their faces and outward appearances do not look human. Their eyes are round and big; their nose is angry, and their mouth enormous. They look entirely like demons. I wonder whether these warriors are drawn like demons rather than like human beings in order to show the fierceness of their acts. I believe that they should be represented as human beings, in a very calm manner, but with the fierceness and the power of a real warrior. Talking about the pictures of our country, a Chinese treatise[143] says that people in these pictures look like supernatural demons.[144] Now that I think about it, this treatise must have referred to warrior pictures, in which people *are* portrayed like demons. As a result, after reading this treatise, people of that country[145] who have never seen anybody from our land, might think that all Japanese faces look exactly like those of demons. People from our land know everything about China, as they read so many books from that land. People from China, on the other hand, do not know anything about our land, as they do not read our books. When, on some rare occasion, a reference is made to our land in one of their books, whatever is written becomes a rule. When someone from a foreign land looks at the people of our country as portrayed in pictures, those images become standards for them. As a result, foreigners who look at the portraits of noblemen looking like mountain rustics, or at the paintings of beautiful women whose faces look ugly, think that all Japanese are shabby and that all their women are unattractive. This is not something that happens only with foreigners. Even people from this land who have once seen in a painting the face of someone who lived in a past that is unknown to them, might think that this is actually the way this ancient person looked in real life!

Again on Paintings, 4[146]

Although, since I do not know anything about painting, it seems that there is nothing further that I should say on the matter without knowing what is good and bad about many things, I can still see very well from the sideline. It is the same thing with all the other arts. Experts say that people with half-knowledge of the arts can see the good and bad points of those arts better than other people. One with some taste for painting would say what I am saying now. Since I have not seen many ancient Japanese and Chinese paintings from different ages, and since I do not know the subject in detail, I will leave it at that. I will speak only about what I usually see in the present age. First of all, among the several genres of monochrome black-and-white paintings *(sumie),* thinly colored *sumie (usuzaishiki),* fully colored paintings *(gokusaishiki),* and others, Indian-ink drawings *(sumie)* stick ink onto the paper and come with a few strokes of the brush; they tend to simplify everything, showing smooth and easy lines. Since the major purpose of these works is to show the strength of the brush, a truly skillful artist will truly have to paint with power. Although there is something attractive in these paintings, the *sumie* of most artists are uninteresting and unpleasant. However, to praise Indian-ink drawings as particularly beautiful is a trend and habit of this age. In reality, there is nothing truly interesting in them. Recently, people in love with the practice of the so-called tea ceremony have concentrated their praise only on these black-and-white paintings. They never choose painting with colors. As a matter of fact, these people are not doing it consciously; they simply guard the tastes established by the ancestors of this art. This is how things have come into being. Everything that is praised in the tea ceremony, including paintings and calligraphy, has no appeal whatsoever, and no beauty. The stubborn preservation and worship of these traditions show the incredible stiffness of this way of thinking. Now, thinly colored *sumie* are appealing, gentle, and beautiful. As for fully colored paintings, there are some which are praiseworthy; sometimes they can be annoying to the point of being loud. Those which are painted with water mixed with a deep blue color are particularly annoying.

When it comes to painting styles, there are several, all based on specific schools that have been active since times long past. Generally speaking, the paintings of these schools follow the tradition of each school, adhering strongly to their rules. They never enquire about the real shapes of the painted objects. The painting of each school follows the school's rules when it comes to good and bad things. It is truly unpleasant to see the face of a nobleman portrayed like a rustic person, or to see the face of a beautiful woman painted plump and ugly. It is also primitive to draw so thickly the lines of the folds in somebody's garments. This is all due to the attempt to show off the power of one's brush. When people draw a pine tree from China, they have a type called

"Chinese pine tree" in their minds. When they have to paint a different pine tree, they learn by imitating the painting of an ancient Chinese master, thinking that this is the way this specific pine tree should be. It is not that in China the pine trees are different; it only means that the painter is unable to paint a common pine tree. And yet, there is a good side to preserving and transmitting traditions—a truly beautiful act. Generally, among the many paintings, the most annoying and unpleasant are Indian-ink drawings painted shabbily, Chinese pine trees, the thick lines of the folds of people's garments, and also images of Bodhidharma,[147] Hotei, and Fukurokuju.[148] It is annoying to look at these paintings once; one would not think of looking at them a second time. Although, in general, to guard ancient rules is a good thing, this all depends on the circumstances and on the things to which they are applied. Painting is definitely not one of the things to which ancient rules should be applied. Not to be able to draw something beautiful that one sees with his eyes and that is not codified by rules shows the stiffness of one's mind. And yet, there are several rules when it comes to the drawing of a house that are quite good, such as, for example, stepping away from the roof and looking inside the house; or, getting behind the clouds and understanding perspective. These are rules that should be respected; if they are not, many bad results follow. To abandon one's paintings to the fancy of the day makes it hard for artists to come up with a good painting.

Moreover, in today's world there are many examples of imitations known as "the China style." Their general rule is to observe the object well and to paint it by imitation, no matter what one plans to represent. People call this kind of painting "live sketches." I personally believe that this is a truly excellent way of painting. However, there are differences between the real object and the painting. Trying to draw something as it really is might actually produce a painting that does not look like the real thing. In this case as well one could end up with a bad painting. This is why each school has its own rules. There are necessarily things that are not included in the principle of painting the truth of things just as they are. This is the beautiful aspect of rules, and the reason why they are so difficult to discard. For example, Japanese landscape paintings are quite good, independent of the school producing them. Chinese paintings of the same genre are extremely bad. One finds in them many rough spots that are unpleasant to the eye. These paintings are bad because they do not follow any rule; they are simply the product of fancy. A road is painted in a place where there should not be any road; a bridge appears where there is no need for one. Besides, boulders, grasses, and trees are painted in the wrong spots. Most paintings have too few in the right spots, and too many in the wrong ones. These are all flaws in a painting. The images of grasses, trees, and rocks rooted deep in the ground, and the form of steep peaks are drawn so unskillfully. One finds these deficiencies even in good paintings. It is because of the presence of specific rules in each school that paintings become appealing.

Furthermore, in Chinese paintings boats are often painted askew—a truly bad habit! Although generally we see boats proceeding diagonally, once this movement is reproduced in a painting, the result is bad. With the diagonal movement the boat does not look as if it were floating flat on the water; it looks as if it is going to capsize, stern up. This failure derives from representing the real boat as it is without following rules. Furthermore, although paintings of birds and insects tend to be extremely precise down to the finest detail, many of them lack the power of flight and movement. Another deficiency is the lack of line drawing in the leaves and stems of painted grasses and trees. Although the practice of avoiding the drawing of contours follows the fact that in reality these contours do not exist, in painting the absence of these lines takes clarity away from the image. In reality, everything comes with an outline where one does not see any; it does not come with a color. If one uses a color such as white to define contours, it becomes difficult to separate objects from each other. This is why it is impossible to avoid the use of lines—something that Chinese paintings have a hard time understanding. Although portraits of people are known as "Chinese paintings," they do not follow the practice of avoiding line drawing. Furthermore, in Chinese paintings the ramifications of trees, the roots of flowers, and the placement of leaves do not follow any rules. Since everything is left to the artist's fancy, there are no regulations. Basically, this is the unappealing side of Chinese paintings. Nevertheless, compared to the paintings of the schools in our land, the Chinese paintings of beasts and birds, insects, fishes, grasses, and plants are drawn with such fine details and with such superior skill that they have an astonishing resemblance to, and look exactly like, their subject matters. Because, in the paintings of our schools, details such as the animals' fur, the birds' wings, the stamens of flowers on grasses and trees, the patterns on leaves, and so on, are drawn coarsely, in many instances our paintings are overwhelmed in comparison to Chinese paintings. This is due to the fact that our paintings are produced for large screens and walls of houses. It would be meaningless to paint with too much fine detail, since these paintings are meant to be looked at from far away. Although this is not a very good practice, it explains why our paintings are drawn with easy strokes of the brush. Yet Chinese paintings, rich in details, look quite superior to ours. Generally speaking, there are merits and deficiencies in the paintings of our schools as well as in Chinese paintings; it is like those instances in which it is difficult to assess who wins and who loses. Moreover, in recent years there have been many examples of paintings that are not concerned with house rules, and that do not rely on Chinese models. Many artists follow their own ideas and go where their tastes take them. Since they decide how to choose what is good and discard what is bad, in the end, one cannot see any good work.

The Beginning of Poetry[149]

Someone asked the question, "What is your definite answer on the beginning of poetry?" I gave the following reply: Since the expression "the beginning of poetry" is nowhere to be found either in the *Kojiki* (Record of Ancient Matters) or in the *Nihongi* (Chronicles of Japan), I can say that the matter is not clear. However, the first poem to be recorded in both works is the famous divine poem, "Many Clouds" *(Yakumo)*.[150] It is recorded in the *Kojiki* as follows:

> When this great deity first built the palace of Suga, clouds rose from that place. He made a song, which said:

Yakumo tatsu	The many-fenced palace of Izumo
Izumo yaegaki	Of the many clouds rising—
Tsumagomi ni	To dwell there with my spouse
Yaegaki tsukuru	Do I build a many-fenced palace:
Sono yaegaki o	Ah, that many-fenced palace![151]

In the *Nihongi* we find the variation *tsumagome ni*.[152] We find also recorded a different character indicating the sound *"mi."*[153]

Since ancient times there have been many distorted theories about the interpretation of this poem—theories that are all ignorant of the past. Therefore, we should not accept them.[154] We should not be led astray by unorthodox theories. In the *Yozai Shō* we find the following explanation: "Since the character *'ya'* (lit., eight) indicates 'a great number' of things, the word *'yakumo'* (lit., eight clouds) is the same as *'yaegumo,'* many layers of clouds. The word *'yae'* (manifold) works in the same way as in the expressions *'yaezakura'* (double-flowered cherry tree) and *'yaeyamabuki'* (double-flowered Japanese yellow rose), which are given this name although they are not necessarily eightfold.

With regard to the word *'izumo,'* since the name Izumo was given to the province after this poem was made, and it actually came from this poem, the first verse *'yakumo tatsu'* (many clouds rising) should not be taken as a pillow-word *(makurakotoba)* of the geographical name Izumo.[155] We should understand *'izumo'* as a contraction of *'izuru kumo'* (rising clouds), a repetition of the preceding *'yakumo'* (many clouds)."[156]

I personally believe that the verse *"Yakumo tatsu"* (many clouds rising) points to the fact that the poet saw those clouds rising, and sang, *"Iyakumo tatsu"* (numberless clouds rising).[157] With regard to the word *izumo*, even the *Gazetteer* indicates that the name of the province derives from this poem.[158] Therefore, in this poem the poet did not sing the name of the province. He simply said, "Rising clouds," or, "clouds that are coming out." To take *izumo* for the name of the province and *yakumo tatsu* as its pillow word is a mistake. This is not a pillow word as in the cases of "sprouting ears of rice" *(yaodate o)*[159] or "my bright Soga" *(masogayo)*.[160] The word *yaegaki* (eight-layered fences) stands for *iyaegaki* (many layers of fences). This does not refer to the real walls of the Suga palace. The poet simply used the word "fence" to point at the clouds. The fact that the poet used the attributive form of the verb *tatsu* (to rise),[161] and did not simply say, *yakumo tachi* (the clouds rise) using the conjunctive form, shows that he composed the poem while he was looking at the clouds. In other words, the expression *izumo yaegaki* indicates the fence of clouds that appeared to the poet while he was looking; it means, "many layered fences of rising clouds." *Tsumagomi ni yaegaki tsukuru* means, "The clouds built many layers of fences in order to hide my wife from sight now." Someone might wonder how clouds can build a fence. However, here we are not dealing with a real act of construction. Seeing the clouds rising, the poet said, "They built a multilayered fence." The word *kaki* (fence) has the same meaning that it took in later ages, as when we people said that clouds of dew rise, hiding things from sight by creating a distance between these things and us. Even abroad people used the expression "Clouds have already risen/ making fences in the sky."[162] It would be a mistake to take these fences as the walls of the Suga palace; they are simply clouds.[163] The repetition, *sono yaegaki o* (ah, those many layers of fences!) is a common feature in the poetry of the ancient age. The repetition of the upper verse has become very popular in songs again; the same technique is used in the contemporary humming tunes of young people.[164] This is the very nature of songs; we see refrains even in the poetry of China.[165] The exclamation *"o"* (ah!) at the end of the poem is the same as the *"o"* at the end of the exchange between the two ancestral deities.[166] Since this was the time when he was building the Suga palace, seeing the rising clouds the poet transformed them in his imagination to "many layers of walls." The whole poem is a song on the clouds.

> Many clouds rising,
> Many layered clouds raising a manifold-fence
>   Hiding my bride from sight,
> Clouds are forming a manifold fence,
> Ah, that manifold fence!

On Songs (Uta)[167]

"Song" *(uta)* is the indeclinable noun of "to sing" *(utafu)*; "to sing" is the inflected form of "song."[168] "To sing" *(utafu)* is the same word as "to appeal to someone" *(uttafu)*.[169] There are many examples of indeclinable nouns that take an inflected form by adding the inflectional suffixes "*ha, hi, fu, he, ho,*" or "*ma, mi, mu, me, mo,* and so on." For example, "dwelling" *(yado)* becomes "to dwell" *(yadoru)*; "room" *(wi)* becomes "to sit down" *(wiru)*; "belly" *(hara)* becomes "to be pregnant" *(haramu)*; "cuts" *(kiza)* becomes "to cut" *(kizamu)*; "negation" *(ina)* becomes "to deny" *(inamu)*; "rest" *(yasu)* becomes "to rest" *(yasumu)*; "bundle" *(tsuka)* becomes "to bundle" *(tsukanu)*; "rope" *(tsuna)* becomes "to tie" *(tsunagu)*. The roots of all these words are indeclinable nouns to which a conjugated suffix is added in order for them to become inflected verbs. For example, the indeclinable noun "song" *(uta)* can become "to sing" *(utafu)*, or "let's sing" *(utawamu)*, or "singing" *(utahi)*, or "sing!" *(utahe)*.[170] Generally, this class of inflected forms ends in either *ra, ri, ru, re,* or, *ma, mi, mu, me,* as we can see from the examples above. Inflected forms ending in *ha, hi, fu, he,* are rare.[171] This is something people should ponder.

Furthermore, there are inflected forms that are made with the addition of two syllables to the indeclinable noun: "taste" *(aji)* becomes "to appreciate" *(ajiwafu)*; "friend" *(tomo)* becomes "to accompany" *(tomonafu)*; "offerings" *(mahi)* becomes "to bribe" *(mahinafu)*, and so on. The meaning remains the same. In later ages it has become difficult to understand which one was the original form: did the indeclinable noun come first, later becoming an inflected form, or did indeclinable nouns come into being by losing the end of inflected forms? Moreover, the word known nowadays as "songs of the Noh theater" *(utahi)* is the transformation of the inflected form "to sing" *(utafu)* into a noun. The following verbs belong to the same class: "to think" *(omofu)*, "to smell" *(nihofu),* "to worship" *(matsuru),* "to cross" *(wataru),* "to fan" *(afugu),* "to proceed" *(omomuku),* and "to lament" *(nageku).* When they are pronounced "thought" *(omohi),* "smell" *(nihohi),* "festival" *(matsuri),* "transit" *(watari),* "fan" *(afuki),* "disposition" *(omomuki),* and "grief" *(nageki),* they are all indeclinable nouns. In other words, they become so thanks to *ki, shi, chi, hi, mi, ri,* and so on. "Song" *(utahi)* is another example. Furthermore, "to teach" *(woshifuru),* "to help" *(tasukuru),* "to establish a procedure" *(tsuizuru),* "to perform" *(shiraburu)* are all inflected forms. They become indeclinable nouns thanks to *e, ke, se, te, ne, he, me, re:* "teaching" *(oshihe),* "help" *(tasuke),* "order" *(tsuide),* and "tune" *(shirabe).*

Question: How do people come to say, "to recite" *(eizuru)* a poem, and "to make" *(yomu)* a poem?

Answer: The Japanese reading of the character *"ei"* is *"nagamuru"* (to sing). It means to compose and recite a poem. *Nagamuru* means "to make something last long" *(nagō suru)*—a long reverberation of the voice *(nagaku koe wo hikite).* This verb is in the same class as "to widen" *(hiromuru),* "to strengthen" *(katamuru),* "to scorn" *(iyashiusuru).* The character *"ei"* fits the meaning of *nagamuru* well. The *Shu-ching* (Classic of Documents) says, "The poem articulates what is on the mind purposefully; song makes language last long."[172] The *Li-chi* (Record of Ritual) states, "Song makes the voice last long. The word "song" means to make the word last a long time." The *Shuo-wen chieh-tzu* (Explanation of Simple and Compound Graphs) says, "The word 'yong' *(ei, nagamuru)* means 'song' *(ge).* It also means to sing a song, to make a poem, or, to make words last long." When I ponder over all these definitions, I realize that originally *utafu* and *nagamuru* meant the same thing, "to sing."

The word *nagamuru* was probably attached to the character *"ei."* Today we commonly use *nagamuru* to indicate the act of looking at something earnestly. The act of staring at something while being deeply immersed in thoughts as a result of grief is expressed in songs through the word *nagamuru.* The verse, "Time I spend staring, lost in thoughts/in the long rains of springtime," is an example.[173] In colloquial language as well the word *nagamuru* is used to express the act of staring, of looking far away. All these examples point toward a meaning that is very different from the meaning of the character *"ei"* with the reading of *nagamuru* as "to sing." The word *nagamuru* expressed with the character *"ei"* does not mean "to look at things." Now that I come to think about it, I realize that in the *Man'yōshū* there are several poems with the indication, "singing *(eizu)* the sky in a poem," "singing the moon," "singing the clouds," "singing the rain," "singing a mountain," "singing the hills," "singing a river," "singing the dew," "singing the leaves," "singing the moss," "singing the grass," "singing the birds," "singing a well," "singing a Yamato harp *(koto).*" All these expressions refer to the act of composing and singing a variety of things in a poem. Both expressions *tsuki wo eizu* and *tsuki wo nagamuru* mean "to compose a poem on the moon" *(tsuki wo yomu).* However, since this is a poem on the act of looking at the moon, *nagamuru* (to sing) came to be identified with the meaning of "to see." I wonder whether by identifying *nagamuru* with the act of looking at various things, the word *nagamuru* came to be used with the meaning of "looking at something." Among the poems mentioned above are also a few poems on things that do not appear in front of the poet's eyes. And yet, to be looking while waiting for the moon conveys the meaning of "looking at the moon," since the poet is in the mood of waiting for the moon, which has not yet appeared. Accordingly, although the expression *sore o nagamuru* meant "to compose a poem on such and such a thing," it came to be used with the meaning of "to look at such and such a thing." Even today, the meaning of *nagamuru* is slightly different from "having a quick look at something." It has the meaning conveyed by the character *"kan"*: to look with great attention, and to ponder over what one sees.

The word *yomu* (to compose a poem) appears in the book on "The Age of the Gods," in which we read, "He composed a verse of poetry, saying" *(utayomi shite notamawaku).*[174] The meaning of the characters *"utayomi shite notamawaku"* is, "he expressed it by singing it." This means that the poet at a certain time composed a poem on events that had occurred earlier, singing them in a song. Although one might think that there are no examples of the use of the character "this" *(kore)* in the grammatical structure of the *Nihongi* (Chronicles of Japan), actually there are many examples. Accordingly, the expression *utayomi shite* does not really mean "to sing this"; it simply means "song." Even in *kanbun* there are many examples in which we find the characters *"utōte iwaku"* (to express singing). Although here we are faced with the difference between a nominal usage—"to express in a song" *(uta ni iwaku)*, and a verbal usage, "to express singing" *(utōte iwaku)*, the meaning of the sentences remains the same: to sing in a song.

Therefore, in the expression *utayomi suru* (to make a song), "song" *(uta)* is the indeclinable noun, and "to make" *(yomu)* is the inflected form. However, we can also say that a conjugated suffix has been added, so that *utayomi* (song) is an indeclinable noun, and *su* (to make) is an inflected form. When one thinks about this matter carefully, one realizes that the character *"uta"* 歌 can be pronounced either *"uta,"* or *"utayomu,"* or *"utayomi suru"*: they all mean the same thing, "to make a song." Therefore, since it already appears in "The Age of the Gods," the expression *uta wo yomu* (to make a song) is quite ancient. However, I have not yet seen any example of the character *"ei"* read as *"yomu."* This must be a more recent usage. Nowadays we find the expression *utayomi suru* used by girls to indicate the act of making a song. It is an ancient expression. When I think about this matter, keeping in mind everything I have said so far, it is hard to tell whether the word *yomu* in the expression *utayomu* which appears in "The Age of the Gods" means "to sing," or whether it simply means "to make a song." As I mentioned earlier, since "song" *(uta)* is the indeclinable noun of the inflected form "to sing" *(utafu)*, it seems that in ancient times *uta* meant "to sing sustaining the voice for a long time." If this is the case, then the word *yomu* in *utayomi suru* sounds as if it meant "to sing." However, if it meant "to sing," it should have been *utōte iwaku* (to express singing). The reason is that, since "to sing" *(utafu)* is the inflected form of "song" *(uta)*, the simple mentioning of the word *utafu* meant "to sing a song" *(uta wo utafu)*. Putting the word *uta* (song) at the beginning of the sentence was like including the meaning of "to sing" *(utafu)* in that very word. If this is correct, then I think that *yomu* meant to produce the song to be sung. Accordingly, this expression would fit well the contemporary usage of *uta wo yomu*—to make a song. Furthermore, today, when we use the word *yomu* to indicate the act of reading a written text, we employ the following two Chinese characters: 読 (to read) and 誦 (to recite). Even these verbs do not simply mean "to look at a text"; they imply an oral recitation. As the *Chou-li* (Rites of Chou) says, "To articulate a tune with the voice is called 'to read'" (Ch. *song*; J. *yomu*).

Additionally, the act of counting something is also expressed with the word *yomu*. In this case as well, we count numbers—two, three, four—aloud. In any event, it is not a mistake to take the word *yomu* in the expression *uta wo yomu* to mean "making a song." When we say *"utafu,"* this verb certainly means to sing sustaining the voice for a long time. When we say *"nagamuru,"* it would be a mistake to interpret it as "seeing." The word *yomu* includes within itself both meanings of "singing" *(utafu)* and "reciting" *(nagamuru)*. However, it also means "to produce," as proof is found in "The Age of the Gods." Moreover, the use of the character *"ei"* to indicate the word *yomu* in *utayomu* is not a mistake; it is actually correct.

Question: I have understood in great detail the meaning of the words *utafu*, *yomu*, *eizuru*, and *nagamuru*. What is the meaning of *shi* (poem) and *uta* (song)?

Answer: The character used in China to indicate "poem" *(shi)* is nothing but what we call *"uta"* in this land; it is a correct fit. It is more correct to read the character *"shi"* as *uta* than applying the reading *uta* to the character 歌 *(uta)*. There is a reason for this that I need to explain in some detail. First of all, since ancient times commentaries of earlier scholars have only been focused on the explanation of the meaning of the characters *"uta"* and *"ei."* They never interpreted the meaning of the words *uta*, *nagamuru*, *yomu*, or what the characters 歌 *(uta)* and 詠 *(ei)* meant. What's the reason? All characters are loan signs; they are far from being essential. Nevertheless, why is it that, from the beginning, Chinese characters and the words of our land were understood as one single thing? This was an enormous mistake. People did not realize that originally characters were borrowed and attached to words—a truly laughable practice! Although people understand that in *kanbun* the Japanese reading of characters does violence to the meaning of those characters, no one seems to realize that Chinese characters do violence to the meaning of the words of our land. It should go without saying that if the Japanese reading of *kanji* harms their meaning, characters harm the language of our land. Therefore, to interpret words according to the characters is like inquiring about the inessential, and forgetting what is truly important. There are characters that fit our language perfectly; others that fit it to a certain degree; and there are characters that do not fit at all. For example, characters of the type of sun *(hi)*, moon *(tsuki)*, mountain *(yama)*, and sea *(umi)* are perfect fits. Characters for "to soften" *(yawaragu)* and "yet" *(imada)* are partial successes. The writing of the words "to think about it" *(omoheraku)* and "if" *(tatohi)* are absolute failures. In words such as "with" *(motte)* and "in other words" *(sunawachi)*, there is a big discrepancy between the words, the *kanji*, and their meanings. Keeping all this in mind, I wonder how it is possible to focus only on the meaning of the character for "song" *(uta)* without asking whether this *kanji* fits the meaning of the word *uta*. It would be useless to concentrate on the meaning of the character if this does not fit the meaning of the word *uta*. We should pay great attention to this matter.

First of all, the "songs" *(uta)* of our land are the "poems" *(shi)* of China. The *Yu-shu Shun tien* (Documents of Yu, Canon of Shun)[175] says, "The poem *(shi)* articulates what is on the mind purposefully *(chi)*; song *(ge*; J. *uta)* makes language *(yan)* last long *(yong)*."[176] In this quotation, poem and song are not two different things. The meaning of this passage is that a poem *(shi)* is the expression of one's will; it is called a song *(uta)* when it is sung for a while. In any case, the character for *uta* means "to sing" *(utafu)* and is the inflected form of *"shi."* Therefore, it has been explained as what "lasts long,"[177] and as "what is recited while sustaining the voice for a long time." As a result, the use of the word *uta* as a reading of the character *"shi,"* and the use of the word *utafu* as a reading of the character *"uta"* are perfect matches between the meaning of the character and the meaning of the word. The character *"shi"* was never used as an inflected form; on the other hand, the character for *uta* has often been used as an inflected form. In later ages, in China as well as Japan, people used the word "song" *(ge; uta)* and meant "poem" *(shi)*. There are many instances in which the expression *ge shi yue* is used. What is the meaning of this expression? Is it "To express something with a poem that is sung?" or is it "To express something by singing a poem?" Or is it like saying "songs and poems" while meaning "poems"? Well, it is all of the above. In later ages, poems *(shi)* came to be directly called "songs" *(uta)*. However, originally things were as I have described them above: "poem" *(shi)* is the indeclinable noun, while "song" *(uta)* is the inflected form. Therefore, in our land, when we mean "song" *(uta)* we should actually write it with the character for "poem" *(shi)*. The reason why we do not do so is that from ancient times we have been composing poems in Chinese in our land. If we were going to use the character *"shi"* to indicate "poems" *(uta)*, then we would be confusing Japanese songs with Chinese poems. Furthermore, since the character *"uta"* fits the meaning of the word "song" perfectly, this character came to be read both as "song" *(uta)* and as "to sing" *(utafu)*. Moreover, the reason why the character for *uta* fits the meaning of "song" so well is, first of all, that, although the character for "poem" *(shi)* means exactly what our word "song" *(uta)* means, the meaning of "song" *(uta)* fits the meaning of the character for *uta* perfectly. The reason is that, as I have already explained, *uta* (song) has the same meaning as *utafu* (to sing). In addition, even in China, when they say "song" *(ge)*, this word becomes an indeclinable noun, thus also coming to mean "poem" *(shi)*. Accordingly, there is no problem whatsoever with the use of the character *"uta."* The same thing applies to the other *kanji* applied to the word *uta*— 哥 and 謌.

Question: If, in order to refer to a Japanese poem, it is sufficient to use the word "song" *(uta)*, how do you explain the existence of the expression, "song from Yamato" *(Yamato uta)*?[178]

Answer: The expression "song from Yamato" is the result of a later age; it did not exist in ancient times. This name was given to songs after poems *(shi)* came from the Chinese land. In China people also called their poems "songs" *(ge; uta)*. Since they also had the same style of poetry as our songs, and since we had been reading the character *"ge"* as *uta* for a long time, it would have been confusing simply to use the word *uta* to single out our poems, as we were also referring to Chinese songs as *uta*. Moreover, the name *Yamato uta* also stands for our local poetic production, in contraposition to Chinese poems *(shi)*. Later on, the character *"shi"* came to be read *Kara uta* (Chinese song), in order to distinguish it from *Yamato uta* (song from the land of Yamato). In the preface to the *Kokinshū*, Ki no Tsurayuki refers to Chinese poems *(shi)* as *"Kara uta."*[179] Poems *(shi)* are the songs of China *(Kara uta)*. That is because songs *(uta)* are the poems *(shi)* of our land. However, in order to be more precise, we should say, *"Kara no uta,"* the songs *of* China. We should not use the expression *"Yamato uta."* The reason is that, while the character *"uta"* exists in China as well, what we call *uta* does not exist in any other country. Accordingly, we should record the word "song" *(uta)* with the characters *"waka"* 倭歌 —the song of Japan. However, while writing the word *waka*, we should pronounce these two characters *"uta"* only. In China they do not call their own poems the poems of China. Ultimately, in order to avoid any confusion with Chinese poems and songs, we should refer to our songs with the characters *"waka"* (倭歌 and 和歌), while pronouncing them *"uta."* Otherwise, we should say *"waka."* When there is no reason for confusion, then it would be better to simply use the character *"uta"* 歌. However, it would be reasonable to use the characters *"waka"* 和歌 when writing in Chinese on a piece of fine paper for poetic purposes. To pronounce these characters *"Yamato uta"* would sound quite vulgar. There is a reason why the expression *"Yamato uta"* appears at the beginning of the preface to the *Kokinshū*.[180] I have mentioned this elsewhere.[181]

With regard to any other things, aside from a few variations between Japan and China, they tend to be the same. For example, Chinese people and people from our land are the same. There is no difference between the mountains of Yamato and Chinese mountains. The water is the same. In all these cases no distinction is made between Japanese and Chinese. We should start talking about a person from Yamato or a person from China only when confusion arises at the time when we go out and meet with the other. No such things as "Japanese water" *(Yamato mizu)* or "Chinese water" *(Kara mizu)* exist, since they are absolutely the same. Only when it comes to language do we find major differences. Therefore, although the content of Chinese songs and poems and of Japanese poems *(uta)* is the same, the language is profoundly different. Accordingly, despite the fact that there are songs *(ge)* in China, no such thing as an *"uta"* exists. Therefore, we should be writing the word *uta* with the characters for *waka* 和歌, Japanese song; there is no need to call it *Yamato uta*, a song from Yamato. Although what I just said is quite logical, in reality the expression *Yamato uta* has been handed down from ancient times. The use of words such as *Wa* (Yamato), *Kan* (Han China), *Yamato* (Japan), and *Morokoshi* (China) is not unreasonable, considering the need to create distinctions because of the confusion arising from the fact that everything was crossing from China to our land. Logically speaking, every single thing that comes from China should be labeled "Chinese" by adding one of the words indicating China—*Tō, Kan,* or *Kara*. To label our local products "Japanese" by adding to the word either *Wa* (和 and 倭) or *Yamato* would be extremely vulgar. This should only be done with things for which there is a concern about confusion between the Chinese and the Japanese counterpart.

Question: Don't you think that the expression "to sing a song" *(uta wo eizuru)* sounds strange with its repetition?

Answer: As you point out in your question, the meaning of the two characters is the same: to sing while sustaining the voice for a long time. We find the quotation, "The word *'ei'* means 'song' *(uta).*"[182] It should say, "to sing a poem" *(shi wo eizuru);* it cannot say, "to sing a song" *(uta wo eizuru)*. In Chinese writings we find the expression *"yong ge."* It does not say, "to sing a song." Literally, it says, "song song." It means, "to make and sing a poem," by using a repetition of two different characters with the same meaning. We also find an expression with the same meaning but reversed characters, *kaei*. The reading *"uta wo eizuru"* is Japanese. No one would understand if you read these two characters *"uta wo nagamuru."* However, since we have the expression *utayomi suru* (to compose a verse of poetry while singing it), there would not be any problem if we read the two characters 詠歌 *"uta wo yomu"* (to make and recite a song). As I have explained in detail above, it is correct to read the character *"ei"* as *"yomu."* Moreover, since in this land we use the character *"uta"* (song) instead of *"shi"* (poem), we can say, *"uta wo eizuru"* (to make and sing a Japanese song) in order to avoid confusing this sentence with *"shi wo eizuru"* (to make and sing a Chinese poem). It is another way to say *"utayomu"* (to make and recite a song), although the meaning of the characters is different. Nowadays it is extremely rare to listen to someone singing a song *(uta wo utafu)*. People only make songs. Accordingly, the word *uta* (song), the character *"ka"* 歌, the word *nagamuru* (to recite), and the character *"ei"* 詠, have taken on meanings that are different from their original meanings. However, taking as proof the expression *utayomi suru*, which appears in the book on "The Age of the Gods," we should be justified in writing the characters *"uta wo eizuru"* and reading them as *"uta wo yomu"*—to make and sing a song. Even today it is quite common in China to sing a poem *(shi wo utafu)*. However, independently from whether a poem is sung or is simply made, they use the characters *"yong"* 詠 and *"ge"* 歌. The same thing should apply to us.

Again on Songs[183]

A person asked me the following question: "How do you explain the fact that people refer to our poetry as either *Yamato uta* or *waka* 倭歌?[184]

The following is my reply: The expression *Yamato uta* is not ancient. It came into existence after people began to write the characters for *waka* 倭歌, as a way of reading these characters.

Question: Then I would like, first of all, to know a little more about the word *waka*.

Answer: In ancient times no one used the word *waka*, which is why it can be found neither in the *Kojiki* (Record of Ancient Matters) nor in the *Nihongi* (Chronicles of Japan): one only finds the word *uta*. The word *waka* came about only after this became a world in which all knowledge was based exclusively on texts from China and we began to write poetry in Chinese. Moreover, because people were writing songs *(uta)* in China as well, confusion arose as to whether people were referring to Chinese or Japanese songs. As a result, the songs of this land came to be called *waka*. There are two interpretations of this name. The first indicates that the name *waka* was modeled after the Chinese practice of differentiating songs *(ge)* in the songs of Qi *(seika)* and the songs of Chu *(soka)*, so that someone called our poetry the songs of Wa *(waka)*, or songs of Yamato. According to the second theory, the name *waka* was made in contraposition to Chinese songs and poems. I personally prefer the second hypothesis since, generally speaking, there are many things that came to be contrasted as either Chinese or Japanese. I mentioned both hypotheses because, although they look the same, their implications are slightly different.

The first documents in which we find the word *waka* are book five of the *Man'yōshū*, "Four *waka* written on the day a farewell party was held at the library" (an event that took place in 730);[185] and book twenty of the same collection, "The former Retired Empress addressed the princes who were following her, and said, 'All princes should present their *waka* to me.'"[186] We find many instances in documents in *kanbun*, in addition to examples found in the several *National Histories* beginning with the *Nihon Kōki* (Japan's Later Chronicles).[187] This is what one would expect. Although the name *waka* is not something that should be recorded, not even briefly, in works in the native *kana* syllabary, after people became used to this word, it came to be seen in tales *(monogatari)* and other works.[188]

Writings dealing only with songs, even if they are in *kanbun*, should simply use the word *uta*. This explains why the *Man'yōshū*, in which the headnotes are all in *kanbun*, records only the word *uta*. There are only two instances in which the word *waka* is used, as I just mentioned. There is a reason for this. The author of the poem in book five wanted to clarify that he was not going to compose a Chinese poem *(shi)*, but a Japanese song *(uta)*. In book twenty, since the request to compose poems was coming from an empress, the poet wanted to avoid confusing his reader into believing that Chinese poems *(shi)* were solicited. With these two exceptions the characters "*waka*" 倭歌 are nowhere to be found. We can see here and there *waka* written with different characters (和歌). However, this word means "poem in response," as we can see in later collections in which the same expression is recorded as *kaeshi* (envoy).[189] The character "*wa*" 和 in this case corresponds to the Chinese word *heyun* (J. *wain*), meaning "rhyme in response."[190] It does not mean "song from Yamato."

A contemporary edition writes the title *Man'yō Waka Shū* (A Collection of Songs in Ten Thousand Leaves). It goes without saying that this is the result of confusion on the part of an ignorant person. The practice of including the word *waka shū* (a collection of Japanese songs) in a title began from the *Kokinshū*. The poetry collection selected by imperial order during the Engi era came to be known as *Kokin Waka Shū* (A Collection of New and Ancient Songs);[191] in the Chinese preface to the collection we find the word *waka* 和歌; in the preface to the *Shinsen Waka* (Songs Newly Selected) by Ki no Tsurayuki, the word *waka* is mentioned.[192] Although this practice was slightly illogical, the use of the word *waka* in books dealing only with songs *(uta)* became increasingly common at a time when the issue of songs was particularly pressing. More and more works used the word *waka* in later ages.

Question: I have understood your explanation of *waka*. Can you please clarify the issue of *Yamato uta*?

Answer: The word *Yamato uta* is not ancient. It is a word that came to be used by attaching this reading to the characters *"waka"* 倭歌. Among words, we have ancient words that originally existed in the past and words that derive from the reading of Chinese characters. For example, the characters *"sōbyō"* came to be read *"kuniihe"* (shrine); the characters *"nagon"* were read *"monomōsutsukasa"* (councilor). These are not ancient words; they are words made out of Chinese characters. *Yamato uta* also belongs to this type of words. To be logical on this point, it would be reasonable to use the characters *"waka"* 倭歌, since there are songs *(uta)* even in China and, also, a confusion between songs and poems in Chinese *(shi)* should be avoided. However, what we call *uta* does not exist in China, and therefore there is no ground for confusion. As a result, the expression *Yamato uta* is troublesome. And yet, it has become a common practice to read the characters *"waka"* as *Yamato uta*—song from Yamato. There are also people who think that this is a naturally ancient expression. I am not arguing that it is necessarily wrong to read these characters *Yamato uta;* I am just saying that we should ponder the issue of origins without being led astray by vulgar theories.

We encounter the word *Yamato uta* for the first time in the *Ise Monogatari* (Tales of Ise), in which we read, "He kept sipping rice wine without applying himself to hunting, putting all his strengths into the composition of songs from Yamato *(Yamato uta).*"[193] The narrator uses the expression *Yamato uta* in order to make a distinction, as this was an occasion when the composition of a Chinese poem was usually required. In the *Genji Monogatari* (The Tale of Genji) as well we find the expression "both Chinese poems and songs from Yamato" whenever poems in Chinese are made and a reason for confusion exists. Otherwise, we usually find only the word "song" *(uta)*. The use of the word *Yamato uta* at the beginning of the preface to the *Kokinshū* is somehow illogical. This is a book entirely dedicated to songs *(uta);* it strives to talk about the very essence of songs. I wish only the word *uta* were used in this book. And yet many interpretations were produced in later ages, and many meanings were attached to the word *Yamato*. These are exaggerations; I find them remarkably groundless and foolish.

The word *Yamato* was not originally attached to *uta*. This combination came about after the compound *waka* was made. *Yamato uta* does not exist in the ancient language. The character *"wa"* 倭 was added simply in order to distinguish our poetry from Chinese songs and poems; it simply means "songs of this land." Whenever there is no reason for confusing our poems with Chinese songs *(Kara uta)*, one should simply use the word *uta*. It was a big mistake to come up with the word *Yamato uta* later, as if this were a wonderful idea. The theory according to which "songs of Yamato are called the poems of the capital" in opposition to "rustic poems" is an unacceptable, vulgar theory.[194] The other theory according to which "*Yamato uta*, written with the characters 大和歌, means a song with softening and unifying powers, since a poem has the strength of enormously calming the human heart," is not worthy of discussion.[195] *Yamato* is simply the name of our land; we should know that it has nothing to do with songs *(uta)*.

On Yamato[196]

Question: There have been several explanations of the name Yamato since ancient times up to the present day. I would like to hear the details of these theories.

Answer: Since the name Yamato should not be connected with our songs *(uta)*, there is no need for me to explain this issue. However, because people became used to the expression *Yamato uta* (song from Yamato), in later ages "Yamato" came to be discussed in works related to poetry. Many theories were presented, which, as a result, caused people to go astray. We should apply ourselves to understanding this matter well.

First of all, Yamato is the name of a province; in other words, it names the region that is known even today as the Yamato province *(Yamato no kuni)*. However, since from the time when Emperor Jinmu began to rule over the land from Kashiwara no Miya all the capitals of the many sovereigns were located in this province, Yamato, being the name of the capital's province, was taken at a later time to be the general term for the whole country.

Question: When did people begin to use the word Yamato? What do you think about the theory according to which "the place was given this name because this was the province where stood the capital of Emperor Jinmu, who was called Kamu-yamato Ihare-biko no Mikoto (Deity of the Ihare District of Divine Yamato)"?

Answer: I do not believe so. The name Yamato goes back to the age of the gods. It is an ancient word that appears in the poem of the deity Yachihoko;[197] it also appears in the sentence, "the sky-seen Land of Yamato" at the time of Nigiwayabi no Mikoto's descent to earth.[198] The name was given to Emperor Jinmu at a later time, and it derived from the name of this land. In "The Chronicles of the Age of the Gods" we find the following paragraph: "And the next child was Sano no Mikoto, also styled Kamu-yamato Ihare-biko no Mikoto. Sano was the name by which he was called when young. Afterwards when he had cleared and subdued the realm, and had control of the eight islands, the title was added of Kamu-yamato Ihare-biko no Mikoto."[199] Although there is a doubtful passage in this quotation, it is nevertheless proof that Kamu-yamato Ihare-biko no Mikoto was not the emperor's original name.[200] A similar indication is given in "The Chronicles of Emperor Jinmu."[201] Moreover, Ihare is also a place-name in the Yamato province. Therefore, it is clear that the name of the province does not derive from the emperor's name.

Question: What do you think about the theory according to which the name Yamato was originally the general term for the whole country but, beginning with the reign of Emperor Jinmu, it also became a particular term indicating the province where the capital was located?

Answer: This is a big mistake. Generally speaking, when it comes to geographical names there are many instances in which names that were originally specific were later used as generic terms. There is no example of a general term that later became a specific one. We might want to think of the examples of the Suruga province, Suruga district, and the village of Suruga; or, the Izumo province, Izumo district, and the village of Izumo; or, the Aki province, Aki district, and the village of Aki; or, the Ōsumi province, Ōsumi district, and the village of Ōsumi. Each one was originally the name of a village that was later used as the name of a district. Furthermore, the name of the district eventually gave the name to the province. Another example would be the name of Tsukushi, which corresponds to today's Chikuzen and Chikugo, and later became the general term for the Kyū province (Kyūshū). Or, when Michinoku was divided and Idewa became an independent province, the name of the district, Idewa, became the general term for the whole province.[202] The same thing can be said with regard to the Kaga province. All these examples show that everything always begins with a specific term that later comes to be used as a general term. There is no need to draw from all these examples in order to realize that even in the ancient language of the age of the gods Yamato was simply the name of a province. It does not appear as a general term until after the reign of Emperor Jinmu.

Question: In the "Chronicles of Emperor Jinmu" we find the following section:

> The Imperial palanquin made a circuit, in the course of which the Emperor ascended the Hill Waki Kamu no Hotsuma. Here, having viewed the shape of the land on all sides, he said:—"Oh! what a beautiful country we have become possessed of! Though a blessed land of inner-tree-fiber, yet it resembles a dragon-fly licking its hinder parts." From this it first received the name of Akizu-shima (lit. the region of harvests). Of old, Izanagi no Mikoto, in naming this country, said:—"Yamato is the Land of Ura-yasu (Bay-easy); it is the Land of Hoso-hoko no Chi-taru (Slender-spears-thousand-good); it is the Land of Shiwa-Kami-Hotsu-ma" (Rock-ring-upper-pre-eminent-true land).[203]

In this passage the name Yamato is mentioned. The names that precede and follow it are all general terms for the whole country. Therefore, it sounds as if Yamato was already the general term for our land since the divine age of Izanagi no Mikoto. How do you explain this?

Answer: All these names refer to one province.[204] This should be clear from reading the phrase that says, "Here, having viewed the shape of the land on all sides." How would it be possible to see the broad expanse of the whole country with one look? The word *masaguni* (blessed land) is actually *masebaguni* (the narrow land). How could the entire country be given this name? "Ura-yasuguni (Bay-easy land), and the other names as well, all refer to one province. The footnote in the *Shaku Nihongi* (Explanation of The Chronicles of Japan) indicating that these are all general terms is well off the mark.[205] Although someone could argue that the Yamato province has no sea and therefore cannot be called "Ura-yasu" (Bay-easy), we should remember that *"ura"* 浦 is simply a loan sign for the word *ura*, which means "heart," as in the expressions *uranaki* (sincere), *uraganashi* (somewhat sad), *urasabishi* (somewhat lonesome).[206] Only later did the name Yamato become a general term for the whole country, as did Akizushima and the other names.

Question: In the "Chronicle of The Age of the Gods," we find the sentence, "Next there was produced the island of Ō-Yamato no Toyo-aki-zu-shima

(Rich-harvest [or autumn]-of-island)."[207] This name sounds like a general term, although it does not include the islands of Tsukushi[208] and Shikoku.[209] What do you think about this?

Answer: First of all, the text says, "Ōyashima" (the eight big islands). This name points to the islands that are divided by the sea, independently of their size; their number is eight. The *Kojiki* lists the following names: Awaji-no-Honosawake island, Iyo-no-Futana island, Oki-no-Mitsugo island, Tsukushi island, Tsu island, Sado island, and Ōyamato-Toyoakizu island.[210] (One version of the *Nihon Shoki* lists the same names.) The *Nihon Shoki* mentions the following names: Ōyamato-Toyoakizu island, Iyo-no-Futana island, Tsukushi island, Oki island, Sado island, Koshi island (I have a doubt about this),[211] Ō island, and Kibinoko island.

Since, among these islands the one called "Ōyamato" indicates all the provinces bordering each other with the exception of the seven islands, it is definitely a general term.[212] However, the name Ōyamato-Akizu-shima is not an ancient word belonging to the age of the gods. It came to be used after the name Akizu-shima became a general term for the entire island. This should be clear also from the quotation that I mentioned above from "The Chronicles of Emperor Jinmu": "From this it first received the name of Akizu-shima." The general terms for the whole country used during the age of the gods were "Ashihara-no-Nakatsu-kuni" (The Central Land of the Reed Plains), "Ōyashima-guni" (The Land of the Big Eight Islands), and so on. Recently, with regard to ancient language it has been argued that Ashihara-no-Nakatsu-kuni was used to indicate this land from heaven, whereas Ōyashimaguni was used to refer to our land when the speaker was speaking from this land. There is no trace of Yamato having been used as a general term; this happened at a later time.

Question: If this is the case, then the text should say, "Ashihara-no-Nakatsu-kuni was produced," and "Ōyashimaguni was produced." Instead, both records mention "Ō-Yamato." Why?

Answer: Since Ashihara-no-Nakatsu-kuni was originally the general term for the whole county, it also included the other seven islands. Since this island (Honshū) does not include the other seven, it would have been difficult to use the names Ashihara-no-Nakatsu-kuni and Ōyashimaguni to refer to it. Originally Yamato was the name of one province; it did not include other provinces. It was only because it became a general term later on that it was adopted to indicate the whole country with the exception of the other seven islands.[213] We find another similar example in Iyo, which was first the name of a province, and was later taken to indicate the entire island of Shikoku. The same thing can be said of Tsukushi (Kyūshū). We should keep all these examples in mind when dealing with this issue.

Question: I understand that originally Yamato was the name of a province. When did it become a general term?

Answer: We should not ask when it happened; it happened naturally. We find the word Yamato used as a general term in the ancient language in the passage from the *Kojiki* that describes a wild goose laying an egg on the island of Hime-jima during the visit of Emperor Nintoku. Consequently, the emperor summoned Takechi no Sukune and asked him a question in the form of a poem: "My elder brother/of gem-cutting Uchi,/you of all others/are the longman of the age./Have you heard/of a wild goose laying its egg/in the land of sky-seen Yamato *(soramitsu/Yamato no kuni ni)*?"[214] We find the same expression in the man's answer to the emperor: "I have never heard/of a wild goose coming here/to lay its egg/in the land of sky-seen Yamato."[215] The *Nihongi* states that "A wild goose has laid an egg on the Mamuta embankment in the province of Kawachi."[216] No matter which version we follow, the places indicated in the *Kojiki* and *Nihongi* are not to be found in the Yamato province. Moreover, since the laying of the egg on the part of the wild goose is a rare event all over this land, "Yamato" stands for the country's general term. Furthermore, since "sky-seen" *(soramitsu)* is a pillow word *(makurakotoba)* of Yamato, it also applies to Yamato as a general term. In both poems from the *Nihongi* we find the expression "Akizushima Yamato" (region-of-harvests Yamato). It is the same thing. If this was already happening at such an early time, we should realize that Yamato must have been used as a general term even earlier.

Question: Is it possible that Yamato was used as a general term on the model of China, where we find many examples of a dynasty giving the name to the entire land?

Answer: How could this be if at the time of the reign of Emperor Nintoku the name was already mentioned in his poem? Although writings from China had already been imported during the reign of that other emperor,[217] Chinese learning had not yet infiltrated our land at all; that was a time when the spirit of the age of the gods had not yet vanished. When one looks at this matter from a later perspective—a time when learning came from Chinese texts in all fields, and everything was influenced by China—one might doubt that even things going back to the age of the gods were modeled after the continent. It is only at a later time, an age of pretended smartness, that differences between our land and foreign land became so extensive. However, the situation during the earliest age was about the same everywhere. People here and there could understand each other on many things. Therefore, the context for the creation of the names of China and the situation leading to the transformation of "Yamato" into a general term must have been very similar.

Question: What is the meaning of the name Yamato?

Answer: The meaning is not clear. Although there have been many theories, past and present, they are all unsatisfactory. Even recently new theories have been proposed, but they do not seem to hit the mark.[218] The most careful thoughts on this matter would lead me to think that Yamato means "a place within the mountains" (yamato 山処). The reason is that in "The Chronicles of Emperor Jinmu" we find the following words of the emperor: "Now I have heard from the Ancient of the Sea that in the East there is a fair land encircled on all sides by mountains *(aoyama yomo ni megushiri).*"[219] This is a reference to the Yamato province. We should keep this passage in mind together with the following poem from the *Kojiki* by Yamatodake no Mikoto: "Yamato/is the crest of the land—/In the close-folded/green-fence/mountains it is hidden:/Yamato, the beautiful."[220] The word *tatanazuku* (close-folded) is *tatanawari tsuku* (adding pile to pile). Moreover, Ōnamuchi no Mikoto's naming of the land "Jewel-fenced-within-land" in "The Chronicles of Emperor Jinmu" comes from the fact that Yamato is hidden inside green mountains, which surround it like a fence.[221] Furthermore, the poem composed by Iwanohime, the consort of Emperor Nintoku, in the *Kojiki,* stating "I pass by Yamato/of the little shields" indicates that Yamato is surrounded by mountains that stand up like shields.[222] Another example to keep in mind are the words of Emperor Jinmu, "a blessed land of inner-tree-fiber," which should be read together with the lines "hidden like inner-tree-fibers" from the long poem on the tomb of Ubara-no-Otome in book nine of the *Man'yōshū.*[223]

Because all the quotations from the ancient language that I mentioned above describe Yamato as the land surrounded by green mountains, it is clear that this is its meaning, "a place within the mountains" *(yamato)*. Basically speaking, ancient documents refer to this province as a place enclosed by mountains, as we have seen above. As a matter of fact, we should realize that the province north of Yamato is called "Yamashiro," which literally means "at the back of the mountains."

Now, there are two interpretations of the meaning of "Yama-to" 山処. One assigns the meaning of place to the *"to"* of Yamato, as in the cases of *tachido* (lit., place to stand on; position), *fushido* (lit., place to lie down; bed), *harahido* (purification place). Although, in the case of Yamato, the *"to"* follows a name rather than the conjunctive form of a verb, its meaning remains the same. *"To"* maintains the same meaning in the words *yado* (dwelling), *sato* (village), and so on. Moreover, the character *"shi"* 止 is read *"to,"* as we can see from the *Private Notes on the Chronicles of Japan:* "In the ancient language 'dwelling' is pronounced *'sumai'* and written with the character *'to* 止.'"[224] We should also keep in mind dictionaries that explain the character *"to"* as "to be" and "to dwell." The *Shuo-wen*[225] explains the character *"chu"* 処 (place) as *"qi"* 止. The *Yu-pian* (The Jeweled Letters) explains the character *"chu"* 処 as *"ju"* 居 (to be).

According to the second interpretation, Yamato is the abbreviation of *yamatsutokoro* (a place of mountains). *"Tsu"* and *"to"* merge to became *"to."* Since both *"toko"* and *"toro"* combined into *"to,"* the four syllables *"tsutokoro"* became one, *"to"*—Yamato. The meaning agrees perfectly with the meaning of the previous interpretation.

Question: What do you think about the following statements from the *Private Notes?* "Heaven and earth separated, and the mud had not yet dried. People lived in the mountains, going back and forth. As a result, they left many footprints in the mud. This is why they called this place 'Yamato' 山跡, footprints on the mountains. The first character is read *'yama'* (mountain); the second (*ato* or footprints) is read *'to* 止.'" A second statement says, "In the ancient language the word for 'to live' was *'to.'* Therefore, Yamato means 'living in the mountains.'"

Answer: Because these theories refer to the fact that Yamato was originally a general term for the whole country, they are both mistaken.[226] Originally Yamato was the name of a province, as I mentioned earlier. Moreover, even if Yamato was originally the name of the entire country, it would still be difficult to believe these theories. The reason is that, first of all, the sentence "the mud had not yet dried; people lived in the mountains," which is used to explain the two etymologies of Yamato, does not make sense. Although in "The Chronicle of the Age of the Gods" we find the phrase "when the land was young,"[227] this passage refers to a time prior to the presence of the two ancestral deities. This was a time when the land of Ōyashima had not yet come into being, let alone people and things. Then how could someone say that people "lived in the mountains"? In addition, there is no reference in any documents to the fact that the land had not yet dried and that people lived in the mountains; and there is no reason why there should be. Both are ungrounded theories. Furthermore, to take these theories as etymologies of a specific province is even more off the mark. Master Keichū's comment on this point is excellent: "I cannot accept the theory of the soft mud since there is no way that the land would not coagulate only in the Yamato province."[228]

However, Keichū accepts the etymology of "footprints on the mountains," arguing that, "since the Yamato province is surrounded by mountains in all four directions, there must have been many footprints in the mountains of people coming and going." He also states in *Yozai Shō* that "In the *Man'yōshū* the name 'Yamato' is often written with the characters 山跡 (footprints on the mountains), especially in the headnotes in book four."[229] However, I do not accept this idea ; I do not think that Yamato became the name of the province just because there were many footprints of people coming and going in the mountains. I would use the same argument against those who support the etymology, "living in the mountains." Not only I do not accept the explanation of "Yamato" as "living in the mountains," but I believe that the meaning of *ato* as "footprints" is baseless. Basically, the theory of the wet mud and footprints on the mountains is based on the ancient practice of writing the characters "*yamato*" 山跡. The idea of "the mud which had not yet dried" derived from the thought of a meaning attached to the character "*ato*" (footprints), and from the idea that people lived in the mountains. The etymology came from putting these two things together. While criticizing this explanation, Keichū still remained attached to the literal meaning of the Chinese characters "*yamato*"—footprints on the mountains.[230]

The fact that in the *Man'yōshū* these characters look like ideographic characters *(seiji)* rather than phonetic ones *(ateji)* is due to the common use made of this combination in ancient times. This usage, however, followed an original practice of employing characters as loan signs. In the remote past, people were not interested in the meaning of characters; in many instances characters were borrowed for their phonetic value. Although the character 跡 is pronounced "*ato*," we find many examples in which "*a*" inside a word is elided. The characters *"yama-ato"* 山跡 were borrowed to write the name Yamato, since the *"a"* of *"ato"* could be absorbed into the *"a"* of *"ma,"* so as to have the elision *"yamato."* This is how Chinese characters were used in the ancient era; they were not necessarily chosen for their meanings.

My predecessors in modern times have been following the explanation of Yamato as "footprints on the mountains."[231] The practice of reading these characters *"yamaato"* in the ritual reading of the preface of the *Kokinshū* during poetry readings is totally baseless.[232] Even if we were to accept as correct the etymology of Yamato as "footprints on the mountains," in songs and other writings from the ancient age we only find the sound "Yamato"; there is no trace of the sound "Yamaato." People who do so are ignorant of the past. Even more so if they believe in this meaning of the name. Nowadays there are many instances of strange habits in the reading of characters. Without thinking about the origin of things, people take the slightest reason as basis for their arguments, coming up with messy, unfamiliar words, so as to surprise and lead foolish listeners astray.

Now, with regard to the present meaning of Yamato as "place within the mountains" 山処, we could use the characters *"yama"* 山 (mountain) and *"to"* 止 (place), and the word would still make sense. However, we cannot accept the theory according to which Yamato would mean "to stop (*shi* 止) at the mountain where people live." The reason is that Yamato means "land located within and surrounded by mountains."

Question: What do you think about the theories that explain the name Yamato as "outside the mountains" 山外, and "the mountains' entrance" 山戸?

Answer: It is hard to believe that Yamato would mean "outside the mountains," since this explanation runs contrary to the ancient language, as I mentioned above.[233] With regard to the second theory, it does not fit the ancient practice of naming.

Question: What is your opinion of the following theory? "When the two ancestral deities created Ōyashima (Japan), they began by producing the great Yamato. Therefore, Yamato means 'the original province of Yashima' (Yashima no moto-tsu-kuni). Yamato is the abbreviation of 'Yashimamoto.'"

Answer: This is a bad theory. The logic of this theory contradicts the reality of the ancient language. At least, theories such as the one on "the footprints on the mountains," although they are incorrect, are close to the spirit of the ancient age. This theory, and others like it, that force a name through a contorted logic, is the result of a pretended smartness on the part of later scholars. All theories that sound so clever are the result of a later age. They never explain the names of the ancient era. Furthermore, with regard to the order in which Yashima was created, the *Kojiki* states that the production of the land began with Awaji and ended with Yamato. Therefore the matter of this order is not settled. To hastily explain the ancient words of the age of the gods based on the *Nihongi*, which is embellished with all sorts of rhetorical flourishes, while going against the *Kojiki*, which is an honest account of the past, is remarkably illogical.

Question: What do you think about the theory according to which Yamato became the general term for the whole country because it was an auspicious name? This theory is based on a quotation from the *Yozai Shō* and the *Shakumyō*:[234] "Mountain (*san* 山) is related to production (*san* 産); to generate things is equivalent to 'to produce' (*san* 産)."[235]

Answer: I have a hard time understanding this explanation. As I mentioned earlier, Yamato became a general term for the entire country before the reign of Emperor Nintoku. During the earliest age this "clever" way of thinking did not exist at all. We have the imperial decree of the Wadō era, "Use a beautiful name,"[236] and the passage from the *Engishiki*, "Give it an auspicious name."[237] However, these are both products of later scholarship; they are not related to the age of the gods. Furthermore, although these quotations indicate a command to assign beautiful characters to names, they do not say to give a place a new name. Although there were discussions on which auspicious characters should be assigned to the name Yamato, it is useless to discuss the issue of good luck and bad luck when it comes to the name itself.

Question: What do you think about assigning the character "*wa*" 倭 to Yamato?

Answer: "Wa" is a name that was assigned to Yamato in China. We find it mentioned for the first time in the section on geography of the *Quian Han shu* (Former History of the Han Dynasty):[238] "The Eastern barbarians are of a quiet nature. They are different from the other barbarians from the south, north, and west. Therefore, Confucius regretted that the Way did not reach that land. It was only natural that he would try to cross over to that land and reach it. The people from Wa dwell in the middle of the ocean across from Korea, separated from all other countries. Sometimes, they come to our land in order to pay their tribute." The same description is repeated in the *Hou Han shu*.[239] "Yamato" always appears abbreviated as "Wa."

The records do not tell us with any certitude the reason why Yamato was given this name. When I think about this issue, I read the passage above in light of the explanation that the *Shuo-wen* gives of the original meaning of the character *"wa"*: "a quiet person." I believe that Pan Ku used this character to name the people from Yamato because "they are of a quiet nature." I cannot be certain about this. Moreover, there is also the following ancient theory from our land:[240] "When someone from our country went over to China, he was asked the name of his land. 'Well, my land . . . *(wanu koku ya to),*' he began to answer. Actually, *wanu* means 'my' *(ware)*, but from that day on our land came to be known as "the Land of Wanu" (Wanukoku; lit., my land)." Although this theory appears in the *Gengenshū*,[241] I have a hard time believing it.

Another theory states that, "If we read the name 'Wanukoku' in Chinese, we have 'Onoko,' a reference to the Onogoro island."[242] I definitely cannot accept this theory. It is too contrived. This is the product of modern Shinto scholars who expound unreasonable and empty ideas. Although they argue that the Onogoro island is the original name of our country, we must remember that this was just one small island; it cannot even be counted among the islands making up Yashima (Japan).[243] It is true that the name of this island survived even during the age of man, as we can see from the poem by Emperor Nintoku,[244] and from a passage from the *Private Notes:* "Nowadays we can see a small island south-west of Awajishima; this is the Onogoro island." However, since the age of the gods this name was never used as the name of our country; there is no trace of this in any document. Therefore, although it is likely that, hearing about "Yashima" and "Yamato," the Chinese people might have named our land by using characters that sounded like these names, there is no reason why foreigners would know a name like Onogorojima, which people from our land had never used since the age of the gods to name our country. This theory is particularly bad. In conclusion, we cannot be certain about the reason why Yamato was called "Wa."

Question: Why is the character *"wa"* 倭 read as "Yamato"?

Answer: Seeing the character *"wa"* in many Chinese documents, people realized that it was used to indicate the name of our land, Yamato. Should you enquire when this practice began, I would say that it is a very ancient one. Since, in the *Kojiki*, all the instances of the name Yamato are already written with this character, people must have become used to this reading very long ago. Because the entire *Record* is written with great attention to the ancient language, whenever a slightly unfamiliar character is used, the editor always adds a note, even to characters that are not particularly controversial, as in the case of the name of the deity "Ame no Tokotachi no Kami" 天之常立神, which is accompanied by the following note: "The reading of the third character is '*toko*'; the reading of the fourth character is '*tachi*.'"[245] The fact that there is no note indicating that the character *"wa"* 倭 should be read "Yamato" shows that this reading was generally known. This is also indicated in the preface.[246] Now, whereas in China the character *"wa"* indicated the whole country, here in our land it was employed as both the general name of the country of Yamato and the specific name of the Yamato province.

Question: How do you explain the fact that "Yamato" is written with both characters *"wa"* 倭 and *"wa"* 和?

Answer: Although the first character has been used all the time, this character was first assigned by the Chinese people to the reading of our land, which they also called "Wanu."[247] Probably because it was not a good name, the character was changed in our land to the second *"wa"* 和. This is why this latter character is nowhere to be found in Chinese texts, not even in later ages, as the name of Yamato. Should you ask for the reason why this character *"wa"* 和 was chosen to indicate the name of our land, I would say that it was probably because it had the same sound as the other character *"wa"* 倭, and because it was a good character. This character was also simply chosen in the ancient era in order to provide the name Yamato with a sign. Since characters were loan signs, there is no need to debate their meaning. The matter was entrusted to circumstances; while using the first character *"wa"* 倭, a time came later on when people decided to distinguish good characters from bad ones, and the name Yamato was reassigned to a more auspicious character. However, with regard to the meaning of the second character *"wa"* 和, we should remember that the explanation according to which "extreme softness is the custom of our land" is the far-fetched interpretation of a later age.

Someone argues that the meanings of the two characters *"wa"* (和 and 倭) are similar, based on the fact that some texts[248] explain the expression, "a quiet nature" from the *Han shu* (History of the Han Dynasty)[249] by adding the character *"wa"* 和, thus saying, "a quiet Yamato nature." However, this is again the product of modern thinking. Moreover, the character *"yō"* 邕 (harmonious) which appears in the decree of Emperor Keitai—"Yamato (日本) is harmonious *(yōyō)*, and each man may do as he pleases in the land; Akitsu is glorified, and the royal territory raised to high honor,"[250]—has the same meaning as the other character *"yō"* 雝, which is explained as follows in notes to a poem from the "Greater Odes" of the *Shi-jing* (Classic of poetry):[251] "the harmonious cry of the phoenix," and "full of harmony." Furthermore, at the beginning of the *Seventeen-Article Constitution* of Prince Shōtoku we find the sentence, "Harmony (*wa* 和) is to be valued."[252] In China the name Yong-zhou was originally the name of the province where the capital was located.[253] This explains why someone at a later time took this name, applying it to the Yamashiro province in our land, which is also known as Yōshū. A note states that the meaning of the character *"yō"* 雍 is "harmony" (*wa* 和),[254] since this character *"yō"* has the same meaning as the other *"yō"* 雝. As, basically speaking, all these factors were related to the character *"wa"* 和, no matter what actually happened, this character was eventually adopted to indicate our land. But I would never go as far as to argue all the ideas mentioned above.

All this thinking took place at a later age; many similarities occurred naturally, of their own accord. Finally, there is a reference to the "land of great harmony" (*taiwa* 太和) in the *Zi hua zi*;[255] this theory is even less reliable than the others.

Question: During which emperor's reign do you think the character for Yamato was changed to the second *"wa"* 和?

Answer: There is no way for me to say with any certitude. However, since I have been asked, I would say that even in the *Nihongi* the character *"wa"* 和 is nowhere to be found, let alone in the *Kojiki*. There is only one instance in book five of the *Nihongi,* but this is a copyist's mistake.[256] If people had already used the second character *"wa"* 和 at that time, they would have definitely used it in the *Chronicles*. However, in the many instances in which the name Yamato was recorded in this document, only the characters *"hi no moto"* 日本 (the sun's origin) and the first *"wa"* 倭 were employed. This kind of mistake was easily made in a later age, when people had become familiar with the second character *"wa"* 和.

Although we find this character used for the first time in the *Shoku Nihongi* (Chronicles of Japan, Continued), no explanation is given of the reasons why such a change took place. When I think about this text again, I realize that, despite Empress Genmei's decree of the Second Day of the Fifth Month 713, "Use a beautiful name when naming all the provinces, districts, and villages of the Five Home Provinces and the Seven Circuits,"[257] there is no trace of the change; the first character *"wa"* 倭 continued to be used. We know from Emperor Shōmu's decree of the Twelfth Month 737, "Twenty-Seventh Day, The name 'Land of Great Yamato' 大倭国 will be written with the characters, 'Fostering Virtue' 大養徳国," and from his decree of the Third Month 747, "Sixteenth Day—After changing the characters indicating the name of the Land of Great Yamato, I am bringing them back to their old form, 大倭国," around this time the first character *"wa"* 倭 was still in use. Until Empress Kōken's decree of the Third Day, Eleventh Month 752, "I appoint Lord Fujiwara Nagate of the Junior Fourth Rank, Upper Grade, Governor of Yamato (Yamato no kami 大倭守)," only the first character *"wa"* 倭 was used to indicate the name Yamato. We find for the first time the name "Land of Yamato" 大和 written with the second character *"wa"* 和 in the imperial decree of the Twenty-Seventh Day, Second Month 758.[258] Beginning from this time, the name Yamato came to be recorded only with the second character *"wa"* 和.

Therefore, this change took place between the Eleventh Month 752 and the Second Month 758. And yet, it seems as if somehow there was a feeling that the second character *"wa"* 和 should not be used. When we think of the decree of 737 in which the change of Chinese characters was clearly spelled out, we understand that the adoption of the character *"wa"* 和 must also have been the object of an imperial decree. However, this is not mentioned in the *Shoku Nihongi*. The decree is not recorded in the *Ruijū Kokushi* (Classified National Histories).[259] The *Shūgaishō* (Gleanings of Mustard)[260] indicates that the character was changed during the Tenpyō Shōhō era (749-756), but it fails to give any proof.

When the characters for Yamato were changed to "Fostering Virtue" 大養徳, the characters for the title "Lord of Yamato" (Yamato no sukune 大倭の宿禰) were also changed (大養徳の宿禰). Therefore, with the adoption of the second character *"wa"* 和 for Yamato, the characters for the title "Lord of Yamato" should have been changed as well. Now, the title was recorded with the first character for *"wa"* 倭 until the Sixth Month 757. The expression "Yamato no sukune" 大和の宿禰, with the second character *"wa,"* appears for the first time in the entry for the Twelfth Month of the same year. It looks as if the character was changed between the Sixth and the Twelfth Month 757. However, in the *Man'yōshū* the second character *"wa"* 和 for Yamato is not used, neither in poetry nor in the headnotes, until book eighteen.[261] In book nineteen, among "the six songs composed as a response to an imperial command at a banquet during the festival of the New Grains on the Twenty-Fifth Day"[262] of the Eleventh Month 752,[263] we find an endnote indicating that "the song above is by the Governor of Yamato (Yamato no kuni no kami 大和国守), Lord Fujiwara no Nagate."[264] This endnote is the first instance in which the second character *"wa"* 和 was used to indicate Yamato in the *Man'yōshū*. In book twenty we find the following headnotes: "The former empress addressed the princes in her retinue and said, 'You shall compose songs in response (*waka* 和歌),' and she immediately recited the following poem;"[265] "The song above was composed on the Fifth Month of 753."[266] This is the first instance in which we find the word *"Yamato uta"* 和歌 (Yamato song) in this poetic anthology.[267] As I mentioned earlier, the entry for the appointment of Lord Fujiwara no Nagate to Governor of Yamato (Yamato no kami 大倭守) appears on the *Kinotomi* (Third) Day of the Eleventh Month 752. The *kinotomi* day corresponds to the Second Day.[268] The fact that in the endnote of Nagate's song the second character *"wa"* 和 was used to indicate the name Yamato, instead of the first character *"wa"* 倭 that was employed in the *Shoku Nihongi*, shows that the shift took place during the Eleventh Month 752. This was a different time from the time when the shift took place in the title "Lord of Yamato" (Yamato no sukune).[269]

Since the order of the songs in the *Man'yōshū* is chronological, we can say that this was the first time when the second character *"wa"* 和 was used in the anthology. However, we should remember that headnotes and endnotes might have been added at a slightly later time.[270] Moreover, since we have only two instances in which this character was used, it is difficult to tell whether these were mistakes on the part of the copyist.[271] Because, in later ages, people got used to always writing the words "Yamato" 大和 and *"waka"* 和歌 with the second character *"wa,"* it is only natural that a sudden slip would occur when writing the first character *"wa"* 倭. Furthermore, I believe that a change taking place between the second and the twenty-fifth day of a month would be too sudden.

Therefore, we cannot rely exclusively on the *Man'yōshū*. Moreover, given the fact that in the *Shoku Nihongi*, when the first character *"wa"* 倭 is used we only find this character, and when we start seeing the second *"wa"* 和 used only this character is consistently used, there is no room for doubting the presence of any mistake. However, since the application of the second character *"wa"* 和 to the title "Yamato no sukune" probably took place at a different time, as the matter could not be left to the fancy of writers, the proof indicating that the first character *"wa"* 倭 was used until the Sixth Month 757 is far from conclusive. As it would be impossible for characters to be used in a title before being used in the name of a place, and as the creation of titles is always posterior, there is no doubt that the character in the name of the land was revised before "Yamato no sukune" 大和の宿禰 began to be written with the second character *"wa"* 和. Therefore, we know that change in the character of the title could not have taken place in the span between the Eleventh Month 752 and the Twelfth Month 757.

I also want to point out that all the references to Yamato in what I have said above are to the name of the Yamato province in the Kinai region, not to the name of the entire country. Beginning with the *Nihongi*, in many instances Yamato as the general term for the country was written with the characters *"hi no moto"* (the sun's origin);[272] it is rarely written with the first character *"wa"* 倭. I wonder whether this might have been the reason for not debating the change of character in the general term for the country. Although later documents write the name of the Yamato province by using the second character *"wa"* 和 exclusively, the first *"wa"* 倭 was not discarded when it came to name other things. In the *Shoku Nihongi*, as well as in later records, the emperor is referred to as "Yamatoneko no Sumera Mikoto" 倭根子天皇.[273] There are many other examples. Until later ages the word *"Yamato uta"* 倭歌 (Yamato song) continued to be written with the first character *"wa."* The general term for the country derived from a different name. Once the second character for *"wa"* 和 was applied to this name, everybody came to use "Yamato" 和.

Question: Among the several Japanese eras there is one called "Wadō" 和銅 (Yamato copper).[274] In book eight of the *Shoku Nihongi* we have two instances of *"Yamato no kuni"* 大和国 (Land of Yamato) written with the second character for *"wa,"*[275] and we also find the word *"Yamato-goto"* 和琴 (Yamato harp).[276] Moreover, *"Yamato-goto"* is also found in book seven of the *Man'yōshū*.[277] How do you explain the use of the second character *"wa"* 和 prior to the Shōhō era (749–756)?

Answer: These are all mistakes on the part of copyists. I have explained the details of this issue in the preceding section.[278] The *"wa"* of Wadō does not mean Yamato; it is a different thing.[279] Although in the index of books five and sixteen of the *Man'yōshū* we find the second character "wa" 和,[280] we must remember that the index is the addition of someone who wrote it at a later time.

Therefore, there is no need for me to debate this issue. You should know that all other instances in which the second character *"wa"* 和 is used prior to 752 are the work of a later person.

Question: Can you explain the name Nippon?[281]

Answer: The original name of our country is "Ōyashima" 大八洲. Nippon is a name created at a later time in order to identify our land for foreigners. This explains why in imperial decrees the emperor is usually referred to as "Ōyashima Tennō" (the emperor of Ōyashima). When the decree is meant for a foreign land, the emperor appears as "Nippon Tennō" (the emperor of Nippon). We can see this tendency in the *Codes*.[282] Although I cannot state with any certainty when this name began to be used, I would say that, looking at the *Nihongi*, all the instances in which the characters "Nippon" appear up to "The Chronicles of Empress Kōgyoku" are revisions made at the time of its compilation. In ancient times this name did not exist. Prior to "The Chronicles of Empress Kōgyoku" the word "Yamato" 倭, written with the first character *"wa,"* was used even when addressing foreign countries.

Now in the entry for autumn, Tenth Day of the Seventh Month 645, when Emperor Kōtoku ascended to the throne, we read the following passage: "Koryŏ, Pèkché and Silla all sent Envoys at the same time bearing tributes.... Kose no Tokuda no Omi addressed the Koryŏ Envoys on the Emperor's behalf, saying:—'This is the mandate of the Emperor of Japan (Nippon Tennō), who rules the world as a God incarnate....' Next he addressed the Pèkché Envoys on the Emperor's behalf, saying:—'This is the mandate of the Emperor of Japan (Nippon Tennō), who rules the world as a God incarnate....'"[283] This is the first instance in which the name "Nippon" was used to indicate our country in a petition shown to foreigners. This is different from instances produced prior to this decree.[284] An entry for 646 states: "The Emperor proceeded to the Eastern Gate of the Palace, where, by Soga, Ōmi of the Right, he decreed as follows:—'The God Incarnate, the Emperor Yamato-neko (Nippon Yamato-neko Sumera-mikoto), who rules the world, gives command to the Ministers assembled in his presence, to the Omi, Muraji, Kuni no Miyakko, Tomo no Miyakko, and subjects of various classes, saying...'"[285] The fact that "Nippon" is mentioned in a decree that was not addressed to foreigners can probably be explained by assuming that this decree was issued at the time when people had begun to use this name. You should know that the name Nippon was recorded elsewhere in addition to the name "Yamato" 倭.

Therefore, the name Nippon began to be used at the time of the reign of Emperor Kōtoku. Many new things were established during his reign. I believe more and more that the use of the new name for the country was related to the fact that this was the time when names began to be given to eras.[286]

When I try to examine these facts in light of Chinese records, I realize that until the Sui dynasty (581–618) only Wa was used to indicate our land. Nippon began to be used in the Tang dynasty (618–907). We find the following statement in the *Tang shu* (Tang History): "Nippon in former times was called Wanu.... In the first year of Xian-heng (670) an embassy came to the court from Japan to offer congratulations upon the conquest of Koguryo. About this time, the Japanese who had studied Chinese came to dislike the name Wa 倭 and changed it to Nippon 日本. According to the words of the Japanese envoy himself, that name was chosen because the country was so close to where the sun rises."[287]

I wonder whether this was the first time that the Chinese people ever heard the name Nippon. "Xian-heng" is the name of an era during the rule of Emperor Kao-cong.[288] The first year of this era corresponds to the ninth year of the reign of Emperor Tenji (670). I wonder whether the envoy mentioned above was the same as the one referred to in the Eighth Year of the "Chronicles of Emperor Tenji": "This year Kujira, the Kawachi no Atahi of Middle Shōkin rank, and others were sent on a mission to the Land of Great Tang."[289] If this is correct, this event took place twenty-four years after the beginning of the Taika era.[290] Although in the meantime there were several diplomatic exchanges between the two countries, it seems that people in China did not hear about the name Nippon. Moreover, since the Chinese record does not point to the first year of the Xian-heng era exactly, they might have heard the name a little earlier. In any event, this would not make any difference.

The Three Korean Kingdoms must have known about our country's new name immediately. And yet the passage from the *Tongguk t'onggam* (Comprehensive Mirror of the Eastern Kingdoms)[291] stating "The land of Wa changed its name to Nippon. According to the words of the Japanese envoy himself, that name was chosen because the country was so close to where the sun rises" was written in the tenth year of the reign of King Munmu of Silla.[292] This corresponds to the first year of the Xian-heng era in Tang China. It looks as if the Korean history was based on the *Tang shu*. This would explain why date and wordings are the same in both documents.

Question: What were the reasons for calling our land Nippon?

Answer: Our land came to be called "the land where the sun rises" because it is the land of the Sun Goddess who shines over the entire world, spreading her favors over all.[293] Moreover, our land naturally came to be called Nippon because, seen from all the Western lands, it is located in the direction from which the sun rises. The *Sui shu* (History of the Sui Dynasty) and the *Zi-zhi tong-jian* (A Comprehensive Mirror for Aid in Government)[294] record the following sentence at the time in the past when an envoy was sent to China: "The Son of Heaven in the land where the sun rises addresses a letter to the Son of Heaven in the land where the sun sets."[295] This event took place during the reign of Empress Suiko.[296] The passage from the *Tang shu* that I mentioned earlier presents the same theory.

We do not find these explanations of the meaning of Nippon in our own records. Since documents written in later ages were based on Chinese texts, I shall not mention them. Generally speaking, Chinese writings on our land are filled with mistakes, and therefore they cannot be taken as historical evidence. However, this all depends on the topics under discussion. The issue of the meaning of Nippon originated in our land and was faithfully transmitted to China, so that I believe no mistake was made. Contrary to the general rule, these Chinese texts help us to restore a tradition that is lost in our country.

The quotation from the *Tang shu* that I mentioned earlier continues as follows: "Some say on the other hand, that Nippon was a small country which had been subjugated by the Wa, and that the latter took over its name."[297] As there is no evidence supporting this statement, no one in our country would say something like this. It can only be a guess on the part of someone in China. Moreover, the theory according to which "the name 'Nippon' was given to our land by the Chinese government during the reign of Empress Wu" is a mistake.[298] The name change took place at the beginning of the Xian-heng era I mentioned earlier. At that time the Chinese people had simply heard of the name change of our country from our envoy. They still did not have any proof of the change. However, they must have learned of the name Nippon from an official letter sent from our emperor to the Chinese emperor, probably at the time of Awata no Mahito's envoy during the reign of Emperor Monmu.[299] This corresponds to the time of Empress Wu. When we think that the name Nippon started to be used from that time even in China, we can only conclude that the theory according to which the name originated in China is a mistaken report.

Question: Is the word "Hi no moto" (sun's origin) ancient?

Answer: As I mentioned earlier, since the concept existed in the past, the characters for "Nihon" 日本 were attached to it, meaning "the sun's origin." However, the name "Hi no moto" did not exist; it was attached later to the characters "Nihon." This explains why the name does not appear in ancient texts. In the *Man'yōshū* we see the characters "Nihon" here and there. The reading of these characters as "Hi no moto" was the work of later people—a mistake on the part of someone who forced this reading upon the characters in order to maintain the five-syllable rhythm of the verse.[300] In ancient songs there are many verses with four syllables. The instances in which the characters "Nihon no" 日本之 appear should all be read "Yamato no" (of Yamato). For example, in the first book of the *Man'yōshū* we have the following song that Yamanoue no Omi Okura composed when he was in Tang China:

Iza kodomo	Quick, boys,
Hayaku Yamato he	Let's set out for Yamato!
Ōtomo no	The pines on the shore
Mitsu no hamamatsu	At Mitsu of Ōtomo
Machikohinuramu	Must long for our return.[301]

We find another example in book eleven:

Yamato no	It is because I expressed my love with such passion
Murofu no kemomo	—As dense as the growth
Motoshigeku	Of the peaches of Murō
Ihite shi mo no wo	In Yamato—
Narazu ha yamaji	That our love is bound to ripen.[302]

Other similar instances should be read in the same way.

There are only a few instances in which the characters "Nihon" should be read "Hi no moto": the verse in the long poem *(chōka)* on Mount Fuji of book five, "the land of Yamato/ of the rising sun";[303] the verses "the land of Yamato/of the rising sun,"[304] and "Yamato/land of the rising sun"[305] from the long poem by the Kōbukuji priest, as it is mentioned in book nineteen of the *Shoku Nihon Kōki* (The Later Chronicles of Japan, Continued).[306] However, even in these instances the poet was not referring to the name of the country. Since the general term for the entire land was already spelled out in Yamato, there is no way that poets would be repeating the name of the same land twice. "Hi no moto" is simply a pillow word introducing the name Yamato.

There are two types of pillow words. One consists in putting the Japanese reading of the characters (Hi no moto), attached to the name "Nihon" 日本, before the name Yamato. Examples of this type are "Harubi no Kasuga" 春日之春日 (Kasuga, the day of spring), and "Tobutori no Asuka" 飛鳥之飛鳥 (Asuka, the flying bird).[307] The second type is an explanation of the name, as in the case of "Hi no mototsukuni Yamato" (Yamato that is the land where the sun rises). In this case, the meaning of the name is emphasized rather than the name itself. No matter what kind of pillow word "Hi no moto" might be, one thing is certain: it *is* a pillow word. "Hi no moto" became the name of our country only at a later time. In the *Nihongi*, whenever the characters "Nihon" 日本 appear, they are always read "Yamato."

Question: When did the characters for Nippon begin to be applied to the name Yamato?

Answer: Whereas the name Nippon began to be used during the reign of Emperor Kōtoku (ca. 645), we do not see it used in the *Kojiki*, which appeared seventy years later, in 712. When we think about this, we realize that at that time "Nippon" was not yet used to indicate "Yamato." The *Kojiki* records events up to the time of the reign of Empress Suiko (r. 592–628). Since during her reign the name Nippon did not yet exist, its characters do not appear. The general term for our country, Yamato, was only written with the first character *"wa"* 倭, following the practice that was customary for the editor. There is not a single instance in which the characters for "Nippon" appear. The reason is that the *Kojiki* focuses on the ancient language rather than on characters.

It was only later, with the *Nihongi*, that Yamato was written with the characters "Nippon" for the first time. The *Chronicles* chose to apply this auspicious name to Yamato because of the interest this work shows in selecting decorative characters in order to embellish its style. In the "Chronicle of the Age of the Gods" we find the sentence "Here and elsewhere the characters for 'Nippon' are to be read Yamato."[308] This note is here because people at that time did not yet have this knowledge.

Now when I examine the content of the *Nihongi*, I notice that the character *"wa"* 倭 is often used to indicate the specific name of the Yamato province, whereas the character for "Nippon" 日本 refers to the general term for the whole country. "Nippon" is also used to indicate the province whenever the name is related to the court. Although this rule does not apply to every single instance, it is a basic rule. The same rule can be applied to people as well. The characters for "Nippon" are used in association with emperors; otherwise, the character *"wa"* 倭 is employed. This argument becomes clear when you open the *Nihongi* again and analyze the following names: Kamu-yamato Ihare-biko no Mikoto 神日本磐余彦の天皇, in which the characters for "Nippon" appear;[309] and Yamatohime-no-Mikoto 倭姫の命, in which the character *"wa"* appears.[310] The name of Yamatodake-no-Mikoto 日本武の尊 includes the characters for "Nippon" because he was considered an emperor.[311] This also explains why *"mikoto"* 尊, a character reserved for gods and emperors, is used in his name, and why his death is recorded with the character *"hō"* 崩, which, again, was reserved for gods and emperors. In other words, these examples show that the *Nihongi* was written with a great concern for Chinese characters.

Question: How do you explain the fact that among the many names of our country, "Nippon" was the one chosen to write the name Yamato?

Answer: Ashihara-no-Nakatsu-kuni was the name given to our land from heaven. The name Ōyashimaguni implies the fact that our country controlled the entire land with its own strengths. Akizushima, attached to the name Yamato, also became the general term for the entire country. The process leading to the creation of these names was different from the one culminating in the formation of the name Yamato. Originally, Yamato was the name of one province. Since it was just one name in a line of names indicating several provinces, Yamato came naturally to be seen as a name in contraposition to other names, even when it became the general term for the whole country. This was the name chosen in order to distinguish our land from foreign countries. This implication is also maintained in the poem by Emperor Nintoku.[312] Moreover, although in the *Nihongi* the name Nihon was used as a general term without any specific reason for doing so, originally the name was devised in order to distinguish our land from foreign countries. It was only logical that the characters for "Nihon" would be specifically used to indicate "Yamato." (In the *Nihongi* "Nihon" somehow is used as a general term in instances in which Japan is distinguished from other lands, as in the book title.)

Question: Was the practice of having the characters "Nihon" and "Yamato" preceded by the character "ō" 大 (great), as in Dai-Nihon 大日本 (great Japan) and "Yamato" 大和, modeled after the Chinese practice of showing respect to the various names of the country, as in the cases of Da Han 大漢 (Great China) or Da Tang 大唐 (Great Tang)?[313]

Answer: No, this is not the case. Emperor Itoku's name was Ō-Yamato-hiko-sukitomo no Mikoto (r. 510–477); Emperor Kōan's name was Ō-Yamato-tarashi-hiko-kunioshihito no Mikoto (r. 392–291); Emperor Kōrei's name was Ō-Yamato-neko-hiko-futoni no Mikoto (r. 290–215); Emperor Kōgen's name was Ō-Yamato-neko-hiko-kunikuru no Mikoto (r. 214–158). We also have the name Oho-Yamato-kuniare-hime no Mikoto[314] written in phonetic style *(kana)*, which clearly indicates that the word ō is an ancient word. How could our country have known about foreign lands during such an ancient age? Moreover, there are many examples of words that are preceded by the word ō (big, great), beside the name Yamato. You should take a look at ancient documents. There are also many words that are preceded by the word *toyo* (abundant). When we look at the names of our country, we see that Yashima and Yamato are preceded by ō, and become Ōyashima and Ōyamato; Ashihara-no-Nakatsu-kuni and Akizushima are preceded by *toyo*, and become Toyoashihara-no-Nakatsu-kuni and Toyoakizushima. These are all ancient names that have existed since the age of the gods. There is no example in China of a word preceded by *toyo*. The origin of this practice is not clear.

    Moreover, in China the emperor's mother was called *"da-hou"* 大后 (J. *taikō*). However, according to the *Kojiki*, in our land the mother of the legitimate heir to the throne was called "Ogisaki" 大后. This proves that the usage of the word ō was not learned from China.[315] On the other hand, the *Nihongi*, having rejected the ancient language, calls the Empress Dowager, "Kōtaigō" 皇太后, on the footsteps of China.[316] It is truly deplorable to see that the ancient language of the age of the gods is doubted in light of a later thinking of pretended smartness which derives everything from China.

    To be truthful, there may be someone who will take issue with my explanation of the word Yamato that I have provided by answering a variety of questions as they were formulated to me. He may think that this tiresome and long discussion is useless to an understanding of the way of poetry. However, as I believe that this might become a key to understanding the meaning of a variety of things, I feel that it was not completely idle talk on my part.

On *Mono no Aware*[317]

Someone asked me the following question: What do you mean by the expression "to know *mono no aware* [the pathos of things]"?

I answered: In the preface to the *Kokinshū* we find the following passage, "The poetry of Yamato has one heart as seed and myriad words as leaves."[318] This "heart" (*kokoro* 心) is the one that knows *mono no aware*. The preface continues, "Because of their many actions people who live in the world express what they think in their hearts by entrusting their feelings to what they see and what they hear."[319] The heart that is mentioned in the sentence "they think in their hearts" is also the heart that knows *mono no aware*. The "one heart" mentioned in the first sentence of the preface is a general concept; the "thinking heart" mentioned in the second is a concrete explanation of the meaning of the general concept. We find another example of what "to know *mono no aware*" means in the following statement from the Chinese preface to the *Kokinshū*: "Their thoughts are easily swayed, their moods alternate between sorrow and happiness."[320]

The reason why all the sentences above are examples of what "to know *mono no aware*" means is that every living creature in the world possesses a feeling heart *(kokoro)*.[321] When there is a heart, by coming in contact with things, one necessarily thinks. Therefore, every single living creature possesses the ability to sing *(uta)*. Because, among all living creatures, man excels over a myriad of beings, when he thinks straight and with a clear heart, his thoughts become extremely deep. Moreover, man is more exposed to deeds and actions than are animals. Since he deals with so many things in real life, all the more numerous are his thoughts. Therefore, it would be unreasonable to think that man can live without songs. When we ask the question why human thoughts are so deep, I can only say that it is because they know *mono no aware*. Whenever a man performs an action, every time he comes in contact with this action, his heart is moved[322] and is unable to stand still. To be moved means to have a variety of sentiments, such as being happy at times, sad at others; or being angry, or joyful, or delightedly interested, or terribly worried, or full of love and hatred, or longing for someone, or being disgusted. In other words, the heart is moved because it knows *mono no aware*.

Let me give you a few examples of what it means to be moved because of knowledge of *mono no aware*. When one encounters something for which he should be happy and has happy thoughts, his happiness derives from the understanding of the essence of that very thing about which he should feel happy.[323] Likewise, when one encounters something for which he should be sad and has sad thoughts, his sadness derives from the understanding of the essence of that very thing about which he should feel sad. Therefore, "to know *mono no aware*" is to discern the nature of happiness or sadness while experiencing the world.[324] When we do not understand the nature of things, there is no feeling thought in our hearts, since we are neither happy nor sad. Without feeling thoughts, songs *(uta)* do not come about.

Therefore, to the extent that every living creature has the ability to discern the nature of things, albeit in different degrees, and has the knowledge of being either joyful or sad, they all have songs in themselves. In understanding the nature of things there is a difference between deep and shallow among living creatures. Since in animals the level of understanding is shallow, it seems, compared to humans, they do not have the ability to discern things. By being superior to things, human beings have a good understanding of the nature of these things, and know how to be moved by them *(mono no aware)*. Even among human beings there are deep thinkers and shallow thinkers. Compared to those who have a deep understanding of *mono no aware* someone might seem to be completely ignorant of it. Because of the enormous difference between these two kinds of people, usually the number of those who lack knowledge of *mono no aware* tends to be big. As a matter of fact, we cannot say that they lack knowledge of *mono no aware*. The difference is one of degree between deep and shallow. Well, a song originates from the depth of one's knowledge of *mono no aware*.

The above is an outline of the meaning of "knowing *mono no aware*." If I need to be more detailed about it, I would say that "to be stirred by external things" is an exact definition of knowing *mono no aware*.[325] Although in common usage "to be stirred" applies only to good feelings, this is actually not the case.[326] Even dictionaries explain the character *"kan"* 感 with the note "to be moved,"[327] saying that it means "sentiment," "deep emotion." It means to be moved by any sorts of feelings while experiencing external reality. However, in our country, "to be stirred" only applies to pleasant feelings. Although it is appropriate to write the verb *mezuru* (to admire something we like) with the character *"kan"* 感, it would be inappropriate to read this character *"mezuru."* The reason is that admiration *(mezuru)* is one among a variety of feelings. Therefore, it is acceptable to write it down with the character for "feeling" *(kan)*. However, since the meaning of "to be stirred" is not limited to feelings of admiration, to refer to the character *"kan"* and to read it *"me-*

zuru" would not exhaust the whole meaning of this character. To be moved by all sorts of feelings, and to be able to have deep thoughts, whether one is happy or sad, are all examples of "being stirred." Therefore, "to be stirred" is nothing but the knowledge of *mono no aware*. I have written in detail about this knowledge in my book *Shibun Yōryō* (Essentials of Murasaki's Work).[328]

Now *aware* is a word meaning "to be stirred deeply." At a later time *aware* was related only to feelings of sadness, and came to be written with the character for "sorrow" (*aware* 哀). However, this character only points at one of the many feelings that are included in the word *aware*; the meaning of *aware* is not limited to sorrow. In the *Man'yōshū* the word *aware* is written with the characters "*awa*" 阿[329] and "*re*" 怜 (compassion). These characters also convey only a partial meaning of *aware* without actually exhausting all its implications. Originally, *aware* was a word expressing a sigh, an articulation of one's innermost feelings irrespective of the social standing of the person experiencing them. It was a word of the same type as "oh!" or "ah!" We can see this by looking at the line in "The Chronicles of Emperor Ninken," "The sentence 吾夫阿怜矣 should be read, '*agatsuma haya to*' (ah, my spouse!)"[330] as well as at the note in "The Chronicles of Empress Kyōgoku" saying that the characters 咄嗟 should be read "*aa*" (ah!).[331] Moreover, there are many examples in *kanbun* in which the characters "*wu hu*" 嗚乎, "*yu jie*" 于嗟, and "*yi*" 猗 are read "*aa*" (ah!). This "ah!" is an expression of sighing. In the *Kogo Shūi* (Gleanings from Ancient Stories) we find the following statement:[332] "At this time the sky cleared up for the first time. Everybody was able to see each other. Their faces were joyful. Stretching out their hands, they sang and danced, and they said, 'Oh *(aware)*, how *(ana)* beautiful, how delightful, how refreshing!'" Although there is some doubt with regard to this passage,[333] it looks like ancient language. This passage is about Amaterasu Ōmikami exiting the heavenly cave.[334] However, the note indicating that "*aware* means 'clear sky' *(ame hare)*" is a hypothesis advanced by a later person; we should not believe it. I mention this etymology here because scholars have been led astray into believing that *aware* means "clear sky."[335] In the passage above, *aware* and *ana* are a repetition of expressions of sighing.

We have the following songs by Yamatodake no Mikoto:

Owari ni	Oh *(aware)*! Thou single pine tree!
tada ni mukaeru	That art right opposite
Hitotsu matsu aware	To Owari—
Hitotsu matsu	Ah me—thou single pine-tree!

> *Hito ni ariseba*   If thou wert a man,
> *Kinu kisemashi o*   Garments I would clothe thee with,
> *Tachi hakemashi o*   A sword I would gird on thee.[336]

> *Yatsume sasu*   In eight-bud-bursting
> *Izumo Takeru ga*   Seaweed-surging Izumo
> *Hakeru tachi*   The Brave wore a sword
> *Tsuzura sawa maki*   All wrapped around with many vines—
> *Sami nashi ni aware*   But without a blade, alas *(aware)*![337]

Moreover, we also have other verses, such as "wife of my longing, alas *(aware)*!"[338] and "Alas *(aware)*! For Kagehime."[339] We also find the expression *aware* in the verses of Shōtoku Taishi, "Alas *(aware)*! For/the wayfarer lying/and hungered for rice."[340] Although in all these poems the word *aware* sounds like "taking pity on someone" and "feeling compassion for someone," these meanings were given to this word later. This is not the meaning that *aware* had in ancient times. In all the examples above, *aware* expressed sighing, as in "Oh, Kagehime!" "Oh, wayfarer!" You should think about this matter with an eye to the following verses, "Oh *(haya)*, my spouse!" recited by Yamatodake no Mikoto,[341] and "Ah *(haya)*, Uneme! Ah *(haya)*, Mimi," recited by the Silla messengers in "The Chronicles of Emperor Ingyō" as they looked at Mounts Unebi and Miminashi.[342]

Now the verb *awaremu* means to think with a sense of sighing *(aware to omou)*. It is the same case as with the verb "to be sad" *(kanashimu)*, which means to think with sadness *(kanashi to omou)*. Therefore, the expression *awaremu* also indicates the fact of being stirred deeply, as when we say that we are moved by this and that. This expression is not limited to love.

However, the use of words changes with the passing of time, and many of them lose their original meaning. The word *aware*, which originally was an expression of sighing, was used in later ages with different meanings, so that its original meaning changed little by little. Let's take a look at the following song from the *Man'yōshū* by Lady Ōtomo no Sakanoue:

> *Hayakawa no*   Oh *(aware)*, my beloved,
> *Se ni iru tori no*   Who feels so lonely
> *Yoshi o nami*   Without a single foothold,
> *Omoite arishi*   Like a bird standing in the rapids
> *Waga ko wa mo aware*   Of the fast-flowing river![343]

In this poem *aware* follows the same phrasing of the poems from the *Kojiki* and the *Nihongi*. Let's also look at the following two anonymous songs:

Nago no umi o	Oh *(aware)*, how moving the ferryman
Asa kogi kureba	Who, like a deer, cries
Watanaka ni	In the middle of the sea,
Kako zo nakunaru	When he rows in the morning his way
Aware sono kako	Through the sea of Nago![344]

Kakikirashi	Oh *(aware)*, how moving this bird,
Ame no furu yo o	The cuckoo
Hototogisu	Crying through the night,
Nakite yukunari	The rain falling,
Aware sono tori	The sky covered with mist![345]

In these two instances, the meaning of *aware* is the same as in all the other poems mentioned above, although the phrasing is slightly different.[346] In these two poems the word *aware* is written with the characters 何怜. Since these two characters are read *"haya"* in "The Chronicles of Emperor Ninken,"[347] you should know that *aware* also articulates a sigh, just like *haya*.

Moreover, in book eighteen of the *Man'yōshū*, Lord Yakamochi, listening to the cry of a cuckoo-bird, wrote the following lines in a long poem *(chōka)*:

Uchi nageki	Never have I stopped to say,
Aware no tori to	Oh *(aware)*, this affecting bird
Iwanu toki nashi	Who grieves![348]

These verses look like a later compositional style, with a different phrasing from the song I quoted earlier. First of all, in the songs of the ancient age, *aware* was an expression of sighing following a noun—Oh, something! *(sore aware)*—that the poet used when he was moved by coming in touch with reality, as in the cases of "Oh, thou single pine tree!" *(hitotsu mastu aware)*, "Oh, the wayfarer!" *(tabibito aware)*, "Oh, how moving is this bird!" *(aware sono tori)*. In the latter phrasing, "Oh, how moving is this bird!" *aware* is still an expression of sighing, as in "Ah, this bird!" *(aa, sono tori)*. However, this expression is somehow different from the contemporary expression *aware no tori* (the poor bird).

Turning our eyes to later poetry, we find the following songs in the *Kokinshū*:

Arenikeri	Ah *(aware)*, how many generations
Aware iku yo no	Has this dilapidated
Yado nare ya	Dwelling witnessed?
Sumikemu hito no	Not a single visit
Otozure mo senu	Comes from the person who used to live here.[349]
Aware mukashibe	Ah *(aware)*, how happy
Ariki chō	To hear of Hitomaro
Hitomaro koso wa	Who people say
Ureshikere	Lived a long time ago . . .[350]

In the *Shūishū* (Collection of Gleanings) we find the following song by Fujiwara no Nagayoshi:

Azumaji no	Opening my way
Noji no yukima o	Through the snowy field path
Wakete kite	Of the Azuma highway,
Aware miyako no	Ah *(aware)*, to look at
Hana o miru kana	The capital's flowers![351]

All these *aware* are absolutely expressions of sighing—a continuation of the same line through to a later age. The everyday expression *appare*[352] is the double consonant form of this *aware*. In the *Kokinshū* we also find the following poem:

Toritomuru	Since they are not something
Mono ni shi araneba	To be grasped by and kept in one's hand,
Toshitsuki o	I have spent my life saying,
Aware ana u to	Ah *(aware)*, how hard
Sugushitsuru kana	These months and years have been![353]

We also find the following verses in a long poem *(chōka)*:

Sumizome no	I cannot exhaust my grief
Yūbe ni nareba	By sighing, "Ah, alas" *(aware aware to)*
Hitori ite	Alone in my room
Aware aware to	When the dark night
Nageki amari	Falls . . .[354]

In these songs as well, *aware* is an expression of sighing. We find the same expression of grief in the words of the *Kagerō Nikki* (The Kagerō Diary), "Thinking, 'Ah, alas' *(aware aware to)*, of the road down the barrier, I was looking far in the distance."[355]

Let's take a look at the following songs from the *Kokinshū*:

Aware chō	Alone these flowers must have bloomed
Koto o amata ni	After spring has gone,
Yaraji to ya	So that I will not address
Haru ni okurete	The many other flowers
Hitori sakuramu	With the sighing expression, "Ah!" *(aware)*.[356]

Aware chō	If the word *aware*
Koto dani nakuwa	Did not exist,
Nani o ka wa	What would help
Koi no midare no	To pull together
Tsukaneo ni semu	My heart confused with love?[357]

Aware chō	This strange word
Koto koso utate	*Aware*
Yo no naka o	Is a shackle
Omoihanarenu	That cannot be discarded
Hodashi narikeri	In this world of passions.[358]

Aware chō	Every time the word
Koto no ha goto ni	*Aware* comes out,
Oku tsuyu wa	Like dew settling on a leaf,
Mukashi o kouru	My tears remind me longingly
Namida narikeri	Of the past.[359]

Let's also look at the following poems from the *Gosenshū* (Later Collection):

Chiru koto no	Forgetting the pain
Uki mo wasurete	Of seeing them scatter,
Aware chō	The word *aware*
Koto o sakura ni	Dwells
Yado shitsuru kana	In the cherry blossoms.[360]

Aware chō	Why do we call it sad,
Koto ni nagusamu	This world of passions
Yo no naka o	In which we live
Nado ka kanashi to	Finding solace
Iite suguramu	In the word *aware*?[361]

Kiku hito mo	Even the person listening
Aware chō naru	To the word *aware*,
Wakare ni wa	When it comes to separation,
Itodo namida zo	Cannot exhaust
Tsukisezarikeru	His tears.[362]

In all these songs the expression *aware chō koto* means "the word *(koto)* known as *aware*." It does not mean "the thing *(koto)* known as *aware*." This should be clear from the verse, "every time the word" *(koto no ha goto ni)*.[363] "The word known as *aware*" is an expression of sighing—"Ah, alas!" *(aware aware to)*, a profound emotion. As we see in the song "After spring has gone," the late-blooming cherry tree wants to be the target of the onlookers' words of sighing admiration, so that the same word will not be addressed to other flowers—"alone these flowers must have bloomed/after spring has gone." You will understand that the meaning of *aware chō koto* is the same in the other poems by comparing them to this one.

In the *Man'yōshū* we find the following anonymous song:

Suminoe no	There is no day
Kishi ni mukaeru	That I do not think of you, saying, "Ah" *(aware)*—
Awajishima	The water's foam *(awa)* at Awaji Island
Aware to kimi o	Across the shore
Iwanu hi wa nashi	Of Suminoe.[364]

In the *Kokinshū* we read:

Yo no naka ni	Where in the world
Izura waga mi no	Is this body of mine?
Arite nashi	While being, it is not—
Aware to ya iwamu	Shall I say, "Ah!" *(aware)* in admiration,
Ana u to ya iwan	Or shall I say "Oh!" *(ana)* in desperation?[365]

In the *Gosenshū* we read:

Aware to mo	I will say neither "Ah!" *(aware)* in admiration,
Ushi to mo iwaji	Nor "Uh!" *(ushi)* in desperation,
Kagerō no	Since this body of mine fades away—
Aru ka naki ka ni	Being and not being,
Kenuru mi nareba	Like shimmering heat haze.[366]

In the *Shūishū* we read:

Aware to mo	If you only said,
Kimi dani iwaba	"Ah!" *(aware),*
Koiwabite	I would not regret
Shinamu inochi mo	Having to die,
Oshikaranakuni	Distraught as I am by love.[367]

Aware to mo	I do not believe
Iubeki hito wa	Anyone
Omōede	Would say, "Ah!" *(aware),* thinking of me.—
Mi no itazura ni	Useless my life continues
Narinubeki kana	While going towards its end.[368]

Konu hito o	While awaiting
Shita ni machitsutsu	The person who does not come,
Hisakata no	No night goes by
Tsuki o aware to	That I do not say, "Ah!" *(aware)*
Iwanu yo zo naki	Beneath the moon high in the sky.[369]

The words *aware to iu* (saying, "Ah!") are an expression of sighing, "Ah, alas!" *(aware aware to)*—the articulation of feelings felt deep in the heart. For example, the expression *hito o aware to iu* means that one is moved by a person and, as a result, makes a sound like sighing. The same meaning also applies to the expressions *waga mi o aware to iu* (sighing over this body of mine), and *tsuki o aware to iu* (sighing over the moon).

Again, in the *Kokinshū* we read:

Yoso ni nomi	Saying, "Ah!" *(aware),* I only looked at
Aware to zo mishi	The plum blossoms

Ume no hana	From afar—
Akanu iro ka wa	Their colors and fragrance of which I never tire,
Orite narikeri	Came forth when I plucked a branch.[370]

Murasaki no	Because of a single clump
Hitomoto yue ni	Of the *murasaki* plant,
Musashino no	As I look at the grasses
Kusa wa minagara	In Musashino
Aware to zo miru	I watch them, saying, "Ah!" *(aware)*.[371]

In the *Shūishū* we read:

Yamazato wa	The snow falls covering the ground
Yuki furishikite	Of the mountain village:
Michi mo nashi	No path can be found.
Kyō komu hito o	Saying, "Ah!" *(aware)*,
Aware to wa mimu	I will look at the person coming today.[372]

Tsukikage o	If I only could
Waga mi ni kauru	Exchange myself,
Mono naraba	With the moonlight
Omowanu hito mo	I would be able to see her, saying, "Ah!" *(aware)*,
Aware to ya mimu	The person who does not think of me.[373]

All these verses *"aware to miru"* (seeing something and saying, "Ah!") are also expressions of sighing deep in the heart at the sight of something.

Again, . . .[374]

These verses *"aware to kiku"* (listening to something and saying, "Ah!") have the same meaning as the other examples above.

Again, in the *Kokinshū* we find the following songs:

Iro yori mo	I think, saying, "Ah!" *(aware)*,
Ka koso aware to	More of their fragrance
Omōyure	Than of their colors:
Ta ga sodefureshi	Who has waved her sleeves
Yado no ume zo mo	On the plum blossoms by the house?[375]

Ware nomi ya	Am I the only one
Aware to omowamu	Thinking, while saying, "Ah!" *(aware)*?

Kirigirisu	The wild pinks
Naku yūkage no	At dusk
Yamatonadeshiko	When the crickets cry.[376]

Tachikaeri	I keep thinking, saying, "Ah!" *(aware)*
Aware to zo omou	Time and time again.
Yoso ni te mo	Like white waves from the offing
Hito ni kokoro o	My heart goes to that person,
Okitsu shiranami	No matter how far she is.[377]

Aware to mo	When I think,
Ushi to mo mono o	Saying either "Ah!" *(aware)* in admiration,
Omou toki	Or "Uh!" in desperation,
Nado ka namida no	Why must tears
Ito nakaruran	Flow down my cheeks?[378]

Chihayaburu	You,
Uji no hashimori	I think of you, saying, "Ah!" *(aware)*,
Nare o shi zo	Keeper of the mighty
Aware to wa omou	Uji bridge,
Toshi no enureba	Since the years go by for both of us.[379]

In the *Shūishū* we find the following song:

Mi o tsumeba	When I reflect upon her feelings
Tsuyu o aware to	I think of her, saying, "Ah!" *(aware)*—
Omou kana	How is she
Akatsukigoto ni	Every time the sun rises,
Ikade okuramu	Tearful dew settling in her eyes?[380]

All these verses *"aware to omou"* (thinking of something and saying, "Ah!") are also expressions of sighing and deep emotions, just like the other examples mentioned above.

Therefore, *"aware to iu"* (saying, "Ah!"), *"aware to miru"* (seeing something and saying, "Ah!"), *"aware to kiku"* (listening to something and saying, "Ah!"), and *"aware to omou"* (thinking of something and saying, "Ah!"), are all sighs over something that moves a person's heart.

Now, in the *Shūishū* we also find the following songs:

Omoi de mo	Although these are the mountains
Naki furusato no	Of my hometown
Yama naredo	That I see not even in my thoughts,
Kakure yuku hata	I can only say, "Ah!" *(aware)*,
Aware narikeri	As they hide from sight.[381]

Toshigoto ni	Although your bloom changes
Saki wa kawaredo	Every year,
Ume no hana	Plum blossoms,
Aware naru ka wa	Your fragrance, that makes me say, "Ah!" *(aware)*,
Usezu zo arikeru	Does not fade away.[382]

Similarly to the verse from Lord Yakamochi's long poem "Oh, this affecting bird!" *(aware no tori)*, in which the poet indicates something that moves him to sighing *(aware)*, in these two examples the poet is stirred by the mountain from his hometown and by the moving fragrance of the plum blossoms, which make him sigh, "Ah!" *(aware)*.

All the words *aware* in the songs above are examples of inflected verbs *(yō)*. *Aware* is also used as an indeclinable noun *(tai)*. We find an example in the following song from the *Gosenshū*:

Atarayo no	Whether I look at the cherry blossoms,
Tsuki to hana to o	Or at the night moon that I do not tire of watching,
Onajiku wa	It is the same—
Aware shireran	I wish I could show them
Hito ni miseba ya	To those who know *aware*.[383]

We find another example in the following song from the *Shūishū*:

Haru wa tada	Spring
Hana no hitoe ni	Blooms simply
Saku bakari	In one petal of the cherry blossoms:—
Mono no aware wa	In autumn *mono no aware*
Aki zo masareru	Is at its highest.[384]

As we have seen from all these examples, although the phrasing of the word *aware* changes, its meaning remains basically the same: to be stirred deeply by experiences and by the surrounding reality of things seen and heard.

In common parlance *aware* is usually interpreted as sorrow, but this is not the case. *Aware* includes a gamut of feelings, including joy, charm, delight, sadness, and love. There are many examples in which the word *aware* is used in relationship to what is interesting and charming. We find in tales and other writings expressions such as "movingly charming" *(aware ni okashiu)* and "movingly happy" *(aware ni ureshiu)*. In the *Ise Monogatari* (Tales of Ise) we read the sentences, "This man, as he was coming every night from his place of exile, played the flute with appeal. His voice was charming; he sang in a moving manner *(aware ni utaikeri)*."[385] The charm of the man's voice as he plays the flute with appeal is *"aware"* (moving). In the *Kagerō Nikki* we read, "Although usually I was quite despondent, there was no limit to how movingly happy *(aware ni ureshiu)* I felt."[386] This sentence calls the joy of fulfillment *"aware"* (moving).

However, in the *Genji Monogatari* and other tales we find many examples in which "charming" *(okashiki)* and "moving" *(aware naru)* stand in antithesis.[387] There is a difference between a general and a specific distinction between the pairs in this antithesis. The general distinction is that, as I mentioned earlier, "charm" is included in *aware*. The specific distinction is that, among the many feelings operating in a person's heart, charm and joy stir the heart in a shallow way, whereas sadness and love move it deeply.[388] This is why a deep feeling is labeled especially *"aware"* (moving)—a fact that explains why, in common parlance, the content of *aware* is believed to be only sadness. For example, among the many flowers of all trees and grasses, the cherry blossoms are singled out as "flowers," while at the same time they are contrasted to the plum blossoms. This is what Genji meant when in the "Wakana" (Spring Shoots) chapter of *Genji Monogatari* he said, "How I would like to put the plum blossoms beside the (cherry) blossoms."[389] It is the same thing with the twelve *ritsu* tones of court music *(gagaku)* in which the *ryo* tones are included at the same time that the six *ritsu* tones and the six *ryo* tones stand beside each other.[390] In other words, the definition of *aware* as the heart's movement because of a specific feeling (sorrow) is derivative. The original definition of *aware* is the stirring up of the heart by all kinds of human feelings. This is why what should be felt deeply inside the human heart is called *"mono no aware."*

Now, with regard to the difference between knowing *mono no aware* and not knowing it, I would say that to know *mono no aware* is to be stirred by the view of the wonderful cherry blossoms, or of the bright moon while facing it. One's feelings are stirred up because he understands, deep in his heart, the moving power of the moon and of the blossoms. The heart that is ignorant of this moving power will never be stirred, no matter how wonderful the blossoms are and how clear the moon is in front of him. In other words, this is what I mean by the phrase "not knowing *mono no aware*."

To know *mono no aware* is to discern the power and essence, not just of the moon and the cherry blossoms, but of every single thing existing in this world, and to be stirred by each of them, so as to rejoice at happy occasions, to be charmed by what one should consider charming, to be saddened by sad occurrences, and to love what should be loved. Therefore, people who know *mono no aware* have a heart; those who do not are heartless. This should be clear from the upper verse of the following song by priest Saigyō:

Kokoro naki	Even one like myself,
Mi ni mo aware wa	Who has no heart,
Shirarekeri	Knows the moving power of things *(aware)*:
Shigi tatsu sawa no	Autumn dusk,
Aki no yūgure	A snipe taking off from the swamp.[391]

We find the following passage in the *Ise Monogatari*: "In the past there was a man. He spent days and months talking to a woman. Since she was not made of wood or stone, she must have taken pity on him, and eventually she was moved *(aware)* by his words."[392] The *Kagerō Nikki* states, "Since even this insensitive heart of mine felt quite strongly, you can imagine how my companion was deeply moved *(aware)* since she was crying."[393] These quotations should give you a taste of what "to know *mono no aware*" means. I have also discussed this topic in detail in *Shibun Yōryō* (Essentials of Murasaki's Work).

The following poem from book nineteen of the *Kokinshū* tells us that songs *(uta)* spring from the knowledge of *mono no aware*:

> A catalogue in the form of a long poem prepared by Ki no Tsurayuki on presenting the old songs to the Emperor:
>
> Since the age/of the awesome gods never ceasing/during reigns profuse/as the joints of black bamboo/men have sung with thoughts/entangled by the spring mists/that drift over Mount Otowa/where echoes sound/unable to sleep/when awakened by the late/night cries of mountain/*hototogisu* echoing/through skies rumbling with/early summer thunderstorms/gazing lovingly/upon the bright brocade of/autumn leaves scattered//upon Tatsuta Mountain/when like the Tenth Month/showers chill winter's portent/like the snow that falls/in

patches on the garden/during winter nights/they felt their hearts melt and fade/ when as the cycle/of the year passed once more or/when especially/moved to express their feelings *(aware chō koto o iitsutsu)*/they wished their lord a/lifespan of one thousand years/the burning desires/of the people of this world/ smoldering like the/molten core of Mt. Fuji/in far Suruga/the tears of those who part too/soon the strand of grief/that binds hearts like skeins of fine/wisteria boughs/these words abundant as the/leaves of eight thousand/grasses upon the meadows . . .[394]

The old songs presented to the emperor are not all by Tsurayuki himself.[395] The old songs mentioned in the catalogue are those to which Tsurayuki refers in the preface, in which he says, "We presented the Emperor with the old songs which are not included in the *Man'yōshū*."[396] The poem above means that each and every song on the seasons, on love, and on miscellaneous topics, which poets have become used to composing since the age of the gods, all spring from one *mono no aware*. In the catalogue of this long poem, among verses on the four seasons, on love, and on miscellanea, we find the lines, "as the cycle/of the year passed once more or/when especially/moved to express their feelings." These lines mean that "all the poems on the seasons, love, and miscellanea mentioned before and after come from an expression of sighing, Ah, alas! *(aware aware to)*, as they deal with the moving power of things *(mono no aware)* according to each and every occasion." This long poem is a catalog singing all the different types of *mono no aware*.

Book eighteen of the *Gosenshū* contains the following passage:

As he was listening somewhere in front of the bamboo blinds to someone talking about this and that, he heard the voice of a woman from the inside saying, "this old man looks as if strangely he knows *mono no aware*." Then, he (Tsurayuki) composed the following song:

Aware chō	Although no sign
Koto ni shirushi wa	Of the word *aware*
Nakeredomo	Was in sight,
Iwa de wa e koso	There was no way it would not come forth
Aranu mono nare	From my words.[397]

Since songs are products of *mono no aware*, it is interesting to see that the woman in the song above would refer to a poetic genius as someone who "looks as if he knew *mono no aware*." The man's answer includes the words *aware chō*, which, as I explained earlier, mean "to sigh after having been stirred by something." The song says that, although to sigh repeating, "Ah, alas!" *(aware aware to)* is of no use in expressing one's feelings, once one cannot endure *mono no aware*, one cannot avoid expressing it. The woman's sentence in the headnote, "He looks as if strangely he knows *mono no aware*," is a roundabout way of saying that "he looks like a poet," knowing that she is actually talking about Tsurayuki. In the answer, he understands the woman's ploy perfectly. What he really means is to say that, although to be a poet is of no use in expressing one's feelings, once *mono no aware* is overwhelming, one cannot avoid being a poet.

In the *Tosa Nikki* (The Tosa Diary) Tsurayuki defines poetry as "an action, in China as well as in our land, performed when one's thoughts become unendurable."[398] In the same diary we find the following sentence: "We were so happy when we reached the capital that the songs we composed were too numerous to record."[399] This line means that, because of their overwhelming joy, they could not bear to hold it in their hearts, and as a result many songs were produced. Joyous thoughts stir up one's heart: this is *mono no aware*. In the book "Dream of the King of Chu" of the *Eiga Monogatari* (A Tale of Flowering Fortunes), the narrator says, "Poetry sets one's heart free; when people are charmed, fascinated, or saddened *(aware)* by something, they all begin by turning to poetry."[400] In this case, as I mentioned earlier, *aware* is singled out as a specific feeling. Generally speaking, feelings deriving from charm and fascination are all *mono no aware*. From all these examples you should know that poetry derives from *mono no aware*.

Question: I have understood that songs *(uta)* come from the knowledge of *mono no aware*. Now, why would someone come up with a song when he is overwhelmed by *mono no aware*?

Answer: Poetry is an action performed when one is overwhelmed by *mono no aware*. To be overwhelmed by *mono no aware* means that someone ignorant of *mono no aware* is not moved even when he comes in contact with *mono no aware*. If one is not moved, no song comes about. For example, despite the frightful roar of the thunder, the deaf man does not think that it is roaring, since he cannot hear. Because he does not think that it is roaring, he is not frightened by it. On the other hand, the person who knows *mono no aware* cannot avoid being moved whenever he comes in contact with *aware*, even when he does not think that it is a moving situation. It is like someone with good hearing who feels the dreadfulness of the thunder even when he makes an effort not to fear it.

Now, when *mono no aware* is so strong that it cannot be contained, it becomes hard to endure it and to control it once it lodges deep in one's heart, despite all efforts to halt it. This is what I mean by being overwhelmed by *mono no aware*. When *mono no aware* becomes so overwhelming, an excess of thoughts springs forth in words of its own accord. The words that come out spontaneously whenever one is overwhelmed by *mono no aware* inevitably prolong themselves and become ornate lines.[401] Soon they are songs *(uta)*. This is also the time when one "sighs" *(nageku)* and "sings" *(nagamuru)*. (I shall discuss this issue later on.)[402] When words create lines that the voice sustains for a long time, the plaintive thoughts *(aware aware to omoi)* tying up one's heart clear up. Although one does not make any conscious effort to say anything, words come out spontaneously. When one is overwhelmed by *aware*, its content comes into expression of its own accord, despite one's efforts not to say anything. It is exactly like master Tsurayuki sang in the poem I mentioned above, "there was no way it would not come out/from my words." Accordingly, when one is overwhelmed by *aware*, a song always comes into being naturally, without any need for thinking about it.

Question: It must be as you say. Whenever one is overwhelmed by *mono no aware*, everything on his mind comes out in words without any conscious thinking. Ordinary language, however, should be sufficient to express one's feelings. I do not understand why these words should be sung, and why poetic language should be used. What are your thoughts on this issue?

Answer: This doubt is only natural on the part of someone living in the modern world. Indeed, you must enquire carefully about the essence of each and every single thing, and ponder with great attention over their meaning. Because, if you look at things with an eye turned to minor details, doubts are bound to be numerous, you must definitely concentrate on the essence of things.

I explained above the process by which a song *(uta)* comes into being. Such a coming into being does not take place through ordinary language. At the same time, the elongation of the voice into a song and the creation of a poetic pattern are not the result of any artificial planning. The expression of what cannot be contained within one's heart comes spontaneously with a pattern in the poetic words that elongates these words into songs. One expresses something in ordinary language only when his feelings *(aware)* are shallow. Whenever his feelings are deep, a pattern comes up naturally that causes the words to be sung. A deep *aware* cannot be satisfied by ordinary language. The same word, once it comes with a singing pattern, cheers up one's heart in a way that no other word can do. A deep feeling that cannot be fully expressed by ordinary language, no matter how detailed the description might be, is fully exposed in its depth by the words' and the voice's patterns when poetic language is employed and a poem is sung. Accordingly, the place where words come with a good degree of patterns, being sustained by the voice for a long time, hides an unfathomably deep *aware*. The person who listens to ordinary language is only mildly moved, no matter how moving the event he is witnessing might be. On the other hand, there is no limit to the depth of what he feels when words come with an ornate pattern, and they are accompanied by a singing voice. This is the natural artfulness *(jinen no myō)* of songs. Here lies the power of poetry to move *(aware)* the frightful spirits.[403]

I believe that, despite this explanation, there might still be someone who is miles away from what I am saying, and still has a hard time understanding my theory. Let me draw from what is near at hand to make an example. When someone is truly sad, to the point that he has a hard time enduring the gloom, no matter how many words he uses to describe his sadness, he cannot put an end to his unbearable feelings. If, on the other hand, he puts all his heart into saying a simple word like, "sad, sad" *(kanashi kanashi)*, no matter if this is common language, whenever he is overwhelmed by unendurable sadness, without even knowing it and without thinking about it, the voice will come to sustain his words, making them into a song, "Oh, how sad, ah, ah!" *(ara kanashi ya, nō nō)*, and his heart will be freed from all pressing sadness. At this juncture his words will be spontaneously assuming a good many ornate patterns; the voice will make them last a long time; they will be similar to a song. In other words, they assume a poetic form. These words take on a meaning that is different from what they mean in ordinary language, thus showing the bottomless depth of *aware* in the patterns of natural expression and in the long-lasting rhythm of the voice. The essence of poetry is made of words that have a pattern of their own that emerges from the inability to further endure the power of *mono no aware*. This is true poetry.

Now, I must also add that there are times when this sudden expressive outburst does not take place unconsciously. There are also instances in which the recitation of a poem is planned. Originally, this action also takes place when one is overwhelmed by *mono no aware*. The reason is that, when one is deeply moved by something and has a hard time keeping it concealed in his heart, and when one finds no satisfaction in expressing these feelings in ordinary language, he finds the utmost consolation by making the content of *aware* into a poetic pattern which he stretches into a sequence and voices into a song. The artfulness of poetry consists in expressing in only three or five lines the depth of one's heart, which cannot be fully articulated in a thousand or even ten thousand words.

Moreover, I must also say that, when it becomes difficult to fully articulate *aware* once one is overwhelmed by it, as I mentioned above, and to express one's feelings, one talks about them by entrusting them to the sound of the wind and the cry of insects caressing the ear; or, one sings his feelings in a song by comparing them to the fragrance of the cherry blossoms and the color of the snow pleasing the eye. This is what the line in the preface to the *Kokinshū*, "People express what they think in their hearts by entrusting their feelings to what they see and what they hear," means.[404] *Mono no aware*, which is difficult to show and cannot be fully articulated in words by saying things just as they are, is easily revealed, even when it concerns the deepest feelings, once it is expressed with the help of metaphors taken from the realm of things seen and heard. The following poem by Emperor Jinmu is an example of "songs in which feelings are entrusted to things":

Mizumizushi	We proud, mighty ones,
Kume no kora ga	We sons of the Kume,
Kakimoto ni	Have by our fence
Ueshi hajikami	A planted ginger tree:
Kuchi hibiku	How it stung my mouth
Ware wa wasurezu	I shall not forget:
Uchiteshi yamamu	I shall smite it and be done.[405]

The emperor composed this song when he subjugated Nagasunehiko. The emperor deeply resented the death of his elder brother, Itsuse no Mikoto, who was killed by a flying arrow at the battle of Kusaesaka. In this poem, the emperor used the image of the bitter taste of ginger biting the tongue and lingering inside the mouth without ever disappearing in order to say that now he will never forget.[406] When we look at later poetry, we find the following song in the *Kokinshū*:

Oto ni nomi	The white dew
Kiku no shiratsuyu	Settling on the chrysanthemum
Yoru wa okite	And I whose nights are made restless by these barren tidings
Hiru wa omoi ni	Will vanish
Aezu kenubeshi	In the morning sun.[407]

Now, as well as in the past, there are an extraordinarily large number of songs like the one above, in which one's feelings are expressed by using the image of some thing.

Furthermore, there is another instance in which the description of one's feelings is entrusted to the representation of external things. One's sentiments are deferred to things when some obstacles prohibit him from showing them openly, once he is overwhelmed by *mono no aware,* as in the case of the following two poems by Isukeyorihime no Mikoto:

Saigawa yo	From Sai River
Kumo tachiwatari	Clouds rise and spread across the sky;
Unebiyama	Unebi Mountain
Konoha sayaginu	Rustles with the leaves of trees:
Kaze fukamu to su	A wind is about to blow.[408]

Unebiyama	Unebi Mountain
Hiru wa kumo toi	In the daytime streams with clouds,
Yū sareba	And when evening falls,
Kaze fukamu to zo	Because of the wind about to blow,
Konoha sayageru	Rustles with the leaves of trees.[409]

These two songs were composed at the time of the death of Emperor Jinmu. As the mother of the princes, Isukeyorihime was saddened over the plot by Tagishimimi no Mikoto to kill his younger brothers. In order to let the princes know about this plot, their mother composed these songs using the images of the wind and the clouds. The princes learned about this event by listening to these poems, and we are told that they made preparations.[410] Tagishimimi was a prince by a different mother. For more details you should take a look at the *Kojiki.* There are many examples like this one, even in later ages. They all express *mono no aware* by entrusting the articulation of feelings to images of things seen and heard.

It might sound as if in this type of poetry things are forced to suit one's feelings, but an examination of the real root of the issue tells us that this is not the case. When one has deep thoughts in his heart, he relates each of them to objects that he sees and hears about. These objects are moving, and poetry comes from using these objects just as they are. Therefore, this is a natural process, free from the beginning of any type of artificiality.

Furthermore, what we call poetry does not simply set the heart free spontaneously, emerging when one is overwhelmed by *mono no aware*. A simple recitation of a song when one is deeply moved *(aware)* does not make one cheerful, and does not bring sufficient satisfaction to that person. Therefore, one finds consolation by making others listen to his song. When others listen and they are moved, then one's heart brightens up considerably. This process also takes place naturally. For example, someone now is having painful thoughts. It is difficult for him to keep these feelings to himself. No matter how much he keeps talking to himself, he cannot cheer up. However, as soon as he shares his feelings with others, he is somewhat relieved. His heart finally brightens up because the people who have been listening to him understand his feelings, and they are moved by them. Accordingly, generally speaking, to feel deeply means that one cannot avoid making others listen to his plea. Whenever one is moved by seeing or hearing something strange, or frightful, or funny, he necessarily wants to share his feelings with others; it is difficult for him to keep them to himself. Although there is no gain, either to oneself or to others, in making other people listen to you, it is only natural that one cannot prevent oneself from talking to others. Songs *(uta)* follow the same reasoning. To make other people listen is not something done on special occasions; it is the essence of poetry.

Those who do not understand this principle argue that real poetry is the expression of one's thoughts just as they are, independently from whether these thoughts are good or bad; they argue that to involve listeners in the process is not real poetry. Although some could agree with this idea momentarily, people who defend this position do not understand the real meaning of poetry. Although the passage in the first dialogue of the *Gumon Kenchū* (Notes of a Fool Asking a Wise Man) is a minor one,[411] when we enquire about the origins of poetry, we see that it is crucial for poetry to have someone listen to and be moved by it. The original nature of poetry is to provide words with patterns and to make them last long with the voice. Poetry has been like this since the age of the gods. There is no better way for someone to cheer up than by knowing that others have listened to his poem and have been moved by it.[412] If the listener is not moved, one's heart will hardly be set free. This rule should be applied to the contemporary world and should be agreed upon. Even if one discloses his feelings to another person, it is of no avail if that person is not moved. One finds consolation precisely in having another person listening to him, sympathizing with him. Accordingly, the fundamental thing in poetry is to have someone listening and feeling *aware*.

This explains why even the poems of the age of the gods are not the expression of the poet's thoughts just as they are. Words come ornate with rhetorical patterns, and they are sung in an appealing and moving voice. When the poet wants to say, "wife" *(tsuma)*, he introduces the pillow word "young grasses" *(wakakusa)*; when he wants to talk about "the night" *(yoru)*, he embellishes the word with the epithet "bead-black" *(nubatama no)*. Here, is not the poet creating rhetorical patterns that are set up in order to make a tune? In later ages the following songs were composed:

Shikishima no	This Chinese robe
Yamato ni wa aranu	Is nowhere to be found in Yamato,
Karakoromo	The spread-out islands—
Koro mo hezu shite	I wish we could meet
Au yoshi mo ga na	Without too much time going by.[413]

Mikanohara	The Izumi river
Wakite nagaruru	Flows gushing from
Izumigawa	The Mika plain—
Itsu miki to te ka	When did I happen to meet her,
Koishikaruramu	Falling in such deep love?[414]

Yoso ni nomi	Will I look at her from afar
Mite ya yaminamu	And stop at that point?—
Kazuraki ya	White clouds trailing over
Takama no yama no	Kazuraki
Mine no shirakumo	And the peak of Mount Takama.[415]

In all these examples the poet expresses his thoughts in only two verses; the remaining three all consist of rhetorical patterns. Someone may argue that these are useless verses. However, the expression of *aware* in two verses is deeply heightened by the three verses of allegedly useless rhetorical patterns. We find many examples of such techniques in the *Man'yōshū*.[416] Here we find the general difference between ordinary language and poetic language.

Although we hear detailed theories about the issue of meaning in common language, which is explained with precision in many words, once it comes to the meaning of *aware*, which can hardly be defined in words, it would be difficult to explain it were it not for poetry.[417] When I am pressed to explain the reason why the depth of *aware* that cannot be defined in words is expressed by poetry, I would answer that this is because poetry comes with rhetorical patterns. Thanks to these patterns, *aware* is displayed in all its depth. A song *(uta)* cannot be explained with the same detail and clarity used to talk about the meaning of things, as we do with our daily language. Moreover, such a deep meaning does not lie within the words of poetry. Poetry simply expresses the moving thoughts kept in one's heart. Although one may be listening to a song with little attention, this song contains a bottomless and limitless amount of moving feelings *(aware)*, thanks to the presence of rhetorical patterns.

On Love Poems[418]

Someone asked me the following question: How do you explain the presence of so many love poems?

I answered as follows: The number of love poems is particularly large beginning with the songs of the most ancient age, which appear in the *Kojiki* and the *Nihongi*. Even in the poetic collections of historical times the number of love poems remains extremely large. Among them, we find an entire section of love poems in the "relationship poems" *(sōmon)* of the *Man'yōshū*. This collection is divided in to three sections: miscellaneous poems *(zōka)*, relationship poems *(sōmon)*, and elegies *(banka)*. In books eight and ten we find the sections of miscellaneous poems on the seasons *(shiki no zōka)* and relationship poems on the seasons *(shiki no sōmon)*. All other poems are known as "miscellanea" *(zō)*; you should know that most of these songs are related to love.[419] To answer your question of why there are so many love poems, I would say that it is because love pierces the human heart more deeply than any other feeling, and therefore it is a phenomenon extremely difficult to endure. As a result, the narratives filled with moving feelings *(aware)* are always numerous in love poems.

Question: Generally speaking, although it seems to be quite illogical, men's deepest aspiration is more towards prosperity and the search for wealth than for love. And yet, why are these desires not sung in poetry?

Answer: There is a difference between "emotions" *(nasake)* and "desires" *(yoku)*. First of all, everything that goes through a person's mind is a kind of emotion. Among these thoughts there are some that make one wish to be this or that—these are desires. Accordingly, emotions and desires never grow apart. Although, generally speaking, desires are a kind of emotion, at the same time they are distinguished from emotions. To be moved by someone, to feel sad or gloomy, or hard-pressed are all examples of emotions. As a matter of fact, people go back and forth from emotions to desires and from desires to emotions. People's thoughts are not a one-way street; they go in different directions. No matter what, songs spring from emotions. Thoughts that go in the direction of emotions are especially sensitive to things, because their moving power is particularly strong. Thoughts that go in the direction of desire are simply searching for one thing. Is it because they do not pierce the human heart so intimately that desires are never as deep as shedding tears at the sound of the birds and at the view of the ephemeral cherry blossoms?

Thoughts of yearning after riches are examples of desires. Since they are far from being moving topics, these thoughts cannot inspire poetry. Although thoughts about love originally spring from desire, they are profoundly emotional. No living creature can avoid them, especially human beings who more than anything else know *mono no aware*. These are the thoughts that move people the most, overwhelming them with *aware*. You should know that other emotions as well, once their moving power is entrusted to this and that image, produce songs *(uta)*.

As I mentioned earlier,[420] it became customary in later ages to say that emotions are a sign of weakness of which one should be ashamed. Emotions seem to be shallower than desires because people often hide them and try to endure them. However, only poetry has preserved the spirit of the ancient age, continuing to sing the true feelings of human beings, just as they are. Poetry is never ashamed of expressing feminine and weak feelings. When, in later ages, people tried to compose outstandingly refined poems, they increasingly concentrated on articulating *mono no aware*. They totally disliked talking about desires, and they never chose them as topics for their songs.

In the rare occurrences in which such poems do appear, they are of the type of "the poem in praise of rice wine" in book three of the *Man'yōshū*.[421] There are plenty of poems like these in Chinese poetry *(shi)*. However, poets of songs *(uta)* truly disdained to treat such topics, and were never drawn to them. They did not find any appeal in making such poems. The reason is that these poets thought that desires were impure and lacked the power to move *(aware)*.

I do not understand why in foreign countries poets are ashamed of emotions filled with *aware,* and why they sing dirty cravings as if these were splendid topics.

Question: How do you explain your statement that poetry does not spring from desires, in light of the fact that in the ancient age we do find songs *(uta)* expressing a desire for eating, drinking, and riches?

Answer: As the proverb says, "Blow a hair and look for injury!"[422] To criticize rashly what someone says, exaggerating something that rarely happens while ignoring the total picture, is what people call a fight. This is something lesser people do all the time. If one wants to say it, he can say that the fire is cold and that the water is hot. However, nothing is unidimensional. One or two exceptions always come up. Things must be resolved with an eye to what is reasonable and with the whole picture in mind. Although there are dark-yellow bulls, doesn't the proverb say "As black as a bull"?

Question: When I look at Chinese texts I notice that the *Li ji* (Book of Rites) talks about the "great desires of man." While dealing with the emotions in a relationship between husband and wife, it looks as if the text considers it a deep relationship. This is only natural considering the fact that a husband loves his wife and a wife has deep feelings for her husband. However, love poems are not necessarily between husband and wife. Someone courts a girl who has been sheltered by parents that do not want the man to get closer to their daughter; someone else turns his eyes to another man's wife, spending an intimate night in her bedchamber, making love. These are all improper and questionable relationships, and yet they are sung in poetry as if they were marvelous accomplishments. What are your thoughts on this issue?

Answer: As I mentioned earlier,[423] no man can avoid falling in love. There are many examples of people, wise men as well as simple ones, who, once their heart begins to go astray with love, act against reason. Eventually, they cause the downfall of their lands and ruin themselves. It would be impossible to count the number of people, past and present, who managed to destroy their reputations because of their behavior. Everyone understands very well that this kind of action is regrettable, and that one should pay special attention and exercise prudence with regard to illicit love. However, not everyone is a saint. It is difficult to do praiseworthy things and have decent thoughts—and I am not thinking only of love—all the time. Among many questionable actions, love is hardly kept in check even if one forces himself to control it. Love is not something that follows one's will. There are many examples in this world of people who could not withstand their sexual drive, even when they knew it was wrong.

Who does not fall in love, deep in one's heart that no one can see? None of those people who pretend to sternly chastise the passions, assuming an air of intellectual superiority, can live without having sexual thoughts, once you start looking deep in their hearts. Especially when one falls in love with someone whom he is forbidden from seeing, the more he tries to endure the situation, knowing that it is inappropriate, the more he becomes weary and gloomy. Since this is not something than can be solved by reason, this is the time when a song *(uta)*, which is deep with moving power *(aware)*, emerges. Therefore, in love poetry we always find many examples of illicit and improper love. This is the logic of poetry from its very beginning.

In any case, poetry responds to external reality when one's feelings are stirred up. It is an expressive act that sings good things as well as bad ones, simply following the poet's heart. The real intent of poetry is not to choose and decide what is improper and what is questionable. Since to stop and to prohibit evil behavior is the job of government and education, they should be the ones warning us against improper love. Poetry is unrelated to teaching; its main purpose is the articulation of *mono no aware*. As poetry belongs to a different category than politics and ethics, it ignores the good and the bad, no matter what these may be. Poetry should not deal with such topics. This being the case, poetry does not sing the praise of evil behavior as if it were good. Poetry simply makes splendid whatever moves the human heart.

You should savor the literature of tales *(monogatari)* with these thoughts in mind, and you should know that this is what they privilege the most. Since I have written in detail about *Genji Monogatari* (The Tale of Genji) elsewhere,[424] quoting words from all the books and giving concrete examples, you should look at these pages while thinking about this issue. Generally speaking, you should be able to understand the way of poetry by looking at this tale.

Question: In China love poems and tales of amorous affairs are rare. On the other hand, books in our country speak only of love. Many are the descriptions of improper love among members of the upper and lower classes. Do you think that the reason why these episodes are not criticized as evil is due to the licentious and flirtatious customs of our land?

Answer: When it comes to love affairs the situation is the same here as in China, in the past as in the present. If you look at Chinese writings through the ages, you will see that nowadays there are many examples of slightly improper love. However, as I mentioned earlier, [425] in that country there is the custom of making a lot of noise when it comes to good and evil. The usual scholars who profess themselves wise disdain and criticize love affairs, writing about them in very hateful and negative terms. In poetry as well they are drawn by local customs. They only express a liking for the manly, heroic spirit; they do not talk about the feminine emotions of love, which they regard as shameful. This way of thinking is nothing but decorative appearance; it does not reflect the real truth of the human heart. However, people who read these writings in later ages did not do any further investigation, and they took this poetry to represent the real state of affairs in that country. It would be foolish to think that the Chinese people are only minimally led astray by love.

Now because our land is a gentle place whose inhabitants do not pretend to be smart, people do not debate the issue of good and evil in any complicated manner. They try to say things just as they are, as we can see from our songs *(uta)* and tales *(monogatari),* which concentrate on the expression of *mono no aware*. This explains why they can write so indifferently and realistically about the many varied feelings of people in love. Moreover, when we look among our writings to the national histories, which were written in our land through the ages in imitation of China, we do not find any difference from the Chinese histories.

Therefore, to think that our land is lax in sexual matters is an erroneous belief on the part of someone who looks only at songs and tales, and does not pay any attention to the national histories. Such a person does not realize that his belief is based on stylistic matters. Although it should not be trusted, does not the *Wei Ji* (History of the Kingdom of Wei) say about our land that "The customs are not lewd"? Not only in love, but in an infinite variety of behaviors, evil people are especially numerous in China. The fact that there are so many rules and prohibitions over there indicates that the country was evil from the very beginning. Since ancient times, in our land people's behavior was neither praised nor blamed; it was simply gentle and tolerant. The reason why we do not hear of too many evil people is because our land is the land of the gods.

Question: Although Buddhist monks should definitely not fall in love, through the ages we find many poems in poetic collections that deal with priests in love; they are never blamed in the way of poetry. How do you explain the fact that monks keep on writing such poems even today, without any hesitation?

Answer: As sexual desire is strictly regulated in Buddhism, this is an issue to which monks should pay enormous attention. Everybody knows this, and to this day it is a pity to see monks involved in this kind of affair. This having been said, I would like to add that decisions about what is good and what is evil should be left to the individual religious lines. Poetry belongs to a different category; it is not required necessarily to follow Confucian and Buddhist teachings. Therefore poetry should not enter into discussions of good and evil behaviors; it should only be concerned with the expression of *mono no aware*, and with the articulation, no matter how, of what is pent up in one's heart.

Because monks have abandoned the secular world and have entered the Buddhist path, they should strictly respect its precepts and should avoid all kinds of improper behavior at all times. It is true that monks should force themselves to exercise prudence and endurance. However, the fact that they are priests does not mean that their worldliness and their human emotions have changed all of a sudden. They are not a buddha or a bodhisattva in human form. The bottom of their hearts is not so pure and unclouded that they can already reach enlightenment. It is only natural that the defilements of this world still linger in them. How could they be free of sexual thoughts? Since it is only logical to think of them as originally human, there is no reason why they should be ashamed of their thoughts. And there is no reason why they should be blamed for them. As long as one is an ordinary human being, failures and mistakes are matters of fact that cannot be avoided. The very strictness of the Buddhist rules towards love derives from the difficulty that any human being encounters when trying to avoid it, and from the ease with which a human being is led astray by love. However, people think that monks should be like buddhas down to the bottom of their hearts. Eventually the monks themselves pretend to be like a buddha—an attitude that makes their behavior all the more sinful.[426]

Let me explain what I mean with an example. A truly honorable holy man draws close for a while to a cherry tree in outstandingly full bloom or to maple leaves in full color and says, "Oh, how beautiful!" Then, on the road he meets a beautiful woman, and apparently he passes her by without even taking a look at her. When I think about these two encounters, I realize that, as the cherry blossoms and maple leaves are worldly delights of color and fragrance, the priest should not turn his attention to them too much. However, because these are not pleasures to which one becomes addicted, the priest cannot be blamed if he is even slightly drawn to them. On the other hand, the sexual appeal of a woman leads human beings astray. Thinking that she will certainly hinder his chances to become a buddha in the next life, the religious person does not even look at the woman. The behavior of this holy man is venerable indeed. However, it would be truly deceitful to think that this was actually what went on inside his heart. The reason is that the beauty of the color and fragrance of the cherry blossoms and maple leaves is limited, so that their appeal to the human heart is shallow.[427] On the other hand, sexual appeal is bottomless and limitless; its impact on the human heart is profoundly deep. Then how could the holy man ignore the beauty of the woman's limitless appeal if he was sensitive enough to praise the cherry blossoms and the maple leaves whose appeal is limited? It would be the same thing as if, for example, someone said that he wanted one hundred golden coins but did not want a thousand golden coins—simply, it does not make any sense.

Someone whose heart is not stirred by the sight of a beautiful woman must be a true buddha indeed! Otherwise, we would call him a heartless person of the likes of stone or wood, inferior even to birds and insects. Among men, monks are singled out as those who do not have a wife. They are constantly concerned with sexual desire. Since they are bound to be oppressed more and more by gloomy thoughts, they produce more moving poems on love than worldly people do. Think of the ancient story about the holy man from the Shiga temple who grasped the hands of the Empress Mother and recited the poem on the "Jeweled Broom."[428] This moving behavior fits the feelings of a priest perfectly. Shall this slight liberation from obsessive thoughts that were mounting deeply in his heart by means of the recitation of this song also be suitable to the Buddhist acts of repentance and display of sins? This is an idle question. A song is a song; it does not need to suit anything.

Notes

Abbreviations

CR   *Chikuma Raiburarī.* Tokyo: Chikuma Shobō.
GBS   *Gendai Bigaku Sōsho.* Tokyo: Keisō Shobō.
KGB   *Kōdansha Gakujutsu Bunko.* Tokyo: Kōdansha.
NKBZ   *Nihon Koten Bungaku Zenshū.* Tokyo: Shōgakukan.
NST   *Nihon Shisō Taikei.* Tokyo: Iwanami Shoten.
SKT   *Shinshaku Kanbun Taikei.* Tokyo: Meiji Shoin.
SNKBT   *Shin Nihon Koten Bungaku Taikei.* Tokyo: Iwanami Shoten.
SNKBZ   *Shinpen Nihon Koten Bungaku Zenshū.* Tokyo: Shōgakukan.
SNKS   *Shinchō Nihon Koten Shūsei.* Tokyo: Shinchōsha.
WBT   *Waka Bungaku Taikei.* Tokyo: Meiji Shoin.

Preface

1. Michael F. Marra, *Kuki Shūzō: A Philosopher's Poetry and Poetics* (Honolulu: University of Hawai'i Press, 2004).

Translator's Introduction: Motoori Norinaga's Poetics

1. This study led Norinaga to the compilation from 1764 to 1798 of a commentary of the *Kojiki* in forty-four books, known as the *Kojiki-den*. Ann Wehmeyer provides an English translation of the first book in Motoori Norinaga, *Kojiki-den, Book 1* (Ithaca, NY: East Asian Program, Cornell University, 1997).

2. Hino Tatsuo, "Motoori Norinaga to Ueda Akinari," in Ariyoshi Tamotsu et al., eds., *Kinsei no Waka, Waka Bungaku Kōza,* vol. 8 (Tokyo: Benseisha, 1994), p. 224.

3. Kanno Kakumyō, *Motoori Norinaga: Kotoba to Miyabi* (Tokyo: Perikansha, 1991), p. 67.

4. *Suzunoya Shū* 1:313.

5. Ki no Tomonori, *Kokinshū* 1:60; English translation by Helen Craig McCullough, *Kokin Waka Shū: The First Imperial Anthology of Japanese Poetry* (Stanford, CA: Stanford University Press, 1985), p. 25.

6. *Gosenshū* 3:117, anonymous.

7. *Shūishū* 1:41, anonymous.

8. McCullough, trans., *Kokin Waka Shū*, p. 3. The original text appears in Okumura Tsuneya, ed., *Kokin Waka Shū*, SNKS 19 (Tokyo: Shinchōsha, 1978): 11.

201

9. Ono Susumu, Satake Akihiro, and Maeda Kingorō, *Iwanami Kogo Jiten* (Tokyo: Iwanami Shoten, 1974), p. 499.

10. For a history of this school, see Peter Nosco, *Remembering Paradise: Nativism and Nostalgia in Eighteenth-Century Japan* (Cambridge, MA: Council on East Asian Studies, Harvard University, 1990). For an account of how the history of this school came into being during the Meiji period, see Susan L. Burns, *Before the Nation: Kokugaku and the Imagining of Community in Early Modern Japan* (Durham, NC, and London: Duke University Press, 2003).

11. Toyoda Kunio, *Nihonjin no Kotodama Shisō*, KGB 483 (Tokyo: Kōdansha, 1980), pp. 184–185.

12. *Man'yōshū* 6:972. Kojima Noriyuki, Kinoshita Masatoshi, and Satake Akihiro, eds., *Man'yōshū*, 2, NKBZ 3 (Tokyo: Shōgakukan, 1972), p. 157. The English translation is by Edwin A. Cranston, *A Waka Anthology, Volume One: The Gem-Glistening Cup* (Stanford, CA: Stanford University Press, 1993), p. 327. See also the translation by Roy A. Miller, "The 'Spirit' of the Japanese Language," *The Journal of Japanese Studies* 3:2 (Summer 1977): 276. For a discussion of the relationship between "things" and "words," see Michael F. Marra, "On Japanese Things and Words: An Answer to Heidegger's Question," *Philosophy East and West* 54:4 (2004): 555–568.

13. Norinaga used this expression in several works, such as *Uiyamabumi* (First Steps up the Mountain, completed in 1798), *Kojiki-den*, and *Kuzubana* (Tokyo: Arrowroot, 1780). See Toyoda Kunio, *Nihonjin no Kotodama Shisō*, pp. 188–189.

14. The original text of *Isonokami no Sasamegoto* appears in Hino Tatsuo, *Motoori Norinaga Shū*, SNKS 60 (Tokyo: Shinchōsha, 1983), pp. 264 and 316–317. Hereafter abbreviated as *IS*.

15. Uetani Hajime, Mizuta Norihisa, and Hino Tatsuo, eds., *Jinsai Nissatsu, Tawaregusa, Fujingen, Mukaukyō*, SNKBT 99 (Tokyo: Iwanami Shoten, 2000), pp. 137–140.

16. Sasaki Nobutsuna, ed., *Nihon Kagaku Taikei*, vol. 7 (Tokyo: Kazama Shobō, 1957), p. 254.

17. Katō Jōken, ed., *Shokyō, Jō*, SKT 25 (Tokyo: Meiji Shoin, 1983): 43. The English translation is by Stephen Owen, *Readings in Chinese Literary Thought* (Cambridge, MA: Harvard University Press, 1992), p. 26.

18. *IS*, p. 323. Likewise, Norinaga read the statement from the *Li-chi* (Record of Ritual) as follows: "Poetry expresses its intent; the act of singing sustains *(nagamuru)* the voice for a long time" (ibid.).

19. This is the definition given of the *shimonidan* verb *nagamu* in Ono Susumu, *Iwanami Kogo Jiten*, p. 946.

20. Hisamatsu Sen'ichi et al., eds., *Keichū Zenshū* 8 (Tokyo: Iwanami Shoten, 1973): 7.

21. The major poetic treatises of Norinaga's time indicated the musical aspect of "songs" *(uta)* as the genealogical moment of poetry. See, for example, the beginning of the first chapter, "The Origin of Poetry" *(Uta no Mimanoto Ron)*, of Kada no Arimaro's (1706–1751) *Kokka Hachiron* (Eight Essays on the Country's Poetry, 1742): "Generally, songs are that which dispels the gloom in one's heart through the length-

ening of words." Hashimoto Fumio, Ariyoshi Tamotsu, and Fujihira Haruo, eds., *Karonshū*, NKBZ 50 (Tokyo: Shōgakukan, 1975), p. 533.

22. On this issue Norinaga was indebted to Kamo no Mabuchi's (1697-1769) *Kanji Kō* (Essay on Poetic Epithets), in which Mabuchi leveled an attack against those who, "without knowing the past of the imperial reigns, explain the language of this land with Chinese phonetics." Hisamatsu Sen'ichi, ed., *Kamo no Mabuchi Zenshū*, vol. 8 (Tokyo: Zoku Gunsho Ruijū Kanseikai, 1978), p. 8.

23. Hosokawa Yūsai followed Liu Xi's explanation in the *Eiga no Taigai Shō*, a commentary of Fujiwara Teika's poetic treatise *Eiga no Taigai* (An Outline for Composing Poetry, after 1223). Keichū quoted the same passage in *Kokin Yozai Shō*. Hino Tatsuo, *Motoori Norinaga Shū*, p. 324, n. 2; Hisamatsu Sen'ichi, *Keichū Zenshū*, vol. 8, p. 7.

24. Uetani Hajime, *Jinsai Nissatsu, Tawaregusa, Fujingen, Mukaukyō*, p. 218.

25. Yoshikawa Kōjirō, Satake Akihiro, and Hino Tatsuo, eds., *Motoori Norinaga*, NST 40 (Tokyo: Iwanami Shoten, 1978), p. 525.

26. Yoshikawa Kōjirō, *Motoori Norinaga*, p. 526.

27. *IS*, pp. 228-230.

28. Hisamatsu Sen'ichi, *Kamo no Mabuchi Zenshū*, vol. 8, pp. 173-174.

29. Ekiken Kai, *Ekiken Zenshū*, vol. 1 (Tokyo: Kokusho Kankō Kai, 1945), p. 40.

30. *IS*, p. 341.

31. Ibid., pp. 244-246.

32. Ibid., pp. 338-343.

33. Ibid., p. 364. The literary scholar Kitamura Kigin (1624-1705) accepts this theory in his commentary of the *Kokinshū*. Yamagishi Tokuhei, ed., *Hachidaishū Zenchū*, vol. 1 (Tokyo: Yūseidō, 1960), p. 7.

34. Hisamatsu Sen'ichi, *Keichū Zenshū*, 8, p. 6.

35. *IS*, pp. 365-367.

36. Ibid., pp. 368-369.

37. Ibid., pp. 369-370.

38. The English translation is by Donald L. Philippi, trans., *Kojiki* (Tokyo: University of Tokyo Press, 1968), p. 248. The original text appears in Nishimiya Kazutami, ed., *Kojiki*, SNKS 27 (Tokyo: Shinchōsha, 1979), p. 169.

39. The poem, from the *Kojiki*, is attributed to Iwanohine no Mikoto, the consort of Emperor Nintoku, who sang it "at the entrance of Nara mountain" during her journey to Yamashiro:

Ao ni yoshi	I pass by Nara
Nara o sugi	Of the blue clay;
Odate	I pass by Yamato
Yamato o sugi	Of the little shields.

English translation by Donald L. Philippi, *Kojiki*, p. 310; Nishimiya Kazutami, *Kojiki*, p. 210.

40. *IS*, pp. 362-363.

41. Hashimoto Fumio, *Karonshū*, pp. 175-176.

42. *IS*, pp. 306-308.

43. Quoted in James J. Y. Liu, *Chinese Theories of Literature* (Chicago and London: University of Chicago Press, 1975), p. 7. See also François Jullien, *La valeur allusive: Des catégories originales de l'interprétation poétique dans la tradition chinoise (contribution à une réflexion sur l'alterité interculturelle)* (Paris: École Française d'Extrême-Orient, 1985), p. 27.

44. Quoted in Haun Saussy, "Syntax and Semantics in the Definition of *Wen*," paper delivered at the Annual Meeting of the Association of Asian Studies (Boston, March 27, 1994), p. 8. See also Jullien, *La Valeur Allusive*, p. 26.

45. "Le terme de *wen* qui a servi de noyau à l'élaboration de la notion de littérature en Chine se prête ainsi à une double enquête, sémantique et symbolique." Jullien, *La valeur allusive*, p. 22.

46. Hisamatsu Sen'ichi, ed., *Kamo no Mabuchi Zenshū*, 19 (Tokyo: Zoku Gunsho Ruijū Kanseikai, 1980), pp. 124-125.

47. Toyoda Kunio, *Nihonjin no Kotodama Shisō*, p. 191. For further information on the role played by the Japanese syllabary in Motoori's philosophy, see Koyasu Nobukuni's *Motoori Norinaga* (Tokyo: Iwanami Shoten, 1992) and *Norinaga Mondai to wa Nani ka* (Tokyo: Seidosha, 1995).

48. Toyoda Kunio, *Nihonjin no Kotodama Shisō*, pp. 194-204.

49. James J. Y. Liu, *Chinese Theories of Literature*, p. 17.

50. François Jullien argues that, in China, analogy takes the place held in the West by "imitation" (mimesis), the explanation of "art" on the ground of its imitation of nature. He gives the example of the analogic force contained in the image of the wind *(feng)* to define the power of words in classical Chinese poetics. In the commentaries of the *Shi jing* (Book of Odes), Confucian hermeneutics privileged the allegorical reading of the wind that stood for the indirectness of poetic expression in its penetrating mission of assisting the government in the process of "culturalization." Rather than an object for imitation, nature was the carrier of influence that, once it scatters the leaves of words *(kotoba),* leads to the transformation and refinement of human nature. The Confucian notion of power—a diffused set of relationships whose order must be maintained more by moral example than by the power of the sword—found in the rhetorical usage of an insinuating wind an indirect way of voicing political criticism, as well as eliciting improvements from rulers and subjects alike. The analogy between the pattern of the "sky" and the pattern of the text was strengthened by the powerful wind of "a moral lyricism" ("lyrisme de la moralité") that was one of the major poles of the Confucian discourse on culture, the other being the "lyricism of void" ("lyrisme de la vacuité") inspired by Buddhist and Daoist aesthetics. See the following statements from the preface to *The Book of Odes*: "The word 'airs' *(feng)* is used here to express the influence of instruction: the wind puts into movement and the instruction causes a transformation.... The notion of 'wind' implies the fact that, like the wind, those above influence and transform those below. Like the wind, those below criticize those above. Through literary expression, complaints are governed by patterning *(wen)*: there is no blame in those who criticize, and those who have ears for

these critical remarks will know how to improve themselves. This is what the word 'airs' implies." The English translation is by Stephen Owen, *Readings in Chinese Literary Thought*, pp. 38 and 46; Jullien, *La Valeur Allusive*, pp. 34, 97–102, and 113.

51. Adapted from James J.Y. Liu, *Chinese Theories of Literature*, pp. 25–26.

52. Jullien, *La valeur allusive*, p. 30.

53. Vincent Yu-chung Shih, trans. and annot. [Liu Hsieh], *The Literary Mind and The Carving of Dragons* (Taipei: Chung Hwa Book Company, 1974), p. 12. See François Jullien on the topic of reciprocity and literary genealogy in China: "Une genèse globale de toute création littéraire est ainsi élaborée en fonction de ces trois termes fondamentaux: le Dao comme totalité cosmologico-morale, le Sage comme premier auteur (en même temps que l'auteur par excellence), le texte canonique comme premier texte (en même temps que le texte par excellence)." Jullien, *La valeur allusive*, p. 40.

54. The expressions "rapprochement analogique" and "projection métaphorique" are from Jullien, *La valeur allusive*, p. 166.

55. From the extensive literature on the subject I will single out Kanno Kakumyō's chapter on "The Meaning of Motoori Norinaga's Theory of *Mono no Aware*," in his *Motoori Norinaga: Kotoba to Miyabi* (Tokyo: Perikansha, 1991), pp. 192–215, and the section "The Poetry of Things" in H.D.Harootunian, *Things Seen and Unseen: Discourse and Ideology in Tokugawa Nativism* (Chicago and London: University of Chicago Press, 1988), pp. 79–105.

56. John H. Moran and Alexander Gode, trans., *On the Origin of Language* (New York: Frederick Ungar, 1966), p. 32.

57. The text is included in Hino Tatsuo, *Motoori Norinaga Shū*, pp. 110–111 (hereafter abbreviated as *SY*). For a reading of this etymology, see Amagasaki Akira, *Kachō no Tsukai: Uta no Michi no Shigaku*, GBS 7 (Tokyo: Keisō Shobō, 1983), pp. 222–241.

58. Ekiken Kai, *Ekiken Zenshū*, 1, p. 45.

59. *IS*, pp. 285–286.

60. Ibid., p. 260. For the original text, see Nishimiya Kazutami, *Kojiki*, p. 30.

61. In the *Kojiki-den* Norinaga reminds his readers that, up to the time of the compilation of the *Man'yōshū*, the word *otoko*, being the counterpart of *otome* (a maiden), only referred to "young men." The extension of the word to indicate all men irrespective of their ages points to a new and later development in the history of this expression. Hino Tatsuo, *Motoori Norinaga Shū*, p. 262, n. 2.

62. *SY*, pp. 131 and 236–237.

63. *SY*, p. 84.

64. Jullien, *La valeur allusive*, pp. 67–73.

65. Sakabe Megumi, *Kagami no Naka no Nihongo: Sono Shikō no Shujusō*, CR 22 (Tokyo: Chikuma Shobō, 1989), pp. 81–82. For a French version, see Megumi Sakabe, "Notes sur le Mot Japonais *hureru*," in *Revue d'Esthetique*, n.s. 11 (1986): 48.

66. This hermeneutical move is reminiscent of attempts by medieval scholars in the West to find the original language of the angels, the privileged creatures that were believed to be able to communicate their thoughts perfectly without the need of relying on

any language. See Umberto Eco, *La ricerca della lingua perfetta nella cultura europea* (Bari: Laterza, 1993).

67. Alexander Gottlieb Baumgarten, *Estetica* (Milan: Vita e Pensiero, 1993), p. 17.

68. Ogyū Sorai, *Distinguishing the Way [Bendō]*, trans. Olof G. Lidin (Tokyo: Sophia University, 1970), pp. 78-80.

69. *IS*, pp. 403-408.

70. Ibid., pp. 408-409. Motoori developed this point further in *Naobi no Mitama* (Rectifying Spirit, 1771). An English translation by H.D. Harootunian appears in Tetsuo Najita, ed., *Readings in Tokugawa Thought* (Chicago: The Center for East Asian Studies, University of Chicago, 1994), pp. 111-127.

71. *IS*, pp. 416-423.

72. Here I am indebted to the explanation given by Hino Tatsuo, who interprets *tai* and *yō* as, respectively, "essence" and "function." Hino Tatsuo, *Motoori Norinaga Shū*, p. 441, n. 11.

73. *IS*, pp. 441-442.

74. Ibid., pp. 458-460.

75. Ibid., p. 467.

76. Ibid., pp. 468-469. Norinaga had already stressed the attention paid by the poets of the *Man'yōshū* to their craft in *Ashiwake Obune*. See Suzuki Jun and Odaka Michiko, eds., *Kinsei Zuisō Shū*, SNKBZ 82 (Tokyo: Shōgakukan, 2000), pp. 335-337.

77. *IS*, p. 471.

78. See, for example, Emperors Tenji and Kōkō, who impersonated a farmer in *Gosenshū* 6:302 and *Kokinshū* 1:21, respectively.

79. *IS*, pp. 480-483.

80. I have hinted briefly at this problem in the epilogue to my *Representations of Power: The Literary Politics of Medieval Japan* (Honolulu: University of Hawai'i Press, 1993), p. 174.

81. Motoori Ōhira (born Inagaki Shigeo) left a diary of the same trip to Yoshino, which is entitled *Ebukuro no Nikki* (The Travel Satchel Diary, 1772). The text appears in Ōno Susumu and Ōkubo Tadashi, eds., *Motoori Norinaga Zenshū: Bekkan,* 3 (Tokyo: Chikuma Shobō, 1993), pp. 5-13.

82. The translation of Norinaga's diary is followed in this volume by a selection of essays in which he discusses places visited during his journey in more detail as well as essays related to Norinaga's notion of poetics.

83. *IS*, pp. 347-350.

84. Hino Tatsuo, *Motoori Norinaga Shū*, p. 352, n. 1.

85. This theory appears in Tanigawa Kotosuga's *Nihon Shoki Tsūshō*. Quoted in Hino Tatsuo, *Motoori Norinaga Shū*, p. 353, n. 3.

86. Hisamatsu Sen'ichi, *Keichū Zenshū*, p. 14. For an account of the philosophy of *yin yang*, see Wing-Tsit Chan, *A Source Book in Chinese Philosophy* (Princeton, NJ: Princeton University Press, 1963), pp. 244-250.

87. Hino Tatsuo, *Motoori Norinaga Shū*, p. 483, n. 7.

88. *IS,* p. 485.

89. An example of contextualization is the "preface" *(kotobagaki)* in poetic anthologies in which the poet, or someone else at a later time, provides the reader with the time, place, and occasion that led to the poem's composition. Another, more large-scale, example is the development of Japanese prose in the early tradition of *monogatari,* in which poems provided the occasion for the unfolding of fiction. Poem-tales *(uta-monogatari),* such as *Ise monogatari* (The Tales of Ise) and *Yamato Monogatari* (The Tales of Yamato), are eloquent examples.

90. Donald L. Philippi, *Kojiki,* p. 91. The original text appears in Nishimiya Kazutami, *Kojiki,* p. 57. The *Nihon Shoki* contains the variation *"tsumagome ni;"* the meaning, however, remains the same.

91. *IS,* p. 266.

92. Yamagishi Tokuhei, *Hachidaishū Zenchū,* 1, p. 10.

93. Quoted in Hino Tatsuo, *Motoori Norinaga Shū,* p. 266, n. 3. Keichū's text appears in Hisamatsu Sen'ichi, *Keichū Zenshū,* 8, p. 14.

94. Quoted in Hino Tatsuo, *Motoori Norinaga Shū,* p. 267, n. 5.

95. Hisamatsu Sen'ichi, *Keichū Zenshū,* 8, p. 14. Interestingly, W.G. Aston is very careful to avoid mentioning the geographical area of Izumo in his translation. His translation reads: "Many clouds arise,/On all sides a manyfold fence,/to receive within it the spouses,/They form a manyfold fence—/Ah! that manyfold fence!" He adds in a note: "The poem no doubt alludes to the meaning ["issuing clouds"] and also to the name of the province, but it seems probable that the primary signification of idzumo here is that given in the translation." W.G. Aston, trans., *Nihongi: Chronicles of Japan from the Earliest Times to A.D. 697* (Tokyo: Tuttle, 1972), pp. 53–54.

96. *IS,* p. 268.

97. Yamagishi Tokuhei, *Hachidaishū Zenchū,* p. 10; Hisamatsu Sen'ichi, *Keichū Zenshū,* vol. 8, pp. 14–15.

98. Benedetto Croce, *La poesia: Introduzione alla critica e storia della poesia e della letteratura* (Milan: Adelphy Edizioni, 1994; 1st ed., 1936), p. 23.

Diary and Poetry: The Sedge Hat Diary

1. The original text, edited by Suzuki Jun, appears in Suzuki Jun and Nakamura Hiroyasu, eds., *Kinsei Kabun Shū, Ge, SNKBT* 68 (Tokyo: Iwanami Shoten, 1997), pp. 155–237. I have also consulted Motoori Norinaga, *Sugagasa no Nikki,* ed. Mibu Tsutomu (Tokyo: Kenkyū sha, 1940), as well as Mishima Takeo and Miyamura Chimoto, trans., *Motoori Norinaga: Sugagasa no Nikki* (Ōsaka: Izumi Shoin, 1995). The title of the diary refers to the traveler's hat.

2. *Man'yōshū* 1:27. Kojima Noriyuki, Kinoshita Masatoshi, and Satake Akihiro, eds., *Man'yōshū,* 1, *NKBZ* 2 (Tokyo: Shōgakukan, 1971), p. 79. Emperor Tenmu composed this poem on the fifth day of the fifth month 679 during an excursion to Yoshino. Edwin Cranston translates this poem as follows: "Goodly men of old/took a good look at its goodness/and pronounced it good:/you too, good fellows, be good enough/to Goodfield's goodliness!" Edwin A. Cranston, *A Waka Anthology, Volume One: The Gem-Glistening Cup* (Stanford, CA: Stanford University Press, 1993), p. 179. In his

commentary on this poem Katō Chikage indicates that the word *yoshi* (good) means "discerning, intelligent, and knowledgeable."

3. Norinaga presents the deities with a poem instead of the customary strips of papers and clothing that travelers offered to the gods in order to be assured safe passage. Norinaga was inspired by the following travel poem by Sugawara no Michizane from *Kokinshū* 9:420. Okumura Tsuneya, ed., *Kokin Waka Shū*, SNKS 19 (Tokyo: Shinchōsha, 1978), p. 162:

Kono tabi wa	I did not bring the proper offerings
Nusa mo toriaezu	For this travel.
Tamukeyama	Mount Offerings
Momiji no nishiki	Has followed the will of the gods
Kami no manimani	By presenting a brocade of maple leaves.

See also the following translation by Helen C. McCullough, *Kokin Waka Shū: The First Imperial Anthology of Japanese Poetry* (Stanford, CA: Stanford University Press, 1985), p. 101: "I have journeyed here/without bringing strips of cloth./Let the gods decide/whether to accept brocades/of red leaves on Offering Hill." The headnote to the poem indicates that this poem was composed "At Mount Tamuke (Mount Offerings) when Emperor Uda traveled to Nara." Mount Tamuke was the site of the Tamukeyama Shrine, which is believed to be south of Mount Wakakusa.

4. This poem echoes the following poem by Ariwara no Narihira from *Kokinshū* 9:411. Okumura Tsuneya, *Kokin Waka Shū*, p. 159:

Na ni shi owaba	If your name befits you,
Iza kototowamu	Please tell me
Miyakodori	Capital bird:
Waga omou hito wa	How is the person
Ari ya nashi ya to	To whom my longing thoughts go?

See also McCullough, *Kokin Waka Shū*, p. 99: "If you are in truth/what your name seems to make you,/I will put to you,/capital-bird, this question:/do things go well with my love?"

5. *Senzaishū* 8:507. Katano Tatsurō and Matsuno Yōichi, eds., *Senzai Waka Shū*, SNKBT 10 (Tokyo: Iwanami Shoten, 1993), p. 154. The headnote to the poem indicates that it was composed at Wasurei during the procession of the Ise Priestess in 1108. Princess Junshi, a daughter of Retired Emperor Shirakawa (r. 1072–1086), served as priestess at the Ise Shrine during the reign of Emperor Toba (r. 1107–1123).

6. Nakazato Tsunemori from the Ise province makes this point in *Ise Meisho Sankō Shō* (Reference to Famous Places in the Ise Province).

7. For an English translation of the *Jinmyōchō*, see Felicia Gressitt Bock, trans., *Engi-Shiki: Procedures of the Engi Era, Books VI–X* (Tokyo: Sophia University, 1972), pp. 113–171.

8. "Two and a half *ri*." One *ri* corresponds to 2.44 miles or 3.93 kilometers.

9. Norinaga expresses his longing for friends who did not join him on the trip to Yoshino.
10. Kamo no Mabuchi (1697–1769) authored an influential commentary of the *Man'yōshū*, titled *Man'yō Kō* (Reflections on The Collection of Ten Thousand Leaves).
11. *Man'yōshū* 1:22. Kojima Noriyuki, *Man'yōshū*, 1, p. 76. Edwin A. Cranston translates poem, headnote, and footnote as follows:

> A poem composed by Mistress Fufuki on seeing the crags on the long mountain flanks of Hata when Princess Tōchi made a pilgrimage to Ise Shrine.
>
> The thrusting, clustered/boulders on the riverbank/bear no trace of grass:/forever young, I too would be/a maiden till the end of time.
>
> We as yet have no detailed information about Mistress Fufuki. However, the *Chronicles* state: "In the fourth year of the emperor [Tenmu; i.e., 676], Wood-Junior/Swine, in spring, on the Fire-Junior/Swine day of the second month, whose first day was Wood-Junior/Swine, Princess Tōchi and Princess Ahe set off on a pilgrimage to Ise Shrine."

Cranston's interpretation of this poem indicates that "the poem sees a divine force in the boulders that keeps them free of grass—an appealing analogue for the smoothness of a young girl's body."
Cranston, *A Waka Anthology*, p. 180. Princess Tōchi was the daughter of Emperor Tenmu and the wife of Prince Ōtomo.
12. *Kokinshū* 10:422, by Fujiwara no Toshiyuki. Okumura Tsuneya, *Kokin Waka Shū*, p. 164. See also McCullough, *Kokin Waka Shū*, p. 102: "It is by his choice/that dewdrops from the blossoms/wet his plumage through./Why then must the bird complain,/'Ah! My wings refuse to dry?'" The word *uguisu* (bush warbler) is hidden behind the expression *ukuhizu* (sadly does not dry).
13. Lit., "Ten *chō*." One *chō* corresponds to 119 yards or 109 meters.
14. *Man'yōshū* 1:43, by the wife of Tagima no Mahito Maro. Kojima Noriyuki, *Man'yōshū*, 1, p. 87. See also Cranston, *A Waka Anthology*, p. 264: "Where is he passing,/My husband, as he goes along?/Today is he crossing/the mountains of Nabari/of the hidden offshore weed?"
15. This is a reference to Emperor Tenmu's journey to the Eastern province on the 22nd day of the sixth month 672 as recorded in the *Nihon Shoki*: "When they were just arriving at the River Yokogawa, a dark cloud overspread the sky to the breadth of more than ten rods." W.G. Aston, trans., *Nihongi: Chronicles of Japan from the Earliest Times to A.D. 697*, vol. 2, p. 306.
16. Norinaga builds this poem around the meaning of the adjective "difficult" (*katashi*) that is found inside the geographical name of the village, Kataka.
17. Lit., "One *jo*." One *jo* corresponds to 3.31 yards or 3.03 meters.
18. Retired Emperor Go-Toba presided over the inauguration ceremony of the Buddha of the Ōno Temple in 1209.
19. A reference to Murōji, also known as "the Koya for women." Women were barred from climbing Mount Koya.

20. Norinaga's journey is taking place in spring, the time for "the flowers' bloom." The word flower *(hana)* refers to the cherry blossoms.

21. A member of Norinaga's Suzunoya School and a Tendai priest, Kaigon was the head of the Kakushōin, a sub-temple within the Raigōji compound in Matsusaka. He died in 1791.

22. Koizumi Ken'an was a good friend of Norinaga and a fellow doctor.

23. Inagake Munetaka was a tofu dealer. Norinaga adopted Munetaka's son Shigeo (1756–1833) after Norinaga's eldest son, Haruniwa, had become blind. Following the adoption, Shigeo came to be known as Motoori Ōhira.

24. Nakazato Tsuneo was adopted into the Hasegawa family, thus becoming one of the richest merchants in Matsusaka.

25. *Man'yōshū* 2:203, by Prince Hozumi (d. 715) who, after the demise of Princess Tajima, composed the following poem on a snowy winter day:

Furu yuki wa	Do not fall so heavily,
Awa ni na furi so	Falling snow,
Yonabari no	Since it must be cold
Ikai no oka no	On the Ikai Hills
Samukaramaku ni	Of Yonabari.

Kojima Noriyuki, *Man'yōshū*, 1, p. 169. See also Cranston, *A Waka Anthology,* p. 277: "O you falling snow,/do not snow so heavily,/lest Yonabari/and the hill of Ikai/should come to feel the cold."

26. *Engishiki* (Procedures of the Engi Era, 905–927), Book 21.

27. *Kokinshū* 1:42, by Ki no Tsurayuki. Okumura Tsuneya, *Kokin Waka Shū*, p. 39. "After some time, he stopped at a house where he used to stay every time he went to Hatsuse. The owner said to him, 'You can rely on this place to spend the night.' He broke off a blossoming branch from a plum tree and recited the following poem:

Hito wa isa	Is that so?
Kokoro mo shirazu	I do not know people's heart—
Furusato wa	Yet in my old place
Hana zo mukashi no	The flowers are fragrant
Ka ni nioikeru	As in the past.

See also McCullough, *Kokin Waka Shū*, p. 22: "I know but little/of what is in someone's heart,/yet at the old place/the fragrance of the blossoms/is the scent of bygone days."

28. This is a reference to a poem by Ōe no Masafusa from *Kin'yōshū* 1:51. Kawamura Teruo, Kashiwagi Yoshio, and Kudō Shigenori, eds., *Kin'yō Waka Shū, Shika Waka Shū*, SNKBT 9 (Tokyo: Iwanami Shoten, 1989), p. 17:

Hatsuseyama	When the flowers on the clouds
Kumoi ni hana no	Of Mount Hatsuse
Sakinureba	Have bloomed,

> *Ama no kawa nami*   I see
> *Tatsu ka to zo miru*   The waves rise on the Milky Way.

29. *Makura no Sōshi*, 124. Matsuo Satoshi and Nagai Kazuko, eds., *Makura no Sōshi*, NKBZ 11 (Tokyo: Shōgakukan, 1974), p. 254: "Once there was a time when, after several days of seclusion, we relaxed during the day. The male attendants and boys who came with us visited the monks in their cells. I spent some time alone leisurely when all of a sudden I was surprised by the loud sound of the conch-shell." See, also, Ivan Morris' translation in *The Pillow Book of Sei Shōnagon*, vol. 1 (New York: Columbia University Press, 1967), p. 128.

30. The word *kanete* (past, before, earlier on) recalls the word *kane* (bell).

31. Such poems include:

> *Hatsuseyama*   Every time I hear
> *Iriai no kane o*   The bell on Mount Hatsuse
>   *Kiku tabi ni*   At dusk
> *Mukashi no tōku*   I am saddened by the thoughts
> *Naru zo kanashiki*   Of a past long gone.

Senzai Waka Shū 17:1154, Fujiwara no Ariie. Katano and Matsuno, *Senzai Waka Shū*, p. 345.

> *Toshi mo henu*   Many years have gone by
> *Inoru chigiri wa*   As I prayed for love
>   *Hatsuseyama*   At Mount Hatsuse:
> *Onoe no kane no*   The bell at the top of the mountain
> *Yoso no yūgure*   Announces someone else's dusk.

Shin Kokin Waka Shū 12:1142, Fujiwara no Teika. Kubota Jun, ed., *Shin Kokin Waka Shū, Ge*, SNKZ 30 (Tokyo Shinchōsha, 1979), p. 56.

32. Tokudō Shōnin.

33. A reference to *Kokinshū* 19:1009. Okumura Tsuneya, *Kokin Waka Shū*, p. 347:

> *Hatsusegawa*   A twin-trunked cedar stands
> *Furukawa no he ni*   Beside the ancient river
>   *Futamoto aru sugi*   Of Hatsuse River—
> *Toshi o hete*   I want to see it again
> *Mata mo aimimu*   After many years have passed,
> *Futamoto aru sugi*   The twin-trunked cedar.

See also McCullough, *Kokin Waka Shū*, p. 227: "The twin-trunked cedar/beside the ancient river, beside Hatsuse River:/the twin-trunked cedar/we two shall see once again/after the years have rolled by."

34. Fujiwara no Teika (1162–1241) was a major poet of the early Kamakura period.

35. Tamakazura, the forgotten daughter of Tō no Chūjo and Yūgao, gives the title to the twenty-second roll of *Genji Monogatari* (The Tale of Genji).

36. This is found in the shrine dedicated to Susa-no-o. Fujiwara no Ietaka (1158–1237) was a poet of the early Kamakura period.

37. A reference to the following poem by Saigyō from *Shinkokinshū*, 1:7. Kubota Jun, ed., *Shin Kokin Waka Shū, Jō, SNKS* 24 (Tokyo: Shinchōsha, 1979), p. 23:

Iwama tojishi	This morning the ice
Kōri mo kesa wa	That closed off the space between rocks
Tokesomete	Has begun to melt:
Koke no shitamizu	The water beneath the moss
Michi motomu nari	Looks for a path to flow.

38. See, for example, the following poem from *Man'yōshū* 7:1095 by Kakinomoto no Hitomaro. Kojima Noriyuki et al., eds., *Man'yōshū, 3, NKBZ* 3 (Tokyo: Shōgakukan, 1972), p. 209:

Mimoro tsuku	When I look at Mount Miwa
Miwayama mireba	Where the gods are worshipped,
Komoriku no	I am reminded
Hatsuse no hibara	Of the field of cypresses
Omōyuru kamo	Of hidden Hatsuse.

39. The gateway at the entrance to a Shinto shrine.
40. Japanese-style bun stuffed with *azuki*-bean paste.
41. Present-day Tō-no-mine.
42. *Man'yōshū* 13:3331. Kojima Noriyuki et al., eds., *Man'yōshū, 3, NKBZ* 4 (Tokyo: Shōgakukan, 1973), p. 430. English translation by Cranston, *A Waka Anthology*, p. 727:

Komoriku no	Hidden
Hatsuse no yama	Hatsuse Mountain,
Aohata no	Green-bannered
Osaka no yama wa	Osaka Mountain—
Hashiride no	In the way they run,
Yoroshiki yama no	How good are these mountains;
Idetachi no	In the way they rise,
Kuwashiki yama zo	How fine are these mountains:
Atarashiki	These precious
Yama no	Mountains—
Aremaku oshi mo	How bitter will be their waste.

43. See, for example, the following *sedōka* from the *Man'yōshū* (7:1282–1284). Kojima Noriyuki et al., eds., *Man'yōshū*, 2, *NKBZ* 2, pp. 251–252:

Hashitate no	As I was thinking that
Kurahashiyama ni	I wanted to see
Tateru shirakumo	The white clouds rising over
Mimaku hori	The ladder-steep
A ga suru nae ni	Mount Kurahashi,
Tateru shirakumo	The white clouds rose.

Or, in Cranston's translation: "White cloud/rising over the mountain,/Kurahashi the ladder-steep,/white cloud/rising at the very instant/I was gazing with desire." *A Waka Anthology*, p. 238.

Hashitate no	I remember the stepping-stones
Kurahashigawa no	On the ladder-steep
Iwa no hashi wa mo	Kurahashi River;
Ozakari ni	I went over them and crossed the river
Waga watashiteshi	When I was young—
Ishi no hashi wa mo	I remember those stepping-stones!

Or, in Cranston's translation: "Across the river,/Kurahashi the ladder-steep,/once on a bridge of stepping-stones/when I was a young man/I went over and across—/on a bridge of stepping-stones." *A Waka Anthology*, p. 238.

Hashitate no	The still sedge
Kurahashigawa no	On the ladder-steep
Kawa no shizusuge	Kurahashi River,
Wa ga karate	I cut as much as I could,
Kasa ni mo amanu	And yet I could not weave a straw hat
Kawa no shizusuge	With the still sedge on the river.

Or, in Cranston's translation: "Down by the river,/Kurahashi the ladder-steep,/still sedge down by the river/I went down and cut,/but I wove no hat for me to wear/from the still sedge down by the river." *A Waka Anthology*, p. 238.

44. Lit., "Fifty or sixty *ken*." Sixty *ken* correspond to one *chō*. One *ken* is about 1.8 meters.

45. See the following poem from *Man'yōshū* 3:290. Kojima Noriyuki, *Man'yōshū*, 1, p. 217:

Kurahashi no	Is it because Mount Kurahashi
Yama o takami ka	Is so high
Yogomori ni	That the light

> *Idekuru tsuki no*   Of the moon coming out every night
> *Hikari tomoshiki*   Is so poor?

See also Cranston, *A Waka Anthology*, p. 274: "Perhaps the loftiness/of Kurahashi's somber peak/is what makes the moon/that lurked hidden all the night/rise with such feeble rays."

46. *P'u-sa ying-luo pen-yeh-ching*, two fascicles.

47. This is a reference to the tomb of Fujiwara no Kamatari (614–669).

48. Norinaga uses the word *kai* in the double sense of "to be worthy of something" and "gorge, ravine."

49. *Man'yōshū* 7:1330. Kojima Noriyuki, *Man'yōshū*, 2, p. 262:

> *Minabuchi no*   The spindle tree standing
> *Hosokawayama ni*   On Mount Hosokawa
> *Tatsu mayumi*   In Minabuchi—
> *Yuzuka maku made*   Let's not tell anyone
> *Hito ni shiraeji*   Until the bow is ready to be used.

This poem puns on the word *mayumi*, which refers to the "spindle tree" as well as to the "bow." The action of making a bow ready by wrapping its handle with the bark of cherry trees *(yuzuka maku)* refers metaphorically to the maturation of a lovers' relationship. Minabuchi is the area where the upper Asuka River flows. This area, presently known as Inabuchi, is located in the Asuka village, Takaichi County, Nara Prefecture.

50. *Man'yōshū* 7:1704, "a poem presented to Prince Toneri." Kojima Noriyuki, *Man'yōshū*, 2, p. 396. Currently the first verse of this poem is read *"fusa taori."* See also Cranston, *A Waka Anthology*, p. 243: "*Breaking a cluster*/drooping Tamu Mountain mist—/How dense it is!/Whence in Hosokawa's stream/the waves splash loud in the shallows?"

51. *Man'yōshū* 1:52. Kojima Noriyuki, *Man'yōshū*, 1, pp. 92–93: ". . . and Yoshino Mountain—/beautiful its name—/soaring beyond the Southern Gate/in the distance, among the clouds." English translation by Ian Hideo Levy, *Man'yōshū: A Translation of Japan's Premier Anthology of Classical Poetry*, vol. 1 (Princeton, NJ: Princeton University Press, 1981), p. 66.

52. *Shūgai Kasen*:

> *Yoshinoyama*   The white clouds on the peak
> *Hana matsu hodo no*   On which my mind has been set
> *Asana asana*   Morning after morning
> *Kokoro ni kakai*   While waiting for the flowers
> *Mine no shirakumo*   Of Yoshino Mountain.

53. *Kokinshū* 17:926, "composed by Lady Ise near a waterfall, during a pilgrimage to the Dragon's Gate." Okumura Tsuneya, *Kokin Waka Shū*, p. 314:

Tachinuwanu	The men who wore
Kinu kishi hito mo	The garment uncut and unsewn
Nakimono o	Are not here—
Nani yamahime no	Why should the lady of the mountain
Nuno sarasuramu	Bleach her cloth?

See also McCullough, *Kokin Waka Shū*, p. 202: "Since they are gone now—/those who were clad in garments/uncut and unsewn—/why should the mountain goddess/persist in bleaching her cloth?"

The holy men *(sennin)* living here were supposed to wear heavenly clothes that did not need any cutting or sewing. The lady of the mountain is the female counterpart of the holy man. She does not need to bleach her clothes—and yet the waterfall, which looks like a bleached cloth, appears to the poet's eyes. At Ryūmon, Bashō wrote the following poems in his travel diary *Oi no Kobumi* (The Records of a Travel-worn Satchel): "A spray of blossoms/on the Dragon's Gate/would be an excellent gift/for tipplers." "Tipplers would be overjoyed/to hear from me/about the bridge of blossoms/across the waterfall." English translations by Nobuyuki Yuasa, *Bashō: The Narrow Road to the Deep North and Other Travel Sketches* (London: Penguin, 1966), pp. 82–83.

54. Norinaga's poem is a tour de force centered around words associated *(engo)* with the notions of "cloth" and "thread": *tachi* means "to cut" and "to stand"; *yora* means "twist" and "without going." The cloth stood as a symbolic analogy *(mitate)* for the waterfall of the Dragon's Gate.

55. *Makura no Sōshi*, 1. Matsuo and Nagai, *Makura no Sōshi*, p. 63: "In spring it is the dawn that is most beautiful. As the light creeps over the hills, their outlines are dyed a faint red and wisps of purplish cloud trail over them." English translation by Ivan Morris, *The Pillow Book of Sei Shōnagon*, vol. 1, p. 1.

56. *Ise Monogatari*, 9. Watanabe Minoru, ed., *Ise Monogatari*, SNKS 2 (Tokyo: Shinchōsha, 1976), p. 23: "Continuing on their way, they came to a mighty river flowing between the provinces of Musashi and Shimōsa. It was called the Sumidagawa. The travelers drew together on the bank, thinking involuntarily of home. 'How very far we have come!' The ferryman interrupted their laments: 'Come aboard quickly; it's getting late.' They got into the boat and prepared to cross, all in wretched spirits, for there was not one among them who had not left someone dear to him in the capital." English translation by Helen Craig McCullough, *Tales of Ise: Lyrical Episodes from Tenth-Century Japan* (Stanford, CA: Stanford University Press, 1968), p. 76.

57. *Kokinshū* 5:828. Okumura Tsuneya, *Kokin Waka Shū*, p. 279:

Nagarete wa	Well, this is what
Imose no yama no	The world of love is about:
Naka ni otsuru	The Yoshino river
Yoshino no kawa no	Whose course falls between
Yoshi ya yo no naka	Mount Imo and Mount Se.

Literally, *imo* means "my beloved wife" and *se* refers to the "beloved husband." The first four verses of the poem are an introduction *(jo)* to the real topic of the composition: the fissures in a relationship between man and woman. See also McCullough, *Kokin Waka Shū*, p. 180: "Let us accept it./Love's course can but remind us/of the Yoshino,/the river falling between Husband Mountain and Wife Hill."

According to the section on "Mount Imose" in Norinaga's *Tamakatsuma*, 9, this poem was inspired by the following poem from *Man'yōshū* 7:1193. Kojima Noriyuki, *Man'yōshū*, 2, p. 231:

Se no yama ni	Has Mount Imo
Tada ni mukaeru	Forgiven
Imo no yama	Mount Se
Koto yuruse ya mo	That stands straight in front of her?
Uchihashi watasu	A bridge I cross between the two.

In this poem the poet uses the bridge as a symbolic analogy *(mitate)* of the actual Mount Funaoka that stands between Mount Imo in the south and Mount Se in the north. Norinaga argues that this poem from the *Man'yōshū* confirms the fact that the mountains in question are located in the Ki province. The relocation of the mountains in the Yoshino area followed the composition of the *Kokinshū* poem mentioned above. Yoshikawa Kōjirō et al., eds., *Motoori Norinaga*, NST 40 (Tokyo: Iwanami Shoten, 1978), pp. 289–292.

58. The Yoshino-no-Yamanoguchi Jinja (the Shrine at the Entrance of the Yoshino Mountain) is mentioned in the ninth book of the *Engishiki*.

59. The spring equinox would correspond to the fourth day of the second month.

60. *Man'yōshū* 3:242, by Prince Yuge, during an excursion to Yoshino. Kojima Noriyuki, *Man'yōshū*, 1, p. 202:

Taki no ue no	I do not think
Mifune no yama ni	That I will live forever
Iru kumo no	Like the clouds trailing
Tsune ni aramu to	Along the crest of Mifune,
Wa ga omowanaku ni	Over the waterfall.

See also Cranston, *A Waka Anthology*, p. 493: "For I know well enough/I shall not be here forever/like the cloud that rests/along the crest of Mifune/over the racing water."

61. Niō are a pair of Buddhist gods, popularly identified as Misshaku and Naraen. Their statues are often found at the entrance to a temple.

62. This is the Main Hall of the Kinpunsenji temple. The original bodies of Zaō Gongen (the Incarnate Zaō) are Shaka, Senju Kannon, and Miroku.

63. Originally a sub-temple of Kinpunsenji, it became the Yoshimizu Shrine in 1875 with the separation of Shinto and Buddhism.

64. After defeating the Hōjō shogunate and restoring power to the emperor's hands during the Kenmu Restoration (1334–1336), Emperor Go-Daigo (1288–1339)

was forced by the troops of shogun Ashikaga Takauji to flee the capital Kyoto and take refuge in Yoshino, where he founded the southern court. In Norinaga's poem, the verb *kumu* (to imagine, to guess) also has the meaning of "scooping up water," as if the poet were capturing the past by drinking at the source of the Yoshimizu-in, which literally means "temple of the good waters."

65. Emperor Go-Murakami (1328–1368) was the seventh son of Emperor Go-Daigo and the second ruler of the southern court.

66. The verb *utsuru* refers to the "transfer" of the emperor from the capital to the Yoshino area, as well as to the emperor's image that "is reflected" in the name of the emperor's dwelling, the temple of good waters.

67. Norinaga was inspired by the following spring poem by Retired Emperor Go-Saga from the *Shoku Gosenshū* 1:78:

Mite mo nao	How enchanting it is,
Oku zo yukashiki	No matter how long one looks at it!
Ashigaki no	Deep into the Yoshino mountain,
Yoshino no yama no	Fenced by the reeds,
Hana no sakari wa	Is the bloom of flowers.

68. This poem appears in the spring section of the *Shin'yō Wakashū* (2:83) preceded by a headnote stating that the emperor composed it while he was living in Yoshino, after he had noticed that "the cherry trees above the clouds" *(kumoi-no-sakura)* had bloomed near the Sesonji temple. *Kumoi* is a term indicating the imperial palace.

69. In 1336 this became the temporary palace of Go-Daigo, whose life came to an end in this building.

70. Emperor Go-Kameyama (1347–1424), the fourth and last emperor of the southern court, was the second son of Go-Murakami and the younger brother of Emperor Chōkei. He returned to Kyoto in 1392, after the reunification of the northern and southern courts, when, under the pressure of shogun Ashikaga no Yoshimitsu, he transferred the imperial regalia to the emperor of the northern court, Go-Komatsu (r. 1392–1412).

71. Also known as the Yamaguchi Jinja, it was considered one of the eight major shrines of Yoshino. The shrine was rebuilt in 1656 after a fire destroyed it in the second month of 1644. It was destroyed again by fire in 1767 and rebuilt in the fourth month of 1776. The shrine is described in the chapter on the battle of Yoshino in the *Taiheiki*: "Suddenly the enemy in the rear pressed forward from Katte-no-myōjin Shrine to the Vajrasattva Hall, the abiding place of the Prince of the Great Pagoda. And thinking that he could not escape, the prince tranquilly clothed his body in a new suit of scarlet-braided armor over an underdress of red brocade, tied the cords of his dragon-head helmet, girded on a short sword, and burst into the middle of the enemy host with twenty mighty men of valor round about him. Although the attackers' numbers were great, they were defeated by this small force, that drove them back in every direction and raised the dust like black smoke as they cut them with their swords,

until like leaves scattering in the wind they ran away to the gorges on the four sides." English translation by Helen Craig McCullough, *The Taiheiki: A Chronicle of Medieval Japan* (New York: Columbia University Press, 1959), p. 177.

72. The name of this mountain comes from the legend according to which Emperor Tenmu was led there by the sound of a *koto*; a heavenly woman was dancing, waving her sleeves. This is considered to be the origin of the Gosechi-no-Mai, the five-maiden dance performed at the imperial palace.

73. The Kunbō-en was built by the tea master Sen no Rikyū (1522–1591) upon the order of Toyotomi Hideyoshi, and it was later rebuilt by Hosokawa Yūsai (1534–1610).

74. *Kokinshū* 2:95, by Sosei, with a headnote indicating that this poem was composed during the poet's visit to the cherry blossom in Kitayama, and was sent to Prince Tsuneyasu. Okumura Tsuneya, *Kokin Waka Shū*, p. 56. See also McCullough, *Kokin Waka Shū*, p. 32: "Today I will press/deep into the hills of spring./If twilight descends,/can it be that I will find/no lodging under blossoms?"

75. In this poem Norinaga plays with the Japanese reading *(take no hayashi)* of the temple's name, Chikurin—"bamboo forest."

76. The plant *yadorigi* (lit., "dwelling plant") is actually a parasite growing on a variety of plants; it was used for medical purposes.

77. This is a reference to the cult of Yumechigae no Kannon—a belief in the power of Kannon to keep all bad dreams from becoming reality.

78. This is the Yoshino Mikumari Shrine. Because of a mispronunciation, since ancient times the deity enshrined there came to be called Mikomori, the god invoked for the birth of children.

79. Norinaga refers to his mixed feelings at the thought of the karma that has led him to the Mikumari Shrine. Tears of joy over fulfilling his dreams come from tears of sadness at the recollection of his late parents. The inspiration for this sentence came from an anonymous poem from *Gosenshū* 17:1188. Katagiri Yōichi, ed., *Gosen Waka Shū*, SNKBT 6 (Tokyo: Iwanami Shoten, 1990), p. 357:

Ureshiki mo	In happiness
Uki mo kokoro wa	In sadness
Hitotsu ni te	The heart is one—
Wakarenu mono wa	Tears
Namida narikeri	Do not diverge.

80. This is a reference to the following poem from *Shūi Waka Shū* 10:595. Masuda Shigeo, ed., *Shūi Waka Shū*, WBT 32 (Tokyo: Meiji Shoin, 2003), p. 117:

Misogi suru	The rope lowered
Kyō kara saki ni	In the sea
Orosu tsuna wa	Today that I perform this purification ceremony
Kami no ukehiku	Is a sign
Shirushi narikeri	That the gods have accepted my plea.

81. The reference appears in the entry for the twenty-ninth day of the fourth month of the second year of the reign of Emperor Monmu (698).
82. *Man'yōshū* 7:1130, "a poem written at Yoshino." Kojima Noriyuki, *Man'yōshū*, 2, p. 218:

Kamu saburu	How sad I am when I look
Iwane kogoshiki	At Mount Mikumari
Miyoshino no	Of fair Yoshino
Mikumariyama o	Standing on the bluff
Mireba kanashi mo	Of divine boulders.

83. One of Norinaga's travel companions, Koizumi Ken'an.
84. This sentence was inspired by the following poem by Nōin from *Shinkokinshū* 2:116. Kubota Jun, *Shin Kokin Waka Shū, Jō,* p. 57:

Yamazato no	When I came and looked
Haru no yūgure	At the mountain village
Kite mireba	At dusk in springtime,
Iriai no kane ni	The flowers scattered
Hana zo chirikeru	At the sound of the bell tolling at sunset.

85. The "flowers" *(hana)* refer to the cherry blossoms, as well as to the poems in Chinese that Norinaga would like to see.
86. The poem is an acrostic. The first syllable of each verse reads *"cha sukoshi,"* which means, "a little tea."
87. *Shinkokinshū* 17:1617. Kubota Jun, *Shin Kokin Waka Shū, Ge,* p. 208. See also William R. LaFleur, *Awesome Nightfall: The Life, Times, and Poetry of Saigyō* (Boston: Wisdom Publications, 2003), p. 118: "'He'll return,' they think,/'when the blossoms are all fallen,' but he for whom they wait/is thinking now he'll/never leave Mount Yoshino."
88. Yoshitsune (1159–1189) was the legendary general who died in exile while fleeing the troops of his brother, the shogun Minamoto no Yoritomo (1147–1199).
89. Toyotomi Hideyori (1593–1615), second son of Toyotomi Hideyoshi. He committed suicide together with his mother, Yodogimi, during the siege of Osaka castle by the troops of the shogun Tokugawa Ieyasu.
90. This is the highest peak in Yoshino. We find a reference to it in *Man'yōshū* 7:1120, "a poem on moss." Kojima Noriyuki, *Man'yōshū*, 2, p. 215:

Miyoshino no	Who weaved
Aoge-ga-mine no	The mat of moss
Kokemushiro	On Aone-no-mine Peak
Tare ka orikemu	Of fair Yoshino?
Tatenuki nashi ni	One cannot distinguish the vertical and horizontal threads.

See also Cranston, *A Waka Anthology*, p. 653: "Who was it wove,/without a thread for warp or weft,/the coverlet of moss/that drapes the heights of Aone,/the Greentop Peak of Yoshino?"

91. "*Maki*" refers to a variety of evergreens, such as cedars and pine trees. However, it stands mainly for cypresses.

92. Sanjō-ga-take of Mount Kinpu.

93. *Man'yōshū* 3:375, written by Yuhara no Ōkimi. Kojima Noriyuki, *Man'yōshū*, 1, p. 145:

Yoshino naru	The ducks cry
Natsumi no kawa no	In the mountain's shade
Kawayodo ni	In the pool
Kamo so nakunaru	Of the Natsumi river
Yamakage ni shite	In Yoshino.

See also Cranston, *A Waka Anthology*, p. 378: "From the river pools/at Natsumi in Yoshino,/from those quiet pools/comes the sound of mallards crying/beneath the shadow of the hills."

94. This is a reference to the *Yamato Meguri* (A Journey to Yamato) by Kaibara Ekiken (1630–1714), a well-known Confucian scholar. Norinaga strongly relied on this work while writing his travel diary.

95. The same cup was circulated among each member of the group and filled with *sake* for everybody to taste.

96. *Man'yōshū* 1:36, written by Kakinomoto no Hitomaro in honor of a visit by Empress Jitō (r. 690–697) to the Yoshino Palace. Kojima Noriyuki, *Man'yōshū*, 1, pp. 83–84: "Many are the lands under heaven/and the sway of our Lord,/sovereign of the earth's eight corners,/but among them her heart/finds Yoshino good/for its crystal riverland/among the mountains,/and on the blossom-strewn/fields of Akitsu/she drives the firm pillars of her palace.//And so the courtiers of the great palace,/its ramparts thick with stone,/line their boats/to cross the morning river,/race their boats/across the evening river./Like this river/never ending,/like these mountains/commanding ever greater heights,/the palace by the surging rapids—/though I gaze on it, I do not tire." English translation by Levy, *Man'yōshū: A Translation of Japan's Premier Anthology of Classical Poetry*, vol. 1, pp. 56–57. See also Cranston, *A Waka Anthology*, pp. 193–194. According to another theory, the Yoshino Palace was located in the village of Miyataki.

97. *Man'yōshū* 6:926, by Yamabe no Akahito. Kojima Noriyuki, *Man'yōshū*, 2, p. 137: "Our great Sovereign/who rules the land in all tranquility,/in fair Yoshino/on the plain of Akizu. . . ." English translation by Cranston, *A Waka Anthology*, p. 311.

98. *Man'yōshū* 6:907. Kojima Noriyuki, *Man'yōshū*, 2, p. 129: "Spreading the fresh branches/along the crest of Mifune/over the waterfall. . . ."

99. This is a reference to a boat with a two-, sometimes three-story cabin.

100. *Man'yōshū* 3:332, by Ōtomo no Tabito. Kojima Noriyuki, *Man'yōshū*, 1, p. 232:

Wa ga inochi mo	My life,
Tsune ni aranu ka	Is it not everlasting?
Mukashi mishi	So that I could go and see
Kisa-no-ogawa o	The brook of Kisa
Yukite mimu tame	Which I saw in the past.

See also Cranston, *A Waka Anthology*, p. 559: "Is there no life in me/such as would last forever—/so that I could go and see the brook of Kisa/as I saw it long ago?" Levy gives the following translation: "Could my life/be granted permanence,/so that I could go again/to see the stream at Kisa/that I saw long ago." Levy, *Man'yōshū*, p. 184.

101. *Man'yōshū* 6:924, by Yamabe no Akahito. Kojima Noriyuki, *Man'yōshū*, 2, pp. 136–137:

Miyoshino no	The voices of the birds
Kisayama no ma no	Make such a racket
Konure ni wa	On the treetops
Koko damo sawaku	In the folds of the Kisa Mountains
Tori no koe kamo	Of fair Yoshino.

See also Cranston, *A Waka Anthology*, p. 310: "In fair Yoshino,/in the vale that lies between/the mountains of Kisa,/from every treetop rise the voices/of the gaily singing birds."

Man'yōshū 1:70, by Takechi no Kurohito, "when the Retired Emperor made an excursion to the Yoshino Palace." Kojima Noriyuki, *Man'yōshū*, 1, p. 99:

Yamato ni wa	I wonder if it has already come
Nakite ka kuramu	Crying to Yamato—
Yobukodori	While calling
Kisa no nakayama	The calling bird
Yobi so koyu naru	Crosses over the Kisa Mountains.

See also Cranston, *A Waka Anthology*, p. 260: "Has it come crying/all the way to Yamato?/A calling bird/went a-calling as it crossed/over the mountains of Kisa." Levy translates this poem as follows: "Has the calling bird/come crying to Yamato?/Its call soars/across Kisa's mountain recesses/and passes toward the capital." Levy, *Man'yōshū*, p. 73.

102. Hitomesenbon (A Thousand Trees in One View).

103. Norinaga was inspired by the following poem from *Senzaishū* (16:1035), composed by Fujiwara no Kintō during a visit to the Daikakuji Temple in Saga. Katano and Matsuno, *Senzai Waka Shū*, p. 310:

Taki no ne wa	Although
Taete hisahiku	The sound of the waterfall
Narinuredo	Has endured for a long time,

| Na koso nagarete | Its name has flown |
| Nao kikoekere | To this very day that I am listening to it. |

104. This is the work of Genkei (fl. late 12th to early 13th c.), a pupil of Unkei (d. 1223).

105. Kanaoka (fl. late 9th to early 10th c.) is said to have been the founder of the *yamato-e* school of painting, and of the Kose school of court painters.

106. Kusunoki no Masatsura (1326–1348), general of the Southern Court and the eldest son of Masashige, was defeated and killed by Kō no Moronao's troops at the battle of Kawachi Shijō Nawate.

107. Shin-Taikenmon-in was a consort of Emperor Go-Daigo and the mother of Emperor Go-Murakami. The poem appears in *Shin'yōwakashū* 19:1365. Kogi Takashi, *Shin'yō Waka Shū: Honbun to Kenkyū* (Tokyo: Kasama Shoin, 1984), p. 246.

108. Emperor Go-Daigo was buried in Yoshino in 1339. His remains were interred facing north towards the capital, as a reminder of the everlasting memory of his reign.

109. *Man'yōshū* 9:1723, by Kinu. Kojima Noriyuki, *Man'yōshū*, 2, p. 402:

Kawazu naku	No matter how heartily I look
Mutsuda no kawa no	At the heart of the willows by the river
Kawayagi no	Along the Mutsuta River
Nemokoro miredo	Where frogs cry,
Akanu kawa kamo	I never get tired of that river.

See also Cranston, *A Waka Anthology*, p. 245: "Riverfrog crying/Mutsuta River bounded/with river willows—/rooted to the spot I gaze/but never tire of the river."

110. *Man'yōshū* 2:142, by Prince Arima. Kojima Noriyuki, *Man'yōshū*, 1, p. 140. See also Cranston, *A Waka Anthology*, pp. 484–485: "When I am at home/I eat my rice heaped in a dish,/but since I am away/on a journey, grass for pillow,/I heap it on leaves of oak." Levy's version: "The rice I would heap/into a lunch box/if I were at home—/since I journey,/grass for pillow,/I heap into an oak leaf." Levy, *Man'yōshū*, p. 104.

111. This is a reference to the One-Thousand-Armed Kannon of the Tsubosaka Temple.

112. This name comes from the twenty-fifth chapter of the *Lotus Sutra*, "The Gateway to Everywhere of the Bodhisattva He Who Observes the Sounds of the World."

113. This is a reference to the stone images of five-hundred arhats.

114. Senka Tennō (r. 535–539) was the third son of Emperor Keitai.

115. *Kokinshū* 20:1080, a song in praise of Amaterasu Ōkami, the Sun Goddess. Okumura Tsuneya, *Kokin Waka Shū*, p. 367. See also McCullough, *Kokin Waka Shū*, p. 241: "Rein in your young horse/at Hinokuma River,/at Hinokuma,/ and let him drink there a while/that I may at least see your back." This poem is a variation of *Man'yōshū* 12: 3097. Kojima Noriyuki, *Man'yōshū*, 3, p. 341:

Sahinokuma	Stop the horse
Hinokumagawa ni	By the Hinokuma River,
Uma todome	The nook of cypresses,
Uma ni mizu kae	And let him drink the water!
Ware yoso ni mimu	Let me see you from far away.

116. Emperor Mommu (r. 697–707) was the son of Empress Genmei and Prince Kusakabe. Prince Kusakabe was the son of Emperor Tenmu and Empress Jitō. Therefore, Mommu was the grandson of Tenmu and Jitō.

117. Emperor Buretsu (r. 498–506), the first son of Emperor Ninken, was the twenty-fifth emperor.

118. This is a reference to the Umeyama Tumulus of Emperor Kinmei (r. 539–571).

119. This is a reference to the tomb of Emperor Tenmu (673–686) and Empress Jitō (r. 690–697). Asuka-no-Kiyomibara-no-Miya was the capital of Emperor Tenmu during the Jinshin insurrection of 672 and continued to be the capital of Empress Jitō until 694, when it was transferred to Fujiwara-no-Miya. Fujiwara-no-Miya continued to be the capital until 710, the year when it was transferred to Nara.

120. Namikawa Seisho (1668–1738) belonged to the school of Itō Jinsai. The five provinces in question are Yamashiro, Yamato, Kawachi, Izumi, and Settsu.

121. The Kawaradera was founded by Empress Saimei (r. 655–661), who used it as her palace. It was considered one of the three major temples of Asuka.

122. The Tachibanadera was built by Empress Suiko (r. 592–628). *Man'yōshū* 16:3822. Kojima Noriyuki, Kinoshita Masatoshi, and Satake Akihiro, eds., *Man'yōshū*, 4, NKBZ 5 (Tokyo: Shōgakukan, 1975), p. 127:

Tachibana no	Did she bind up her hair,
Tera no nagaya ni	The young girl with loose hair
Wa ga ineshi	With whom I slept
Unaihanari wa	In the row house
Kami agetsuramu ka	Of the Tachibana temple?

See also Cranston, *A Waka Anthology,* p. 755: "She whose hair hung loose/when I led her to the longhouse/and slept with her there/at the Temple of the Orange Tree—Has she now bound up her locks?"

123. *Kokinshū* 18:933. Okumura Tsuneya, *Kokin Waka Shū*, p. 317:

Yo no naka wa	What is constant
Nani ka tsune naru	In this world?
Asukagawa	Asuka River, the River of Tomorrow—
Kinō no fuchi zo	Yesterday's pools
Kyō wa se ni naru	Are today's rapids.

See also McCullough, *Kokin Waka Shū*, p. 205: "In this world of ours/what is there of constancy?/Yesterday's deep pool/in the River of Tomorrow/today becomes a rapid."

124. Twelfth day, tenth month, second year of the reign of Emperor Jomei (630): "The Emperor removed (the palace) to a place near the Hill of Asuka [Asuka-no-Oka]. This was called the Palace of Okamoto." Aston, *Nihongi*, vol. 2, p. 165.

125. The Okamoto Palace was transformed into a temple, the Okadera, in 663. The temple is also known as Ryūgaiji.

126. Pilgrims wore a sleeveless, one-layer robe as an overcoat in order to avoid damaging their clothes.

127. This is a verse in praise of Kannon that puns on an alternative name of the temple, Tsuyuokadera, the Temple of the Dewy Hill. The poem is found in *Saigoku Sanjūsansho Goeika*:

Kesa mireba	When I looked this morning
Tsuyuokadera no	I saw the dew in the moss of the garden
Niwa no koke	Of the Temple of the Dewy Hill—
Sanagara ruri no	It shined like the blaze
Hikari narikeri	Of lapis lazuli.

128. Lit., "Five or six *sun*." One *sun* corresponds to 1.2 inches or 3.03 centimeters.

129. The construction of the Asukadera began in 588, following the request of Soga no Umako. It was completed in 596. The main image of Shaka Nyorai was enshrined in 606. Known as the Asuka Daibutsu, or the Great Buddha of Asuka, this is Japan's most ancient bronze statue.

130. Irukatsuka is thought to be the tomb of Soga no Iruka (d. 645).

131. The seventh son of Emperor Kanmu, Junna reigned from 823 to 833.

132. A reference to this mountain is found in the *Engishiki*.

133. *Man'yōshū* 2:159. Kojima Noriyuki, *Man'yōshū*, 1, p. 147: "Scarlet leaves on Kami Hill/that our Lord, sovereign/of the earth's eight corners,/gazed on when evening came/and went to view when morning came—/if he were here/he would go view them today, he would gaze on them tomorrow. . . ." English translation by Levy, *Man'yōshū*, p. 111.

134. Nakatomi no Kamatari (614–669) led a punitive expedition against Soga no Iruka, opening the path to the Taika reform. He was given the name Fujiwara, thus becoming the ancestor of one of Japan's most powerful political families.

135. This name is written with the characters of "Fujiwara."

136. She was known as Lady Ōtomo, since she belonged to the Ōtomo clan.

137. *Man'yōshū* 2:103, a poem presented by the emperor to Lady Fujiwara. Kojima Noriyuki, *Man'yōshū*, 1, p. 123:

Wa ga sato ni	A big snow has fallen
Ōyuki fureri	On my village—
Ōhara no	Only later will it fall
Furinishi sato ni	On your old-fashioned village,
Furamaku wa nochi	Ōhara.

See also Cranston, *A Waka Anthology*, p. 490: "Here in *my* village/we have had a great snowfall,/but in Great Pastures,/*your* tumbledown old village,/snow will fall later, if at all." Levy's translation: "A great snow has fallen/on my village./Only later will it fall/on the antiquated village,/your Ōhara." Levy, *Man'yōshū*, p. 88.

138. *Man'yōshū* 1:52, a poem on the Imperial Well at the Fujiwara Palace. Kojima Noriyuki, *Man'yōshū*, 1, pp. 92–93: "Our Lord, sovereign/of the earth's eight corners,/child of the high-shining sun,/founds her great palace/on the fields of Fujii,/of the rough wisteria cloth,/and stands there on the banks/of Haniyasu Pond.//Around her she sees/Yamato's green Kagu Hill/standing lush/toward the Eastern Gate,/a hill of spring,/and this hill, Unebi,/rising newly verdant/towards the Western Gate,/young and fresh,/and Miminashi,/that hill of green sedge,/standing towards the Northern Gate,/superb, like a very god,/and Yoshino Mountain—beautiful its name—/soaring beyond the Southern Gate/in the distance, among the clouds.//Here in the divine shadows/of high-ruling heaven,/in the divine shadows/of heaven-ruling sun,/may these waters gush forever,/the crystal waters/of the imperial well." English translation by Levy, *Man'yōshū*, pp. 64–66.

139. Kenzō (r. 485–487) was enthroned in this capital.

140. *Man'yōshū* 12:2860. Kojima Noriyuki, *Man'yōshū*, 3, p. 289:

Yatsurigawa	Water
Minasoko taezu	Never stops running
Yuku mizu no	At the bottom of the Yatsuri River—
Tsugite so kouru	As my love never stops,
Kono toshikoro o	No matter how many years . . .

141. Emperor Kōtoku (r. 645–654) ordered the construction of the Abe Temple in 645.

142. Monju Bosatsu represents the wisdom and realization of all buddhas. This is a reference to the Monju-in, a sub-temple of the Abe temple.

143. This is a reference to the Kusabaka Tumulus.

144. Abe no Seimei (921–1005) was a master of divination *(onmyōji)*.

145. Empress Suiko (r. 592–628) was the third daughter of Emperor Kinmei. She was the first female to become emperor. This is a reference to the Ishibutai Tumulus.

146. Emperor Yōmei reigned from 585 to 587.

147. *Nihon Shoki*, fifth month, fourteenth year of Empress Suiko's reign (606): "The Imperial commands were given to Kuratsukuri no Tori, saying: '. . . We grant thee the rank of Dainin, and We also bestow on thee twenty chō of water-fields in the district of Sakata in the province of Afumi. . . .' With the revenue derived from this land, Tori built for the Empress the Temple of Kongō-ji, now known as the nunnery of Sakata in Minabuchi." English translation by Aston, *Nihongi*, vol. 2, pp. 134–135.

148. *Man'yōshū* 1:171. Kojima Noriyuki, *Man'yōshū*, 1, p. 154:

Takahikaru	The divine child
Waga hi no miko no	Of the high shining sun

Yorozuyo ni	Was meant to rule
Kuni shirasamashi	For numberless generations—
Shima no miya ha mo	Oh, the Shima palace!

See also Levy, *Man'yōshū*, p. 117: "O the Garden Palace/where our child/of the high-shining sun/was meant to rule the land/for ten thousand generations!"

149. The scholar Abe no Nakamaro (701-770) went to China as a foreign student in 716 and died in China. He is the author of the following famous poem, written while looking at the moon in China (*Kokinshū* 9:406; Okumura Tsuneya, *Kokin Waka Shū*, p. 155):

Ama no hara	When I look far away
Furisake mireba	At the plain of heaven,
Kasuga naru	I see the moon that has come out
Mikasa no yama ni	From Mount Mikasa
Ideji tsuki kamo	In Kasuga.

See also McCullough, *Kokin Waka Shū*, p. 97: "When I gaze far out/across the plain of heaven,/I see the same moon/that came up over the hill/of Mikasa at Kasuga."

150. *Shunrai Zuinō*, in Hashimoto Fumio, Ariyoshi Tamotsu, and Fujihira Haruo, eds., *Karon Shū*, p. 173:

Seri tsumishi	Does the ancient proverb
Mukashi no hito mo	"To pick up parsley"
Wagagoto ya	Apply to me?
Kokoro ni mono wa	Nothing is going
Kanawazarikemu	The way I would like it to go.

This proverb comes from the legend of a man who was in love with an empress who used to eat parsley. The man thought that he might have a chance to conquer the lady's heart if he only provided the woman with parsley, but his efforts were in vain.

151. This is a reference to the Dainenji temple of Daifuku.

152. Kibi no Makibi (695?-775) went to China in 716 as a student. On his return he served under Empresses Kōken (r. 749-758) and Shōtoku (r. 764-770), rising to the post of Minister of the Right, Second Senior rank.

153. This poem was inspired by the following poem that the *Taikōki* (An Account of the Chancellor, 16) attributes to Toyotomi Hideyoshi (1537-1598):

Itsushika to	When, when will I ever see them,
Omoiokurishi	I spent so many days thinking—
Yoshinoyama no	Today my eyes are dyed
Hana o kyō shi mo	With the colors of the flowers
Misomenuru kana	On Mount Yoshino.

154. This pond was located near Mount Kagu and the Fujiwara Palace. See note 138: *Man'yōshū* 1:52.

155. This shrine was dedicated to the Eight Great Dragon Kings (Hachidai-ryūō), whom people worshipped in times of drought in order to elicit rainfall. For a variation of the prayer to the Dragon Kings, see *Kinkai Wakashū* 619, by Minamoto no Sanetomo. Higuchi Yoshimaro, ed., *Kinkai Waka Shū*, SNKS 44 (Tokyo: Shinchōsha, 1981), p. 176:

Toki ni yori	At times,
Sugureba tami no	When it becomes excessive,
Nagekinari	It only brings grief to people:
Hachidai-ryūō	Please, Eight Great Dragon Kings,
Ame yametamei	Put an end to this rain!

156. *Man'yōshū* 1:2, composed by the emperor when he ascended Mount Kagu and viewed the land. Kojima Noriyuki, *Man'yōshū*, 1, p. 64. The English translation is by Cranston, *A Waka Anthology*, p. 164: "In Yamato/there are crowds of mountains,/but our rampart/is Heavenly Mt. Kagu:/when I climb it/and look out across the land,/over the land-plain/smoke rises and rises;/over the sea-plain/seagulls rise and rise./A fair land it is,/Dragonfly Island,/the land of Yamato." See also Levy, *Man'yōshū*, p. 38: "Many are the mountains of Yamato,/but I climb heavenly Kagu Hill/that is cloaked in foliage,/and stand on the summit/to view the land./On the plain of land,/smoke from the hearths rises, rises./On the plain of waters,/gulls rise one after another./A splendid land/is the dragonfly island,/the land of Yamato." The original text reads: "Yamato ni wa/murayama aredo/toriyorou/Ame no Kaguyama/noboritachi/kunimi o sureba/kunihara wa/keburi tachitatsu/unahara wa/kamame tachitatsu/umashi kuni so/Akizushima/Yamato no kuni wa."

157. *Man'yōshū* 10:1883. Kojima Noriyuki, *Man'yōshū*, 3, pp. 60–61:

Momoshiki no	Is this leisure time
Ōmiyabito wa	For the inhabitants of the court
Itoma are ya	Of the one hundred stones?
Ume o kazashite	Here they have gathered,
Koko ni tsudoeru	Adorning their hair with plum blossoms.

158. Kongōsen Vajra Mountain was also called Takamayama, the Mountain of High Heaven.

159. The Kongōzanji was built in the Nara period.

160. This mountain is also known as Nijōzan.

161. *Ise Monogatari*, 67. Watanabe Minoru, *Ise Monogatari*, p. 82. The following is the English translation by McCullough, *Tales of Ise*, pp. 114–115: "Around the Second Month of a certain year, a man set out with a group of companions on a pleasure jaunt to the province of Izumi. Mount Ikoma in Kawachi, swathed in restless, billowing clouds, slipped in and out of sight as they traveled. After an overcast morning, the sky cleared around noon, and they saw fallen snow, pure and white, blanketing the treetops. Gazing at the scene, one of the company recited,

> *Kinō kyō*　　　　　　It was through reluctance
> *Kumo no tachimai*　　To reveal the woods in bloom
> *Kakurou wa*　　　　　That yesterday and today
> *Hana no hayashi o*　　Clouds soared and swirled
> *Ushi to narikeri*　　　And the mountain hid itself."

See also *Man'yōshū* 12:3032. Kojima Noriyuki, *Man'yōshū*, 3, pp. 326–327:

> *Kimi ga atari*　　　　I will keep looking
> *Mitsutsu mo oramu*　In your direction—
> *Ikomayama*　　　　　Oh, clouds, do not trail
> *Kumo na tanabiki*　　Over Ikoma Mountain,
> *Ame wa furu tomo*　　Even if rain falls down.

162. *Man'yōshū* 6:921. Kojima Noriyuki, *Man'yōshū*, 2, p. 135:

> *Yorozuyo ni*　　　　Will I ever get tired to look at it
> *Mitomo akane ya*　　Even ten thousand years?
> *Miyoshino no*　　　　The imperial palace
> *Tagitsu kafuchi no*　　Of fair Yoshino
> *Ōmiyatokoro*　　　　Surrounded by deep pools.

See also Cranston, *A Waka Anthology*, p. 297: "Though ten thousand years/should pass, how should I weary/of fair Yoshino,/of gazing at the palace/by the deep and seething pools?"

163. The word *fumi* means both "writing, record, document" and "to step on, to set foot on." Norinaga rejoices at the thought of having been able to set foot on Mount Kagu.

164. This is a reference to the Shrine of the Heavenly Rock-Cave in Minaminura, where the Sun Goddess Amaterasu is enshrined. The shrine was made of a cave where Amaterasu allegedly concealed herself, throwing the whole land into utter darkness.

165. A shrine mentioned in the *Engishiki*.

166. *Man'yōshū* 1:52, the poem of the Imperial Well at the Fujiwara Palace; see note 138. See also *Man'yōshū* 1:201, by Kakinomoto no Hitomaro, at the time of the temporary enshrinement of Prince Takechi at Konoe. Kojima Noriyuki, *Man'yōshū*, 1, pp. 168–169:

> *Haniyasu no*　　　　　The waters of the hidden marsh
> *Ike no tsutsumi no*　　Running on the banks
> *Komorinu no*　　　　　Of Haniyasu pond
> *Yukue o shirani*　　　Do not know where to go—
> *Toneri wa matou*　　　The officials lose their way.

See also Cranston, *A Waka Anthology*, pp. 222–223: "Pent within banks,/waters of the hidden marsh/of Haniyasu Pond:/with no direction for them now/the courtiers wander dazed." Or, in Levy's translation: "Not knowing where they will drift,/like the hidden puddles that run/on the banks of Haniyasu Pond,/the servingmen stand bewildered." Levy, Man'yōshū, p. 130.

167. Yakushi, "Medicine Master," was a popular buddha whose full name was Yakushi-ruikō, Emerald Light of the Master of Medicine. He is the Buddha of the Land of Emerald in the East. Among his twelve vows was the vow to cure diseases. Also known as Kenkōji, the Toyoradera was originally the residence of Soga no Iname (d. 570), who converted it into a temple during the reign of Emperor Kinmei (r. 539–571) and called it Mukuharadera, the Temple Across the Field.

168. See the entry for the tenth month, thirteenth year of the reign of Emperor Kinmei (552), on the introduction of Buddhism to Japan. King Syöng-myöng of Pekche presents Emperor Kinmei with an image of Shakyamuni in gold and copper, several flags and umbrellas, and a number of volumes of sutras. "The Emperor said:— 'Let it be given to Iname no Sukune, who has shown his willingness to take it, and as an experiment, make him to worship it.' The Oho-omi knelt down and received it with joy. He enthroned it in his house at Oharida, where he diligently carried out the rites of retirement from the world, and on that score purified his house at Muku-hara, and made it a Temple." English translation by Aston, Nihongi, vol. 2, p. 67.

169. The well is mentioned in an old folk song *(saibara)*: "In front of the Kazuragi temple/To the west of the Toyora Temple/At the Enoha well/The white walls are immersed/Ooshitodo, oshitodo/This being so/May the country flourish/May our houses prosper/Ooshitodo, toshitondo/Ooshitondo, toshitondo." English translation by Hilda Katō, "The *Mumyōshō* of Kamo no Chōmei and Its Significance in Japanese Literature," in M*onumenta Nipponica* 33:3–4 (1968): 379, n. 142. Kamo no Chōmei (1155?–1216) mentioned the Enoha well in his poetic treatise, *Mumyōshō* (The Nameless Treatise), and quotes the following poem (English translation by Katō, p. 379):

Furinikeru	Grown ancient through the years
Toyora no tera no	At Toyora temple
Enoha i ni	Lies the Enoha well
Nao shiratama o	Pearl-glittering
Nokosu tsukikage	Moonlight is all that is left.

170. Norinaga refers to the province of Settsu. The entry from the *Nihongi* on the tenth month of 552 mentioned above continues as follows: "After this a pestilence was rife in the Land, from which the people died prematurely. As time went on it became worse and worse, and there was no remedy. Okoshi, Mononobe no Ohomuraji, and Kamako, Nakatomi no Muraji, addressed the Emperor jointly, saying:—'It was because thy servants' advice on a former day was not approved that the people are dying thus of disease. If thou dost now retrace the steps before matters have gone too far, joy will surely be the result! It will be well promptly to fling it away, and diligently to seek happiness in the future.' The Emperor said:—'Let it be done as you advise.' Accordingly officials took the image of Buddha and abandoned it to the current of the Canal of Naniwa. They also set fire to the Temple, and burnt it so that nothing was

left." English translation by Aston, *Nihongi,* vol. 2, p. 67. On the Canal of Naniwa (Naniwa-horie), see also the entry tenth month, eleventh year of the reign of Emperor Nintoku (A.D. 323) from *Nihongi:* "The plain north of the Palace was excavated, and the water from the south diverted into the Western Sea. Therefore that water was called by the name Hori-ye [excavated estuary, or canal]." English translation by Aston, *Nihongi,* vol. 1, p. 281.

171. *Man'yōshū* 13:3266. Kojima Noriyuki, *Man'yōshū,* 3, p. 396:

"Haru sareba/hana sakioori/akizukeba/ni no ho ni momitsu/umasake o/kamunabi-yama no/obi ni seru/Asuka no kawa no/hayaki se ni/ouru tamamo no/uchinabiki/kokoro wa yorite/asatsuyu no/kenaba kenubeshi/koishiku mo/shiruku mo aeru/komorizuma kamo

[When spring comes,/the flowers bloom and scatter;/when autumn comes,/the maple leaves are all red;/like the jeweled algae growing/in the fast rapids/of the Asuka River/surrounded by the sacred mountain/my heart is drawn to one direction;/longingly I think of her/to the point that I do not care should I melt away/like the morning dew;/it was so worthy to meet her,/my hidden wife!]"

172. *Man'yōshū* 3:235, by Kakinomoto no Hitomaro, at the time when the sovereign went to Hikazuchi Hill, the Hill of Thunder. Kojima Noriyuki, *Man'yōshū,* 1, p. 199:

Ōkimi wa	Since our sovereign
Kami ni shi maseba	Is a god,
Amakumo no	She builds a temporary palace
Ikazuchi no ue ni	Above the thunder
Iori seru kamo	In the heavenly clouds.

See also Cranston, *A Waka Anthology,* p. 196: "Our great Sovereign/is a very god indeed:/see how high amidst/the clouds of heaven she now dwells/encamped upon the thunder!" Levy's version: "Our Lord,/a very god,/builds her lodge/above the thunder/by the heavenly clouds." Levy, *Man'yōshū,* p. 151.

173. *Man'yōshū* 8:1419, by Princess Kagami. Kojima Noriyuki, *Man'yōshū,* 2, p. 299:

Kamunabi no	Do not cry so painfully,
Iwase no mori no	Calling bird,
Yobukodori	In the forest
Itaku na naki so	Of sacred Iwase—
Waga koi masaru	My love only increases.

174. *Man'yōshū* 13:3289. Kojima Noriyuki, *Man'yōshū,* 3, pp. 407–408:

"Miwakashi o/Tsurugi no ike no/hachisuba ni/tomareru mizu no/yukuenami/aga suru toki ni/aubeshi to/aitaru kimi o/na ine so to/haha kikosedomo/aga kokoro/ kiyosumi no ike no/ike no soko/are wa wasureji/tada ni au made ni

[Without knowing where to go/like the water gathering/on a lotus leaf/of beloved/ Tsurugi-no-ike,/I met you/as I was told we should meet,/and yet my mother says/ that I should not fall asleep—/my heart is as deep/as the bottom of the pond,/the pure pond—/I will not forget/until we meet again.]"

175. Emperor Kōgen (r. 214-158 B.C.) was the first son of Emperor Kōrei (r. 290-215 B.C.).

176. See *Nihon Shoki*, tenth month, tenth year of the reign of Emperor Tenmu (681): "In this month the Emperor intended to hunt on the plain of Hirose. A temporary palace had been constructed, and his baggage made ready, but in the end the Imperial car did not proceed thither. Only those from the rank of Princes of the Blood down to the Ministers all stayed at Karunoichi and inspected the equipage and the saddle-horses." English translation by Aston, *Nihongi*, vol. 2, p. 353. See also *Man'yōshū* 2:207, by Kakinomoto no Hitomaro, on the death of his wife. Kojima Noriyuki, *Man'yōshū*, 1, p. 172: "I did not know what to say,/what to do,/but simply could not listen/and so, perhaps to solace/a single thousandth/of my thousand-folded longing,/I stood at the Karu market/where often she had gone, and listened,/but could not even hear/the voices of the birds/that cry on Unebi mountain...." English translation by Ian Hideo Levy, *Man'yōshū*, p. 134.

177. This is a reference to the Misemaruyama Tumulus.

178. This shrine is mentioned in the *Engishiki*.

179. Kōbō Daishi (774-835), the founder of Shingon Buddhism in Japan, was active at the beginning of the Heian Period. Prince Shōtoku (574-622) was the son of Emperor Yōmei (r. 585-587).

180. The man mispronounces the name of the Sarusawa Pond that is located in front of the southern gate of Kōfukuji.

181. The headquarters of the Hossō sect of Buddhism, Kōfukuji was transferred by Fujiwara no Fubito from Asuka to Nara when this city became the capital of Japan in 710. This was the tutelary temple of the Fujiwara clan.

182. She was the regent for Emperor Chūai from 201 to 269 B.C.

183. *Man'yōshū* 1:52. English translation by Cranston, *A Waka Anthology*, p. 644. See also note 138.

184. Emperor Itoku (r. 510-477 B.C.) was the second son of Emperor Annei (r. 549-511 B.C.).

185. Emperor Jinmu (r. 600-585 B.C.), the alleged first emperor of Japan, ascended the throne in this capital.

186. See *Man'yōshū* 1:29, by Kakinomoto no Hitomaro, while passing the ruined capital at Ōmi. Kojima Noriyuki, *Man'yōshū*, 1, p. 80: "Since the reign of the Master of the Sun/at Kashiwara by Unebi Mountain,/where the maidens/wear strands of jewels,/ all gods who have been born/have ruled the realm under heaven,/each following each/

like generations of the spruce,/in Yamato/that spreads to the sky. . . ." English translation by Levy, *Man'yōshū*, p. 53.

187. This is the tomb of the third emperor, Annei.
188. In 1699 the shogun Tokugawa no Yoshitsuna had issued the order to restore imperial tombs.
189. See note 120.
190. This temple, Jimyōji, gives an alternative name to Mount Unebi.
191. Suizei (r. 581–549 B.C.), second emperor of Japan, was the third son of Emperor Jinmu.
192. The tumulus of Emperor Annei.
193. The first emperor of Japan (r. 660–585 B.C.), according to the *Kojiki* and *Nihon Shoki*.
194. "His tomb is to the north of Mount Unebi, atop the oak ridge." English translation by Donald L. Philippi, *Kojiki* (Tokyo: University of Tokyo Press, 1968), p. 185.
195. The *Shoku Nihon Kōki* mentions the fact that in 843 people worshipped the tomb of Emperor Seimu (r. 131–190) in the village of Heijō as if it were Jingū's.
196. "Seventy-sixth year of Jinmu's reign (585 B.C.), Spring, third month, eleventh day. The Emperor died in the palace of Kashiha-bara. His age was then 127. The following year, Autumn, the twelfth day of the ninth month, he was buried in the Misasagi N.E. of Mount Unebi." English translation by Aston, *Nihongi*, vol. 1, p. 135.
197. *Man'yōshū* 1:13, poem of the three hills by Naka no Ōe (the Emperor of the Ōmi Palace). Kojima Noriyuki, *Man'yōshū*, 1, p. 71:

Kaguyama wa	Longing for Mount Unebi,
Unebi o oshi to	Mount Kagu
Miminashi to	Fought against
Aiarasoiki	Mount Miminashi.
Kamiyo yori	Since the age of the gods
Kaku ni arurashi	Things like this seem to have happened:
Inishie mo	If in the past
Shika ni are koso	Things were like this,
Utsusemi mo	Even people nowadays
Tsuma o	Seem to be fighting
Arasourashiki	Over a wife.

See also Cranston, *A Waka Anthology*, p. 171: "Kagu Mountain/was in love with Unebi,/and with Miminashi/quarreled over her./From the age of the gods/things have been this way, it seems./Since in ancient times/such already was the way,/we mortals too,/it seems,/quarrel over our wives." Levy's version: "Kagu Hill/loved Unebi's manliness,/and Miminashi, with jealousy,/rebuked her./So it has been/since that age/ of the gods./So it was/in ancient times,/and in our day too/mortals struggle for their mates." Levy, *Man'yōshū*, pp. 44–45.

198. Norinaga was inspired by *Kokinshū* 19:1055, by Sanuki. Okumura Tsuneya, *Kokin Waka Shū*, p. 359:

Negigoto o	It is because the shrine
Sa nomi kikikemu	Has listened to prayers
Yashiro koso	So easily
Hate wa nageki no	That at the end it has become
Mori to narurame	A forest of complaints.

See also McCullough, *Kokin Wakashū*, p. 236: "That the shrine is called/a Forest of Trees of Sighs—/is it not because/its deities have granted/so many sad petitions?"

199. *Man'yōshū* 16:3788. Kojima Noriyuki, *Man'yōshū*, 4, p. 109. Kazurako was the name of a girl who, courted by three men, did not have the heart to choose and as a result threw herself in a pond and died. The three men gathered at the side of the pond and each of them composed a poem. The first poem is the following, in which the name of the girl, Kazurako, is artfully concealed in the verb *kazuku* (to dive in, to be submerged):

Miminashi no	How hateful
Ike shi urameshi	The Miminashi Pond!
Wagi moko ga	I wish the water had dried up
Kitsutsu kazukaba	When my beloved
Mizu wa karenamu	Came and drowned.

200. The Miwa Shrine is considered the most ancient one in Japan. It houses the god Ōmononushi, also known as Ōkuninushi.

201. Norinaga was inspired by *Shikashū* 1:29, by Ise Taiyū. Kawamura, Kashiwagi, and Kudō, *Kin'yō Waka Shū, Shika Waka Shū*, p. 228:

Inishie no	The double cherry trees
Nara no miyako no	Of the ancient capital
Yaezakura	Nara
Kyō kokonoe ni	Today must extend their fragrance
Nioinuru kana	To the imperial palace.

202. This is a reference to the god Ōtataneko, son of Ōkininushi-no-Mikoto.

203. This line was inspired by *Man'yōshū* 1:259, by Kamo Taruhito. Kojima Noriyuki, *Man'yōshū*, 1, pp. 207–208:

Itsu no ma mo	When
Kamusabikeru ka	Did they become so venerably aged?
Kaguyama no	Moss grows
Hokosugi ga ure ni	On the tip of the cedar's branches,
Koke musu made ni	Similar to the edge of a halberd's blade, on Mount Kagu.

See also Levy, *Man'yōshū*, p. 159: "When did Kagu's halberd cedar/turn so venerably aged/that moss spreads on its roots?"

204. *Kokinshū* 18:982, with the first line *"waga io wa"* (my temporary dwelling). Okumura Tsuneya, *Kokin Waka Shū*, pp. 332–333. See also McCullough, *Kokin Waka Shū*, pp. 214–215: "I live in a cell/at the foot of Mount Miwa./If you should miss me,/please come and pay a visit—/the gate where the cedar stands."

205. This was the capital of Emperor Kinmei (r. 539–571).

206. *Kokinshū* 19:1009. See note 33.

207. These slopes are found along the old Ise highway connecting the Yamato and Ise provinces.

208. See note 21.

209. Kitabatake Akiyoshi (d. 1383?), third son of the general and historian Kitabatake Chikafusa (1293–1354), conquered the Ise province and built his castle in Tage.

210. A member of the Kitabatake family has served as provincial governor *(kokushi)* of Ise for several generations.

211. Kitabatake Tomonori (1528–1576) was an eighth-generation descendant of Kitabatake Akiyoshi. He was defeated and ordered to commit ritual suicide in 1576 by Oda Nobunaga, who put an end to the Kitabatake clan after more than a 240-year history.

212. The "last leaves" *(sueba)* refer to Norinaga himself, who was the last descendant *(matsuyō)* of a family that had served Lord Kitabatake Tomonori. Aside from being a hymn to the past glory of Tomonori, the poem also refers to the blessings of Norinaga's ancestors, which are now reaching him.

213. This is the eleventh-generation ancestor of the Motoori family, who followed the sad destiny of his lord Kitabatake Tomonori. Norinaga was seven generations removed from Sōsuke.

214. The temple is located in the Ibuta district of the city of Matsusaka.

215. A reference to Mount Kinpu in Yoshino.

Diary and Poetry: Songs on "Aware"

1. Book One, Spring, *Shinpen Kokka Taikan,* vol. 9, *Shikashū Hen 5, Kashū,* 129. The last verse, *aware fukaki,* refers to the tree's power to be moved (to feel), as well as to the tree's power to move the observer.

2. Book Two, Fall, 657. See *Kokinshū* 5:805, anonymous:

Aware to mo	Why are my tears
Ushi to mo mono o	Flowing ceaselessly,
Omou toki	Whenever I am
Nado ka namida no	Either moved to joy
Ito nagaruramu	Or feeling depressed?

See also Helen C. McCullough, *Kokin Waka Shū: The First Imperial Anthology of Japanese Poetry* (Stanford, CA: Stanford University Press, 1985), p. 804: "Why, when one is in love,/should a threadlike stream of tears/flow without ceasing,/not only when one is sad,/but also when one feels joy?"

3. Book Two, Fall, 670. See *Shinkokinshū* 16:1539, by Minamoto no Mitsuyuki:

Kokoro aru	If only people
Hito nomi aki no	With sensitivity
Tsuki o miba	Would look at the autumn moon,
Nani o ukimi no	What will a depressed person like myself
Omoide ni semu	Take as his memento?

4. Book Two, Fall, 673. See *Kokinshū* 4:193, by Ōe no Chisato, "composed for a poetic match at the house of Prince Koresada:"

Tsuki mireba	When I gaze upon the moon
Chiji ni mono koso	I am saddened
Kanashikere	By a thousand things,
Wagami hitotsu no	Though autumn does not come
Aki ni wa aranedo	For me alone.

See also McCullough, *Kokin Waka Shū*, p. 51: "Autumn does not come/for me alone among men—/yet I am burdened/with a thousand vague sorrows/when I gaze upon the moon."

5. Book Two, Fall, 679. See *Kokinshū* 17:867:

Murasaki no	Because of a single clump
Hitomoto yue ni	Of the purple *murasaki* plant
Musashino no	I am deeply moved by the sight
Kusa wa minagara	Of all the grasses
Aware to zo miru	On the Musashi plain.

See also McCullough, *Kokin Waka Shū*, p. 867: "Because of this one/precious *murasaki* plant,/I feel affection/for all the grasses and shrubs/growing on Musashi plain."

See *Ise Monogatari* 41:

Murasaki no	When the *murasaki*'s hue
Iro koki toki wa	Is strong and deep,
Me no haru ni	One can distinguish
No naru kusaki zo	No other plant
Wakarezarikeru	On the vast plain.

Trans. McCullough, *The Tales of Ise*, p. 99.

See *Genji Monogatari*:

Te ni tsumite	When shall I pluck
Itsushika mo min	And hold in my hand
Murasaki no	The young field plant

>   *Ne ni kayoikeru* Whose roots join the roots
>   *Nobe no wakakusa* Of the *murasaki*?

English translation by Norma Field, *The Splendor of Longing in the Tale of Genji* (Princeton, NJ: Princeton University Press, 1987), p. 161. Field indicates that the *Kokinshū* poem, "Murasaki no" "is thought to be the source of the phrase *murasaki no yukari*, which refers to one who is related to the beloved or to the transfer of affection from the beloved to the kin. The strength of the dye and its capacity to stain its surroundings was a metaphor for human relationships." (Ibid., p. 162).

6. Book Two, Fall, 721. See, *Shoku Shūishū* 9:696, by Fujiwara no Michinobu:

>   *Shigure suru* This is limited only to tonight,
>   *Koyoi bakari zo* As the showers fall:
>   *Kaminazuki* Tears
>   *Sode ni mo kakaru* Falling on my sleeves
>   *Namida narikeru* During the godless month.

7. Ibid., 731. The seventh-century Fuwa Barrier (lit., "the indestructible, impenetrable barrier") was created in northern Japan in order to stop invasions from the north on the part of brave Ainu warriors.

8. Ibid., 759. See *Shūishū* 9:511, anonymous:

>   *Haru wa tada* Spring is nothing but
>   *Hana no hitoe ni* The blooming
>   *Saku bakari* Of flowers:
>   *Mono no aware wa* When it comes to the moving power of things,
>   *Aki zo masareru* Autumn is by far superior.

See also the response to the poem above by Kunaikyō in *Shinkokinshū* 18:1805:

>   *Take no ha ni* The moving power of things
>   *Kaze fukiyowaru* Which is felt so deeply at dusk,
>   *Yūgure no* When the wind blowing through the bamboo leaves
>   *Mono no aware wa* Weakens,
>   *Aki to shi mo nashi* Is not only limited to autumn.

9. Ibid., 761. See *Kokinshū* 6:342, by Ki no Tsurayuki, "when he was asked by the emperor to make a song":

>   *Yuku toshi no* How much I regret
>   *Oshiku mo aru ka na* The passing year,
>   *Masukagami* When I think that even my features,
>   *Miru kage sae ni* Which I see in a clear mirror,
>   *Kurenu to omoeba* Come to an end.

See also McCullough, *Kokin Waka Shū*, p. 82: "My heart fills with gloom/as I watch the year depart,/for shadows descend/even on the face I see/reflected in the mirror."

10. Book Two, Fall, 767. See *Kokinshū* 18:971, anonymous, "a song composed by a man who lived in the village of Fukakusa, who sent it to someone living there, when he had to go to the capital":

Toshi o hete	If I go away
Sumikoshi sato o	From the village
Idete inaba	Where I lived for so long a time,
Itodo Fukakausa	It will certainly become a wild field,
No to ya narinamu	"Deep Grass," increasingly deeper.

See also McCullough, *Kokin Waka Shū*, p. 212: "This Fukakusa,/my home for so long a time—/if I go away,/will it become a wild field,/'Deep Grass' deeper than ever?" *Kokinshū* 18:972, "Reply:"

No to naraba	If it becomes a wild field
Uzura to nakite	I will spend the years
Toshi wa hemu	Crying like a quail:
Kari ni dani ya wa	Won't you come at least briefly
Kimi wa kozaramu	For some hunting?

See also McCullough, p. 212: "If it be a field,/I will spend the years crying/like a calling quail,/and surely you will at least/come briefly for some hunting." *Senzaishū* 4:259, by Fujiwara no Shunzei:

Yū sareba	As evening falls,
Nobe no akikaze	From along the moors the autumn wind
Mi ni shimite	Blows chill into the heart,
Uzura naku nari	And the quails raise their plaintive cry
Fukakusa no sato	In the deep grass of Fukakusa village.

The English translation is by Earl Miner, *An Introduction to Japanese Court Poetry* (Stanford, CA: Stanford University Press, 1968, p. 25).

11. Book Two, Fall, 772.
12. Ibid., 785. See *Go-Toba-In Goshū* 1544:

Hatsukari no	The first geese
Tokoyo no aki o	Abandon
Sumisutete	The autumn of everlasting darkness:
Yamaji harukani	Far away on a mountain path,
Yūgure no koe	Their voices in the dusk.

13. Book Two, Fall, 843.

14. Ibid., 963.

15. Book Three, Love Songs, 1046. See *Ise Monogatari,* 71. The English translation is by McCullough, *The Tales of Ise,* p. 118.

> *Chihayaburu*   To see this person
> *Kami no igaki mo*   From the imperial court,
> *Koenubeshi*   I should be willing
> *Ōmiyabito no*   To cross the sacred fence
> *Mimaku hoshisa ni*   Of the mighty gods.

His reply:

> *Koishiku wa*   If you are so inclined,
> *Kite mo miyo kashi*   Pray come,
> *Chihayaburu*   For the mighty gods
> *Kami no isamuru*   Forbid no one
> *Michi naranaku ni*   To travel the path of love.

16. Book Three, Love Songs, 1245. See *Kokinshū* 11:502:

> *Aware chō*   If there were not the word,
> *Koto dani naku wa*   Aware,
> *Nani o ka wa*   What could we use
> *Koi no midare no*   As a cord to bind
> *Tsukaneo ni semu*   The disorder of love?

See also McCullough, *Kokin Waka Shū,* p. 117: "Were our speech to lack/the soft, sorrowful sigh, "Ah,"/what might I employ/as a cord/to bind and tame/love's agonized disorder?"

17. Book Three, Love Songs, 1266. See *Kokinshū* 13:670, by Taira no Sadafun:

> *Makura yori*   It was a love
> *Mata shiru hito mo*   Of which no one knew
> *Naki koi o*   Aside from my pillow:
> *Namida sekiaezu*   Unable to control my tears,
> *Morashitsuru ka na*   I let the secret out.

See also McCullough, *Kokin Waka Shū,* p. 149: "Only my pillow/knew of a passion hidden/from those around me,/but the tears I could not stop/have let the secret escape."

See also *Senzaishū* 12:739, by Priest Chōe:

> *Aware to mo*   Will only my pillow
> *Makura bakari ya*   Know
> *Omouran*   How pitiable I am?

Notes to Pages 99–100

Namida taesenu	The sight of a night
Yowa no keshiki o	Spent with unceasing tears.

18. Book Three, Love Songs, 1276.
19. Ibid., 1287.
20. Book Three, Miscellanea, 1318.
21. Ibid., 1351.
22. Ibid., 1399. See *Fūgashū* 10:1005:

Uchitsuke ni	How moving it is
Aware naru koso	To have been moved so deeply
Aware nare	At first sight,
Chigiri nara de wa	When I think that, were it not for our destiny,
Kaku ya to omoeba	It would never have been like this!

23. Book Three, Love, 1421. See *Ise Monogatari*, 9, by Ariwara no Narihira:

Suruga naru	I do not meet you,
Utsu no yamabe no	Neither in my dreams,
Utsutsu ni mo	Nor when I am awake,
Yume ni mo hito ni	Beside Mount Utsu, "Awakening Mountain,"
Awanu narikeri	In Suruga.

See also McCullough, *The Tales of Ise,* p. 75: "Beside Mount Utsu/in Suruga/I can see you/neither waking/nor, alas, even in my dreams."

Shinkokinshū 10:981, by Fujiwara no Ietaka:

Tabine suru	Allow safe passage
Yumeji wa yuruse	On the path of dreams,
Utsu no yama	As I rest on my journey!
Seki to wa kikazu	I have heard of no barrier on Mount Utsu,
Moru hito mo nashi	And no one guards it.

24. Book Three, Miscellanea, 1498.
25. Ibid., 1588. The "Three Dusks" *(Sanseki)* in question are *Shinkokinshū* 4:361 by Jakuren, 362 by Saigyō, and 363 by Fujiwara no Teika:

1)	*Sabishisa wa*	Lonesomeness
	Sono iro to shi mo	Does not come
	Nakarikeri	With any color:
	Maki tatsu yama no	Autumn dusk
	Aki no yūgure	On the mountain where black pines rise.

2)	*Kokoro naki*	Even a person such as myself,
	Mi ni mo aware wa	Without sensitivity,

>   *Shirarekeri*   Knows *aware:*
>   *Shigi tatsu sawa no*   Autumn dusk
>   *Aki no yūgure*   On a marsh where a snipe rises.
>
> 3)   *Miwataseba*   When I look far in the distance,
>   *Hana mo momiji mo*   There are
>   *Nakarikeri*   No flowers and no maple leaves:
>   *Ura no tomaya no*   Autumn dusk
>   *Aki no yūgure*   On the fishermen's huts in the bay.

For a discussion of the "Three Dusks," see Kōji Kawamoto, *The Poetics of Japanese Verse: Imagery, Structure, Meter* (Tokyo: University of Tokyo Press, 2000), pp. 26–42. See also *Gyokuyōshū* 14:1964:

>   *Tsuki mireba*   When I gaze upon the moon,
>   *Itodo aware zo*   Aware
>   *Masarikeru*   Exceeds all measure,
>   *Ukiyo ni sumeru*   Since I think of all the things
>   *Tagui to omoeba*   Living in this painful world.

26. Book Four, Ancient Styles, 1967. The god Tsukiyomi was also known as Tsukuyomi-no-Mikoto. "Then when he [Izanagi] washed his left eye, there came into existence a deity named Amaterasu Ōmikami. Next, when he washed his right eye, there came into existence Tsukuyomi-no-Mikoto." English translation by Donald L. Philippi, *Kojiki* (Tokyo: University of Tokyo Press, 1968), p. 70. The expression *"tabi no kenagami"* (since I have spent many days on a journey) appears at the end of *Man'yōshū* 6:941, a long poem by Yamabe no Akahito, as he was passing Karani island:

>   . . . *shima no sakizaki*   . . . since, wherever I went,
>   *Kuma mo okazu*   Passing all capes of the island
>   *Omoi so a ga kuru*   I kept on thinking
>   *Tabi no kenagami*   How many days I had spent on my journey.

Essays

1. *Tamakatsuma* (The Jeweled Basket, 1793–1801) 14:84. Yoshikawa Kōjirō, Satake Akihiro, and Hino Tatsuo, eds., *Motoori Norinaga, NST* 40 (Tokyo: Iwanami Shoten, 1978), pp. 477–478.

2. *Nihon Shoki,* Twenty-fifth year of the reign of Emperor Suinin, Third Month: "Now Amaterasu no Ōkami instructed Yamatohime no Mikoto, saying: 'The province of Ise, of the divine wind, is the land whither repair the waves from the eternal world, the successive waves. It is a secluded and pleasant land. In this land I wish to dwell.'" English translation by W. G. Aston, *Nihongi: Chronicles of Japan from the Earliest Times to A.D. 697* (Tokyo: Tuttle, 1972), vol. 1, p. 176.

3. Suruga-no-fu, or Surugafu, corresponds to today's Shizuoka.

4. Motoori Norinaga, *Tamakatsuma* 3:17. *Motoori Norinaga*, pp. 86–87.

5. This is a reference to the *Sugagasa Nikki*.

6. Kamuyaimimi-no-Mikoto is the son of Emperor Jinmu and the elder brother of Emperor Suizei. "At this time Kamuyaimimi-no-Mikoto called [his birthright] to his younger brother Takenunapakamimi-no-Mikoto, saying: 'I was unable to kill the enemy, and it was you who finally killed him. Therefore, even though I am the older brother, it is not right for me to be the first. For this reason, be the first and rule the kingdom. I will help you and will serve as a priest.'" Translation by Donald L. Philippi, *Kojiki*, p. 54.

7. The three volumes of *Ryōboshi* appeared in manuscript form in 1797. The author is also known as Tsukui Naoshige.

8. *Tamakatsuma* 12:63. *Motoori Norinaga*, pp. 394–396.

9. English translation adapted from Donald L. Philippi, *Kojiki* (Tokyo: University of Tokyo Press, 1968), pp, 55–56.

10. *Kokin Rokujō* 4:

Katakoi wa	An unrequited love
Kurishiki mono to	Is truly painful!—
Mikomori no	I appeal
Kami ni urehete	To the God of Mikomori
Shirasete shi gana	And let him know.

11. *Makura no Sōshi*, 266, chapter on deities. Matsuo Satoshi and Nagai Kazuko, *Makura no Sōshi*, p. 417: "The God of Mikomori delights me." Translation by Ivan Morris, *The Pillow Book of Sei Shōnagon* (New York: Columbia University Press, 1967), vol. 1, p. 235.

12. *Man'yōshū* 7:1130. See translation of *Sugagasa no Nikki*, footnote 82.

13. This reading appears in the Kan'ei edition of the *Man'yōshū*.

14. Zaō Gongen is a bodhisattva in fierce form whom En no Gyōja perceived after a thousand-day confinement on Mount Kinpu.

15. For the personal relation of Motoori Norinaga's family to the Mikumari Shrine, see the translation of *Sugagasa no Nikki*, poem 26.

16. *Tamakatsuma* 12:85. *Motoori Norinaga*, p. 405.

17. Norinaga was forty-two years old when he visited Yoshino in the first year of the An'ei era (1772).

18. Lit., "Ho-musubi-no-kami." *Tamakatsuma* 4:83. *Motoori Norinaga*, pp. 139–140.

19. Lit., *magagoto* (crooked things). "Thus, at last, Izanami-no-kami, because she had borne the fire-deity, divinely passed away." Trans. Philippi, *Kojiki*, p. 57.

20. Lit., *iwa-kakuru* (to hide in a cave).

21. "After each had finished speaking, Izanagi-no-Mikoto said to his spouse: 'It is not proper that the woman speak first.' Nevertheless, they commenced procreation and gave birth to a leech-child. They placed this child into a boat made of reeds and floated it away." Trans. Philippi, *Kojiki*, p. 51.

22. Lit., *Ananiyashi*. "After having agreed to this, they circled around; then Izanami-no-Mikoto said first: '*Ananiyashi*, how good a lad!' Afterwards, Izanagi-no-Mikoto said: '*Ananiyashi*, how good a maiden!' After each had finished speaking, Izanagi-no-Mikoto said to his spouse: 'It is not proper that the woman speak first.'" Philippi, *Kojiki*, p. 51.

23. *Tamakatsuma* 2:26. Motoori Norinaga, pp. 56–57.

24. *Tsuki no sawari* (lit., the monthly obstacle) refers to a woman's monthly periods, which forced women to keep away from sacred areas because of impurities related to blood.

25. Poetess of the middle Heian period and one of the Thirty-six Poetic Geniuses of Japan.

26. A reference to the *Tao te ching* (Classic of the Way and Integrity).

27. This English translation is by Robert E. Morrell, who argues that *wakō dōjin* is "the doctrine that the buddhas and bodhisattvas 'moderate the light (of their wisdom) and identify with the dust (of the human world),' i.e., they assume human forms for the sake of benefiting sentient beings. The phrase can be traced to the *Tao Te Ching* IV: '. . . we should attemper our brightness, and bring ourselves into agreement with the obscurity of others' (Legge, tr.)." Robert E. Morrell, *Sand and Pebbles (Shasekishū): The Tales of Mujū Ichien, A Voice for Pluralism in Kamakura Buddhism* (Albany: State University of New York Press, 1985), p. 305, n. 124.

28. *Fūgashū* 19:2112. Tsugita Kasumi and Iwasa Miyoko, eds., *Fūga Waka Shū* (Tokyo: Miai Shoten, 1974), p. 398. Watarai no Tomomune (1265–1341) was a priest at the Outer Shrine of Ise.

29. This is a reference to the Buddhist theory of "original ground and manifest trace" *(honji suijaku),* according to which the Shinto gods are manifestations of an original buddha. See, for example, the following poem from *Goshūishū* 20:1177, written by Fujiwara no Tokifusa on the fence of the Kibune Shrine during a visit. Kubota Jun and Hirata Yoshinobu, eds., *Go-Shūi Waka Shū*, SNKBT 8 (Tokyo: Iwanami Shoten, 1994), p. 383:

Omou koto	Manifesting himself as trace
Naru kawakami ni	On the upper river,
Ato tarete	Answering everybody's requests,
Kibune wa hito o	The God of Kibune
Watasu narikeri	Takes everybody to the shore of salvation.

30. This is a reference to the Buddhist notion of *"hōben"* (Sk. *upāya*), an expedient means or device with the goal of saving sentient beings.

31. *Tamakatsuma* 9:30. Motoori Norinaga, pp. 289–292.

32. Emperor Kōtoku (r. 645–654) supervised the Taika reforms. The edict in question is part of the reforms that Kōtoku promulgated on the first day of the second year of his reign (645), after all the ceremonies for the new year were over: "The Home provinces shall include the region from the River Yokogaha at Nabari on the east, from Mount Senoyama in Kii on the south, from Kushibuchi in Akashi on the

west, and from Mount Afusaka-yama in Sasanami in Afumi in the north." English translation by Aston, *Nihongi*, vol. 2, p. 207.

33. *Man'yōshū* 1:35, by princess Ahe, who composed the poem when crossing Mount Se. In this poem the princess, later known as Empress Genmei, is moved by the memory of her dead husband, Prince Kusakabe, the son of Empress Jitō. The poem was probably composed in 690, one year after Prince Kusakabe's death, during Empress Jitō's journey to the Kii province in the Ninth Month. Kojima Noriyuki et al., *Man'yōshū*, 1, p. 83:

Kore ya kono	Oh, here it is
Yamato ni shite wa	The famous Mount Se,
Aga kouru	Said to be along the path toward Ki!—
Kiji ni ari to iu	The mountain of the beloved husband whom I loved
Na ni ou Senoyama	In Yamato.

See also Cranston, *A Waka Anthology*, p. 272: "Is this then the spot/for which I yearned in Yamato,/the famous mountain/said to lie along the road to Ki,/Senoyama, Husband Peak?" Or, in Levy's version, "Ah, here it is,/the one I loved back in Yamato:/the one they say lies by the road to Ki/bearing his name,/Se Mountain,/mountain of my husband." Ian Hideo Levy, *Man'yōshū: A Translation of Japan's Premier Anthology of Classical Poetry*, vol. 1 (Princeton, NJ: Princeton University Press, 1981), p. 56.

34. *Man'yōshū* 7:1098. Kojima Noriyuki et al., *Man'yōshū*, 2, p. 210:

Kiji ni koso	People say that Mount Imo, the Mount of the Beloved Wife,
Imoyama ari to ie	Is along the path toward the land of Ki—
Tamakushige	The jeweled comb box
Futagamiyama mo	Mount Futagami, Two-Peak Mountain,
Imo koso arikere	Has also its female peak!

35. *Man'yōshū* 13:3318. Kojima Noriyuki et al., *Man'yōshū*, 3, p. 421: "While saying, Let's pick up the ear shells/along the coast/of the land of Ki,/I crossed Mount Imo and Mount Se. . . ."

36. *Man'yōshū* 4:544. Kojima Noriyuki et al., *Man'yōshū*, 1, p. 322:

Okureite	Rather than be left behind
Koitsutsu arazuwa	In my yearning,
Ki no kuni no	I wish I were
Imose no yama ni	On Mount Imose, the Mountain of Husband and Wife,
Aramashimono o	In the land of Ki.

See also Levy, *Man'yōshū*, pp. 266–267: "Rather than be left behind/longing for you,/would that I could be/Imo and Se Mountains—/'husband and wife'—/there in the land of Ki."

Man'yōshū 7:1208. Kojima Noriyuki et al., *Man'yōshū*, 2, p. 235:

Imo ni koi	As I cross the mountain
Aga koeyukeba	Thinking longingly of my beloved,
Senoyama no	How envious I am
Imo ni koizute	To see Mount Se standing apart from Mount Imo
Aru ga tomoshisa	Without any thought of love.

See also *Man'yōshū* 7:1193, 1195, 1209, 1210, and 1247.

37. Kenshō (1130–1210) was a poet and a theoretician of the Rokujō School of poetry. The *Shūchūshō* is a poetic treatise compiled between 1185 and 1190.

38. In this work in three volumes compiled in 1696, the scholar and monk Keichū (1640–1701) classified poems from twenty-one collections according to their topography.

39. *Man'yōshū* 3:285, by Tajihi Kasamaro when he crossed Mount Se on his way to the land of Ki. Kojima Noriyuki et al., *Man'yōshū*, 1, p. 216:

Takuhire no	I want to say her name badly,
Kakemaku hoshiki	My beloved wife!—
Imo no na o	How about trading her name
Kono Senoyama ni	With Mount Se,
Kakeba ika ni aramu	The Mountain of the Beloved Husband?

See also Levy, *Man'yōshū*, p. 168: "I would speak my wife's name,/trailing it/like a scarf of mulberry./How would it be if I hung her name/on Se Mountain,/'Husband's Mountain'?"

40. *Man'yōshū* 3:286, by Kasuga Oyu, as a response to Kasamaro's poem mentioned in the previous note. Kojima Noriyuki et al., *Man'yōshū*, 1, p. 216:

Yoroshinahe	Now you say it!
Waga se no kimi ka	My beloved husband
Oikinishi	Will never call 'beloved wife'
Kono Senoyama o	This mountain of Se
Imo to wa yobaji	That for so long has been called Husband's Mountain.

See also Levy, *Man'yōshū*, p. 285: "It is fit that my man/should bear the name/of Se Mountain,/'Husband's Mountain.'/Let us not call it 'wife.'"

41. *Man'yōshū* 7:1098.
42. Ibid. 7: 1193. See translation of *Sugagasa Nikki*, footnote 57.
43. *Kokinshū* 5:828. See translation of *Sugagasa no Nikki*, footnote 57.

Nagarete wa	Well, this is what
Imose no yama no	The world of love is about:
Naka ni otsuru	The Yoshino River

Yoshino no kawa no	Whose course falls between
Yoshi ya yo no naka	Mount Imo and Mount Se.

44. Kaibara Ekiken (1630–1714), a well-known Confucian scholar, wrote a variety of works on the topography of Japan, including the *Yamato Meguri* (A Journey to Yamato), which had a great influence on Norinaga's study of the Yamato area.

45. In the *Kokin Waka Rokujō* (Six Volumes of Japanese Poems Ancient and Modern; late tenth century), the verse "Yoshino no kawa no" is replaced by "Yoshino no taki no."

46. *Gyokuyō Waka Shū* 8:1278:

Naka ni yuku	I wish the Yoshino River
Yoshino no kawa wa	Which flows in between
Asenanan	Would become shallow:
Imosenoyama o	I must try to cross
Koete mirubeku	The Imose Mountains.

47. Reply:

Imoseyama	I see not even the shadow
Kage dani miede	Of the Imose Mountains:
Yaminubeku	I think the Yoshino River
Yoshino no kawa wa	Which must come to an end,
Nigore to zo omou	Is muddy.

48. *Man'yōshū* 7:1193. See translation of *Sugagasa no Nikki*, footnote 57.

Se no yama ni	Has Mount Imo
Tada ni mukaeru	Forgiven
Imo no yama	Mount Se
Koto yuruse ya mo	That stands straight in front of her?
Uchihashi watasu	A bridge I cross between the two.

49. *Man'yōshū* 7:1209. Kojima Noriyuki et al., 2, *Man'yōshū*, 235:

Hito naraba	If you are human,
Haha ga manago so	Mother's love is the highest:
Asa mo yoshi	Mount Imo Younger Sister and Se Elder brother
Ki no kawa no he no	Nearby the Ki River
Imo to Se no yama	The place of hemp robes.

50. *Tamakatsuma* 12:1. Motoori Norinaga, pp. 375–376.

51. According to his *Diary to Wakayama in the Eleventh Year of the Kansei Era*, Motoori traveled to Wakayama during the First and Second Month of 1799. He de-

parted on the 23rd Day of the First Month. He reached Senoyama on his way back, probably on the 25th Day of the Second Month.

52. The ninth book of *Tamakatsuma* is entitled "Hana no Yuki" (Snow Flowers). The reference is to the passage translated above.

53. The sentence appears in the headnote to *Man'yōshū* 1:35, composed by Princess Ahe "when crossing Mount Se."

54. *Man'yōshū* 13:3318.

55. *Tamakatsuma* 1:3. Motoori Norinaga, pp. 12-13.

56. *Kokinshū* 5:300, by Kiyowara no Fukayabu. Okumura Tsuneya, *Kokin Waka Shū*, p. 118. See also McCullough, *Kokin Waka Shū*, p. 73: "Since autumn herself/is the traveler crossing/the sacred mountain,/she makes her own offerings,/to the Tatsuta River."

57. The section in question is book 8 of the *Kokinshū* on "parting." *Kokinshū* 8:388, composed by Minamoto no Sane, "as several people, who had gone from Yamazaki to the sacred forest *(kamunabi no mori)*, came and now regretted to have to say good-by and return home." Okumura Tsuneya, ed., *Kokin Waka Shū*, SNKS 19 (Tokyo: Shinchōsha, 1978), p. 148:

Hitoyari no	Since this is not a path
Michi naranaku ni	I was ordered to take,
Ōkata wa	In general,
Yukiushi to iite	I say how hard it is to go—
Iza kaerinamu	Let's go back together!

See also McCullough, *Kokin Waka Shū*, pp. 92-93: "No one forces me/to undertake this journey./I think on the whole/I will call it too trying/and turn around and go back."

58. According to the *Yozaishō*, Keichū's commentary on the *Kokinshū*, Keichū believed that Mount Kannabi was the Ikazuchi-no-oka of Asuka, in the district of Takaichi.

59. Norinaga refers to Kamo no Mabuchi's commentary on the *Kokinshū*, the *Kokinshū Uchigiki*.

60. *Kokinshū* 5:283, topic unknown. Okumura Tsuneya, *Kokin Waka Shū*, p. 113:

Tatsutagawa	Maple leaves float
Momiji midarete	In random patterns
Nagarumeri	In the Tatsuta River:
Wataraba nishiki	If I crossed it,
Naka ya taenamu	Will the brocade tear in half?

See also McCullough, *Kokin Waka Shū*, p. 70: "Were one to cross it,/the brocade might break in two—/colored autumn leaves/floating in random patterns/on the Tatsuta River." The poem is followed by an interpolation saying, "According to someone, this poem was composed by the Nara Emperor." There are several theories trying to identify this emperor, which include Emperors Mommu, Shōmu, and Heizei.

61. Longing for the ancient capital, Emperor Heizei (r. 806-809) moved back to Nara in 809 after relinquishing the throne to Emperor Saga (r. 809-823).
62. *Kokinshū* 5:284, anonymous. Okumura Tsuneya, *Kokin Waka Shū*, p. 113:

Tatsutagawa	Maple leaves float
Momijiba nagaru	In the Tatsuta River:
Kamunabi no	Showers must be falling
Mimuro no yama ni	On the sacred
Shigure furusashi	Mimuro mountain.

See also McCullough, *Kokin Waka Shū*, p. 70: "Late autumn showers/must be falling at Mimuro,/the divine mountain,/for colored leaves are floating/on the Tatsuta River." The poem is followed by a note pointing at a different version of the poem. It says, *"Asukagawa/momijiba nagaru"* (Maple leaves float/in the Asuka River). Scholars believe that the Asuka version of the poem is more ancient than the one included in the *Kokinshū*.
63. Mount Mimuro is located in the Heguri prefecture of the Yamato province.
64. *Shūishū* 7:389. Masuda Shigeo, *Shūi Waka Shū*, p. 73.
65. *Tamakatsuma* 2:10. Motoori Norinaga, pp. 48-49.
66. See also Felicia Gressitt Bock, trans., *Engi-Shiki: Procedures of the Engi Era, Books VI-X* (Tokyo: Sophia University, 1972), p. 115.
67. This appears in the third book of the *Engishiki*.
68. See note 57.
69. *Tamakatsuma* 5:48. Motoori Norinaga, pp. 168-169.
70. This mountain is located between the city of Ikoma in the Nara prefecture and Hiraoka in eastern Ōsaka.
71. *Man'yōshū* 9:1747, composed when all the lords of the court went down to Naniwa. Kojima Noriyuki et al., *Man'yōshū*, 2, pp. 412-413:

Shirakumo no	Cherry blossoms
Tatsuta no yama no	Blooming
Taki no ue no	On Ogura Peak,
Ogura no mine ni	On top of the rapids
Sakioru	Of Mount Tatsuta
Sakura no hana wa...	By the white clouds...

See also Cranston, *A Waka Anthology*, p. 328: "Where white clouds rise/above soaring Tatsuta/and the mountain torrent/plummets down Ogura's peak,/blossoming cherries/burgeon in great swirls of bloom...." This mountain is believed to correspond to the peak on the border between the city of Kashiwara of the Osaka prefecture and the Nara prefecture.
72. Norinaga refers to the essay *Yoshi ya Ashi ya* that Ueda Akinari (1734-1809) appended to Kamo no Mabuchi's *Ise Monogatari Koi* of 1793.
73. Norinaga refers to *Tamakatsuma* 1:3.

74. *Tamakatsuma* 2:11. Motoori Norinaga, pp. 49–50.
75. *Man'yōshū* 4: 598. Kojima Noriyuki et al., *Man'yōshū*, 1, p. 339. See also Levy, *Man'yōshū*, p. 284: "One may die from longing, too./Like the hidden current/in the Minase River,/unperceived, I grow thinner/with each month,/with each day."
76. *Man'yōshū* 11: 2712, with the first verse, "Kototoku wa." Kojima Noriyuki, *Man'yōshū*, 3, pp. 250–251.
77. *Man'yōshū* 11:2817. Kojima Noriyuki, *Man'yōshū*, 3, p. 274.
78. *Kokinshū* 15:760. Okumura Tsuneya, *Kokin Waka Shū*, p. 260. See also McCullough, *Kokin Waka Shū*, p. 167: "Denied a meeting,/my passion but increases./What a fool I was/to fall so deeply in love/with the shallowest of streams!"
79. *Kokinshū* 15:793, anonymous. Okumura Tsuneya, *Kokin Waka Shū*, p. 269. See also McCullough, *Kokin Waka Shū*, p. 174: "If there were never/the slightest flow of water/in the dry river/of our love, then I would think/the channel doomed to vanish."
80. *Man'yōshū* 10:2007. Kojima Noriyuki et al., *Man'yōshū*, 3, p. 90. The *Man'yōshū* text says *"ama tsu shirushi to."*
81. This is a classification according to topics of the *Six National Histories*. It was compiled by Sugawara no Michizane (845–903) in 890.
82. *Tamakatsuma* 6:41. Motoori Norinaga, pp. 192–193.
83. The poet Fujiwara Teika quotes this poem in his *Genji Monogatari Okuiri* (An Entry into the Depth of the *Tale of Genji*, 1227), a commentary of the *Tale of Genji*, while discussing the chapter "Usugumo" (Wisps of Clouds). Teika takes this poem to be the source of Genji's statement "Is it a floating bridge of dreams?" The poem's author and source remain unknown. See also Haruo Shirane's translation: "Is it because/the affairs of men and women/are like a floating bridge of dreams/that my melancholy thoughts do not cease/even when I cross to visit you?" Haruo Shirane, *The Bridge of Dreams: A Poetics of 'The Tale of Genji'* (Stanford, CA: Stanford University Press, 1987), p. 192.
84. *Man'yōshū* 3:335, by Ōtomo no Tabito, commander of Dazaifu in the island of Kyūshū. Kojima Noriyuki, *Man'yōshū*, 1, p. 233. The lower verse in the original text says, *"Se ni wa narazu te/fuchi ni ari koso."* The word *wada* in *"Ime-no-Wada"* literally refers to a curved shape, like a bay or a bow. See also Levy, *Man'yōshū*, p. 185: "I trust/my journey won't be long;/may Ime no Wada,/the Abyss of Dreams,/not turn into rapids/but still be an unmoving pool."
85. *Man'yōshū* 7:1132. Kojima Noriyuki et al., *Man'yōshū*, 2, p. 218.
86. "The divine place, deep into the mountains and quiet;/the scenic place, remote and secret;/clouds coil around the gorge of Mibune, the Three Boats;/the mist opens into view the Province of the Eight Boulders;/leaves become yellow, bidding farewell to summer;/*katsura* flowers bloom whitish, welcoming the arrival of autumn;/now, I stand in the area of Ime-no-Wada, the Bay of Dreams;/a thousand years of ancient reverberations come flowing." Eguchi Takao, ed., *Kaifūsō* (Tokyo: Kōdansha, 2000), pp. 262–263.
87. A two-volume commentary of *The Tale of Genji* by Yotsutsuji Yoshinari (1329–1402), who compiled between 1362 and 1367.

88. "Yume no Ukihashi" (The Floating Bridge of Dreams) is the title of the fifty-fourth and last chapter of *Genji Monogatari*.

89. This poem appears in the fourth book of the *Sagoromo Monogatari* (The Story of Sagoromo). In this poem Sagoromo discloses his love for his beloved Genji no Miya.

90. *Tamakatsuma* 6:3. Motoori Norinaga, p. 172.

91. *Kokinshū* 15:257. Okumura Tsuneya, *Kokin Waka Shū*, pp. 104–105. The poem is preceded by the following headnote: "Although he did not intend to, he exchanged amorous vows with a person living in the western wing of the residence of the Empress of the Fifth Ward. However, some time after the Tenth Day of the First Month, she hid herself somewhere else. He knew about her new whereabouts, but he could not meet her. In the spring of the following year, on a night when the moon was particularly beautiful and the plum trees were in bloom, thinking longingly of last year, he went to the western wing of that residence. Lying down on the bare floor until the moon sank, he recited the following poem, Lord Ariwara no Narihira." This poem also appears in *Ise Monogatari*, *dan* (chap.) 4. See also McCullough, *Kokin Waka Shū*, p., 165: "Is this not the moon?/And is this not the springtime,/the springtime of old?/ Only this body of mine/the same body as before...."

92. In *Seigo Okudan* (Conjectures on *The Tales of Ise*) Keichū introduces the two major interpretations that give two different answers to its initial questions. If we give an affirmative answer to the questions, then this means that, although the poet's perception of moon and spring are different, moon and spring are phenomenologically the same. And yet, the poet is the one who has changed even less, since he is perceptually and phenomenologically the same. If the answer is negative, then, this year the moon is not as beautifully misty as last year, and spring this year is not as appealing as last year's. Moon and spring have totally changed, whereas the poet's longing for the woman remains the same. In *Ise Monogatari Koi* (Ancient Meaning of *The Tales of Ise*), Kamo no Mabuchi follows the second interpretation.

93. "The poetry of Ariwara no Narihira tries to express too much content in too few words. It resembles a faded flower with a lingering fragrance." Trans. Helen C. McCullough, *Kokin Waka Shū*, p. 7.

94. Helen C. McCullough takes the plum blossoms to be the object of the poet's stare. The original text, however, is less reductive. "He stared at the flowers from every conceivable standing and sitting position, but it was quite helpless to try to recapture the past." Translation by Helen C. McCullough, *Tales of Ise: Lyrical Episodes from Tenth-Century Japan*, (Stanford, CA: Stanford University Press, 1968), p. 71.

95. *Shin Kokinshū* 16:1449. Kubota Jun, *Shin Kokin Waka Shū*, *Ge*, p. 152. In this poem Fukayabu laments his old age.

96. *Tamakatsuma* 5:44. Motoori Norinaga, pp. 165–166.

97. *Kokinshū* 16:861. Okumura Tsuneya, *Kokin Waka Shū*, p. 292. This poem appears in the last *dan*, chap. 125, of the *Ise Monogatari* (The Tales of Ise). See also McCullough, *Kokin Wakashū*, p. 188: "Composed when he was ill and failing.— Upon this pathway,/I have long heard others say,/man sets forth at last—/yet I had not thought to go/so very soon as today."

98. This comment appears in Keichū's (1640–1701) *Seigo Okudan* (Hypothetical Judgments on *The Tales of Ise*, 1692).

99. Keichū uses the Buddhist expression *kyōgen kigo*, which literally means "floating phrases and fictive utterances."

100. *Tamakatsuma* 6:18. Motoori Norinaga, pp. 180–181.

101. Norinaga reproduces the style used by Sei Shōnagon in the chapter on "Flowering Trees" (Ko no Hana wa) from *Makura no Sōshi* (The Pillow Book), 44. Matsuo and Nagai, *Makura no Sōshi*, pp. 125–127: "Plum blossoms, whether light or dark, and in particular red plum blossoms, fill me with happiness. I also like a slender branch of cherry blossoms, with large petals and dark read leaves. . . ." Trans. Ivan Morris, *The Pillow Book of Sei Shōnagon*, vol. 1, p. 42.

102. They are also known as "Kiri-ga-yatsu" from the name of a place in Kamakura where they first bloomed.

103. Norinaga uses the expression *"arite yo no naka"* (being in the world), a quotation from *Kokinshū* 2:71. Okumura Tsuneya, *Kokin Waka Shū*, p. 49:

Nokorinaku	It is because they scatter
Chiru zo medetaki	Without leaving a trace
Sakurabana	That cherry blossoms delight us so,
Arite yo no naka	Since to linger in the world to the end
Hate no ukereba	Is depressing.

See also McCullough, *Kokin Waka Shū*, p. 27: "It is just because/they scatter without a trace/that cherry blossoms/delight us so, for in this world/lingering means ugliness."

104. *Tamakatsuma* 13:9. Motoori Norinaga, pp. 412–413.

105. *Man'yōshū* 20:4500, by Ichihara no Ōkimi. Kojima Noriyuki, *Man'yōshū*, 4, p. 445. In the original text the fourth line reads, *"kokoro mo shinoni."*

106. *Man'yōshū* 17:3916, by Yamabe no Akahito. Kojima Noriyuki, *Man'yōshū*, 4, p. 171:

Tachibana no	Will the fragrance that I smell
Nioeru ka ka mo	From the flowers of the orange tree
Hototogisu	Disappear
Naku ya no ame ni	In the rainy night in which
Utsuroinuramu	The cuckoo bird sings?

Man'yōshū 18:4111, a long poem *(chōka)* by Ōtomo no Yakamochi. Kojima Noriyuki, *Man'yōshū*, 4, pp. 272–273:

. . . *shirotae no*	. . . in the white mulberry
Sode ni mo kokiire	Sleeve I will put the flower and,
Kaguwashimi	Because of its fragrance
Okite karashimi . . .	I will leave it there until it withers . . .

107. *Man'yōshū* 10:2233, with the first verse, "Takamatsu ni." The word for

mushroom *(matsu no ko)* is hidden in the first and second verse: "Taka**matsu no/ko**no mine." Kojima Noriyuki, *Man'yōshū*, 3, p. 139.

108. *Armillaria matsudake,* written with the characters for "mushroom of the pine tree."

109. The characters for *ka* (芳) and *take* (茸) are similar and could easily be mistaken while transcribing the text.

110. *Tamakatsuma* 6:11. *Motoori Norinaga*, pp. 176–177. The Shishinden is the main hall of the imperial palace in Kyoto. It is also known by the honorific term "Nanden," or Southern Exposure.

111. Also known as *Teiō Hennenki* (Chronicles of Emperors and Kings), this work is an abbreviated history of India, China, and Japan in twenty-seven volumes. It was edited by monk Eiyū in the Kamakura period. Apparently, Norinaga thought that the *Rekitai Hennen Shūsei* and the *Teiō Hennenki* were different works.

112. Emperor Kanmu (r. 781–806) was the second son of Emperor Kōnin. The capital was moved to Kyoto in 794.

113. Emperor Ninmyō (r. 833–850) was the second son of Emperor Saga.

114. Prince Shigeaki (906–954) was a son of Emperor Daigo (r. 897–930).

115. Minamoto no Kintada (889–948) was a grandson of Emperor Kōko (884–887). He is considered to be one of Japan's Thirty-Six Poetic Geniuses.

116. The *Bankiroku* was compiled in 1158.

117. Emperor Murakami (r. 946–967) was the fourteenth son of Emperor Daigo.

118. Kujō Koremichi (1093–1165) wrote this work for Emperor Nijō (r. 1158–1165) in order to acquaint him with court ceremonies.

119. Since the last part of this essay is unrelated to the main topic for discussion, I am appending it here as a footnote: "The same work states that 'nowadays, the upper nobility is not provided with any private houses. Without manors how could they deal with public and private matters? When I think about how the recent trend to give the upper nobility land has annihilated the system of public stipend, it is beyond my power to understand how they can serve.' Moreover, the same record says that 'recently, they are wearing rigid things on top of more rigid things. I do not understand how people can use underpants, and the buckle to keep crown and the daily headgear in place. To get dressed up to meet people is a painful and sickening experience, and all this in order to associate with one or two people wearing unbearable colors!'"

120. *Tamakatsuma* 4:36. *Motoori Norinaga*, p. 116.

121. This is a reference to Keichū's (1640–1701) *Kokin Yozai Shō* (A Treatise on the Excess Material of the *Kokinshū*, 1692).

122. *Wakana* I. The English translation of the title is by Royall Tyler, trans., *The Tale of Genji*, vol. 2 (New York: Viking, 2001), p. 575.

123. *Tamakatsuma* 5:23. *Motoori Norinaga*, p. 148.

124. Shikishima (lit., "the scattered islands") is a name for Japan.

125. "Poetry is thus of great antiquity, but it was not until the reign of the Nara Emperor that composition became widespread. (It may have happened because His Majesty was especially skilled in the art.)" Trans. McCullough, *Kokin Waka Shū*, p. 6.

126. "Since then, one or two people have been acquainted with the poetry of antiquity and understood the true nature of the art." Trans. McCullough, ibid., p. 6.

127. "Hitomaro is dead, but poetry lives." Trans. McCullough, ibid., p. 8.

128. This is a reference to the *mana* preface by Ki no Yoshimochi (d. 919), as opposed to the *kana* preface by Ki no Tsurayuki (ca. 868–ca. 945).

129. "After Emperor Heizei's time, Japanese poetry was cast aside and ignored. There were masters of the elegant style, like the Ono Consultant [Takamura], and of the refined style, like the Ariwara Counselor [Yukihira], but all were known for their proficiency in Chinese poetry; it was not our art (lit., 'this way') that brought them to prominence." Trans. McCullough, *Kokin Waka Shū*, p. 258.

130. "By fortunate chance, we live in a time when Japanese poetry is taking on a new life, and we rejoice that our art (lit., 'our way') flourishes again." Trans. McCullough, ibid., p. 259.

131. *Tamakatsuma* 4:77. *Motoori Norinaga*, pp. 135–136.

132. *Tsurezuregusa* 137. Kidō Saizō, ed., *Tsurezuregusa, SNKS* 10 (Tokyo: Shinchōsha, 1977), pp. 153–154: "Are we to look at cherry blossoms only in full bloom, the moon only when it is cloudless? To long for the moon while looking on the rain, to lower the blinds and be unaware of the passing of the spring—these are even more deeply moving. Branches about to blossom or gardens strewn with faded flowers are worthier of our admiration. Are poems written on such themes as 'Going to view the cherry blossoms only to find they had scattered' or 'On being prevented from visiting the blossoms' inferior to those on 'Seeing the blossoms'? People commonly regret that the cherry blossoms scatter or that the moon sinks in the sky, and this is natural; but only an exceptionally insensitive man would say, 'This branch and that branch have lost their blossoms. There is nothing worth seeing now.'" English translation by Donald Keene, *Essays in Idleness: The Tsurezuregusa of Kenkō* (New York: Columbia University Press, 1967), p. 115. Kenkō is the Buddhist name of Urabe no Kaneyoshi (1283–after 1352), who was born in the family in charge of the Yoshida Shrine in Kyoto. He served Emperor Go-Nijō (r. 1301–1308) before taking the tonsure and becoming a recluse. Kenkō entered the poetic school of Nijō Tameyo (1250–1338), becoming one of the Four Kings (Shitennō) of poetry.

133. *Tsurezuregusa* 7. Kidō Saizō, *Tsurezuregusa*, p. 27: "We cannot live forever in this world; why should we wait for ugliness to overtake us? The longer man lives, the more shame he endures. To die, at the latest, before one reaches forty, is the least unattractive. Once a man passes that age, he desires (with no sense of shame over his appearance) to mingle in the company of others. In his sunset years he dotes on his grandchildren, and prays for long life so that he may see them prosper. His preoccupation with worldly desires grows even deeper, and gradually, he loses all sensitivity to the beauty of things, a lamentable state of affairs." English translation by Donald Keene, *Essays in Idleness*, p. 8.

134. *Tamakatsuma* 4:78. *Motoori Noninaga*, pp. 136–137.

135. A reference to Confucian scholars.

136. A reference to Buddhist monks.

137. *Tamakatsuma* 14:38. *Motoori Norinaga*, pp. 457–458.

138. Norinaga refers to paintings by the literati *(bunjinga)*.
139. *Tamakatsuma* 14:39. *Motoori Norinaga*, p. 458.
140. Ibid. 14:40. *Motoori Norinaga*, p. 458.
141. Norinaga refers to *ukiyo-e* prints of beauties *(bijinga)*.
142. *Tamakatsuma* 14:41. *Motoori Norinaga*, pp. 458–459.
143. A reference to *Wu tsa tsu* (J. *Gozasso;* The Five Sections, 1619).
144. Lit., "*yasha* and *rasetsu.*" *Yasha* (Sk. *yakṣa*) are a kind of demon of fearsome appearance who harms and even eats men. *Rasetsu* (Sk. *rākṣasa*) are also a kind of demon said to bewitch and eat men.
145. China.
146. *Tamakatsuma* 14:42. *Motoori Norinaga*, pp. 459–463.
147. The first patriarch of Zen in China.
148. Hotei and Fukurokuju are two of the Seven Deities of Good Fortune.
149. *Isonokami no Sasamegoto* (Personal Views on Poetry, 1763), 1:6. Hino Tatsuo, ed., *Motoori Norinaga Shū*, SNKS 60 (Tokyo: Shinchōsha, 1983), pp. 265–268.
150. The poem is attributed to the deity Susa-no-wo.
151. English translation by Donald L. Philippi, *Kojiki*, p. 91. See also W. G. Aston's translation: "Many clouds arise,/on all sides a manifold fence,/to receive within it the spouses,/they form a manifold fence—/ah! That manifold fence!" Aston, *Nihongi*, vol. 1, pp. 53–54.
152. Aston argues that while *tsumagomi* is intransitive (my spouse is hidden), *tsumagome* is transitive (it hides my spouse). *Nihongi*, p. 54.
153. 徵 indicating *mi*, and 昧 indicating *me*.
154. Norinaga refers to theories such as the one advanced by Kitamura Kigin (1624–1705) in his *Hachidaishū Shō* (A Treatise on the Eight Imperial Collections, 1682), in which the "eight clouds" *(yakumo)* and the "eight fences" *(yaegaki)* are related to the eight-tailed dragon slain by the deity Susa-no-wo after his descent to Izumo.
155. *Makurakotoba* is a poetic rhetorical technique consisting of fixed expressions that work as epithets. They express some quality of the word they modify.
156. Keichū argues that the word *izumo* in this poem is the attributive form *(rentaikei)* of the verb *izu* (to come out) plus the noun *kumo* (clouds).
157. Norinaga follows the etymology advanced by the Shinto scholar Tanigawa Kotosuga (1709–1776) who, in the fifth book of his *Nihon Shoki Tsūshō* (A Compendium Treatise on the *Chronicles of Japan*, 1762), argued that the word *yatsu* (eight) derives from *iyatsu* (many ports).
158. Norinaga refers to the *Izumo Fudoki* (The Gazetteer of the Izumo Province, 733).
159. *Man'yōshū* 16:3842, by Lord Heguri. Kojima Noriyuki, *Man'yōshū*, 4, p. 136:

Warawadomo	Everybody,
Kusa wa na kari so	Do not cut the grass!
Yahotade o	Cut the smelly armpit hair
Hozumi no Aso ga	Of Lord Hozumi—
Wakikusa o kare	The sprouting ears of rice!

254 Notes to Pages 137–139

160. This is a reference to a poem that Empress Suiko sent in reply to Soga no Umako during a banquet. The exchange is recorded in the *Nihon Shoki,* Seventh Day of the First Month, Twentieth Year of Suiko's reign (612): "My bright Soga!/The sons of Soga—/were they horses,/they would be steeds of Hiuga:/were they swords,/they would be good blades of Kure./Right indeed/seems the Great Sovereign/to have in her service/the sons of Soga!" Trans. (with a slight modification) Aston, *Nihongi,* vol. 2, p. 143.

161. The attributive form *(rentaikei)* implies the presence of an understood *toki* (when), thus giving the verse the following meaning: "When I was looking, I saw many clouds rising."

162. Lit., "people's land"—a reference to China. The quotation comes from the forty-fourth chapter of the *San-kuo yen-yi* (Romance of the Three Kingdoms).

163. Kitamura Kigin, Keichū, and Tanigawa Kotosuga all interpreted the fences as real walls rising into the sky like clouds.

164. Norinaga argues that the ancient technique of the refrain was abandoned during the Heian period, only to surface later again in the popular music *(imayō).*

165. Examples can be found in the *Kuo-feng* (Airs of the Sate) of the *Shi-jing* (Classic of Poetry).

166. This is a reference to the poetic exchange in the *Kojiki* between Izanagi and Izanami at the time of the production of the land. "Then Izanagi no Mikoto said first: 'Ah, what a cute girl!' *(Ana ni yashi, e otome o).* Afterwards, his spouse, little sister Izanami no Mikoto, said: 'Ah, what a handsome lad!' *(Ana ni yashi, e otoko o)."* See also Philippi's translation in *Kojiki,* p. 51.

167. *Ashiwake no Obune* (A Small Boat amidst the Reeds, 1757). Suzuki Jun and Odaka Michiko, eds., *Kinsei Zuisō Shū,* NKBZ 82 (Tokyo: Shōgakukan, 2000), pp. 274–287.

168. Norinaga uses the words *tai* (which includes nouns and pronouns) and *yō* (which includes verbs, adjectives, and all particles that can be conjugated).

169. This etymology comes from Norinaga's teacher, Hori Keizan (1688–1757), who articulated it in his *Fujingen* (Things that Cannot Be Exhausted in Words).

170. Norinaga refers to the verb forms: negative *(mizenkei),* conjunctive *(renyōkei),* final *(shūshikei),* attributive *(rentaikei),* perfect *(izenkei),* and imperative *(meireikei).*

171. Here Norinaga stresses the specificity of the concept he intends to discuss, songs.

172. English translation by Stephen Owen, *Readings in Chinese Literary Thought* (Cambridge, MA: Council on East Asian Studies, Harvard University, 1992), p. 26, with a slight modification ("purposefully" instead of "intently").

173. *Kokinshū* 13:616, by Ariwara no Narihira. Okumura Tsuneya, *Kokin Waka Shū,* p. 217:

   Oki mo sezu   Until dawn I spent the night
  Ne mo sede yoru o   Not awake
   Akashite wa   Nor asleep—

| *Haru no mono to te* | Time I spend staring, lost in thoughts |
| *Nagame kurashitsu* | In the long rains of springtime. |

See also McCullough, *Kokin Waka Shū*, p. 615: "Having passed the night/neither waking nor sleeping,/I have spent the day/brooding and watching the rain—/the unending rain of spring." The word *nagame* works as a pivot word *(kakekotoba)* with the meanings of (1) "to stare while being immersed in thoughts" and (2) "long rains" *(nagaame)*.

174. This expression precedes the poem "Many Clouds Rising" *(Yakumo tatsu)* by Susa-no-wo in the *Nihon Shoki*. See Aston, *Chronicles of Japan*, vol. 1, p. 53.

175. A reference to the *Classic of Documents*.

176. English translation, with a slight modification, by Owen, *Readings in Chinese Literary Thought*, p. 26.

177. This is the explanation of the character *"ge" (uta)* in the *Shuo-wen chieh-tzu* (Explanation of Simple and Compound Graphs).

178. The Chinese reading of *"Yamato uta"* is *waka*.

179. "Now, there are six Japanese poetic *(uta)* styles. No doubt the same is true of Chinese poetry *(Kara uta)*." Trans. McCullough, *Kokin Waka Shū*, pp. 3–4.

180. "Japanese poetry *(Yamato uta)* has the human heart as seed and myriads of words as leaves." Trans. McCullough, ibid., p. 3.

181. This reference is currently unidentified.

182. This is a quotation from the *Shuo-wen chieh-tzu* (Explanation of Simple and Compound Graphs).

183. *Isonokami no Sasamegoto* 2:27–29. Hino Tatsuo, *Motoori Norinaga Shū*, pp. 347–353.

184. Whereas Ki no Tsurayuki's preface to the *Kokinshū* begins with the words *Yamato uta* (song from Yamato), the Chinese preface to the same collection by Ki no Yoshimochi begins with the word *waka* 和歌. The nuance is lost in the English translation, in which both terms appear as "Japanese poetry." See McCullough, *Kokin Waka Shū*, pp. 3 and 256.

185. *Man'yōshū* 5:876. Kojima Noriyuki et al., *Man'yōshū*, 2, p. 88. See also Levy, *Man'yōshū*, p. 381.

186. *Man'yōshū* 20:4293. Kojima Noriyuki et al., *Man'yōshū*, 4, p. 371. The Retired Empress was Genshō (r. 715–724).

187. This is a reference to the entry of the Nineteenth Day of the Ninth Month 808.

188. Norinaga argues that in Japanese writings such as *monogatari* (tales) and *nikki* (diaries) one should use the native word *uta* rather than the Chinese cognate *waka*.

189. For an example, see *Man'yōshū* 1:24. Kojima Noriyuki et al., *Man'yōshū*, 1, p. 77: "Poem by Prince Omi, deeply moved upon hearing this and replying *(kotafuru uta* 和ふる歌*)*. English translation by Levy, *Man'yōshū*, p. 50. See also *Man'yōshū* 3:402. Kojima Noriyuki et al., *Man'yōshū*, 1, p. 254: "Poem written in immediate response *(kotafuru uta)* by Ōtomo Sarugamaro." Levy, *Man'yōshū*, p. 207.

190. Norinaga refers to the Chinese practice of incorporating a rhyme from the original poem in one's response to that poem.

191. The Engi era goes from 901 to 923. There are two theories with regard to the alleged date of composition of the *Kokinshū*, 905. One indicates 905 as the year when Emperor Daigo (r. 897–930) issued the order for the composition of an imperial anthology. According to the second theory, 905 marks the date of the completion of the *Kokinshū*. It is unclear which theory Norinaga followed.

192. The *Shinsen Waka* is a selection of 280 poems from the *Kokinshū*, with an addition of eighty new poems.

193. *Ise Monogatari, dan* 82. Watanabe Minoru, *Ise Monogatari*, p. 97. See also McCullough's translation: "Though the prince would go out hawking during these visits, the hunts themselves did not greatly interest him, and were indeed little more than pretexts for sipping wine and composing verse." *The Tales of Ise*, pp. 124–125.

194. This theory, mentioned in the *Nihon Shoki Tsūshō* (An Explanation of the Chronicles of Japan), is attributed to the Shinto scholar Asai Shigetō.

195. The master of linked poetry *(renga)* Sōgi (1421–1502) advanced this hypothesis in his commentary on the *Kokinshū*, the *Kokin Waka Shū Ryōdo Kikigaki* (The Verbatim Notes of Both Scholars [Tsuneyori and Sōgi] on the *Kokinshū*, 1472).

196. *Isonokami no Sasamegoto* 2:30–53. Hino Tatsuo, *Motoori Norinaga Shū*, pp. 353–392.

197. Norinaga refers to a long poem *(chōka)* written by Ōkuninushi bidding farewell to his jealous wife Suseribime: "Your head drooping,/like the lone reed of *susuki* grass/of Yamato/you will weep." Trans. (with a slight modification) Philippi, *Kojiki*, p. 109.

198. Norinaga refers to an entry from the *Nihon Shoki*, First Day of the Fourth Month of the Thirty-first Year (630 B.C.) of the reign of Emperor Jinmu. "Finally, when Nigi-haya-hi no Mikoto soared across the Great Void in a Heaven-rock-boat, he espied this region and descended upon it. Therefore he gave it a name and called it Sora-mitsu-Yamato (Sky-saw-Yamato)." Trans. Aston, *Nihongi*, vol. 1, p. 135.

199. English translation by Aston, ibid., p. 108.

200. The doubtful passage is probably related to the unexplained connection between Emperor Jinmu and the Ihare district of Yamato.

201. "The Emperor Kami Yamato Ihare-biko's personal name was Hiko-hoho-demi." Aston, *Nihongi*, vol. 1, pp. 109–110.

202. As a matter of fact, on the Twenty-third Day of the Ninth Month 712 the district of Idewa broke lose from the province of Echigo, so that a district became a province, maintaining the same name.

203. *Nihon Shoki*, First Day of the Fourth Month of the Thirty-first Year (630 B.C.) of the reign of Emperor Jinmu. Trans. Aston, *Nihongi*, vol. 1, pp. 134–135.

204. Norinaga argues that Yamato, Akizushima, and so on do not refer to the entire country, but only to the Yamato province. Keichū and Tanigawa Kotosuga also supported this theory.

205. The *Shaku Nihongi*, in twenty-eight volumes, is a commentary of the *Nihon Shoki* written by Urabe Kanekata at the end of the Kamakura period.

206. In his commentary of the *Man'yōshū*, the *Man'yō Daishōki* (A Stand-in's Chronicle of the *Man'yōshū*, 1690), Keichū explains the word *urayasu* of *Man'yōshū* 14:3504 as "tranquil" *(kokoroyasu ni)*. Kojima Noriyuki et al., *Man'yōshū*, 3, p. 488. The poem says,

Haru no saku	Not one night
Fuji no uraba no	Have I slept
Uraysasu ni	With tranquility on the tip of my heart—
Sanuru yo so naki	The tip of the leaves of the wisteria flowers blooming in spring—
Koro o shimoeba	Because of my thoughts for her.

207. English translation by Aston, *Nihongi,* vol. 1, p. 13.

208. This is a reference to the island of Kyūshū.

209. The inquirer feels that the name Ō-Yamato no Toyo-aki-zu-shima refers to the entire island of Honshū.

210. These islands correspond to Awajishima, Shikoku, Oki, Kyūshū, Iki, Tsushima, Sadogashima, and Honshū. See Philippi, *Kojiki,* pp. 53–54.

211. The doubt is due to the fact that "Koshi" refers to the Hokuriku region and therefore cannot be an island. In the *Nihon Shoki Tsūshō*, Tanigawa Kotosuga wondered whether this might be a reference to the island of Hokkaidō (Ezoshima).

212. Norinaga means that Ōyamato-Akizushima is the general term for the island of Honshū.

213. Norinaga argues that Yamato became the general term for the island of Honshū.

214. English translation by Cranston, *A Waka Anthology,* pp. 43–44. See also the translation by Philippi, *Kojiki,* p. 320.

215. "Divine Child/of the high-shining sun,/it is but proper/you deign to ask me,/you do well indeed/to deign to ask me:/I of all others/am the longman of the age./I have never heard/of a wild goose coming here/to lay its egg/in the land of sky-seen Yamato." Trans. Cranston, *A Waka Anthology,* p. 44.

216. Fifth Day of the Third Month of the Fiftieth Year (362 A.D.) of Emperor Nintoku's reign, "A man of Kawachi informed the Emperor, saying:—'A wild goose has laid an egg on the Mamuta embankment.' That same day a messenger was sent to see. He said:—'It is true.' The Emperor hereupon made a song, in which he inquired of Takechi no Sukune, saying:—'O Aso of Uchi!/Thou, beyond all others,/a man distant of age—/Thou, beyond all others,/a man long in the land—/hast thou not heard/that a wild goose has laid an egg/in Akitsushima/the land of Yamato?' Takechi no Sukune made a song in reply, saying:—'Our great Lord/who rules tranquilly,/right is he, right is he/to ask me./For in Akitsushima, in the land of Yamato,/never have I heard/that a wild goose has laid an egg.'" Trans. Aston, *Nihongi,* vol. 1, pp. 294–295.

217. Norinaga refers to the reign of Nintoku's predecessor, Emperor Ōjin (r. 270–310), when, according to the *Kojiki* and the *Nihon Shoki,* Confucian scriptures were imported to Japan.

218. An example might be the etymology that Kaibara Ekiken (1630–1714) presented in his *Nihon Shakumyō* (Japanese Etymologies, 1699), according to which the name Yamato means "outside the mountains" (*yamato* 山外) because it is located in the outskirts of Mount Ikoma.

219. English translation by Aston, *Nihongi*, vol. 1, p. 110.

220. *Yamato wa/kuni no mahoroba/tatanazuku/aokaki/yamagomoreru/Yamato shi uruwashi*. English translation by Cranston, *A Waka Anthology*, p. 23. See also Philippi's translation: "Yamato is/the highest part of the land;/the mountains are green partitions/lying layer upon layer./Nestled among the mountains,/how beautiful is Yamato!" (*Kojiki*, p. 248). Yamato-takeru no Mikoto sang this poem in the plain of Nobo, where he died thinking of the sword he had left with his beloved.

221. Aston, *Nihongi*, vol. 1, p. 135.

222. "I pass by Nara/of the blue clay; I pass by Yamato/of the little shields." Trans. Philippi, *Kojiki*, p. 310.

223. *Man'yōshū* 9:1809. Kojima Noriyuki, *Man'yōshū*, 2, p. 441. "*Utsuyufu no*" is a pillow word of *komoru* (to be hidden). By indicating the presence of the pillow word in Emperor Jinmu's account of the land, Norinaga wants to stress the hidden nature of Yamato, the land hidden inside the mountains.

224. The *Nihongi Shiki*, which was compiled during the Heian period, is an account of how to read the *Nihon Shoki*.

225. A reference to the *Shuo-wen chieh-tzu* (Explanation of Simple and Compound Graphs).

226. Norinaga implies that, if we accept the theory according to which Yamato owes its name to the footprints left in the mud, then Yamato cannot refer only to the Yamato province but must refer to the whole country, as it would be unthinkable that the land coagulates in some regions and not others.

227. Philippi, *Kojiki*, p. 47.

228. Keichū's criticism appears in his *Kokin Yozai Shō* (A Treatise on the Excess Material of the *Kokinshū*, 1692).

229. Despite the presence of the quotations marks, in the last quotation Norinaga is paraphrasing rather than quoting literally.

230. Norinaga argues that the character "*ato*" has nothing to do with its literal meaning. According to him, it simply stands as a sign indicating the sound "*to*."

231. Both Keichū in *Kokin Yozai Shō* and Kitamura Kigin (1624–1705) in *Haichidai Shūshō* (A Treatise on the Eight Imperial Collections, 1682) accepted this etymology.

232. This practice was based on Sōgi's commentary of the *Kokinshū*, the *Kokin Waka Shū Ryōdo Kikigaki*.

233. Norinaga cannot accept this theory because it gives Yamato the opposite meaning from the one that he defends, "a land inside the mountains."

234. A reference to Kaibara Ekiken's (1630–1714) *Nihon Shakumyō* (Japanese Etymologies, 1699).

235. This theory argues that the name Yamato includes the character "mountain" (Chinese pronunciation, *san* 山), a character that is homophonous with "creation" (*san* 産). Therefore, the name Yamato is an extremely auspicious name.

236. This is a reference to an order by Empress Genmei to use characters with beautiful names when naming geographical areas. The edict was issued in 713.

237. This is a reference to volume twenty-two of the *Engishiki* (Procedures of the Engi Era, 901–922), in which we find an ordinance to use two beautiful characters when naming a place.

238. This is a reference to the *Han shu* (History of the Han Dynasty) by Pan Ku.

239. This is the *History of the Latter Han Dynasty,* ca. 445.

240. This theory is mentioned in the *Shaku Nihongi* (Explanation of the Chronicles of Japan).

241. The *Gengenshū* (An Anthology of Origins, 1337), a text in eight volumes by Kitabatake Chikafusa (1293–1354), explains the origins of Japan based on quotations from the *Kojiki* and the *Nihon Shoki.*

242. Onogoro island was the island that Izanami and Izanagi created by lowering the jeweled spear from the Heavenly Floating Bridge. It became the base of operations for the creation of the world. "They stirred the brine with a churning-churning sound; and when they lifted up the spear again, the brine dripping down from the tip of the spear piled up and became an island. This was the island Onogoro." Trans. Philippi, *Kojiki,* p. 49.

243. This is a critique of Tanigawa Kotosuga who, in *Nihon Shoki Tsūshō,* argued that Onogorojima is Japan's original name.

244. *Kojiki,* Book Three:

Oshiteru ya	When from the cape
Naniwa no saki yo	Of far-shining Naniwa
Idetachite	I set forth,
Waga kuni mireba	Going out to view the land,
Awashima, Onogoroshima . . .	Awa Island, Onogoro island . . .

Trans. Cranston, *A Waka Anthology,* p. 35. See also the translation by Philippi, *Kojiki,* p. 306.

245. As this note was designed to provide the correct reading of the Chinese characters, it was not included in the English translation. "Next, when the land was young, resembling floating oil and drift-like a jellyfish, there sprouted forth something like reed-shoots. From these came into existence the deity Umashi Ashi Kabi Hikoji no Kami; next, Ame no Tokotachi no Kami. These two deities also came into existence as single deities, and their forms were not visible." Trans. Philippi, ibid., p. 47.

246. "If expressed completely in ideographic writing, the words will not correspond exactly with the meaning, and if written entirely phonetically, the account will be much longer. For this reason, at times ideographic and phonetic writing have been used in combination in the same phrase, and at times the whole matter has been recorded ideographically. Thus, when the purport is difficult to gather, a note has been added to make it clear; but when the meaning is easy to understand, no note is given." Trans. Philippi, *Kojiki,* p. 43,

247. The name "Wei-nu Guo" appears in the chapter on the Eastern barbarians

from the *Hou Han shu* (History of the Latter Han Dynasty). This designation was particularly disliked in Japan because of its literal meaning, "land of the slaves from Yamato."

248. An example would be the *Shuo-wen chieh-tzu* (Explanation of Simple and Compound Graphs).

249. "The Eastern barbarians are of a quiet nature. They are different from the other barbarians from the south, north, and west."

250. *Nihon Shoki*, Eighth Day of the Twelfth Month of the Seventh Year (513) of the reign of Emperor Keitai. English translation adapted from Aston, *Nihongi*, vol. 2, p. 12.

251. This is a reference to the song "Great Dignity" from *The Major Odes*: "Full of harmony was he in his palace;/full of reverence in the ancestral temple." Translation by James Legge, *The Chinese Classics, IV, The She King* (Hong Kong: Hong Kong University Press, 1960), p. 447.

252. English translation in Ryusaku Tsunoda, Wm. Theodore de Bary, and Donald Keene, eds., *Sources of Japanese Tradition* (New York: Columbia University Press, 1964), vol. 1, p. 48. This is a quotation from the *Analects* of Confucius 1:12. James Legge translates the character *"wa"* 和 as "natural ease." James Legge, *The Chinese Classics* (Hong Kong: Hong Kong University Press, 1970), vol. 1, p. 143.

253. This is a reference to the city of Chang-an.

254. This is a reference to the Chinese dictionary *Kang-xi zi-dian*.

255. In this Taoist text the "Land of Great Harmony" was one of the lands of utopia. No text has been found linking this Taoist place to Yamato, the "land of harmony" 和国.

256. Norinaga refers to the entry of the Sixth Year (92 B.C.) of the reign of Emperor Sujin: "Before this the two Gods, Amaterasu no Ōkami and Yamato no Ōkunidama, were worshipped together within the Emperor's Great Hall" (trans. Aston, *Nihongi*, vol. 1, p. 151). Yamato is written with the second character *"wa"* 和 in the 1770 edition of the *Nihon Shoki*. The most ancient manuscript records the first *"wa"* 倭.

257. This is a reference to the Kinai region.

258. "The Governor of the province of Yamato 大和, Lord Ōtomo Inakimi of the Junior Fourth Rank, Lower Grade, presented a report to the empress." Ujitani Tsutomu, ed., *Shoku Nihongi, Chū* (Tokyo: Kōdansha, 1992), p. 184.

259. This work was edited by Sugawara no Michizane (845–903) in 892.

260. This is a dictionary in three volumes edited by Tōin Kinkata (1291–1360).

261. The four books from 17 to 20 were compiled between 746 and 759. Book 18 includes poems composed from the Twenty-third Day of the Third Month 730 to the Eighteenth Day of the Second Month 750.

262. *Man'yōshū* 19:4273–4278.

263. This date corresponds to January 3, 753, of the Gregorian calendar.

264. This is the endnote *(sachū)* of *Man'yōshū* 19:4277.

265. *Man'yōshū* 20:4293. Kojima Noriyuki, *Man'yōshū*, 4, p. 371. The empress in question was probably Genshō (r. 715–724), although another theory indicates Empress Genmei (r. 707–715).

266. This is footnote to *Man'yōshū* 20: 4293, the song that Prince Toneri composed in response to the empress' command.

267. Norinaga seems not to have realized that the meaning of *waka* in this case is not "poem from Yamato," but "envoy" written as a response to another poem. This passage contradicts his explanation of the use of the word *Yamato uta* in his essay "Again on Songs."

268. Actually, it corresponds to the Third.

269. In other words, the character in the name of the Yamato land (Yamato no kuni 大和国) changed in the Eleventh Month 752; the character in the title "Lord of Yamato" (Yamato no sukune 大和の宿禰) took place between the sixth and the Twelfth Month 757.

270. Norinaga is referring to the group of songs from number 4273 to 4278.

271. In the second case it cannot be a mistake for *wa* 倭, since the term *waka* does not refer to Yamato, but simply means "poem in response."

272. The decree of 513 by Emperor Keitai that Norinaga mentioned above is an example: "Yamato (日本) is harmonious."

273. W.G. Aston explains this term as follows: "This title is found in the Japanese names of the ancient Emperor Kōrei and his two successors. It also occurs in the Japanese names of the Empresses Genmei and Genshō in the early part of the eighth century. Here Yamato-neko is used by the Emperor himself, although it was no part of his name. It would appear therefore that it had become, to some extent, a common name, like Pharaoh or Caesar." *Nihongi*, vol. 2, p. 210, n. 2.

274. The Wadō era from 708 to 715 covers the reign of Empress Genmei.

275. Entries Nineteenth Day of the Eighth Month 721 and Thirteenth Day of the Eighth Month 721.

276. Entry Twenty-seventh Day of the First Month 721.

277. The word appears in the headnote to *Man'yōshū* 7:1328.

278. Norinaga argued that the use of the second character *"wa"* 和 in the name Yamato took place after the Eleventh Month 752 (prior to the First Month 757).

279. In a note to the entry on the Eleventh Day of the First Month 708 in the *Shoku Nihongi* Norinaga argues that the word *Wadō* should be read *"Niki akagane"* (pure copper).

280. The word *Yamato-goto* appears in the index to *Man'yōshū* 5:810 and 16:3817.

281. This is the Chinese reading of "Hi-no-moto" (the sun's origin), and the current name for Japan (together with Nihon).

282. This is a reference to *Kushiki-ryō* (Public Codes), which is part of the *Yōrō-ryō* (Codes of the Yōrō Era, 718–757).

283. English translation by Aston, *Nihongi*, vol. 2, p. 198.

284. For example, in the entry for the Fourth Day of the Tenth Month 632, Ōtomo Umakai addresses the Chinese envoy, referring to the Japanese emperor as "Sumeramikoto no Mikado." See Aston, *Nihongi*, vol. 2, p. 166.

285. English translation by Aston, *Nihongi*, vol. 2, p. 210. The entry is Fifteenth Day of the Second Month 646.

286. The first era in Japanese history is the Taika era (645–649), which was created at the time of Emperor Kōtoku's ascension to the throne.
287. English translation in Wm. Theodore de Bary, ed., *Sources of Japanese Tradition*, vol. 1, pp. 10–11.
288. Kao-cong reigned from 649 to 683.
289. Adapted from Aston, *Nihongi*, vol. 2, p. 292. This is the entry for the Twelfth Month 669.
290. Actually, it would be twenty-five years.
291. The Confucian scholar Itō Tōgai (1670–1736) mentioned this history of Korea in his *Heishokutan*. Norinaga was actually quoting from Tōgai's work.
292. Munmu was king of Silla from 661 to 681.
293. As a footnote, Norinaga adds the poem below from the *Gyokuyō Waka Shū*, book 20 (Collection of Jeweled Leaves, ca. 1313). See Tsugita Kasumi, ed., *Gyokuyō Waka Shū* (Tokyo: Iwanami Shoten, 1989), p. 432.

Waga kuni wa	Since our land
Amaterukami no	Descends from
Sue nareba	The Goddess shining in the sky,
Hi no moto to shi mo	It came to be called
Ifu ni zo arikeru	The origin of the sun.

294. This work was composed by Si-ma Guang in 1084.
295. English translation in Wm. Theodore de Bary, ed., *Sources of Japanese Tradition*, vol. 1, p. 10.
296. See the "Chronicles of Empress Suiko," Autumn, Third Day of the Seventh Month 607: "The Dairai, Imoko Wono no Omi, was sent to the Land of Great Tang." Aston, *Nihongi*, vol. 2, p. 136.
297. English translation in de Bary, ed., *Sources of Japanese Tradition*, vol. 1, p. 11.
298. This theory appears in the *Gengenshū* as a quotation from the *Kuo-di Zhi*, a geographical record of the Tang dynasty.
299. Norinaga refers to the entry for the Eighteenth Day of the First Month 701 from the *Shoku Nihongi*.
300. Norinaga refers to *Man'yōshū* 13: 3295 in the 1643 Kan'ei edition of the work, in which Yamato no is spelled out "Hi no moto no."
301. *Man'yōshū* 1:63. Kojima Noriyuki, *Man'yōshū*, 1, p. 97. English translation by Cranston, *A Waka Anthology*, p. 346. See also Levy, *Man'yōshū*, p. 70: "Come lads, make speed/for Yamato! The pines/on the beach/by Ōtomo's noble cove/wait for us in longing." The Kan'ei edition of the *Man'yōshū* says, "Haya Hi no moto e."
302. *Man'yōshū* 11:2834. Kojima Noriyuki, *Man'yōshū*, 3, p. 278. The Kan'ei edition records the verse "Hi no moto no."
303. *Man'yōshū* 3:319. Kojima Noriyuki, *Man'yōshū*, 1, p. 227: *Hi no moto no/ Yamato no kuni no/shizume to mo/imasu kami ka mo*.... Cranston translates these verses as follows: "Here in Yamato/land of the rising of the sun,/guardian of its peace,/abides this living god forever...." Cranston, *A Waka Anthology*, p. 315.

304. *Hi no moto no/Yamato no kuni wo* 日本乃 野馬台能国遠.
305. *Hi no moto no/Yamato no kuni wa* 日本乃 倭之国波.
306. Entry of the Twenty-ninth Day of the Third Month 849.
307. See, for example, *Man'yōshū* 1:78. Kojima Noriyuki, *Man'yōshū*, 1, p. 102. Translation by Levy, *Man'yōshū*, p. 75:

Tobu tori no	If I depart, and leave behind
Asuka no sato wo	The village of Asuka,
Okite inaba	Where the birds fly,
Kimi ga atari wa	I shall no longer be able
Miezu ka mo aramu	To see the place where you abide.

308. Adapted from Aston, *Nihongi*, vol. 1, p. 13.
309. This is the name of Emperor Jinmu.
310. This is the name of the daughter of Emperor Suinin (r. 29 B.C.-70 A.D.).
311. Prince Yamatodake never ascended the throne. However, he was considered an emperor because he was the son of Emperor Keikō (r. 71-130) and the father of Emperor Chūai (r. 192-200).
312. Norinaga refers to the poem he mentioned earlier about the wild goose laying its egg in the land of Yamato rather than in some foreign country.
313. This theory appears in the dictionary *Yakubun Sentei* by the Confucian Ogyū Sorai (1666-1728).
314. This is the great-granddaughter of Emperor Annei (r. 549-511 B.C.) and the consort of Emperor Kōrei (r. 290-215 B.C.).
315. In the *Kojiki*, the title of "queen mother" accompanies Isukeyorihime (consort of Emperor Jinmu), Hibasuhime (consort of Emperor Suinin), Okinagatarashihime (consort of Emperor Chūai), and Iwanohime (consort of Emperor Nintoku).
316. Eighth Day of the First Month 581 B.C.: "Kami-Nunagaha-mimi no Mikoto assumed the rank of Emperor. He made his capital at Katsuraki. It was called the palace of Takaoka. He honored the Empress by granting her the title of Kōtaigō (Empress Dowager)." Aston, *Nihongi*, vol. 1, p. 140. The consort of Emperor Jinmu becomes Empress Dowager on the year of her son's (Emperor Suizei) ascension to the throne.
317. *Isonokami no Sasamegoto* 1:12-14. Hino Tatsuo, *Motoori Norinaga Shū*, pp. 280-315.
318. Norinaga follows Kenshō's (1130?-1209?) reading of this sentence as presented in *Kokin Wakashū Kenshō Chū* (Kenshō's Notes on the *Kokinshū*, 1191), according to whom the preface states, *hitotsu kokoro* (one heart), rather than the commonly accepted *hito no kokoro* (the human heart). In McCullough's translation, "Japanese poetry has the human heart as seed and myriads of words as leaves." *Kokin Waka Shū*, p. 3.
319. "It comes into being when men use the seen and the heard to give voice to feelings aroused by the innumerable events in their lives." McCullough, *Kokin Waka Shū*, p. 3.
320. "Japanese poetry plants its roots in the earth of the heart and produces its flowers in the groves of words. People cannot remain passive when they live in the

world: their thoughts are easily swayed, their moods alternate between sorrow and happiness. A poem is a response in words to an emotion stirring the heart." McCullough, *Kokin Waka Shū*, p. 256.

321. Norinaga creates a variation on the third sentence of Ki no Tsurayuki's preface: "The song of the warbler among the blossoms, the voice of the frog dwelling in the water—these teach us that every living creature sings." McCullough, *Kokin Waka Shū*, p. 3.

322. Lit., "the feeling heart moves." This is a quotation from the Great Preface to the *Shi-jing* (Classic of Poetry). "The feelings move inwardly, and are embodied in words. When words are insufficient for them, recourse is had to sighs and exclamations. When sighs and exclamations are insufficient for them, recourse is had to the prolonged utterances of song." Translation by James Legge, *The Chinese Classics, IV, The She King* (Hong Kong: Hong Kong University Press, 1960), p. 34. See, also Owen's translation: "The affections are stirred within and take on form in words. If words alone are inadequate, we speak them out in sighs. If sighing is inadequate, we sing them." Stephen Owen, *Readings in Chinese Literary Thought* (Cambridge, MA: Council on East Asian Studies, Harvard University, 1992), p. 41.

323. For Norinaga, knowledge of *mono no aware* is equivalent to knowledge of the nature of phenomena.

324. Norinaga gives the following poetic example from *Minamoto no Shigeyuki Shū* (The Collection of Minamoto no Shigeyuki, ca. 1000):

Aware oba	Although I thought I did not know
Shiraji to omoedo	The meaning of *"aware,"*
Mushi no ne ni	My heart
Kokoro yowaku mo	Will surely weaken
Narinubeki kana	At the sound of the chirping insects.

325. "To be stirred by external things" *(mono ni kanzuru)* is a quotation from the "Record of Music" of the *Li ji* (Book of Rites): "When the human mind is moved, some external thing has caused it. Stirred (*kan* 感) by external things into movement, it takes on form in sound." "A human being is born calm: this is his innate nature endowed by Heaven. To be stirred by external things and set in motion is desire occurring within that innate nature." English translations by Owen, *Readings in Chinese Literary Thought*, pp. 50–51 and 53.

326. During the Edo period *kanzuru* referred only to positive feelings. It was not used in relation to sorrow or hatred.

327. A reference to the *Kang-xi zi-dian*.

328. Written in 1763, this analysis of *Genji Monogatari* (The Tale of Genji) is included in Hino Tatsuo, *Motoori Norinaga Shū*. See sections on pp. 61-63, 84-89, 112-140, 159-163, 195-201, 215-224, and 235-241.

329. This character was created in Japan *(kokuji)*. It is not recorded in dictionaries of Chinese characters, and it does not have any particular meaning.

330. Fourth Day of the Ninth Month 493. This is the lament of a woman living at

Mitsu in Naniwa. "Woes me *(aware),* my youthful spouse! For me too he is an elder brother." Aston, *Nihongi,* vol. 1, p. 396.

331. *Nihongi,* Sixth Month 645.

332. The *Kogo Shūi* is a work compiled by Inbe no Hironari in 807 lamenting the loss of power of the Inbe family at the hands of the Nakatomi (Fujiwara). See also Genchi Katō and Hikoshirō Hoshino, trans., *Kogoshūi: Gleanings from Ancient Stories* (London: Curzon Press, 1972), p. 23: "The Sun-Goddess coming forth from the Rock-Cave now illumined the sky and consequently the spectators were enabled to distinguish one another's faces once more. Overflowing with joy, they loudly cried:

'*Ahare! Ahare!*' (signifying that the sky is now illuminated)

'*Ana omoshiroshi!*' ('O how delightful it is again clearly to see one another's faces!')

'*Ana tanoshi!*' ('What joy to dance with outstretched hands!')

'*Ana sayake oke!*' ('How refreshing and reviving! just like the rustling sound of breezes softly whispering in bamboo grass, or through the leaves of the trees playing sweet melodies of natural music!')."

333. Norinaga does not explain the nature of his doubts.

334. Norinaga refers to the *Kojiki* myth of the Sun Goddess who concealed herself in a heavenly rock-cave, leaving the land completely dark. A ruse by several deities forced Amaterasu out of her hiding place, thus restoring light to the entire land. See Philippi, *Kojiki,* pp. 81–86.

335. The etymology that relates the word *aware* to the joy felt at the time when light was restored to the world thanks to the reappearance of the sun (Amaterasu) in the sky is found in Kaibara Ekiken's *Nihon Shakumyō* (Japanese Etymologies, 1699). Norinaga himself accepted this theory in an earlier work, *Aware Ben* (A Discussion of *Aware*, 1758).

336. English translation by Aston, *Nihongi,* vol. 1, p. 209. In this episode, which appears in "The Chronicles of Emperor Keikō," Yamato Takeru returns to a lone pine of Cape Otsu where he had forgotten his sword while having a meal. He sang this poem upon finding the sword. The event is recorded on the Seventh Day of the Tenth Month 110.

337. English translation by Cranston, *A Waka Anthology,* p. 20. In this episode from the *Kojiki,* Yamato Takeru exchanges swords with Izumo Takeru and gives him a false one. "As they were unsheathing their swords, Izumo Takeru was unable to unsheathe the imitation sword. Then Yamato Takeru no Mikoto, unsheathing his sword, struck and killed Izumo Takeru. Then he made a song saying: The many-clouds-rising/Izumo Takeru/wears a sword/with many vines wrapped around it,/but no blade inside, alas!" Philippi, *Kojiki,* pp. 236–237.

338. "*Omoizuma aware.*" This song, which appears in the *Kojiki,* is sung by Prince Karu, who was exiled to the hot spring of Iyo. For an English translation of the poem, see Cranston, *A Waka Anthology,* p. 52, and Philippi, *Kojiki,* p. 339.

339. "*Kagehime aware.*" This poem appears in "The Chronicles of Emperor Buretsu," Eighth Month 497. In this poem Kagehime, daughter of Mononobe no Arakai, laments the death of her beloved, Heguri no Shibi. For an English translation of the poem, see Aston, *Nihongi,* vol. 1, p. 402.

340. *"Ii ni ete/koyaseru/sono tabito aware."* This song appears in "The Chronicles of Empress Suiko," First Day of the Twelfth Month 613. Prince Shōtoku composed this poem upon feeding and clothing a starving man on the hill of Kataoka. For an English translation of the poem, see Aston, *Nihongi*, vol. 2, pp. 144-145.

341. *"Azuma haya."* The episode is narrated in the "Chronicles of Emperor Keikō." Yamatodake no Mikoto's concubine, Oto-tachibana-hime, throws herself into the sea in order to pacify the god of the sea, and to assure her beloved a safe passage. Aston, *Nihongi*, vol. 1, p. 206. See also Philippi, *Kojiki*, pp. 241-242.

342. *"Uneme haya Mimi haya."* Eleventh Month 453. This episode refers to the envoys from Silla who had come to pay their respect at the time of the death of Emperor Ingyō. "Now the men of Silla had always loved Mount Miminashi and Mount Unebi, which are hard by the capital city. Accordingly, when they arrived at the Kotobiki Hill, they looked back, and said:—'Uneme haya! Mimi haya!' This was simply because they were unpracticed in the common speech, and therefore corrupted Mount Unebi, calling it Uneme, and corrupted Mount Miminashi, calling it Mimi." Aston, *Nihongi*, vol. 1, p. 326.

343. *Man'yōshū* 4:761, by Ōtomo no Sakanoue no Iratsume. Kojima Noriyuki, *Man'yōshū*, 1, p. 383. In his commentary on the *Man'yōshū*, the *Man'yō Daishōki*, Keichū argues that *"waga ko"* refers to the lady's lover rather than to a child. See also Levy, *Man'yōshū*, p. 331: "Oh my child/who loved me helplessly/like a hovering bird/over quick river shallows!"

344. *Man'yōshū* 7:1417. Kojima Noriyuki, *Man'yōshū*, 2, p. 283.

345. *Man'yōshū* 9:1756. Kojima Noriyuki, *Man'yōshū*, 2, p. 417.

346. Norinaga refers to the fact that, rather than ending with the exclamation *aware*, these two poems end with a noun that is preceded by *aware*.

347. See note 330.

348. *Man'yōshū* 18:4089. Kojima Noriyuki, *Man'yōshū*, 4, pp. 259-260.

349. *Kokinshū* 18:984, anonymous. Okumura Tsuneya, *Kokin Waka Shū*, p. 333. See also McCullough, *Kokin Waka Shū*, p. 215: "Utterly ruined!/Ah, how many long years/might the house have seen?/Not even a visit now/from the one who lived here once." In the *Kokinshū Tōkagami* (A Telescope on the *Kokinshū*; completed in 1793, published in 1797), Norinaga translates the second verse of this poem in the idiom of his time as follows: *"Aa, aware"* (Oh, how moving!).

350. *Kokinshū* 19:1003. Okumura Tsuneya, *Kokin Waka Shū*, pp. 343-344. This is a quotation from a long poem by Mibu no Tadamine. For an English translation of the poem, see McCullough, *Kokin Waka Shū*, pp. 223-225.

351. *Shūishū* 16:1049. Masuda Shigeo, *Shūi Waka Shū*, p. 197.

352. *Appare* is an exclamation indicating admiration.

353. *Kokinshū* 17:897. See, also, McCullough's translation: "We are powerless/to seize time and make it stay,/so I have spent them/in constant grief and hardship—/all these passing months and years." *Kokin Wakashū*, p. 197. In the *Kokinshū Tōkagami* Norinaga interprets the lower verse "how quickly/these hard months and years have passed!"

354. *Kokinshū* 19:1001, anonymous. Okumura Tsuneya, *Kokin Waka Shū*, pp.

340–341. For an English translation of the poem, see McCullough, *Kokin Waka Shū*, pp. 220–221.

355. Entry of the Twentieth Day of the Sixth Month 970: "I was taut with emotion as we rode down from the barrier. The vista stretched on into the distance...." Edward Seidensticker, *The Gossamer Years (Kagerō Nikki): A Diary by a Noblewoman of Heian Japan* (Tokyo: Tuttle, 1973), p. 83.

356. *Kokinshū* 3:136, by Ki no Toshisada, "seeing a cherry tree blooming in the Fourth Month." Okumura Tsuneya, *Kokin Waka Shū*, p. 68. See also McCullough, *Kokin Waka Shū*, p. 40: "Was it unwilling/that some of our praise should go/to all the others—/this tree blooming by itself/after the passing of spring?"

357. *Kokinshū* 11:502. Okumura Tsuneya, *Kokin Waka Shū*, p. 188. See also McCullough, *Kokin Waka Shū*, p. 117: "Were our speech to lack/the soft, sorrowful sigh, "Ah,"/what might I employ/as a cord to bind and tame/love's agonized disorder?"

358. *Kokinshū* 18:939, by Ono no Komachi, with the last verse *"hodashi narikere."* Okumura Tsuneya, *Kokin Waka Shū*, p. 319. See also McCullough, *Kokin Waka Shū*, p. 206: "It is nothing more/than a detestable chain/preventing escape/from a melancholy world—/this thing they call emotion."

359. *Kokinshū* 18:940, anonymous. Okumura Tsuneya, *Kokin Waka Shū*, p. 319. See also McCullough, *Kokin Waka Shū*, p. 206: "The dew that appears/on each leafy utterance/of the word called "ah"—/what is it but fallen tears/shed in memory of the past?"

360. *Gosenshū* 3:133. Katagiri Yōichi, *Gosen Waka Shū*, p. 44.

361. *Gosenshū* 16:1192. Katagiri Yōichi, *Gosen Waka Shū*, p. 358.

362. *Gosenshū* 20:1395. Katagiri Yōichi, *Gosen Waka Shū*, p. 424.

363. *Koto no ha* stands for the currently used term *kotoba* (word).

364. *Man'yōshū* 12:3197. Kojima Noriyuki, *Man'yōshū*, 3, p. 363.

365. *Kokinshū* 18:943. Okumura Tsuneya, *Kokin Waka Shū*, p. 320. See also McCullough, *Kokin Waka Shū*, p. 207: "For one in this world/life means being here today/and gone tomorrow./Might we call it saddening,/or shall we call it bitter?" McCullough takes the word *aware* to mean "sad," rather than an exclamation indicating awe in front of the mystery of life, as Norinaga interprets this term.

366. *Gosenshū* 17:1191. Katagiri Yōichi, *Gosen Waka Shū*, p. 358.

367. *Shūishū* 11:686, by Minamoto no Tsunemoto. Masuda Shigeo, *Shūi Waka Shū*, p. 132.

368. *Shūishū* 15:950, by the Regent Ichijō. Masuda Shigeo, *Shūi Waka Shū*, p. 179. See also Steven D. Carter, trans., *Traditional Japanese Poetry: An Anthology* (Stanford, CA: Stanford University Press, 1991), p. 219: "I can't even think/of a soul who might tell me,/'How I pity you'—/and so I go on living,/but wasting my life away."

369. *Shūishū* 18:1195, by Ki no Tsurayuki. Masuda Shigeo, *Shūi Waka Shū*, p. 227.

370. *Kokinshū* 1:37, by Monk Sōsei. Okumura Tsuneya, *Kokin Waka Shū*, p. 37. See also McCullough, *Kokin Waka Shū*, p. 21: "Blossoms of the plum/admired only from afar:/I plucked you and now/I know the fascination/of your colors and fragrance."

371. *Kokinshū* 17:867. Okumura Tsuneya, *Kokin Waka Shū*, p. 295. See also McCullough, *Kokin Wakashū*, p. 190: "Because of this one/precious *murasaki* plant, I feel affection/for all the grasses and shrubs/growing on Musashi plain."

372. *Shūishū* 4:251, within the original text, *"yuki furitsumite"* (the snow falls and piles up). Masuda Shigeo, *Shūi Waka Shū*, p. 46.

373. *Shūishū* 13:793, by Mibu no Tadamine. Masuda Shigeo, *Shūi Waka Shū*, p. 152.

374. This space is blank in the original text. Evidently Norinaga was unable to find any song containing the expression *aware to kiku* (listening to something, and saying "Ah!") in the first three imperial anthologies, *Kokinshū* (905), *Gosenshū* (951), and *Shūishū* (1005-1007). As a matter of fact, none of these songs exists. We find such song in the "Aoi" chapter of *Genji Monogatari* (The Tale of Genji). Ishida Jōji and Shimizu Yoshiko, eds., *Genji Monogatari*, 2, SNKS 13 (Tokyo: Shinchōsha, 1977), p. 97:

Hito no yo o	Listening, while saying, "Ah!" *(aware)*,
Aware to kiku mo	Of this human world
Tsuyukeki ni	My eyes are moist with tears—
Okururu sode o	Much more so when I think
Omoi koso yare	Of the sleeves you sent me.

See, also R. Tyler's translation: "The sad news I hear, that a life can pass so soon, brings tears to my eyes,/but my thoughts go first of all to the sleeves of the bereaved." Murasaki Shikibu, *The Tale of Genji*, trans. Royall Tyler (New York: Viking, 2001), vol. 1, p. 179. The same expression also appears in *Shikashū* 1:47 (Collection of Verbal Flowers, 1151-1154). Kawamura and Kashiwagi, *Kin'yō Waka Shū, Shika Waka Shū*, p. 233:

Konu hito o	I share the same longing
Machikaneyama no	With the sparrow calling
Yobu kodori	The person who does not come
Onaji kokoro ni	To Machikaneyama—Wait Mountain,
Aware to zo kiku	As I listen to him while I say, "Ah!" *(aware).*

375. *Kokinshū* 1:33. Okumura Tsuneya, *Kokin Waka Shū*, p. 36. See also McCullough, *Kokin Waka Shū*, p. 20: "More than the color/it is the fragrance I find/a source of delight./Whose sleeve might have brushed against/the plum tree beside my house?"

376. *Kokinshū* 4:244, by Monk Sōsei. Okumura Tsuneya, *Kokin Waka Shū*, p. 100. See also McCullough, *Kokin Waka Shū*, p. 61: "Can it be fitting/that none but I should stand here/to feel emotion?/Wild pinks blowing where crickets/chirr in the gathering dusk!"

377. *Kokinshū* 11:474, by Ariwara no Motokata. Okumura Tsuneya, *Kokin Waka Shū*, p. 180. See also McCullough, *Kokin Waka Shū*, p. 112: "Over and over,/like white waves from the offing,/my fond thoughts return/to an absolute stranger/who has carried off my heart."

378. *Kokinshū* 15:805, anonymous. Okumura Tsuneya, *Kokin Waka Shū*, p. 273. See also McCullough, *Kokin Waka Shū*, p. 176: "Why, when one is in love,/ should a threadlike stream of tears/flow without ceasing/not only when one is sad/ but also when one feels joy?"

379. *Kokinshū* 17:904, anonymous. Okumura Tsuneya, *Kokin Waka Shū*, p. 307. See also McCullough, *Kokin Wakashū*, p. 198: "When I tell the years,/I feel deep pity for you,/faithful guardian/mounting watch over the bridge/at Uji of mighty name."

380. *Shūishū* 12:730, anonymous. Masuda Shigeo, *Shūi Waka Shū*, p. 140.

381. *Shūishū* 6:350, by Yuge no Yoshitoki. Masuda Shigeo, *Shūi Waka Shū*, p. 65.

382. *Shūishū* 16:1013, anonymous. Masuda Shigeo, *Shūi Waka Shū*, p. 190.

383. *Gosenshū* 3:103, by Minamoto no Saneakira, with the verse *"kokoro shireran"* (people who know the heart of things). Katagiri Yōichi, *Gosen Waka Shū*, p. 35.

384. *Shūishū* 9:511, anonymous. Masuda Shigeo, *Shūi Waka Shū*, p. 96.

385. *Ise Monogatari, dan* 65. Watanabe Minoru, *Ise Monogatari*, p. 80. See also McCullough, trans., *Tales of Ise*, p. 113: "Each night the youth returned from his place of exile, played his flute with great feeling, and sang melancholy ballads in a moving voice."

386. This line appears in the entry for the Twelfth Day of the Third Month 970. "And even I, despondent though I usually am, was swept up in the happiness of the occasion"; Edward Seidensticker, *The Gossamer Years*, p. 80. "Forgetting that I had ever been sad, I experienced a happiness beyond comparison"; Sonja Arntzen, trans., *The Kagerō Diary: A Woman's Autobiographical Text from Tenth-Century Japan* (Ann Arbor: Center for Japanese Studies, The University of Michigan, 1997), p. 193.

387. We find an example at the beginning of Sei Shōnagon's *Makura no Sōshi* (The Pillow Book). Matsuo and Nagai, *Makura no Sōshi*, p. 63: "In summer the night is charming *(okashi)*, particularly with the full moon. Darkness is charming, as well as the many fireflies scattered here and there, or just one or two glittering in the night. In autumn dusk is particularly moving *(aware nari)*, the setting sun getting closer and closer to the edge of the mountains. How moving it is to see groups of birds, of three or four, two or three, hurriedly flying to their nests!"

388. In an original note Norinaga quotes the following poem from the *Shinkokinshū* (5:1402, by Kiyohara Fukayabu) as an explanation of his statement that joy is a shallow feeling:

Ureshiku wa	One
Wasururu koto mo	Can easily forget
Arinubeshi	Joy.—
Tsuraki zo nagaki	The pain of love, however,
Katami narikeru	Is a long-lasting memento.

389. "When her (Onna San no Miya's) answer seemed a little late in coming, he (Genji) went back in and showed off his (plum) flowers (to Murasaki). 'This is how blossoms should smell,' he said. 'If only one could give cherry blossoms this perfume, I doubt that people would care any longer for any other kind.' And he went on, 'I suppose

these catch the eye because there is little else now to look at. I should like to put them beside cherry blossoms at their best.'" Translation by Royall Tyler, *The Tale of Genji*, vol. 2, p. 595. Tyler adds the following note: "Genji may be explaining his attraction to Onna San no Miya: despite Murasaki's cherry blossom beauty she lacks Onna San no Miya's perfume (rank)."

390. The *ryo* tones are the sad, negative, feminine ones associated with *yin;* the *ritsu* tones are the sunny, positive, masculine ones associated with *yang.*

391. *Shinkokinshū* 4:362. Kubota Jun, *Shin Kokin Waka Shū*, Jō, p. 133. In this poem *"kokoro naki"* (a heartless person) refers to the fact that, having taken the tonsure, Saigyō has made a vow to discard all kinds of feelings in order to embrace a life of religious detachment. The poetics of *mono no aware* explain Norinaga's disdain for the Buddhist faith that forces believers to detach themselves from feelings, which he considered to be the root of all knowledge. See also Carter, *Traditional Japanese Poetry*, p. 161: "Even one who claims/to no longer have a heart/feels this sad beauty:/snipes flying up from a marsh/on an evening in autumn."

392. *Ise Monogatari, dan* 96. Watanabe Minoru, *Ise Monogatari*, p. 113. See also McCullough, *Tales of Ise*, pp. 135–136: "Once there was a man who wooed a lady with such persistence that she gradually began to return his affection. (Not being made of stone or wood, she could scarcely have helped feeling sorry for him.)"

393. Entry around the Twentieth Day of the Sixth Month 970. "Dull though my emotions had become, I was moved to tears by the beauty of the scene, and my companion even more strongly"; Edward Seidensticker, *The Gossamer Years*, p. 83. "I think it is useless to try and explain such feelings, and it seemed all the more so for my companion who was also moved to tears"; Sonja Arntzen, *The Kagerō Diary*, p. 197.

394. *Kokinshū* 19:1002. Okumura Tsuneya, *Kokin Waka Shū*, pp. 341–342. English translation by Laurel Rasplica Rodd and Mary Catherine Henkenius, *Kokinshū: A Collection of Poems Ancient and Modern*, pp. 340–341. See also McCullough, *Kokin Waka Shū*, pp. 221–222, in which the verses in question, *"aware chō/koto o iitsutsu"* are underplayed: "men utter prayers/for our sovereign's long life."

395. The *Kokin Eiga Shō* (Essays on the Splendors of the *Kokinshū*) argues that the old poems in the *Kokinshū* were all composed by Tsurayuki—an argument denied by Keichū in the *Kokin Yozai Shō*.

396. "Thus it happened that, desirous of preserving the memory of the past and of renewing what has grown old, and also having in mind both a personal inspection and a transmission to posterity, he (Emperor Daigo) addressed Major Private Secretary Ki no Tomonori, Mifumidokoro Librarian Ki no Tsurayuki, Former Kai Lesser Clerk Ōshikōchi Mitsune, and Right Gate Guards Aide Mibu no Tadamine and caused them to present him with old poems missing from the *Man'yōshū*, and also with compositions of their own." English translation by McCullough, *Kokin Waka Shū*, p. 7.

397. *Gosenshū* 18:1271, Katagiri Yōichi, *Gosen Waka Shū*, p. 385. As a footnote Norinaga adds the following poem by Saigyō from *Sankashū* 679 (The Mountain Hut), with *"bakari ka"* in the last line of the original text. Gotō Shigeo, ed., *Sankashū*, p. 184:

Kakimidaru	It is my habit
Kokoro yasumenu	When my heart, distraught by love
Kotogusa wa	Cannot stand still,
Aware aware to	To simply sigh, saying,
Nageku bakari zo	"Ah, alas!" *(aware aware to).*

398. This line appears in the entry for the Ninth Day of the Second Month 935. It follows the poem composed in Naniwa by Tsurayuki's wife on their dead daughter. "She began to weep. How must the listening father have felt? Such poems are not composed for pleasure. Both in China and in our land, they spring from emotion too strong to be borne." McCullough, *Kokin Waka Shū*, p. 288.

399. This line appears in the entry for the Sixteenth Day of the Second Month 935, after crossing the Katsura River. "Too much elation at returning to the capital had resulted in too much poetry." McCullough, *Kokin Waka Shū*, p. 290.

400. This sentence appears after the poetic exchange between Fujiwara no Michinaga and the nurse Koshikibu after the death of Michinaga's daughter, Kishi, at age nineteen during childbirth. "We are told that poetry gives voice to what is in the heart—and the reason, I imagine, is that composition seems to be the first resort of people of all types whenever they confront something delightful *(okashiki)*, splendid *(medetaki)*, or pathetic *(aware)*." English translation by William H. McCullough and Helen Craig McCullough, *A Tale of Flowering Fortunes: Annals of Japanese Aristocratic Life in the Heian Period* (Stanford: Stanford University Press, 1980), vol. 2, p. 683.

401. Norinaga uses the word *aya*, which means literally, "pattern." This was Norinaga's understanding of the word *bun* used by the Sorai school as a literary term.

402. Norinaga refers to section 25 of *Isonokami no Sasamegoto* (pp. 338–343) on the word *nagamuru*.

403. Norinaga has the preface to the *Kokinshū* in mind: "It is song that moves heaven and earth without effort, stirs emotions in the invisible spirits and gods, brings harmony to the relations between men and women, and calms the hearts of fierce warriors"; translation by McCullough, *Kokin Waka Shū*, p. 3. In a footnote Norinaga mentions the following passage from the *Nihon Shoki* in order to stress the moving power of poetic words. According to Norinaga, the Sun Goddess was moved to leave the Heavenly Rock by the beauty *(uruwashiki* 麗美*)* of the deity's words. The passage appears in "The Chronicles of the Age of the Gods": "Futo-dama no Mikoto, ancestor of the Imbe no Obito, was thereupon made to take these things in his hand, and, with lavish and earnest words of praise, to recite a liturgy. When the Sun-Goddess heard this, she said:—'Though of late many prayers have been addressed to me, of none has the language been so beautiful as this.' So she opened a little the Rock-door and peeped out. Thereupon the God Ama no Tajikara-wo no Kami, who was waiting beside the Rock-door, forthwith pulled it open, and the radiance of the Sun-Goddess filled the universe." Translation by Aston, *Nihongi*, vol. 1, p. 49.

404. See note 320.

405. English translation by Cranston, *A Waka Anthology*, p. 16, who follows the *Kojiki* version, with the variations *"mitsumitsushi,"* and *"ware wa wasureji."* Cranston

uses the word "pepper tree" instead of "ginger tree." See also Aston's translation: "My mouth tingles/with the ginger planted/at the bottom of the hedge/by the glorious/sons of warriors—/I cannot forget it:/let us smite them utterly"; *Nihongi*, vol. 1, p. 127. This poem is recorded on the Fourth Day of the Twelfth Month 663 B.C.

406. "The Imperial army at length attacked Naga-sune-hiko and fought with him repeatedly, but was unable to gain the victory. . . . Ever since Itsuse no Mikoto was hit by an arrow at the battle of Kusaka and died, the Emperor bore this in mind, and constantly cherished resentment for it. On this campaign it was his desire to put all to death, and therefore he composed these verses, saying . . ." Aston, *Nihongi*, vol. 1, pp. 126–127.

407. *Kokinshū* 11:470, by monk Sosei. Okumura Tsuneya, *Kokin Waka Shū*, p. 179. See also McCullough, *Kokin Waka Shū*, p. 111: "Though I but know you/through others, love has made me/like chrysanthemum dew,/rising by night and by day/fading into nothingness."

408. Translation by Cranston, *A Waka Anthology*, p. 18.

409. Ibid. These two poems appear in Book Two of the *Kojiki*. After the death of Emperor Jinmu, his consort, Isukeyorihime, sings these two songs in order to warn her two sons of Tagishimimi no Mikoto's plot to kill them. The poems are preceded by the following explanation: "After the emperor's death, the elder half-brother Tagishimimi no Mikoto took as wife Isukeyorihime, the empress, and plotted to kill the three younger brothers. At this time their mother Isukeyorihime, suffering in anguish, warned her sons of the danger in a song." Philippi, *Kojiki*, p. 183.

410. "Then her sons, hearing and understanding, took alarm." Philippi, *Kojiki*, p. 184.

411. Compiled by Nijō Yoshimoto (1320–1388) in 1363, this is a dialogue between the inquirer Nijō Yoshimoto and the poet Ton'a (1289–1372). In the answer to the first dialogue Ton'a argues for a need of rhetorical skills in the composition of poetry. According to Ton'a, poets must craft poetic expression so as to make it beautiful to the listeners' ears. Ton'a, however, does not explain why poets should care for style, which is probably why Norinaga had some reservations about this dialogue.

412. As a footnote Norinaga adds the following poem by Jien (1155–1225) from his poetry collection, the *Shūgyokushū* (The Collection of Gathered Jewels; edited in 1328–1346):

Ureshi kanashi	To whom shall I tell
Waga omou koto o	My thoughts,
Tare ni iite	Joyous as well as sad,
Sa wa sa ka to dani	And let him know
Hito ni shiraremu	That things are like this and like that?

413. *Kokinshū* 14:697, by Ki no Tsurayuki. Okumura Tsuneya, *Kokin Waka Shū*, p. 240. See also McCullough, *Kokin Waka Shū*, p. 154: "I long for a way/to meet you as constantly/as in far Cathay/people dress in gorgeous robes/foreign to Yamato's isles." The first three verses are a preface *(joshi)* to the actual poem, which develops in

verses four and five. The connection between the two sections of the poem is brought about by the word *koromo,* which means "robe," as well as "even the time" *(koro mo).* In the *Kokinshū Tōkagami,* Norinaga calls the preface "the pattern of words" *(kotoba no aya).*

414. *Shinkokinshū* 11:996, by the Middle Councilor Kanesuke. Kubota Jun, *Shin Kokin Waka Shū,* Ge, p. 11. The first three verses are a preface introducing the actual poem (fourth and fifth verses). The connection between the two images is provided by the word *izumi,* which, besides being a poetic spot *(utamakura)* in the Yamashiro province (Izumigawa), also means "when did I see you?" *(itsu mi).*

415. *Shinkokinshū* 11:990, anonymous. Kubota Jun, *Shin Kokin Waka Shū,* Ge, p. 9.

416. See, for example, the "allegorical poems" *(hiyuka)* of book seven, the "relationship poems on the seasons" *(shiki no sōmonka)* of book ten, and the "expressions of thoughts by reference to things" *(kibutsu chinshi)* of books eleven and twelve.

417. Following the philosophy of Ogyū Sorai (1666-1728), Norinaga contrasts two different *kokoro* (meaning, heart) in this sentence: the prosaic *"kokoro"* 意 of things that can be theorized and exhaustively treated in words; and the poetic *"kokoro"* 情 of feelings that words never succeed in articulating fully.

418. *Isonokami no Sasamegoto* 2:71-76. Hino Tatsuo, *Motoori Norinaga Shū,* pp. 420-433.

419. As a footnote Norinaga adds the following song by Jien from his poetic collection, the *Shūgyokushū:*

Koi to iu	If people did not possess
Kokoro no hito ni	The heart
Nakariseba	Known as love,
Aru kai mo araji	To be would be worthless—
Aki no yūgure	Autumn dusk.

420. Norinaga refers to sections 66 and 67 of *Isonokami no Sasamegoto,* on the alleged femininity of the emotions. Hino Tatsuo, *Motoori Norinaga Shū,* pp. 408-413.

421. Norinaga refers to a sequence of poems by Ōtomo no Tabito, governor-general of Dazaifu. *Man'yōshū* 3:338-350.

422. It means to take pleasure in disclosing people's faults.

423. Norinaga refers to the beginning of this essay.

424. Norinaga refers to his work *Shibun Yōryō* (Essentials of Murasaki's Work, 1763).

425. Norinaga refers again to section 66 of *Isonokami no Sasamegoto* on the originally feminine nature of the passions.

426. According to Norinaga, the sinfulness of the monk lies in the fact that he pretends to be someone that he is not.

427. Norinaga means that it is shallow in comparison to the appeal of a woman.

428. This episode is narrated in the *Taiheiki* (The Record of the Great Peace, 1375-1379). A monk over eighty years of age is captivated by the beauty of the

Kyōgoku empress, whom he meets by chance. Hoping to see her again, he travels to the capital and stands in the garden of the Imperial Palace in Kyoto. Moved by the sight of the monk, the empress allows him to take her hands in his. Thus, the monk is liberated from his sexual desires. He recites the following poem:

Hatsuharu no	At the first day of spring
Hatsune no kyō no	Of the first Day of the Rat
Tamabahaki	I take in hand
Te ni toru kara ni	The jewel broom, and all my soul
Yuragu tama no o	Tingles with the tinkling gems.

This song, by Ōtomo no Yakamochi, appears in *Man'yōshū* 20:4493 (Kojima Noriyuki, *Man'yōshū*, 4, p. 442), with the variation *"yuraku"* in the last verse; translation by Cranston, *A Waka Anthology*, p. 481. While the *Taiheiki* states that the monk's gloom lifted after he took the empress' hands in his, Norinaga argues that the song brought about the liberation of the holy man from his passions. Yamashita Hiroaki, ed., *Taiheiki*, 5, *SNKS* 78 (Tokyo: Shinchōsha, 1988), pp. 324–326.

Glossary

aa 阿々
aa (Ch. *wu hu*) 嗚呼
aji honfushō 阿字本不生
aji hongen setsu 阿字本元説
Akizuno 蜻蛉野
ame hare 天晴
ame no shita no sōmyō 天の下の惣名
Ame no Tokotachi no Kami 天之常立神
amehare 天晴
ametsuchi no koe 天地の声
ana 阿那
Aruga Chōhaku 有賀長伯
Aruga Chōsen 有賀長川
Asai Shigetō 浅井重遠
Ashiwake Obune 排蘆小船
aware 阿波礼
Aware Ben 安波礼弁
aya 文
aya 阿夜

Bendō 弁道
bigaku 美学
Bo Juyi 白居易
bokujū 僕従
bun 文

chi 志
chō-rinri 超倫理

daoti 道体
Daxu 大序
dong 動

ei 詠

eizuru 詠ずる

feng 風
Fujingen 不尽言
Fujitani Mitsue 富士谷御杖
Fujiwara Michitoshi 藤原道俊
Fujiwara Shunzei 藤原俊成
Fujiwara Teika 藤原定家

gan 感
ge 歌
Genji Monogatari Tama no Ogushi 源氏物語玉の小櫛
ge shi yue 歌詩曰
Goi Kō 語意考
gojū onzu 五十音図
Gosenshū 後撰集

Hachidaishū Shō 八代集抄
Hannyakyō Ongi 般若経音義
heyun 和韻
hi 日
hinaburi 夷曲
hi no moto 日本
Hi no mototsukuni Yamato 日の本つ国のやまと
Hokekyō Ongi 法華経音義
Hori Keizan 堀影山
Hosokawa Yūsai 細川幽斎
Hyakunin Isshu Kaikanshō 百人一首改観抄

ichigyō ichigi ha 一行一義派
ichion ichigi ha 一音一義派
iki o nagaku suru 息を長くする

imada 未
Imoseyama 妹背山
Isonokami no Sasamegoto 石上私淑言
itsura no koe 五十聯の音
itsuwari 偽り
iya 弥
iyaegaki 弥重垣
iyatsu 弥津
izu 出づ
Izumo 出雲
izumo iyaegaki 出雲弥重垣
izuru kumo 出づる雲

jigi 字義
jinen no myō 自然の妙
ji no koe 字の声

Kada no Arimaro 荷田在満
kadoku setsuwa 歌徳説話
kaei 歌詠
kaeshi 返し
Kagerō-no-ono 蜻蛉の小野
kagō 嘉号
Kaibara Ekiken 貝原益軒
kami no kotoba 神語
kami no yo 神世
Kamo no Mabuchi 賀茂真淵
kan 観
kan 感
Kan 漢
Kanji Kō 冠辞考
Kara 漢
kari no mono 仮[借]の物
Kawagita Tanrei 川北丹霊
kazari 潤色
Keichū 契沖
Kenshō 顕昭
Ki no Tsurayuki 紀貫之
Kitamura Kigin 北村季吟
koe 声
koe o nagaku hiku 声を長く引く
Kogo Shūi 古語拾遺
Kojiki 古事記

Kojiki-den 古事記伝
Kokindenju 古今伝授
Kokin-jo Chū 古今序註
Kokinshū 古今集
Kokin Waka Shū Ryōdo Kikigaki 古今和歌集両度聞書
Kokka Hachiron 国歌八論
kokoro 情
kokoro kotoba 意詞
kokorozashi o iu 言志
kokuji 国字
konata no kotoba no gi 此方の言の義
Korai Fūteishō 古来風躰抄
kore 之
kotau 和ふ
kotauru uta 答歌
koto 言
koto 事
kotoba 言葉
kotoba no aya 詞の文
kotoba no kokoro 言の意
kotodama 言霊
kotodama no shingon 言霊の真言
kudoku 功徳
kumo 雲

lian lei 連類
Liu Xie 劉勰

makoto 実
makoto no kokoro 実の情
Man'yōshū 万葉集
Minasegawa 水無瀬川
moji 文字
moji no giri 文字の義理
moji no koe 文字の声
moji no sata 文字の沙汰
mono ni kanzuru 物に感ずる
mono no aware 物のあはれ
Morikawa Akitada 森川章尹
Morokoshi no kashi 唐の歌詩
moto no kokoro 本の意
moto no tai 本の体
Motoori Norinaga 本居宣長

Glossary

Motoori Ōhira　本居大平
motte　以

nagaiki　長息
nagaiki　長生
nagaiku　奈我以久
nagamu　詠
nagamuru　奈我牟流
nageku　奈宜久
nagon　納言
nahoku　直く
naisekaisei　内世界性
Nakazato Tsunemori　中里常守
Naobi no Mitama　直毘霊
nasake　情
Nihon Shakumyō　日本釈名
Nihon Shoki Tsūshō　日本書紀通証
Nihongi Shiki　日本紀私記
ni no machi no koto　二の町のこと
Nippon　日本
nochi no yo no gakumonzata　後世学問沙汰

Ogyū Sorai　荻生徂徠
omoheraku　以為
ongi setsu　音義説
onna warabe no kotomeki　女童べの言めき
onozukara kotoba　おのずから詞
Ōyashimaguni　大八洲国

Reizei Tamemura　令泉為村

sakashidachitaru setsu　賢しだちたる説
sama/sugata　様／姿
Senzaishū　千載集
shi　詩
Shibun Yōryō　紫文要領
Shi ming　釈名
Shinkokinshū　新古今集
shi wo eizuru　詠詩
Shoku Nihongi　続日本紀
shu　主

Shūchūshō　袖中抄
Shūishū　拾遺集
Shu jing　詩経
sōbyō　宗廟
Sōgi　宗祇
Sugagasa no Nikki　菅笠日記
Sunao　古質
sunawachi　則
Suzuki Shigetane　鈴木重胤
Suzunoya Shū　鈴屋集

Tachibana Moribe　橘守部
tai　体
taiwa　太和
takumi　巧
Tamakatsuma　玉勝間
Tamaki Masahide　玉木正英
Tanigawa Kotosuga　谷川士清
tansoku　嘆息
tatohi　仮使
Tatsutagawa　立田川
tiandao　天道
tianwen-renwen　天文人文
Tō　唐
tonau　唱ふ
tuo wu, jie wu yi yin huai　託物借物意引懐
tsu　津
tsuki　月

Uiyamabumi　宇比山踏
uji hongen setsu　宇字本元説
umi　海
uta　歌
utahi　謡
uta wo eizuru　詠歌
utayomi shite notamawaku　歌之日
utōte iwaku　歌日

Wa　和
Wadō　和銅
wain (Ch. heyun)　和韻
waka　倭歌
waka　和歌

Waka Yaegaki 和歌八重垣
Wei-nu Guo 倭奴国
Wenxin Diaolong 文心雕龍
wu 物
wuchang 五常
wuxing 五行

xing 性
xing 興

yae 八重
yaeyamabuki 八重山吹
yaezakura 八重桜
yairo 八色
yakigumo 焼雲
yakumo 八雲
yakumo tatsu 八雲立つ
yama 山
Yamashiro 山背
yamata no orochi 八岐大蛇
Yamato 夜麻登
Yamato 和
Yamato 山跡
Yamato 山外

Yamato 山戸
Yamato 山処
Yamato no kuni 大和の国
Yamato uta 夜麻登干多
Yamazaki Ansai 山崎闇斎
yan 言
yang 陽
Yashimamoto 八洲元
yatsu 八
yawaragu 和
Yi jing 易経
yin 蔭
yō 用
yoku 欲
yomu 詠む
yong 詠
yong ge 詠歌
Yong-zhou 雍州
Yōshū 雍州
yōyō 邕邕
yuan 原

zhi 質

Bibliography

Amagasaki Akira. *Kachō no Tsukai: Uta no Michi no Shigaku.* GBS 7. Tokyo: Keisō Shobō, 1983.

Arntzen, Sonja, trans. *The Kagerō Diary: A Woman's Autobiographical Text from Tenth-Century Japan.* Ann Arbor: Center for Japanese Studies, University of Michigan, 1997.

Aston, W. G., trans. *Nihongi: Chronicles of Japan from the Earliest Times to A.D. 697.* Tokyo: Tuttle, 1972.

Baumgarten, Alexander Gottlieb. *Estetica.* Milan: Vita e Pensiero, 1993.

Bock, Felicia Gressitt, trans. *Engi-Shiki: Procedures of the Engi Era, Books VI–X.* Tokyo: Sophia University, 1972.

Burns, Susan L. *Before the Nation: Kokugaku and the Imagining of Community in Early Modern Japan.* Durham, NC, and London: Duke University Press, 2003.

Carter, Steven D., trans. *Traditional Japanese Poetry: An Anthology.* Stanford, CA: Stanford University Press, 1991.

Chan, Wing-Tsit. *A Source Book in Chinese Philosophy.* Princeton, NJ: Princeton University Press, 1963.

Cranston, Edwin A. *A Waka Anthology, Volume One: The Gem-Glistening Cup.* Stanford, CA: Stanford University Press, 1993.

Croce, Benedetto. *La poesia: Introduzione alla critica e storia della poesia e della letteratura.* Milan: Adelphi Edizioni, 1994; 1st ed., 1936.

Eco, Umberto. *La ricerca della lingua perfetta nella cultura europea.* Bari: Laterza, 1993.

Eguchi Takao, ed. *Kaifūsō.* Tokyo: Kōdansha, 2000.

Ekiken Kai, ed. *Ekiken Zenshū,* 1. Tokyo: Kokusho Kankō Kai, 1945.

Field, Norma. *The Splendor of Longing in the Tale of Genji.* Princeton, NJ: Princeton University Press, 1987.

Gotō, Shigeo, ed. *Sankashū.* SNKS 49. Tokyo: Shinchōsha, 1982.

Harootunian, H. D. *Things Seen and Unseen: Discourse and Ideology in Tokugawa Nativism.* Chicago and London: University of Chicago Press, 1988.

Hashimoto Fumio, Ariyoshi Tamotsu, and Fujihira Haruo, eds. *Karonshū.* NKBZ 50. Tokyo: Shōgakukan, 1975.

Higuchi Yoshimaro, ed. *Kinkai Waka Shū.* SNKS 44. Tokyo: Shinchōsha, 1981.

Hino Tatsuo, ed. *Motoori Norinaga Shū.* SNKS 60. Tokyo: Shinchōsha, 1983.

——. "Motoori Norinaga to Ueda Akinari." In Ariyoshi Tamotsu et al., eds. *Kinsei no Waka, Waka Bungaku Kōza* 8. Tokyo: Benseisha, 1994.

Hisamatsu Sen'ichi, ed. *Kamo no Mabuchi Zenshū,* 8. Tokyo: Zoku Gunsho Ruijū Kanseikai, 1978.
——, ed. *Kamo no Mabuchi Zenshū,* 19. Tokyo: Zoku Gunsho Ruijū Kanseikai, 1980.
—— et al., eds. *Keichū Zenshū,* 8. Tokyo: Iwanami Shoten, 1973.
Ishida Jōji and Shimizu Yoshiko, eds. *Genji Monogatari,* 2. *SNKS* 13. Tokyo: Shinchōsha, 1977.
Jullien, François. *La Valeur allusive: Des catégories originales de l'interprétation poétique dans la tradition chinoise (Contribution à une réflexion sur l'alterité interculturelle).* Paris: École Française d'Extrême-Orient, 1985.
Kanno, Kakumyō. *Motoori Norinaga: Kotoba to Miyabi.* Tokyo: Perikansha, 1991.
Katagiri Yōichi, ed. *Gosen Waka Shū. SNKBT* 6. Tokyo: Iwanami Shoten, 1990.
Katano Tatsurō and Matsuno Yōichi, eds. *Senzai Waka Shū. SNKBT* 10. Tokyo: Iwanami Shoten, 1993.
Katō, Genchi, and Hikoshirō Hoshino, trans. *Kogoshūi: Gleanings from Ancient Stories.* London: Curzon Press, 1972.
Katō, Hilda. "The *Mumyōshō* of Kamo no Chōmei and Its Significance in Japanese Literature." *Monumenta Nipponica* 33:3–4 (1968): 321–430.
Katō Jōken, ed. *Shokyō, Jō. SKT* 25. Tokyo: Meiji Shoin, 1983.
Kawamoto, Kōji. *The Poetics of Japanese Verse: Imagery, Structure, Meter.* Tokyo: University of Tokyo Press, 2000.
Kawamura Teruo, Kashiwagi Yoshio, and Kudō Shigenori, eds. *Kin'yō Waka Shū, Shika Waka Shū. SNKBT* 9. Tokyo: Iwanami Shoten, 1989.
Keene, Donald, trans. *Essays in Idleness: The Tsurezuregusa of Kenkō.* New York: Columbia University Press, 1967.
Kidō Saizō, ed. *Tsurezuregusa. SNKS* 10. Tokyo: Shinchōsha, 1977.
Kogi Takashi. *Shin'yō Waka Shū: Honbun to Kenkyū.* Tokyo: Kasama Shoin, 1984.
Kojima Noriyuki, Kinoshita Masatoshi, and Satake Akihiro, eds. *Man'yōshū,*1. *NKBZ* 2. Tokyo: Shōgakukan, 1971.
——, eds. *Man'yōshū,* 2. *NKBZ* 3. Tokyo: Shōgakukan, 1972.
——, eds. *Man'yōshū,* 3. *NKBZ* 4. Tokyo: Shōgakukan, 1973.
——, eds. *Man'yōshū,* 4. *NKBZ* 5. Tokyo: Shōgakukan, 1975.
Koyasu Nobukuni. *Motoori Norinaga.* Tokyo: Iwanami Shoten, 1992.
——. *Norinaga Mondai to wa Nani ka.* Tokyo: Seidosha, 1995.
Kubota Jun, ed. *Shin Kokin Waka Shū, Ge. SNKS* 30. Tokyo Shinchōsha, 1979.
——, ed. *Shin Kokin Waka Shū, Jō. SNKS* 24. Tokyo: Shinchōsha, 1979.
Kubota Jun and Hirata Yoshinobu, eds. *Goshūi Waka Shū. SNKBT* 8. Tokyo: Iwanami Shoten, 1994.
LaFleur, William R. *Awesome Nightfall: The Life, Times, and Poetry of Saigyō.* Boston: Wisdom Publications, 2003.
Legge, James. *The Chinese Classics.* Volume 1. Hong Kong: Hong Kong University Press, 1960.
——. *The Chinese Classics, IV: The She King.* Hong Kong: Hong Kong University Press, 1960.

Levy, Ian Hideo. *Man'yōshū: A Translation of Japan's Premier Anthology of Classical Poetry*. Volume 1. Princeton, NJ: Princeton University Press, 1981.

Liu, James J. Y. *Chinese Theories of Literature*. Chicago and London: University of Chicago Press, 1975.

Marra, Michael F., ed. *A History of Modern Japanese Aesthetics*. Honolulu: University of Hawai'i Press, 2001.

———, ed. *Japanese Hermeneutics: Current Debates on Aesthetics and Interpretation*. Honolulu: University of Hawai'i Press, 2002.

———. *Kuki Shūzō: A Philosopher's Poetry and Poetics*. Honolulu: University of Hawai'i Press, 2004.

———. *Modern Japanese Aesthetics: A Reader*. Honolulu: University of Hawai'i Press, 1999.

———. "On Japanese Things and Words: An Answer to Heidegger's Question." *Philosophy East and West* 54:4 (2004): 555–568.

———. *Representations of Power: The Literary Politics of Medieval Japan*. Honolulu: University of Hawai'i Press, 1993.

Masuda Shigeo, ed. *Shūi Waka Shū*. WBT 32. Tokyo: Meiji Shoin, 2003.

Matsuo Satoshi and Nagai Kazuko, eds. *Makura no Sōshi*. NKBZ 11. Tokyo: Shōgakukan, 1974.

McCullough, Helen Craig, trans. *Kokin Waka Shū: The First Imperial Anthology of Japanese Poetry*. Stanford, CA: Stanford University Press, 1985.

———, trans. *The Taiheiki: A Chronicle of Medieval Japan*. New York: Columbia University Press, 1959.

———, trans. *Tales of Ise: Lyrical Episodes from Tenth-Century Japan*. Stanford, CA: Stanford University Press, 1968.

McCullough, William H., and Helen Craig McCullough, trans. *A Tale of Flowering Fortunes: Annals of Japanese Aristocratic Life in the Heian Period*. 2 vols. Stanford, CA: Stanford University Press, 1980.

Miller, Roy A. "The 'Spirit' of the Japanese Language." *The Journal of Japanese Studies* 3:2 (Summer 1977): 251–298.

Minemura Fumito, ed. *Shinkokin Waka Shū*, NKBZ 26. Tokyo: Shōgakukan, 1974.

Mishima Takeo and Miyamura Chimoto, trans. *Motoori Norinaga: Sugagasa no Nikki*. Osaka: Izumi Shoin, 1995.

Morrell, Robert E. *Sand and Pebbles (Shasekishū): The Tales of Mujū Ichien, A Voice for Pluralism in Kamakura Buddhism*. Albany: State University of New York Press, 1985.

Morris, Ivan, trans. *The Pillow Book of Sei Shōnagon*. 2 vols. New York: Columbia University Press, 1967.

Mostow, Joshua S. *Pictures of the Heart: The Hyakunin Isshu in Word and Image*. Honolulu: University of Hawai'i Press, 1996.

Motoori Norinaga. *Kojiki-den, Book 1*. Translated by Ann Wehmeyer. Ithaca, NY: East Asian Program, Cornell University, 1997.

———. *Sugagasa no Nikki*. Edited by Mibu Tsutomu. Tokyo: Kenkyūsha, 1940.

Murasaki, Shikibu. *The Tale of Genji*. 2 vols. Translated by Royall Tyler. New York: Viking, 2001.
Nishimiya Kazutami, ed. *Kojiki*. SNKS 27. Tokyo: Shinchōsha, 1979.
Nosco, Peter. *Remembering Paradise: Nativism and Nostalgia in Eighteenth-Century Japan*. Cambridge, MA: Council on East Asian Studies, Harvard University, 1990.
Ogyū, Sorai. *Distinguishing the Way [Bendō]*. Translated by Olof G. Lidin. Tokyo: Sophia University, 1970.
Ōkubo Tadashi, ed. *Motoori Norinaga Zenshū*. Volume 15. Tokyo: Chikuma Shobō, 1969.
Okumura Tsuneya, ed. *Kokin Waka Shū*. SNKS 19. Tokyo: Shinchōsha, 1978.
Ōno Susumu and Ōkubo Tadashi, eds. *Motoori Norinaga Zenshū: Bekkan*, 3. Tokyo: Chikuma Shobō, 1993.
Ōno Susumu, Satake Akihiro, and Maeda Kingorō, eds. *Iwanami Kogo Jiten*. Tokyo: Iwanami Shoten, 1974.
Owen, Stephen. *Readings in Chinese Literary Thought*. Cambridge, MA: Harvard University Press, 1992.
Philippi, Donald L., trans. *Kojiki*. Tokyo: University of Tokyo Press, 1968.
Rimer, J. Thomas, and Jonathan Chaves, eds. *Japanese and Chinese Poems to Sing: The Wakan Rōei Shū*. New York: Columbia University Press, 1997.
Rodd, Laurel Rasplica, and Mary Catherine Henkenius, trans. *Kokinshū: A Collection of Poems Ancient and Modern*. Princeton, NJ: Princeton University Press, 1984.
Rousseau, Jean-Jacques. *On the Origin of Language*. Translated by John H. Moran and Alexander Gode. New York: Frederick Ungar, 1966.
Sakabe Megumi. *Kagami no Naka no Nihongo: Sono Shikō no Shujusō*. CR 22. Tokyo: Chikuma Shobō, 1989.
———. "Notes sur le mot japonais *hureru*." *Revue d'Esthetique*, n.s. 11 (1986): 43–49.
Sasaki Nobutsuna, ed. *Nihon Kagaku Taikei*, 7. Tokyo: Kazama Shobō, 1957.
Saussy, Haun. "Syntax and Semantics in the Definition of *Wen*." Paper delivered at the Annual Meeting of the Association of Asian Studies, Boston, March 27, 1994.
Seidensticker, Edward, trans. *The Gossamer Years (Kagerō Nikki): A Diary by a Noblewoman of Heian Japan*. Tokyo: Tuttle, 1973.
Shinpen Kokka Taikan Henshū Iinkai, ed. *Shinpen Kokka Taikan*. CD-ROM, Ver. 2. Tokyo: Kadokawa Shoten, 2003.
Suzuki Jun and Nakamura Hiroyasu, eds. *Kinsei Kabun Shū, Ge*. SNKBT 68. Tokyo: Iwanami Shoten, 1997.
Suzuki Jun and Odaka Michiko, eds. *Kinsei Zuisō Shū*. NKBZ 82. Tokyo: Shōgakukan, 2000.
Toyoda Kunio. *Nihonjin no Kotodama Shisō*. KGB 483. Tokyo: Kōdansha, 1980.
Tsugita Kasumi, ed. *Gyokuyō Waka Shū*. Tokyo: Iwanami Shoten, 1989.
Tsugita Kasumi and Iwasa Miyoko, eds. *Fūga Waka Shū*. Tokyo: Miai Shoten, 1974.
Tsunoda, Ryusaku, Wm. Theodore de Bary, and Donald Keene, eds. *Sources of Japanese Tradition*. Volume 1. New York: Columbia University Press, 1964.
Uetani Hajime, Mizuta Norihisa, and Hino Tatsuo, eds. *Jinsai Nissatsu, Tawaregusa, Fujingen, Mukaukyō*. SNKBT 99. Tokyo: Iwanami Shoten, 2000.

Ujitani Tsutomu, ed. *Shoku Nihongi, Chū*. Tokyo: Kōdansha, 1992.
Watanabe Minoru, ed. *Ise Monogatari*. SNKS 2. Tokyo: Shinchōsha, 1976.
Yamagishi Tokuhei, ed. *Hachidaishū Zenchū*, 1. Tokyo: Yūseidō, 1960.
Yamashita Hiroaki, ed. *Taiheiki, 5*. SNKS 78. Tokyo: Shinchōsha, 1988.
Yoshikawa Kōjirō, Satake Akihiro, and Hino Tatsuo, eds. *Motoori Norinaga*. NST 40. Tokyo: Iwanami Shoten, 1978.
Yuasa, Nobuyuki. *Bashō: The Narrow Road to the Deep North and Other Travel Sketches*. London: Penguin, 1966.

Index of First Lines

Aga yuki wa, 122
Aimineba, 120
Akanaku ni, 54
Aki o hete, 97
Akugareshi, 98
Ama no hara, 226n.149
Ame fureba, 34
Ao ni yoshi, 203n.39
Are hateshi, 98
Arenikeri, 177
Ari to shi mo, 68
Atarayo no, 183
Atotoite, 100
Atsumete wa, 100
Aware chō/hito mo nagisa ni, 99
Aware chō/koto dani naku wa, 178, 238n.16
Aware chō/koto koso utate, 178
Aware chō/koto ni nagusamu, 179
Aware chō/koto ni shirushi wa, 186
Aware chō/koto no ha goto ni, 178
Aware chō/koto o amata ni, 178
Aware kimi, 51
Aware mukashibe, 177
Aware naru/utsu no yamabe no, 100
Aware naru/uzura no koe mo, 97
Aware oba, 264n.324
Aware to mo/iubeki hito wa, 180
Aware to mo/iwanu kokoro no, 98
Aware to mo/kikaba hitoyo wa, 99
Aware to mo/kimi dani iwaba, 180
Aware to mo/makura bakari wa, 99
Aware to mo/makura bakari ya, 238n.17
Aware to mo/omowaba kami mo, 98
Aware to mo/ushi to mo iwaji, 180

Aware to mo/ushi to mo mono o, 182, 234n.2
Aware to wa, 99
Azumaji no, 177

Chigiri are ya, 57
Chihayaburu/kami no igaki mo, 238n.15
Chihayaburu/Uji no hashimori, 182
Chiru koto no, 178
Chiyorozu no, 7

Furinikeru, 229n.169
Furusato ni, 48
Furu yuki wa, 210n.25
Futamoto no, 90

Hakanashi ya, 123
Hana mitsutsu, 60
Hana to nomi, 54
Haniyasu no, 228n.166
Hare yaranu, 110
Haru no saku, 257n.206
Harusame ni, 35
Haru sareba, 230n.171
Haru wa tada, 183, 236n.8
Hashitate no/kurahashigawa no/Iwa no hashi wa mo, 213n.43
Hashitate no/kurahashigawa no/Kawa no shizusuge, 213n.43
Hashitate no/kurahashiyama ni, 213n.43
Hatsuharu no, 274n.428
Hatsukari no, 237n.12
Hatsusegawa/furukawa no he ni, 91, 211n.33
Hatsusegawa/hayaku no yo yori, 42

Hatsuseyama/iriai no kane o, 211n.31
Hatsuseyama/kumoi ni hana no, 210n.28
Hayakawa no, 175
Hisakata no, 121
Hito naraba, 245n.49
Hito no yo o, 268n.374
Hitori ite, 96
Hito wa isa, 210n.27
Hitoyari no, 246n.57

Ie ni areba, 68
Ima wa mata, 57
Ime-no-Wada, 122
Imo ni koi, 244n.36
Imoseyama/kage dani miede, 245n.47
Imoseyama/naki na mo yoshi ya, 49
Inishie no/ato wa furinishi, 66
Inishie no/fukaki kokoro o, 79
Inishie no/kokoro o kumite, 51
Inishie no/Nara no miyako no, 233n.201
Inishie no/sore ka aranu ka, 89
Iro yori mo, 181
Itozakura, 38
Itsu no ma mo, 233n.203
Itsushika to/omoikakeshi mo, 77
Itsushika to/omoiokurishi, 226n.153
Iwama tojishi, 212n.37
Iza kodomo, 168
Iza kyō wa, 54

Kaeraji to, 67
Kaerimiru/Hotoke mo aware, 100
Kaerimiru/yosome mo ima o, 68
Kage miru mo, 96
Kaguyama wa, 232n.197
Kakikirashi, 176
Kakimidaru, 271n.397
Kamunabi no/iwase no mori no, 230n.173
Kamunabi no/Mimuro no kishi ya, 118
Kamunabi no/yama o sugiyuku, 116
Kamu saburu, 219n.82
Katakoi wa, 241n.10
Katasogi no, 111

Kawanoe no, 36
Kawazu naku, 222n.109
Kawazura no, 37
Kaze kiou, 98
Kesa mireba, 224n.127
Kiji ni koso, 243n.34
Kikiwataru, 70
Kiku hito mo, 179
Kimi ga atari, 228n.161
Kimi masade, 93
Kinō kyō/furimi furazumi, 39
Kinō kyō/kumo no tachimai, 228n.161
Kochitaku wa, 120
Koi ni mo so, 120
Koishiku wa, 238n.15
Koi to iu, 273n.419
Koke no tsuyu, 67
Koko nite mo, 52
Kokonoe no, 67
Kokoro aru/hito ika naramu, 96
Kokoro aru/hito nomi aki no, 235n.3
Kokoro kara, 37
Kokoro naki, 185, 239n.25
Komoriku no, 212n.42
Konogoro no, 39
Kono tabi wa, 208n.3
Konu hito o/Machikaneyama no, 268n.374
Konu hito o/shita ni machitsutsu, 180
Kore ya kono, 243n.33
Kurahashi no, 213n.45

Makura yori, 238n.17
Mikanohara, 193
Miminashi no, 233n.199
Mimoro tsuku, 212n.38
Minabuchi no, 214n.49
Minasegawa, 121
Mi o tsumeba, 182
Misogi suru, 218n.80
Mite mo nao, 217n.67
Miwakashi o, 230n.174
Miwataseba/hana mo momiji mo, 240n.25

Index of First Lines

Miwataseba/tada shirakumo zo, 4
Miyoshino no/Aoge-ga-mine no, 219n.90
Miyoshino no/hana wa hikazu mo, 52
Miyoshino no/Kisayama no ma no, 221n.101
Miyoshino no/yamabe ni sakeru, 4
Miyoshino no/yama yori fukaki, 57
Miyoshino no/Yoshino no yama no, 4–5
Mizumizushi, 190
Momoshiki no/ōmiyabito o, 78
Momoshiki no/ōmiyabito wa, 227n.157
Moto yori mo, 110
Mukashi mishi, 124
Murasaki no/hitomoto yue ni, 181, 235n.5
Murasaki no/iro koki toki wa, 235n.5
Murasaki no/tsuki wa nani zo no, 96
Mushi no ne ka, 96

Nagarete no, 66
Nagarete wa, 215n.57, 244n.43
Nago no umi o, 176
Naka ni yuku, 245n.46
Na mo takaku, 42
Na ni shi owaba, 208n.4
Negigoto o, 233n.198
Nezame shite, 99
Nobe no tsuyu, 97
Nokorinaku, 250n.103
No to naraba, 237n.10
Nugitsuredo, 44
Nugu mo oshi, 94

Ōkimi wa, 230n.172
Oki mo sezu, 254n.173
Okureite, 243n.36
Omoi de mo, 183
Omoiizuru, 55
Omoiyaru, 89
Omoudochi, 83
Omou koto, 242n.29
Oshiteru ya, 259n.244
Oto ni nomi, 191

Owari ni, 174

Sabishisa wa, 239n.25
Sahinokuma, 223n.115
Saigawa yo, 191
Sakiniou, 52
Samo koso wa, 88
Sasanokuma, 71
Se no yama ni, 216n.57, 245n.48
Seri tsumishi, 226n.150
Shibashi to te, 35
Shigure suru, 236n.6
Shikishima no, 193
Shirakumo no, 247n.71
Shiranami no, 117
Shirayuki no, 98
Shitagusa no, 93
Sue taenu, 114
Sugi no kado, 90
Suminoe no, 179
Sumizome no, 177
Suruga naru, 239n.23

Tabigoromo/sode koso nureru, 58
Tabigoromo/tamoto tōrite, 36
Tabine suru, 239n.23
Tachibana no/nioeru ka ka mo, 250n.106
Tachibana no/tera no nagaya ni, 223n.122
Tachikaeri, 182
Tachinuwanu, 215n.53
Tachiyorade, 49
Takahikaru, 225n.148
Takamato no, 126
Takane yori, 59
Take no ha ni, 236n.8
Taki no ne wa, 221n.103
Taki no ue no, 216n.60
Takuhire no, 244n.39
Tamadasuki, 84
Tani fukaku, 47
Tatsutagawa/momijiba nagaru, 247n.62
Tatsutagawa/momiji midarete, 246n.60

Te ni tsumite, 235n.5
Te o orite, 101
Tobu tori no, 263n.307
Toki ni yori, 227n.155
Toritomuru, 177
Toriyorou, 79
Toshigoto ni, 183
Toshi mo henu, 211n.31
Toshi o hete, 237n.10
Towaba ya na, 97
Tsui ni yuku, 124
Tsuki mireba/chiji ni mono koso, 235n.4
Tsuki mireba/itodo aware zo, 240n.25
Tsukikage o, 181
Tsuki ya aranu, 123

Uchi nageki, 176
Uchi taori, 47
Uchitsuke ni, 239n.22
Ukeyo nao, 33
Ume no hana, 126
Unebiyama/hiru wa kumo toi, 191
Unebiyama/mireba kashikoshi, 84
Uraburete, 120
Urayamashi, 54
Ureshi kanashi, 272n.412
Ureshiki mo, 218n.79
Ureshiku wa, 269n.388
Utsushite mo, 40

Wa ga inochi mo, 221n.100
Waga kuni wa, 262n.293
Wa ga sato ni, 224n.137

Wa ga seko wa, 38
Waga yado wa, 90
Wakareyuku, 34
Wakarutomo, 80
Warawadomo, 253n.159
Ware nomi ya, 181

Yakumo tatsu, 26, 27, 136
Yamato ni wa, 221n.101
Yamato no, 168
Yamato wa, 12, 154, 258n.220
Yamazato no, 219n.84
Yamazato wa, 181
Yatsume sasu, 175
Yatsurigawa, 225n.140
Yo no naka ni, 179
Yo no naka wa/ime no watari no, 122
Yo no naka wa/nani ka tsune naru, 223n.123
Yoki hito no, 33
Yoroshinahe, 244n.40
Yorozuyo ni, 228n.162
Yoshino naru, 220n.93
Yoshinoyama/hana matsu hodo no, 214n.52
Yoshinoyama/hiru mishi hana no, 57
Yoshinoyama/kiesenu yuki to, 5
Yoshinoyama/yagate ideji to, 59
Yoso ni ninu, 97
Yoso ni nomi/aware to zo mishi, 180
Yoso ni nomi/mite ya yaminamu, 193
Yoyo o hete, 52
Yuku toshi no, 236n.9
Yū sareba, 237n.10

Index

Abe no Nakamaro, 76, 226n.149
Abe no Seimei, 76
Aruga Chōhaku, 25
Aruga Chōsen, 3
Asai Shigetō, 24, 256n.194
Ashiwake Obune (A Small Boat amidst the Reeds), 3, 7–8, 206n.76
aware, x, 13, 188–194, 195, 196, 197; etymologies, 17–18, 174; songs on, 96–101
Aware Ben (A Discussion of *Aware*), 18, 265n.335

Bankiroku (Record of a Watchman), 127
Baumgarten, Alexander Gottlieb, 20
Bendō (Distinguishing the Way), 20
Bo Juyi, 16, 19

Ebukuro no Nikki (The Travel Satchel Diary), 206n.81
Eiga Monogatari (A Tale of Flowering Fortunes), 187
Eiga no Taigai (An Outline for Composing Poetry), 203n.23
Engishiki (Procedures of the Engi Era), 41, 72, 87, 158, 210n.26

Fūgashū (Collection of Elegance), 110, 111
Fujingen (Things that Cannot be Fully Expressed in Words), 7, 254n.169
Fujitani Mitsue, 15
Fujiwara no Ietaka, 43, 212n.36
Fujiwara no Michitoshi, 13
Fujiwara no Nagayoshi, 177

Fujiwara no Shunzei, 13
Fujiwara no Teika, x, 43, 203n.23, 248n.83

Gengenshū (An Anthology of Origins), 159, 262n.298
Genji Monogatari (The Tale of Genji), 43, 123, 128, 148, 184, 197, 212n.35
Genji Monogatari Okuiri (An Entry into the Depth of the *Tale of Genji*), 248n.83
Genji Monogatari Tama no Ogushi (The Jeweled Comb of the *Tale of Genji*), 3
Goi Kō (Reflections on the Meaning of Words), 15
Go-Daigo, Emperor, 51, 52, 53, 67, 216n.64, 222n.108
Go-Kameyama, Emperor, 53, 217n.70
Gokinai Shi (An Account of the Five Provinces in the Kinai Region), 72
Go-Murakami, Emperor, 51, 53, 217n.65
Gosenshū (Later Collection), 4, 178, 180, 183, 186
Gumon Kenchū (Notes of a Fool Asking a Wise Man), 192
Gyokuyōshū (Collection of Jeweled Leaves), 114

Hachidaishū Shō (A Commentary on the Eight Imperial Collections), 25
Hannyakyō Ongi (Sound and Meaning in the Heart Sutra), 15

Index

Han shu (History of the Han Dynasty), 160
Hokekyō Ongi (Sound and Meaning in the Lotus Sutra), 15
Hori Keizan, 7, 9, 254n.169
Hosokawa Yūsai, 9, 203n.23
Hyakunin Isshu Kaikanshō (Revised Views on One Poem by a Hundred Poets), 3

Inagake Munetaka, 41, 210n.23
Inagake Shigeo, 41, 210n.23. *See also* Motoori Ōhira
Ise Meisho Sankō Shō (Reference to Famous Places in the Ise Province), 208n.6
Ise Monogatari (Tales of Ise): Norinaga's quotations from, 49, 79, 124, 148, 184, 185
Ise Monogatari Koi (Ancient Meaning of *The Tales of Ise*), 249n.92
Isonokami no Sasamegoto (Personal Views on Poetry), 3, 17; and *aware*, 18; and Chinese characters, 7
Itō Tōgai, 262n.291
Izumi Shikibu, 110–111
Izumo Fudoki (The Gazetteer of the Izumo Province), 137

Jien, 272n.412, 273n.419
Jinmu, Emperor, 149–150, 190, 191; tomb of, 87, 106–107
Jinmyōchō (Register of Deities), 35, 87, 107, 108, 118

Kada no Arimaro, 202n.21
Kagerō Nikki (The Kagerō Diary), 178, 184, 185
Kaibara Ekiken (Atsunobu), 10, 18, 61, 113–114, 220n.94
Kaifūsō (Fond Recollections of Poetry), x, 122
Kaigon, 41, 91, 210n.21

Kakai Shō (Treatise on Rivers and Seas), 122, 248n.87
Kakinomoto no Hitomaro, 62, 82
Kamo no Mabuchi, 10, 14–15, 203n.22, 209n.10
Kanji Kō (Essay on Poetic Epithets), 203n.22
Kawagita Tanrei, 15
Keichū, 3–4, 5, 6, 8, 11–12, 25, 27, 112, 113, 117, 123, 124–125, 128, 156, 257n.206; Norinaga's critique of, 9, 24–25
Kenkō, 129–130, 252n.132
Kenshō, 112, 263n.318
Ki no Tsurayuki, 5–6, 21, 24, 42, 43, 147, 186, 187, 188
Kitabatake Akiyoshi, 234n.209
Kitabatake Chikafusa, 259n.241
Kitabatake Tomonori, 92, 234n.211, 234n.212, 234n.213
Kitamura Kigin, 26, 27, 203n.33, 253n.154
Kogo Shūi (Gleanings from Ancient Stories), 18, 174, 265n.332
Koizumi Ken'an, 41, 56, 210n.22
Kojiki (Records of Ancient Matters), 3, 12, 13, 15, 18, 25, 87, 108, 136, 152, 153, 154, 158, 169, 171, 191, 194; Yamato name, 160
Kojiki-den (The Transmission of the *Kojiki*), 10, 201n.1; 202n.13, 205n.61
Kokin Eiga Shō (Essays on the Splendors of the *Kokinshū*), 270n.395
Kokin-jo Chū (Notes on the Preface to the *Kokinshū*), 26
Kokinshū (Collection of Ancient and Modern Poems), 4, 5, 21, 24; Norinaga's quotations from, 37, 49, 54, 71, 90, 91, 116, 117, 120, 123, 124, 128, 144, 172, 176–177, 178, 179, 180–181, 182, 185, 190, 191, 211n.33

Kokinshū Tōkagami (A Telescope on the *Kokinshū*), 266n.349, 266n.353, 273n.413
Kokin Waka Rokujō (Six Volumes of Japanese Poems, Ancient and Modern), 114, 115
Kokin Wakashū Kenshō Chū (Kenshō's Notes on the *Kokinshū*), 263n.318
Kokin Waka Shū Ryōdo Kikigaki (The Verbatim Notes of Both Scholars), 24, 256n.195, 258n.232
Kokin Yozai Shō (Excess Material of the *Kokinshū*), 8, 24, 26, 128, 136, 158, 203n.23
Kokka Hachiron (Eight Essays on the Country's Poetry), 202n.21
Kokugaku (School of National Learning, or Nativism), 6
Korai Fūteishō (Poetic Styles Past and Present), 13
Kose no Kanaoka, 67
kotoage, 6–7
kotodama, 6, 15
Kuki Shūzō, ix
Kusunoki no Masatsura, 67
Kuzubana (Arrowroot), 202n.13

Li ji (Book of Rites), 139, 196, 202n.18, 264n.325
Liu Xi, 9
Liu Xie, 16

Makura no Sōshi (Pillow Book), 108
Man'yō Daishōki (A Stand-in's Chronicle of the *Man'yōshū*), 257n.206, 266n.343
Man'yō Kō (Reflections on The Collection of Ten Thousand Leaves), 209n.10
Man'yōshū (Ten Thousand Leaves), x, 5, 8, 13, 195; and *aware*, 174, 175, 176; and *kotodama*, 6; and love poems, 194; and Nihon, 168; Norinaga's quotations from, 33, 36, 38, 41, 47, 50, 62, 68, 75, 78, 81, 82, 84, 108, 112, 113, 116, 119, 120, 121, 122, 126, 147, 179; and *waka*, 24; and Yamato, 162, 163
Matsuo Bashō, x
Minamoto no Shigeyuki Shū (Collection of Minamoto no Shigeyuki), 117, 264n.324
Minamoto no Yoshitsune, 59, 64, 67
mono no aware, x, 5, 11, 16, 17–19, 21, 23, 28, 172–194, 195, 197, 199
Morikawa Akitada, 3
Motoori Haruniwa, 210n.23
Motoori Norinaga: and *aya*, 13–14; and etymology, 9–10, 17–18; and intentionality, 8; and *kotodama*, 7; and Nijō school, 4–5; perfect language, 21; and philology, 3, 8–9, 11–12, 23–28; and *uta-makura*, x
Motoori Ōhira, 23
Motoori Sōsuke, 93
Murasaki Shikibu, 123

Nakatomi no Kamatari, 75, 224n.134
Nakazato Tsunemori, 208n.6
Nakazato Tsuneo, 41, 210n.24
Namikawa Seisho, 72, 86, 223n.120
Naobi no Mitama (Rectifying Spirit), 206n.70
Nihongi Shiki (Private Notes on the Chronicles of Japan), 11, 155
Nihon Kōki (Japan's Later Chronicles), 74, 147
Nihon Shakumyō (Japanese Etymologies), 10, 18, 158, 265n.335
Nihon Shoki (Chronicles of Japan), 11, 12, 15, 26, 73, 81, 87, 152, 153, 158, 161, 164, 171, 194, 209n.15; and Nippon, 165, 169
Nihon Shoki Tsūshō (A Compendium Treatise on the *Nihon Shoki*), 9, 206n.85

Nijō Tameyo, 252n.132
Nijō Yoshimoto, 272n.411
Nishida Kitarō, 22

Ogyū Sorai, 7, 20, 263n.313, 273n.417
Ōno Susumu, 6
Ono no Takamura, 114

Quian Han shu (Former History of the Han Dynasty), 158

Reizei Tamemura, 3
Rekitai Hennen Shūsei (The Collection of Chronicles of Various Generations), 127, 251n.111
Rinji Saishiki (Special Festivals), 118
Rousseau, Jean-Jacques, 17
Ruijū Kokushi (Classified Histories of the Land), 121, 162
Ryōboshi (A Record of Imperial Tombs), 107

Saigyō, x, 60; Norinaga's quotations from, 58–59, 185
Sakabe Megumi, 19
Sandai Jitsuroku (The True Records of Three Reigns), 107
San-kuo yen-yi (Romance of the Three Kingdoms), 254n.162
Seigo Okudan (Conjectures on The Tales of Ise), 123
Sei Shōnagon, 42
Senzaishū (Collection of a Thousand Years), 11; Norinaga's quotations from, 34
Shaku Nihongi (Explanation of The Chronicles of Japan), 151, 256n.205, 259n.240
Shibun Yōryō (Essentials of Murasaki's Work), 3, 17; and aware, 17–19, 174, 185
Shi jing (Book of Odes), 19, 20, 161, 204n.50, 254n.165, 264n.322
Shi ming (Explanation of Terms), 9

Shinkokinshū (New Collection of Ancient and Modern Poems), 4, 11, 124
Shinsen Waka (Songs Newly Selected), 147
Shin-Taikenmon-in, 67
Shōchi Tokai Hen (An Exposition of Places of Scenic Beauty), 112, 244n.38
Shoku Kōki (The Later Chronicles, Continued), 107, 118
Shokukokinshū (Collection of Ancient and Modern Times Continued), 114
Shoku Nihongi (Chronicles of Japan, Continued), 8, 56, 107, 108, 161, 163, 164
Shūchūshō (Notes in the Sleeve), 112, 113
Shūgaishō (Gleanings of Mustard), 162
Shūgyokushū (The Collection of Gathered Jewels), 272n.412, 273n.419
Shūishū (Collection of Gleanings), 4, 118, 177, 180, 181, 182, 183
Shu jing (Book of Documents), 7, 139
Shuo Wen Jie Zi (Explanations of Simple and Compound Graphs), 14, 139, 155, 159, 255n.182
Sōgi, 24, 256n.195
Sugagasa no Nikki (The Sedge Hat Diary), x, 23, 106
Sui shu (History of the Sui Dynasty), 167
Suzuki Shigetane, 15
Suzunoya Shū (The Collection of the House of Bells), 3

Tachibana Moribe, 15
Taiheiki (The Record of the Great Peace), 273n.428
Takahashi Mushimaro, 6–7
Takeguchi Eisai, 106, 107, 241n.7
Tamakatsuma (The Jeweled Comb Basket), 3
Tamaki Masahide, 9
Tanigawa Kotosuga, 9, 10, 26, 206n.85, 253n.157, 257n.211, 259n.243

Tao te ching (Classic of the Way and Integrity), 111
Tōin Kinkata, 260n.260
Tongguk t'onggam (Comprehensive Mirror of the Eastern Kingdoms), 166
Tosa Nikki (The Tosa Diary), 187

Ueda Akinari, 119
Uiyamabumi (First Steps Up the Mountain), 9–10, 202n.13

Xu Shen, 14

Waji Shōranshō (Rectification of Japanese Names), 6
Waka Yaegaki (The Manifold Fence of Waka), 25
Watarai no Tomomune, 111

Wei Ji (History of the Kingdom of Wei), 198
Wenxin Diaolong (The Literary Mind and Carving of Dragons), 16, 19
Wu tsa tsu (J. *Gozasso*; The Five Sections), 132, 253n.143

Yamazaki Ansai, 25
Yi jing (The Book of Changes), 16
Yōrō-ryō (Codes of the Yōrō Era), 165, 261n.282
Yoshida Yoroshi, 122
Yoshino Hyakushu, x
Yu-pian (The Jeweled Letters), 155

Zhouyi (Book of Changes), 14
Zi-zhi tong-jian (A Comprehensive Mirror for Aid in Government), 167

About the Author

MICHAEL F. MARRA is a professor of Japanese literature, aesthetics, and hermeneutics at the University of California, Los Angeles. He has served on the faculties of Osaka University of Foreign Studies, University of Tokyo, University of Southern California, and University of Kyoto. Among his publications are *The Aesthetics of Discontent: Politics and Reclusion in Medieval Japanese Literature* (1991); *Representations of Power: The Literary Politics of Medieval Japan* (1993); *Modern Japanese Aesthetics: A Reader* (1999), a companion volume to a *History of Modern Japanese Aesthetics* (2001); *Japanese Hermeneutics: Current Debates on Aesthetics and Interpretation* (2001); and *Kuki Shūzō: A Philosopher's Poetry and Poetics* (2004).

HAWAI

Production Notes for Marra / *The Poetics of Motoori Norinaga*
Cover design by Santos Barbasa Jr.
Interior design by University of Hawai'i production staff
with text and display in Sabon
Composition by inari information services
Printing and binding by The Maple-Vail Book Manufacturing Group
Printed on 60# Glatfelter Offset, B18, 420 ppi

THE POETICS OF
Motoori Norinaga